Women Serial and Mass Murderers

WOMEN SERIAL AND MASS MURDERERS

A Worldwide Reference, 1580 through 1990

by

Kerry Segrave

McFarland & Company, Inc., Publishers
Jefferson, North Carolina, and London

British Library Cataloguing-in-Publication data are available

Library of Congress Cataloguing-in-Publication Data

Segrave, Kerry, 1944–
    Women serial and mass murderers : a worldwide reference, 1580 through 1990
/ by Kerry Segrave.
        p.   cm.
    [Includes index.]
    Includes bibliographical references.
    ISBN 0-89950-680-1 (lib. bdg. : 50# alk. paper) ∞
    1. Women murderers — Biography — Dictionaries.   2. Serial murders —
History — Dictionaries.   3. Mass murder — History — Dictionaries.
I. Title.
HV6515.S44   1992
364.1′523′092 — dc20
[B]   91-50949
                                                                              CIP

Manufactured in the United States of America

McFarland & Company, Inc., Publishers
    Box 611, Jefferson, North Carolina 28640

Contents

Introduction   1

Amy Archer-Gilligan   10
Johanna Healy Bacher   14
Velma Barfield   15
Elizabeth Bathory   20
Mrs. Leon Bearce   24
Martha Beck   26
Marie Becker   32
Kate Bender   35
Patricia Bolin   39
Harjit Kaur Bhuller Brar   42
Marie de Brinvilliers   44
Inez Campbell   51
Patty Cannon   52
Opal Juanita Collins   56
Patricia Columbo   59
Glenda Cooper   64
Mary Ann Cotton   66
Anna Cunningham   74
Lillie May Curtis   78
Rachal David   81
Nellie Dcyzheski   87
Catherine Deshayes   89
Nannie Doss   92
Amelia Dyer   98
Lillian Edwards   102
Christine Falling   105

Susanna Fazekas   112
Elizabeth Fiederer   118
Priscilla Ford   120
Lafonda Fay Foster and Tina Marie Hickey Powell   126
Edna Fuller   134
Janie Lou Gibbs   136
Sister Godfrida   138
Delfina Gonzales and Maria Gonzales   140
Gesina Gottfried   142
Gwendolyn Graham   147
Belle Gunness   155
Anna Hahn   162
Violet Hultberg   167
Mary Jane Jackson   169
Marie Jeanneret   172
Hélène Jegado   177
Annie Jones   182
Roxanne Jones   183
Charlotte Juenemann   186
Kathleen King   188
Tillie Klimek   192
Christa Lehmann   197
Anjette Lyles   199
Alma May McAninch   203
Carol MacDonald   206

v

Sarah Malcolm   208
Martha Marek   210
Rhonda Belle Martin   213
Daisy Louisa de Melker   218
Elsie Nollen   224
Maureen O'Donohue   226
Bonnie Parker   228
Marie Pasos   232
Popova   233
Dorothea Montalvo
   Puente   234
Florence Ransom   243
Vera Renczi   246
Martha Rendall   248
Sarah Jane Robinson   250
Amelia Sach and
   Annie Walters   254
Antoinette Scieri   257

Lydia Sherman   260
Mamie Shey Shoaf   264
Della Sorenson   265
Mariam Soulakiotis   270
Hieronyima Spara   273
Marybeth Tinning   275
La Toffania   282
Jane Toppan   284
Ruth Urdanivia   290
Sophie Ursinus   295
Waltraud Wagner   296
Marie Walkup   298
Margaret Waters   300
Jeanne Weber   303
Catherine Wilson   308
Martha Hasel Wise   313
Anna Zwanziger   318

Index   323

Introduction

Multicides committed by women are different from those committed by men. Different types of victims are targeted. Different places are selected to carry out the murders. Different methods to kill are utilized.

The average woman mass murderer kills for the first time when she is 31.4 years old and continues to kill for five years before finally being apprehended by the police. By that time she has murdered just slightly fewer than 17 people. With very few exceptions the murders take place in the residence of the killer or (what is less likely) that of the victim. Often murderer and victim share a residence. Almost never is a victim killed in the street or in a public place. The most popular murder weapon is arsenic.

Of the 17 victims that the average woman murderer claims, the majority are selected from her immediate or extended family. Others have close ties to the woman as employers, friends, or suitors. A large percentage of the average mass murderer's victims come from the powerless groups: the very young, such as toddlers, and the very old or ill, such as nursing home or hospital patients.

During the five-year spree, people around the woman probably have had indications that all was not normal. Gossip has probably spread around the neighborhood. However, after the death of one of her victims a doctor would have conducted a cursory exam, at most, and ascribed death to natural causes. Upon her arrest, regardless of whether she confesses, the mass killer shows little or no remorse for her actions. When she comes to trial she is adjudged sane, convicted, and sentenced to a long prison term.

At least this is the picture that emerges when an average is taken of the murderers profiled in this book. In computing this average I have not included La Toffania, Hieronyima Spara, Catherine Deshayes, Popova, or Susanna Fazekas. Data on these women are a little more vague than for the others. The number of their victims is also extremely high, which is as much a function of their time, place, and role as agent, as anything else. While these numbers are huge, they may not be exaggerations; however they remain anomalies.

For the 83 women whose birthdates are known or can be reasonably

1

estimated, six killed for the first time when under 20 years of age; 29 were in their twenties, 33 were in their thirties, 11 were in their forties, and 4 were in their fifties when they first turned to murder.

This book profiles women who have killed at least three people—not counting themselves in the case of murder-suicide. It covers women from all over the world and extends from 1580 to 1990. Women such as Caril Fugate, who accompanied Charles Starkweather on his killings in 1957–58, and Myra Hindley, who aided English killer Ian Brady, have been excluded. These women were guilty of murder in law but were passive participants. Both were traditional in the sense that they functioned in the stereotypical role of cheerleader for their men. Had they never met Starkweather and Brady there is nothing to indicate they would have been petty criminals, let alone murderers.

A few of the females in this book, such as Bonnie Parker and Martha Beck, also worked with men, but these women were all equal—or dominant—partners in murder. Had Parker not met Clyde Barrow and Beck not met Raymond Fernandez, there was an excellent chance they would have followed the same road they did.

In many ways female killers are more interesting than their male counterparts. Before committing murder, anyone, male or female, must overcome the socialization process we are all subjected to that attempts to check such behavior. Females have more levels of this process to overcome. While males are socialized not to commit murder, this is partly undone by the fact that males *are* socialized to be violent. They must, like Boy Scouts, always be prepared, for it is this group that will be sent off by the government to fight in wars. Thus males are conditioned and socialized to not commit murder but conditioned to be able to go somewhere and kill on command during a state of war. This obviously means that highly contradictory signals are being sent out, with the result that many men murder and many are mass murderers. Statistics for murder, not just multicides, show that only 10 to 15 percent of murders are committed by females, indicating just how confusing the signals are for men, or how successful the conditioning of females in this area has been. The percentage of female killers has been fairly constant across time and across countries. No statistics are available specifically for multicides, but there is nothing to indicate that the percentage of females would be higher.

Since they don't function as potential combat troops—not yet anyway—women don't get the type of pro-aggression training that men do. If anything, passivity training is sharpened. This is to make women particularly tractable towards men. A disadvantaged group like American blacks have a much higher homicide rate than that of dominant whites. Yet women, also a disadvantaged group, have a much lower rate.

All of this conditioning makes it much, much more difficult for females to emerge as killers. And compared to men, relatively few do. When they commit mass murder they do it in ways quite different from men in terms of victims targeted and weapons used. This is not surprising since murder, like almost everything else in our society, is at least in part a social construct.

Poison, especially arsenic, was for a long time a popular murder method for both men and women. As long as science could not conclusively and efficiently show the presence of arsenic in the body, the killer was assured of getting away with the crime. That changed around the 1830s or 1840s, when forensic science became able to detect poison in the body of the victim even years after death.

Despite this, arsenic continued to be the weapon of choice among female mass killers. Of the 84 cases in this book at least 35 used poison, and 30 or more of those used arsenic. This figure is more impressive if one factors out the 25 cases of women who murdered their own children in a one-day rampage. Then it becomes at least 30 arsenic killers out of 59. In contrast, over the past 25 years 57 to 60 percent of all murders in the United States have been committed by firearms.

Murders involving stabbing and cutting instruments bring the total to 80 percent, and adding murders with blunt instruments and fists, hands, and feet brings the total to slightly over 90 percent. Poison is today part of the "everything else" category—less than 10 percent.

One reason that arsenic may be favored by women is that in a sense it is a nonviolent method—at least in comparison to gunning somebody down, stabbing them to death, bludgeoning open their skulls, and so on. These methods are more "masculine" in nature. Women in this book have used such methods, but they don't predominate. Of the 12 women who have targeted the particularly defenseless, not including their own children, not one of them employed arsenic. The more helpless a victim is, the more likely it is that the woman will kill aggressively.

A few killers did use various other poisons. Those that have targeted mainly their immediate family as victims have generally used arsenic. If arsenic is a passive way of killing in the sense that the killer simply hands the victim a spiked bowl of soup or a laced mug of coffee and waits for the arsenic to work, from the victim's point of view, the result is extremely violent. Death by arsenic is more painful than the more overtly violent methods. The victim is gripped by searing stomach pains, wracked by convulsions, has violent diarrhea and, in some cases, paralysis of the extremities. Some victims in this book took up to a year to expire. Some who survived were rendered permanently paralyzed. The killer often deliberately administered judicious doses of poison to ensure that the victim lingered long and painfully.

Serial killer Henry Lee Lucas claimed he killed 500 during his career.

Police put the toll at around 100. This is another example of a "masculine" trait—competition and bragging—carried over into something as perverse as multicides. Lucas said he had murdered every way there was, except by poison. This simply underlines poisoning as a female way to kill.

Traditionally the female role in our society is to be a nurturer, caregiver, nurse, cook, food server, and so on. While living precisely these roles, many of these women have dosed somebody and then "cared" for them as they died over a period of hours, days, weeks, months, or even a year. Perhaps these females are rebelling at some level against their role as an inferior. As they went on their murderous way, were they mocking their place, sending up their role in a particularly gruesome manner? Were they striking back at a male-dominated world that gave them little opportunity except as breeding machines and quasi-servants, or servants in fact? Obviously there is more than a little sadism involved when one orchestrates such a lengthy and painful demise for someone, as so many of these killers did. A number of them were praised by those around them for their self-sacrificing nursing efforts toward their victim—at least until the truth came out.

With the exception of those few who seemed to murder for financial gain, a motive is missing, at least one that would make some sort of sense to the average person. While most people can perhaps understand how one person could be driven in some way to murder another, it is a much larger leap to empathize, however minimally, with the person who kills again and again over many years.

Hatred of men is an underlying factor, and is present perhaps more often than generally assumed. Some women like La Toffania and Hieronyima Spara openly expressed hatred for men; in other cases it must be implied. This hatred is also fairly obvious for the women whose crime consisted of mass-murdering their children on one particular day. These mothers could not overcome their conditioning enough to target their husbands, but they could overcome it enough to kill a part of him—his children.

A major difference between male and female mass murderers is that women are more apt to target powerless people. Few if any males have made a practice of wholesale killing of only toddlers and young children. Few if any have singled out very old, bedridden people. Yet many women have. Part of the reason for this may be simple opportunity; it is women mainly who come in contact with these groups as sitters, caregivers, and so on. It may also be a reflection of the position of females in the "pecking order." If it is safer to aggress against those lower on that pecking order, then this propensity of women to target the powerless is logical. It is when murdering members of these groups that women don't use arsenic.

Only a handful of the women profiled employed more typically "male" methods of aggressive murder; the few women who worked with men in some fashion also tended to use "male" methods. It is only among these that one can find examples of women who murdered at a place other than their residence, the victim's residence, or their place of employment. Still, there are no female mass murderers like Richard Speck, Ted Bundy, the sniper who killed from the Texas tower, or the man who killed in the McDonalds near San Diego. Women simply don't go into the street and mass-murder total strangers. There are no female counterparts to a Bundy or a Gacy, to whom sex or sexual violence is a part of the murder pattern. There are no women who desecrate the body afterward by cutting off parts or ripping it open and eating the insides, and so on. There have been numerous men who have done this. The only equivalent would seem to be whatever satisfaction might accrue to a woman nursing her victim as the victim dies slowly and painfully from a dose of poison.

A woman like Marie de Brinvilliers murdered strangers by going into hospitals where she did charity work and "practiced" her poisoning skills on the poor. But that's not quite like a Richard Speck type. The sole exception is Priscilla Ford, who drove her car down a busy Reno, Nevada, sidewalk one day cutting down pedestrians. She went into the streets and killed perfect strangers. No other mass-murdering woman has ever done that.

In some cases the ineptitude of the authorities has been obvious. While it is easy to look at a case like that of Jeanne Weber and assume it could never happen again, maybe it could. Much more recently, Christine Falling and Gwendolyn Graham have gone on long murder streaks which, in retrospect, should have been stopped much sooner. The average physician probably doesn't have the mindset to approach each body with the thought in the back of his mind that murder may be involved; in the vast majority of cases, it isn't. And the idea that a woman may be a killer, a mass killer even, is probably harder to accept than the same conclusion about a man.

Money has often been a strong motivation for killing. The women in this book are well represented by females who murdered again and again for money. Other reasons were sometimes involved, but financial gain was central. Belle Gunness, Kate Bender, Patty Cannon, the Gonzales sisters, and Amy Archer-Gilligan turned murder-for-money into a virtual business. Gunness lured men to her farm using matrimonial ads. They didn't leave. Kate and Patty both headed operations which involved robbing and killing travelers who stopped at the inns they operated. The Gonzales sisters robbed and killed customers at their brothel, but for the most part they dispatched the female inmates to control the others and weed out the old, unproductive ones. Amy preyed on the elderly at the nursing home she owned. Residents at her home paid a fixed amount of money for life care, and Amy set out to ensure that period was as short as possible. Sarah Malcolm took three lives in the course of a single robbery.

Women like Sarah Jane Robinson, Daisy de Melker, Anjette Lyles, and Velma Barfield have also been obsessed enough with money to kill for it. They limited their victims to immediate family members, for the most part. Between them they rid themselves of six husbands. Catherine Wilson, Martha Marek, and Gesina Gottfried selected victims equally from family and others such as friends, suitors, and acquaintances. Anna Hahn specialized in picking up very old men and having them bequeath their assets to her. If she couldn't manage that she would borrow money from a victim, ensuring he died before repayment was demanded.

Women who killed family members and friends all used poison to do in their victims. The others used much more violent methods, except for Amy. Gunness, Bender, Cannon, and the Gonzales sisters were violent killers. Interestingly, all but the Gonzales sisters had men as accomplices, or at least passive intimates, well aware of what was happening. Kate set up victims for her father and brother, while Patty headed her own gang of male thugs.

Nannie Doss, Lydia Sherman, Della Sorenson, Janie Lou Gibbs, Martha Wise, Christa Lehmann, Opal Collins, Patricia Columbo, Anna Cunningham, Tillie Klimek, Rhonda Martin, and Marybeth Tinning almost exclusively limited their victims to members of their nuclear or extended families. Overwhelmingly the preferred murder weapon was arsenic, administered through food or drink prepared by the killer for the victim. Many had strife-ridden marriages, although it is unclear whether this contributed to murderous actions or whether the women were unstable to start with, thus contributing to or causing their poor marriages. Some of these killers confessed and some confessed partially, but most did not. Generally they showed little or no remorse for what they did. These 12 women dispatched among them 18 husbands, 29 of their own children, seven other children such as stepchildren, four mothers, one father, four cousins, five in-laws, one brother, one sister, one aunt and one uncle.

The murderous intermediary, or agent, has pretty much passed into history, with the last reported case being the bizarre Hungarian Fazekas story from the 1920s. The heyday for such people was in Europe from the late 1600s to the early 1700s. Arsenic was the ideal killer. Odorless, tasteless, and colorless, it couldn't be detected in the body at that time. So prevalent did murder by poison become, especially in the European upper-class, that the position of "food taster" evolved. People were hired to do nothing but taste food destined for elite stomachs. So chaotic did life become that royalty finally had to step in and put a stop, more or less, to the practice.

Those who desired to do somebody in had only to go to a person like Toffania, Spara, Deshayes or Popova to purchase the necessary poison and instructions in its use. While most of them killed occasionally themselves, they primarily supplied the equipment and knowledge. Deshayes did murder a huge number of babies as part of satanic rites.

One common thread that tied these women together is their immense and intense hatred of men. Popova bragged of never murdering a woman among her 300 victims. Virtually all of Toffania's and Spara's kills were male. Both hated men. Fazekas dispensed her poison and its lore only to females. A few of those did go on to murder people of their own gender, but the vast majority were males. These women despised men, and they got even.

Lust is a motive that figures only to a minor extent as a driving force of female mass killers. Vera Renczi operated like the legendary black widow spider, taking on a mate and then dispatching him. Tired of being single, Anna Zwanziger took extreme measures to try and land a husband. Florence Ransom let her jealousy toward her husband's former wife get the better of her. In her midfifties, Marie Becker suddenly started running around with much younger men. She could only attract them with money, but murder provided that. Sophie Ursinus turned to homicide to prevent a lover from leaving her and to get rid of an old husband. When Martha Beck met Raymond Fernandez through a dating club, she soon came to dominate him. What had been mere swindling on his part became swindling-cum-murder by the pair, underpinned by a dark sexuality. Sex was one of several motives underlying Mary Ann Cotton's propensity to kill anyone and everyone close to her.

Neither Martha Rendall, Margaret Waters, Amelia Dyer, Amelia Sach and Annie Walters, Jeanne Weber, Christine Falling, Jane Toppan, Sister Godfrida, Marie Jeanneret, Gwendolyn Graham, Waltraud Wagner, nor Dorothea Puente employed arsenic in targeting especially defenseless victims. Five of them committed murder by the very physical means of strangulation or suffocation. This difference may emerge as a result of the victim being so helpless. Perhaps the fact that the killer has no fear of the victim somehow provokes a more direct murder method.

These women had a variety of motives for their crimes. Some were baby farmers, women who took in babies from women who couldn't afford them or didn't want them. The woman giving up the child paid a fee to the woman "adopting" the child. Baby farming was most prevalent in Victorian England. The farmers killed the babies, pawned the clothes, and kept the proceeds. Some women seemed to enjoy killing, even attaining a state akin to sexual arousal. And some of these women were mentally disturbed.

For some women no reason, however illogical, existed for their killing sprees. Helene Jegado simply didn't like her victims. Almost anything could be perceived by her as a slight. She was quick to respond to slights in a murderous fashion. Antoinette Scieri and Marie de Brinvilliers enjoyed killing. The latter was able to murder scores due to her privileged position in the upper class. Carrying enjoyment further, Elizabeth Bathory and Mariam Soulakiotis each murdered hundreds by personally administering gruesome and barbarous tortures. Bathory had the power of her class position behind her, while Soulakiotis was aided by the power of religion. On the surface, money motivated Soulakiotis but the pleasure of murder seemed to dominate, for she never did anything with the money she got except accumulate it. Bonnie Parker, Mary Jane Jackson, and the Lafonda Foster-Tina Powell pair were basically down-and-out types who on occasion exploded with a display of brutal, vicious behavior culminating in murder. Priscilla Ford, battling mental demons, went on a short rampage in her car, cutting down pedestrians on a busy street. The murders committed by these women were all aggressive. They were senseless and violent.

Some women profiled in this book have included their own children among their victims; however, they were usually only a part of the victim list. Usually the children were murdered over a long period of time, one by one. A group of 25 women are distinguished by the fact that they dispatched three or more of their own children in a short period of time on one bloody day. The only exception is Charlotte Juenemann who let her children starve to death—a process that took a week or so. These women claimed no other victims, but sometimes took their own lives as well.

While for Edna Fuller, Marie Pasos, Mamie Shoaf, Alma McAninch, Nellie Dcyzheski, and Roxanne Jones the motives are complex and numerous, living in grinding poverty seemed to be the major spur to kill. For Johanna Bacher, Violet Hultberg, Elsie Nollen, Carol MacDonald, and Mrs. Bearce, marital problems of one kind of another called for an extreme reaction. Marie Walkup, Harjit Brar, Inez Campbell, Ruth Urdanivia, Annie Jones, Charlotte Juenemann, Elizabeth Fiederer, and Lillian Edwards appear to have become mentally disturbed shortly before the killings, while Patricia Bolin, Lillie Curtis, Kathleen King, Glenda Cooper, Maureen O'Donohue, and Rachal David appear to have been mentally disturbed for much longer periods.

None of these 25 women used arsenic as a weapon, which may be due to the position of power these women held over their defenseless children. Being relatively powerful, they could use a more physical, powerful method to kill. Of the 11 females living under the strain of poverty or marital problems, eight took their own lives along with those of their children. These women also utilized more "humane" methods of killing. Almost half chose asphyxiation, a painless death compared to the other methods employed. Among the 14 women with mental difficulties, six committed suicide, while eight either did not attempt it or failed if they did. These women selected the most brutal and vicious methods of killing their children; the longer the mental disturbance had existed, the more brutal the method of murder, and the mother was less likely to commit suicide. Only one of these mothers used asphyxiation, while one woman manually strangled her offspring. Another threw hers from a tall building to their deaths, and yet another hanged hers from a beam in the cellar.

One school of thought suggests that aggression turned outward is murder, while aggression turned inward is suicide. In many of these cases the woman's hatred of her husband comes to the fore. Unable or unwilling to attack or kill him, she turns instead to herself and her children, murdering them as a way of seeking revenge, getting even for real or imagined grievances against her husband. Those with marital problems best illustrate this theory. While notes left behind may express "love" and so on for husband and children, the hatred of the husband and the murder of his children — his creations — as an act of revenge is all too obvious.

Amy Archer-Gilligan

(1873–1962). *Place:* Windsor, Connecticut. *Time:* 1907–1916. *Age:* 34–43.
Victims: 20–40(?). *Method:* Arsenic poisoning.

Her name was Amy Archer-Gilligan, but she was known simply as
"Sister" Amy to the people who lived in her home for the aged. She claimed
to labor long and hard cooking, cleaning, and washing, but something was
amiss, because the elderly died at a much higher rate — close to seven times
higher — than at other institutions.

Over the period from 1907 to 1916, when the authorities caught up with
her, Amy probably murdered between 20 and 40 people. Several bodies had
been exhumed with poison found in all of them. The motive was fairly
simple — greed. Despite the number of probable victims, Amy was tried and
convicted on only one count of murder.

Little information has been reported on this woman's early life. She
was born around 1873 and married James H. Archer sometime in the 1890s.
Her only child, a daughter Mary, was born in 1898. Before 1907 she
operated a home for the aged at Newington, Connecticut. By all accounts
her life was quiet and uneventful, with no hint of wrongdoing.

In 1907 the Archer family moved to Windsor, a few miles from Hart-
ford, where Amy set up and ran the Archer Home for Elderly and Indigent
Persons. Here Amy seemed to take up her murderous ways. During the
home's first years, from 1907 to the end of 1910, only 12 residents of the
home died. From 1911 to 1916, however, a total of 48 people died at the
home, which only accommodated 14. Since a normal rate for this period
was calculated to be about eight deaths, some concluded that as many as
40 residents were murdered.

Amy seems to have led a life full of hard work, with little financial gain
in return. The money needed to set up the home may have come from a be-
quest she received upon the death of her parents. Around 1911 Mr. Archer
died, and it may have been at that point that Amy turned to murder. The
cause of Mr. Archer's death is unknown. Amy said that when he died he
left "his property to some one other than myself." This seems unlikely. By
the time of her arrest in 1916, Amy had married Michael W. Gilligan and
buried him. When his body was exhumed, it was found to contain arsenic.

Suspicion was first aroused when Franklin Andrews, a resident of the home died suddenly on May 30, 1914. Mr. Andrews had paid $1,000 for life care at the institution, which in his case turned out to be only a matter of months. The day of his death, he was observed walking on the grounds and doing some work around the garden. He appeared to be in the best of health. At eleven o'clock that night Amy phoned Andrews's sister, Mrs. Pierce, to say he was ill but it wouldn't be necessary to come to the home until morning. When Mrs. Pierce arrived the next day, Amy told her that her brother had died ten minutes after the phone call but that Mrs. Pierce couldn't see the body because it had been sent out for embalming.

While examining her brother's belongings, Mrs. Pierce found a letter from Amy asking for a $500 loan and requesting that he tell no one about it. She reported her suspicions to a Hartford newspaper and to the police. An investigation of sorts followed, but Andrews's body was not examined at the time. Once Amy came under suspicion, the deaths at the home ceased for half a year, but they resumed again by the end of 1914.

The investigation dragged on, and it was almost two years before police did the obvious and exhumed the bodies of Andrews, four other former residents of the home, and Mr. Gilligan. All were found to have died from arsenic poisoning. Death certificates for those exhumed had listed such causes of death as gastric ulcers and apoplexy. Amy was arrested in May of 1916 and charged with the murder of Andrews. At that time police considered 20 deaths at the home to be suspicious but proceeded on only the one count.

Amy, it was claimed, operated a simple scam: she requested that new residents pay $1,000 for life care in advance and then dispatched them as quickly as possible. The high death rate at the home was a fairly well known fact; on the eve of Amy's arrest Connecticut governor Marcus Holcomb said, "I've heard rumors about the Windsor home for two years, but no newspaper, State Official or private citizen ever approached me on the matter" [2].

As evidence against Amy, the police found large quantities of arsenic stashed away in the house. Mrs. Archer-Gilligan had also purchased some just two days before Andrews's death. Only a few days before Andrews died, Amy wrote to a potential new resident, Mrs. Gowdy, that "There will be a vacancy very soon." Mrs. Goudy took Andrews's spot and herself shortly afterward became another victim of arsenic poisoning.

Upon her arrest Amy stated, strangely, "I am not guilty and I will hang before they prove it against me" [8]. She also issued a statement to the press through her attorney. She claimed that certain of her neighbors expected to profit from her inmates and that they kept the agitation against her going. Amy also stated, "From inmates in the home I heard stories told on the streets of Windsor that they would be poisoned if they remained at the home and one day an old gentleman did become excited and declared I had drugged a glass of hot lemonade given him for a cold. He asked the doctor to analyse the lemonade and the physician did so by drinking it right before him. And the doctor, he's alive today. . . . Many inmates died, but that is not strange, because they were all old and feeble. Most of them were ailing from diseases other than those which usually accompany advanced age. . . . I am as innocent of wrongdoing to any person who has ever been an inmate of my home in either thought, word or deed, as any child 5 years old" [11].

Prosecutor Hugh Alcorn called the case "the biggest crime that ever shocked New England and the worst poison plot this country has ever known." Coroner Dr. Arthur Wolff seconded that opinion and added, "The motive appears to be cupidity" [6].

Dr. Howard King attended most of the deaths at the home, including Andrews's and defended Amy, feeling that the arsenic could have been placed in Andrews's body by "ghouls to incriminate Mrs. Gilligan." He added that Amy was a victim of persecution and was disliked by a number of townspeople. "Mrs. Gilligan is in some respects a little queer but I do not think it is possible that she committed the crime," said King [8]. He was one of the few who supported her. The doctor had been under fire in the community and the press for not realizing what was happening at the home.

Amy was found guilty of murder in the first degree in July 1917 and sentenced to hang. After her lawyer appealed on technical grounds, a new trial was ordered, with the same result. This time she was sentenced to life in prison. At the first trial the only defense put forward was that somebody else put arsenic in the victims' bodies after death. At the second trial a different tack was taken. Lawyers claimed Amy wasn't morally responsible for her crimes because she was a drug user. At no time was a plea of insanity considered.

Strangely, no evidence of wealth was uncovered during the trials. Amy claimed to own real estate worth around $9,000 that was mortgaged for half that amount. On her arrest, various creditors slapped liens totaling an additional $2,500 on the property.

In 1923 Amy was reexamined by court psychiatrists. Declared insane, she was committed to a Connecticut hospital for the insane where she stayed until her death in 1962 at the age of 89.

Sources

1. "Dig Up More Bodies in Hunt for Poison." *New York Times,* May 12, 1916, p. 8.

2. "Governor Heard Rumors." *New York Times,* May 14, 1916, p. 9.

3. "Inmates of Old Home Poisoned, Police Say." *New York Times*, May 9, 1916, p. 11.

4. "Mrs. Gilligan Says She Is Persecuted." *New York Times,* May 11, 1916, p. 4.

5. Nash, Jay Robert. *Look for the Woman.* New York: M. Evans, 1981, pp. 10–11.

6. "New England Poison Mystery." *Chicago Tribune,* May 12, 1916, p. 3.

7. "Sentence of Hanging for Mrs. Gilligan." *New York Times,* July 14, 1917, p. 14.

8. "Suspect Poisoning of Other Inmates." *New York Times*, May 10, 1916, p. 5.

9. Wilson, Colin. *Encyclopedia of Murder.* New York: Putnam, 1962, pp. 231–32.

10. "Woman Dead at 89 Was Doomed in '17 Poison Slayings." *New York Times,* April 24, 1962, p. 28.

11. "Woman Keeper of 'Death House' Issues a Plea." *Chicago Tribune,* May 11, 1916, p. 5.

Johanna Healey Bacher

(1891–1922). *Place:* Greenwich, Connecticut. *Time:* March 26, 1922. *Age:* 31. *Victims:* 4. *Method:* Knife.

When Johanna Healey married Henry Bacher, the hoped-for happy marriage soon turned into a tragedy. Bacher, once divorced at the time, was a carpenter and boxer by trade. The couple probably married near the end of World War I. They lived in Greenwich, Connecticut, and had three children; in the year they died, Margaret was 4, Johanna was 3, and Henry, Jr., was 15 months.

In March 1922, the couple had been separated for some time. Henry had initiated divorce proceedings charging Johanna with "intolerable cruelty." Friends of the woman noticed she was depressed over the issue. She finally procured some rat poison, but someone informed the police. On March 23, Police Chief Andrew Talbot had Johanna and her three children brought to police headquarters for a little talk. At first Johanna denied having any poison, but under questioning she relented and told Talbot she bought the poison to kill her children. Johanna explained that she was afraid Henry would obtain custody of the children. It seems that Bacher and members of his family had been annoying and harassing Johanna. Talbot offered Johanna any assistance he could and made her promise she would never commit such a rash act. Talbot told her he would send for her again in a few days. Before the family departed, the chief gave each child a box of candy.

During the evening of March 26, 1922, Johanna took a butcher knife and slit the throats of her three children. Then she took her own life in a similar fashion. Before killing herself, Johanna threw a paper bag addressed to Talbot out of her window into the street. It contained her bank book, insurance papers, and a letter stating her intentions. A passerby found the bag near midnight and took it to the police station.

Source

"Slays 3 Children, Ends Her Own Life." *New York Times,* March 28, 1922, p. 6.

Velma Barfield

(1932–1984). *Place:* Lumberton, and St. Pauls, North Carolina. *Time:* 1971(?)–1978. *Age:* 39–46. *Victims:* 4–5(?). *Method:* Arsenic poisoning.

During the six years she spent on death row, Velma Barfield gained national attention as forces opposed to capital punishment rallied to her defense. This woman was an obvious choice to try and gain converts to their position. Velma was middle aged, a grandmother, and religious. Her own community was deeply shocked that such a "nice woman" could be a mass murderer.

Born Margie Velma Bullard on October 23, 1932, in Cumberland County, North Carolina, Velma lived out her life in small rural communities in southwestern North Carolina. She was the oldest daughter and second oldest child of nine fathered by loom repairman Murray Bullard. Stories about her childhood are contradictory. Some of the more negative ones may have been exaggerated as part of the lobbying effort to save her from execution. A 1984 article stated that Velma claimed her father beat her, some of her siblings, and their mother, who was unable to protect the children from her husband's anger. Velma also claimed her father raped her when she was 13. Mr. Bullard died in 1972. Of her childhood and the beatings she said, "Sometimes he couldn't find what he was looking for, and he would just go right off on one of us. ...Things that went on inside our home when I grew up were kept inside" [3].

In 1978, shortly after her conviction, Barfield told a reporter that up until young adulthood she was close to her father. "Dad never called me by my name. He always called me Sug or Honey," Barfield recalled with a smile [1]. When told of her claims of an abusive and cruel childhood, her brother Jimmy Bullard, a Baptist minister, exclaimed, "That's not true! We had a good childhood." Two of her brothers felt her charge of rape was a lie [2].

After finishing the tenth grade, Velma dropped out of high school during the eleventh grade. As soon as she turned 17 she eloped with Thomas Burke, a textile plant worker who later got a job driving a Pepsi-Cola truck. For the next 15 years life unfolded quietly for the couple. Velma had a son, Ron, when she was 19. A daughter Kim was born three years later. The family bought a small house. Kim recalled them as an all–American family during those years, going to the lake for picnics and to the beach on weekends. Everyone in the family loved everyone else.

It all changed for the worse around 1966, when Burke sustained head injuries in an auto accident. He lost his job and he began to drink, first socially but then heavily. To keep the family together financially, Velma worked first in a textile mill and later in a department store. According to Velma, her husband had become an abusive alcoholic. Because of the tension she was experiencing, Velma got a prescription for tranquilizers from her family doctor. Soon she was taking more than prescribed. To avoid detection Velma would go from doctor to doctor for prescriptions and would have them filled at different drugstores in the area. By routinely mixing drugs or doubling and tripling doses, Velma became hooked on a variety of prescription drugs, from painkillers to antidepressants to tranquilizers, from Valium to Tylenol III with codeine.

It got so bad that, according to Kim, "While she was on drugs she always had different personalities — argumentative, sad or happy. I'd come home from school, she might be passed out with her face bleeding from something she fell against" [3]. Thomas was treated for alcoholism in a hospital. On his release relations between the couple were so strained that they barely spoke to each other. Burke burned to death in his bed in 1969. Velma always denied playing any part in his death. The state prosecutor at her 1978 trial believed she murdered him. Even Kim was unsure, commenting, "It's always been a question in the back of my mind whether Mama had anything to do with Daddy's death too, but I never asked her" [2].

Jennings Barfield married Velma in 1970. Six months later, in March 1971, he was dead from what were then thought to be natural causes. When his remains were exhumed years later his body was found to be full of arsenic. Again Velma always denied being responsible for his death.

Velma continued to consume large quantities of drugs. Over the period from 1972 to 1975, she had to be treated at a hospital four times for drug overdoses. After the death of her second husband she moved back home to live with her mother. During this time Barfield led a very religious life. A member of the First Pentecostal Holiness Church, she taught Sunday school, did volunteer work in the church office one morning a week, and attended services twice a week.

By 1974 the cost of her drug habit was too much to handle. She pretended to be her mother and borrowed $1,000 from a loan company using the name Lillie Bullard. When letters from the company demanding payment started to arrive, the puzzled Lillie got upset. A couple of days after Christmas that year Velma put some arsenic-based ant killer into her mother's Coca-Cola. Lillie died on December 30. An autopsy found nothing suspicious and the cause of death was assigned to natural causes.

While arsenic can easily be detected in a person, alive or dead, an autopsy will not routinely uncover its presence. Specific tests must be done.

Two years later, Velma took a job as a live-in nurse-companion to 85-year-old Dollie Edwards in Lumberton. Dollie's niece, Alice Storms, was impressed by Barfield's performance on the job, finding the house to be always neat and clean. Alice's father, Stewart Taylor, a farmer in nearby St. Pauls, was also impressed. He was about seven years older than Velma and separated from his wife. He and Velma began seeing each other. Toward the end of February 1977, Velma laced Dollie's morning cereal and coffee with rat poison. After three days of agony, during which Velma carefully tended her, Dollie died on February 28, 1977. At the funeral for her employer Barfield cried openly and grieved as much as any member of Dollie's family.

Velma was unemployed until she was hired as a live-in housekeeper by Margie Pittman, who was looking for somebody to care for her parents, 80-year-old John Henry Lee and his 76-year-old wife Record Lee. Pittman's pastor recommended Barfield for the job. Margie's sister Sylvia Andrews thought of Velma as a very Christian person and said that family was very pleased with Barfield's work as a housekeeper for the Lees.

Not so long after she started work Velma came across a blank check while housecleaning. The temptation was too great to resist. Velma forged the check for $50 in Mrs. Lee's name, apparently to feed her drug habit. John Henry discovered the theft and threatened to prosecute Velma. Mr. Lee suddenly became violently ill. For several days he suffered the agonies of violent diarrhea, vomiting, and convulsions and died on June 4, 1977. Doctors ascribed his demise to gastroenteritis, not suspecting that Velma had spiked John Henry's tea and beer with ant poison. Velma, who had nursed him during his final days, made another show of great grief at the funeral, weeping and wailing as she consoled the widow. She then put some arsenic into Mrs. Lee's tea, but not enough to kill her, before resigning her position in October 1977.

Stewart Taylor and Velma had grown closer and planned to marry when Taylor got his divorce. However, the relationship soured in November 1977, when Taylor discovered Velma had forged a $195 check on his account. They fought about the issue. Stewart threatened to prosecute but apparently tempers cooled, for they continued to see each other. In January of the next year Velma forged another check on Taylor's account.

On January 31, the couple went to a Rex Humbard gospel meeting. Later that evening at Taylor's home, she dosed Taylor's beer with ant poison. Hours later she called his daughter, Alice Storms, to report that her father was ill. When Storms suggested she come over Velma kept her at bay by saying, "Don't you worry. I'll take care of everything" [3]. After several days of extreme agony, Taylor died. Only when he was on the verge of death did Velma cash the forged check she had been holding. Velma sent an ornate wreath to Taylor's funeral that was identical to the one she had sent to John Henry's. After the services Velma asked for and received Taylor's wedding ring, as well as $400 that the family gratefully gave her. Storms would later say, "You're looking at a big fool that got conned" [3].

Taylor's family couldn't understand how he could be healthy one day and dead a few days later. They pushed for and finally got tests beyond those conducted during a routine autopsy. The results of these showed Taylor's tissues to be full of arsenic. Barfield was arrested and, much to the surprise of District Attorney Joe Britt, admitted to poisoning Taylor as well as Lee, Edwards, and her own mother.

The other bodies were exhumed, along with Jennings's remains. All were found to contain arsenic. Velma maintained that she never intended to kill anyone but only wanted to make and keep them ill until she could repay the money she had stolen from them. That way she also hoped to earn their gratitude by nursing them back to health. Barfield needed the money she stole, she said, to pay for the various drugs she was addicted to.

Speaking about the murders, Velma maintained she hadn't killed Jennings: "The four, that was all. . . . It was kind of like something they have done to you, and you want to do something back. In none of the cases did I feel like it would kill them. . . . I was not myself" [1].

Velma had stolen money from three of her victims, but not from Dollie Edwards. When Britt asked her to explain that murder, Velma said, "I can't explain. . . . There was no reason. . . . But, I figured it would kill her when I gave it to her" [2].

Velma was put on trial only for the murder of Taylor, since his was the only one that took place after North Carolina's new capital punishment statute was in effect. The previous law had been declared unconstitutional. The defense was a plea of insanity. However, even defense witnesses said they didn't think the defendant was insane. During the trial Record Lee's family came to see Britt. They were worried because the elderly woman had been vomiting for a long time. A lock of her hair was analyzed and found to contain arsenic. The jury took 70 minutes to find Velma guilty of first-degree murder. That same jury then heard arguments to decide the degree of punishment. Britt portrayed Velma as callous and malicious. If ever a case deserved the imposition of the ultimate penalty, he argued, this one did. The jury agreed, after three hours of deliberations in December 1978, to sentence Velma to death.

Immediately after the trial Velma stated, "I am guilty. Personally, I don't want an appeal. . . . I want one thing to be said, I hold nothing against anybody—the jurors, the judge, the district attorney, anybody who testified against me. But I wonder how many of them oppose abortion, which I feel is premeditated murder" [1]. But appeal she did.

During her time in prison awaiting trial in 1978, Velma claimed to have undergone a religious transformation which resulted in an "inward change." A group of supporters formed, including evangelist Billy Graham's wife Ruth, that was dedicated to getting Velma's execution commuted. It was said that Velma counseled and supported younger inmates in their adjustment to prison life. Rising at 3:30 in the morning to read the Bible and answer the up to one hundred letters she received weekly, Velma usually gave up her allotted daily hour of outdoor exercise time due to the volume of her work. Not everyone was impressed. Margie Pittman said, "She's got religion now, they say. Well, she had religion before. So we all thought" [3].

Almost six years elapsed before all avenues of appeal were exhausted. "I've known all the time it would come to this," said Velma, "but that doesn't make it easy. People don't think murderers deserve any chance to live" [3]. On the night of her execution, several hundred opponents of capital punishment gathered outside the prison to protest. Velma declined to request a specially prepared last meal. Instead of that night's regular prison menu of liver and macaroni, she opted for a final meal of Coca-Cola and Cheez Doodles. In the early morning of November 2, 1984, Velma was wheeled into the execution chamber, where at 2 A.M. she was given a lethal injection of procuronium bromide. Barfield became the first woman executed in the United States since 1962.

A relative of one of Velma's victims, speaking of Barfield's murders and crime in general in southwestern North Carolina, commented, "We're used to killings here. People stab each other. They shoot each other, but this. ... This is just unbelievable" [1].

Sources

1. Carroll, Ginny. "Confessed Poisoner Awaits Death." *The News and Observer* [Raleigh, N.C.], December 10, 1978, pp. 1, 6.
2. Kuncl, Tom. *Ladies Who Kill.* New York: Pinnacle, 1985, pp. 134–36.
3. Levin, Eric. "Cunning Poisoner—Or Redeemed Christian." *People*, October 29, 1984, p. 85–86, 89.
4. "No Clemency for Woman; Execution Set." *Chicago Tribune,* September 28, 1984, p. 12.
5. Pearsall, Chip. "Barfield Jury Calls for Death." *The News and Observer* [Raleigh, N.C.], December 3, 1978, pp. 1, 20.
6. Schmidt, William E. "Woman Executed in North Carolina." *New York Times,* November 2, 1984, pp. A1, A20.

Elizabeth Bathory

(1560–1614). *Place:* Hungary. *Time:* 1580s(?)–1610. *Age:* 20s–50. *Victims:* 300–650. *Method:* Torture.

Hungary's Elizabeth Bathory is often called "Countess Dracula" after her habit of killing young women, draining their blood, and then bathing in it. Legend has it that she took up this practice in 1600 or later, after the death of her husband. According to the story, a servant who was brushing Bathory's hair caused her mistress some discomfort by accidentally pulling too hard. Elizabeth slapped the servant and drew blood, some of which landed on Elizabeth's arm. Servants wiped it off, but Bathory was convinced that spot on her arm was left paler and more translucent—signs of beauty in those days—than the surrounding area. After that incident, Bathory took to bathing regularly in blood.

This story is probably completely in error. Accomplices who testified at Bathory's trial made no mention of blood baths at all. Elizabeth's start as a torturer and murderer also came much earlier. She may have been only 20, too young to worry about the effect of age on her skin. Most of her victims were drained of blood, but that was a natural result of prolonged torture. Blood sacrifice was also a common part of sorcery and witchcraft, both of which Bathory believed in strongly. She surrounded herself with practitioners of these black arts. Bathory murdered and tortured because she enjoyed killing, and her position in the aristocracy allowed her to get away with it for a long time.

Elizabeth was born in Hungary in 1560. Her father Gyorgy was a soldier, while her mother Anna was the sister of the king of Poland. When their daughter was 11 years old, the Bathorys arranged a future marriage for her with Ferencz Nadasdy. The Nadasdy family was almost as well connected and powerful as the Bathorys. The wedding took place on May 8, 1575, when Elizabeth was 15. She kept her own name after the ceremony, as a sign that her family had more status than the Nadasdy clan.

The Bathory family contained Satan worshippers, lesbians, drunks, sadists who tortured servants, murderers, and those who practiced incest. Elizabeth herself was subject to stabbing pains in her head and behind her eyes. Sometimes she was taken by "fits." These were called "possession" by some, but they may have been bouts of epilepsy, which ran in the family.

The couple settled into their man residence, Castle Csejthe, in north-western Hungary, after the wedding. In addition, they had a few other resi-dences. Whenever she moved from one place to another, Elizabeth's first order of business was to set up a torture chamber in a convenient spot. Life was boring for the vain Elizabeth, since Ferencz was often away from home for months at a time. She dabbled in witchcraft, sorcery, and alchemy as she moved from castle to castle. Wanton and promiscuous, she engaged in many affairs, with women as often as with men.

Five or six times a day Bathory would take out her jewels and change her clothes again and again. Hours were spent admiring herself in front of a mirror. Servants would paint her face carefully each day. Other servants spent their time making cosmetics for her. She consumed various drugs and medicines to alleviate her headaches.

Ferencz's mother often grilled her daughter-in-law about why she was not pregnant. Elizabeth did have children, but not until a decade after her wedding. Her start in torture and murder seems to have begun after these confrontations with her mother-in-law. Her resentment would be taken out on her servants by sticking pins into them. Elizabeth also bit them and ex-posed them, smeared with honey, to ants and bees. She was probably about 20 at the time. Ferencz was said to have sometimes joined in this torturing of servants when he was home. Living in fear of his spouse, Ferencz was content as long as he could have his mistresses on the side.

Over the years, Bathory's sadistic practices grew, and she branched out from servants to strangers. A handful of trusted employees functioned as agents. They scoured the countryside to find suitable young females and return them to the castle. Some were enticed with the promise of jobs as maids. If that didn't work they were drugged into submission or simply physically overpowered. Those who entered the castle never returned. Rumors about the evil Bathory spread throughout the neighboring villages, but nothing was ever done. The women who were taken away were always of low birth. At the time peasants in general were badly treated and had no real rights; the authorities would not trouble a woman of high birth, like Bathory, over some missing peasants. Relatives of the victims had no power to force action. They kept quiet.

Ferencz died in 1600 (1604 in some accounts). Elizabeth's murderous ways may or may not have escalated after his death. Her own servants often became victims of torture alongside women abducted from the country-side.

Bathory used a variety of implements such as needles, knives, whips, and red-hot pokers.

The victims were stripped naked and held down by accomplices. Pins were stuck into their nipples or under their nails. Elizabeth would sometimes tear a girl's breasts to shreds, or her vagina would be burned with candles. Some victims were beaten with cudgels. Pins were stuck into their upper and lower lips. Some were dragged naked outside into the snow where cold water was poured on them until they froze to death. Torture would last for hours, during which time Bathory talked, shouted, and paced the room. Before going into a final faint she would scream, "More, more still, harder still" [5].

A cylindrical cage with long iron spikes in it was constructed on Bathory's orders. The victim would be forced inside, and the cage was raised off the floor by means of a pulley. One of the servants would stab at the girl with a red-hot poker. In trying to avoid the poker the girl would impale herself on the spikes inside the cage. While this was going on, Elizabeth would stand on a stool screaming out sexual obscenities at the victim" [4].

Keys and coins were heated red-hot, and the victim would be forced to hold them in her hands. Bodies were cut with scissors. Helpers cut off fingers. One victim had a strip of flesh removed, which she was forced to grill and eat. Bathory was big on flesh biting. She would rip out a piece of flesh with her teeth from breasts, cheeks, and shoulders. Bodies were sometimes buried, sometimes left to rot, and sometimes just thrown over the castle walls at night to be devoured by animals from the woods before morning.

Bathory would burn breasts, cheeks and other parts of the victim at random. From time to time she would yank open their mouths so violently the corners would split open. As she stuck needles into their skin Elizabeth would screech, "The little slut—if it hurts, she's only got to take them out herself" [5].

Elizabeth made the mistake of starting to spirit away young women who, if not from her own class, were not as low-born as peasants. Some of the mothers of these girls began to ask questions and raise a fuss. Hungary's King Matthias—his father attended Bathory's wedding—finally yielded to pressure and ordered an investigation to be headed by Count Thurzo, who was Bathory's closest neighbor. The count staged a late-night raid on the castle on December 29, 1610. He caught Bathory and her helpers in the middle of a torture-and-murder session.

The trial was held in 1611. It involved 80 counts of murder, which was the number of bodies the raiders managed to find. Estimates on the number of people killed by Bathory over the years range from 300 to 650. Half a dozen of Elizabeth's servants were convicted and executed. Some were tortured before death. Bathory was the only one not required to be present at the trial. She was allowed to remain in her apartment at the castle, under heavy guard.

Once she was convicted of murder, Elizabeth's high connections saved her from the fate of her servant accomplices. Instead of being executed she was walled up in her apartment. The windows and door were sealed up except for tiny slits in the stone for ventilation and a larger slit for passing plates of food to her. Bathory lived in this solitary fashion with no communication of any kind until her death on August 21, 1614. The exact date is uncertain, since her death was not detected until plates of food went untouched for a long time.

Sources

1. *Crimes and Punishment,* vol. 8. New York: Marshall Cavendish, 1985, pp. 1217–18.

2. Green, Jonathon. *The Greatest Criminals of All Time.* New York: Stein & Day, 1980, p. 268.

3. Masters, R. E. L. *Perverse Crimes in History.* New York: Julian, 1963, pp. 12–24.

4. McNally, Raymond T. *Dracula Was a Woman.* New York: McGraw-Hill, 1983.

5. Penrose, Valentine. *The Bloody Countess.* London: Calder & Boyars, 1970.

Mrs. Leon Bearce

(1901–?). *Place:* Lake George, New York. *Time:* June 20, 1931. *Age:* 30. *Victims:* 3. *Method:* Knife.

Mr. and Mrs. Leon Bearce operated a small tourist camp in New York state in the early 1930s. In 1930 their camp was close to the community of Glen Falls. However, that summer the body of a young waitress was found hanging in a tree, a suicide. Thinking the resultant publicity would be bad for business, Leon Bearce moved his camp down the highway, nearer to Lake George, for the 1931 season.

His marriage had gone sour by then. Mrs. Bearce and Leon separated for some months early in 1931. In fact, action for a formal separation had been instituted by Mrs. Bearce, with a court date set for June 19. Whatever problems existed between the couple were not made public except for Leon's assertion that his wife had been acting "queerly" for several months. Their court case was postponed, and around the middle of June Mrs. Bearce moved back in with her husband to attempt a reconciliation. It was an attempt that went bad almost immediately and then turned into a tragedy.

Around 6:30 P.M. on June 20, 1931, the couple's four-year-old daughter Dena ran up to her father who was working on the grounds of the camp. Her throat was slashed and blood gushed forth. Dena pointed to her throat and screamed, "Mamma done it." Leon grabbed his daughter and raced into town for medical help. It was too late, however; Dena died a couple of hours later.

Returning to the camp with the police, Leon and the authorities began to search the woods for the remaining children after they found the Bearce home empty. In a clump of bushes they found the couple's 10-month-old twins, George and Joyce, with their throats slashed. Both were dead.

Standing nearby was Mrs. Bearce, who was taken into custody without a struggle. The bloody knife was still in her possession. The woman told the arresting officer, "If that knife hadn't been so dull I'd have used it on myself and finished the job" [3]. At the police station, Mrs. Bearce explained that she was worried over the possibility of a divorce. She said her husband believed her to be crazy and threatened to have her sent to an

24

asylum. Rather than be separated from her children Mrs. Bearce decided, she said, to kill them and then to commit suicide. Regaining her composure quickly after the murders, Mrs. Bearce slept soundly in jail and ate well, apparently unaware of the severity of her situation, before her worst fear came true. She was committed to an asylum.

Sources

1. "Mother, Alleged Killer of Three Children, Calm." *The Knickerbocker Press,* June 23, 1931, p. 3.
2. "Mother Kills 3, Fearing Asylum." *New York Times,* June 22, 1931, p. 5.
3. "Mother Slays 3 Small Children." *The Knickerbocker Press,* June 22, 1931, pp. 1, 14.

Martha Beck

(1920–1951). *Place:* United States. *Time:* 1947–1949. *Age:* 27–29. *Victims:* 4–20(?). *Method:* poison (barbiturates), beating, shooting, drowning.

Overweight and emotionally unstable, Martha Beck might have lived out her life quietly—if unhappily—had it not been for a practical joke played on her. A friend sent her name to a dating club, or lonely hearts club as they were then known, and Beck met Raymond Fernandez. Fernandez was usually content to swindle women he met in that fashion but the pair formed an odd alliance and their deeds soon escalated to include murder as Beck came to dominate Fernandez.

Martha was born in 1920 and had a traumatic childhood. At the age of 13 she was raped, perhaps many times, by her brother. Overweight since she was a teen-ager, the plain-looking Beck weighed about 200 pounds and was very much a misfit. In 1947 she was living in Pensacola, Florida, where she worked as a nurse. Although she was only 27 years old, Martha had already been divorced three times. Her last husband was Alfred Beck, whom she had married in 1944. From these marriages she had two children which a judge had ordered removed from her custody on the grounds that she was an unfit mother. One may have been the illegitimate child of a long-distance bus driver who had committed suicide rather than marry Martha.

Working in Pensacola, Beck had been superintendent of a crippled children's home and then was employed as a registered nurse at a city maternity hospital. Beck was fired from that job in 1947.

Sometime in October 1947, Martha received a pitch in the mail from Mother Dinene's Friendly Club for Lonely Hearts which promised the usual—true happiness in a blissful marriage. All this would be Martha's for just a five dollar fee. Beck sent in the money and claimed she was "witty, vivacious and oozed personality." No mention was made of her weight, divorces, or children [4]. She soon received a reply in the form of a charming letter from one Raymond Fernandez.

Of Spanish-American descent, Ray was born in Hawaii, or perhaps in Spain, in 1914. The epitome of a seedy, sleazy gigolo, he had gold teeth, a cheap toupee covering his sparse hair, and a pencil moustache. By all accounts he had led a quiet and law-abiding life until 1945, when he suffered a serious head injury in a shipboard accident when a metal door struck his head.

Fernandez underwent a profound personality change; he started to believe he possessed supernatural powers. He also thought he could hypnotize people from afar and make women fall in love with him. Before the accident he was described as "woman-shy," but afterward he became a highly successful gigolo. Ray preyed on women he met through dating clubs, bilked them of their assets, and moved on to his next victim. His success was prodigious; he counted about 100 such victims from 1945 until he met Martha late in 1947.

Beck was so impressed by the one letter from Fernandez that she traveled from Pensacola to his New York City apartment to meet him in November or December of 1947. When they met, Ray was actually living in the apartment of Mrs. Jane Thompson. The couple had recently gone on a trip to Spain, from which only Fernandez had returned. Thompson may or may not have been murdered, but with this possible exception Ray was not a murderer. His only brush with the law up to that time was one brief jail term for theft.

At the first meeting Ray was put off with Martha on a number of counts. Beck was fat, ugly, had no clothes sense and, worst of all, she had no money. Martha, however, was mad for Fernandez from the start; within hours of meeting they had sex. Ray soon tried to ditch her but Beck would not be easily shunted aside. She dramatically tried to commit suicide by gassing herself.

Uncharacteristically, Ray took her back. The one trump card she held, it seems, was a voracious and insatiable sex drive that coincided with Raymond's. At their trial the couple's sex habits would be much discussed and labeled as "degenerate" — so degenerate, in fact, that even the sensationalist press couldn't print the details.

Not only did Fernandez take Martha back, he also explained exactly how he made his living. None of this bothered Beck, who replied, "That's all right, I don't mind darling. We can work together. I can pretend I am your sister. We can be together always. And I can help to persuade the women to put their trust in you" [1].

The suave Fernandez had never needed any help before, but he agreed to take Martha along. The couple worked the northeastern United States and bilked an average of one or two women a month out of their assets. They continued to find all of their likely marks through lonely hearts clubs. Surprisingly, dragging his 200-pound "sister" around with him did nothing to detract from Ray's success in charming women.

One of the lucky women who escaped alive was Esther Henne of Pennhurst, Pennsylvania. Henne was a 41-year-old teacher who was married to Ray during March 1948. "He was courteous for the first four days of our married life, then he became irritable and gave me tongue lashings because I wouldn't sign over my insurance policies and my teacher's pension fund," said Henne.

Esther left Ray at the end of March as her fear of him increased. During their one month of married life Martha lived with the couple; Ray told Henne that Martha was his brother-in-law's sister-in-law. But, said Henne, "they acted too lovingly to be relatives." Esther lost several pieces of jewelry and $500 in cash stolen by Beck and Fernandez [5].

Several sources claim the couple murdered up to 20 victims during their relatively short time together. Ultimately police charged them with only three murders and did not pursue investigations into other possible murders.

Details of only one other case have been reported, but this murder can be fairly credited to the pair. On August 14, 1948, Ray married Myrtle Young in Chicago. The newlyweds adjourned to their boarding house in Chicago, accompanied by the ever-present Beck. Claiming that her brother was shy, Martha insisted on sharing the bed with Myrtle. Not surprisingly, Young protested this unusual wedding-night suggestion. The annoyed and forceful Beck then gave the bride an overdose of barbiturates. Young was unconscious for 24 hours. When she awoke, the still very groggy and dazed woman was put on a bus bound for her hometown of Little Rock, Arkansas. Soon thereafter she died. Young yielded $4,000 and an automobile.

Beck was possessive of Fernandez; her jealousy peaked when Ray serviced these other women sexually, even though she knew it was part of his work. Perhaps it was these jealous rages which led the couple to escalate from swindling to swindling and murdering.

Toward the end of 1948, Raymond met Janet Fay, an Albany, New York, widow in her sixties. Fay fell for Fernandez and was soon telling friends she had met someone with whom she was in love. After his arrest Ray would boast that he had gotten $6,000 out of Fay. The woman was last seen in Albany on January 2, 1949. She had gone to Fernandez's apartment in Long Island on the promise of an imminent marriage. When Janet arrived, Beck took care of her. "I bashed her head in with a hammer in a fit of jealousy," she later confessed to police. "I turned to Raymond and said: 'Look what I've done.' Then he finished the job off by strangling her with a scarf" [1]. The date was January 4, 1949.

The couple then had sex, with Fay's body on the floor beside them. When they finished they cleaned up the blood, put the body into a truck, and stored it at the home of Ray's real sister. A few days later they collected the body and took it to a house they had newly rented in Queens, New York, where they cemented it into the basement floor. After waiting for four days for the cement to completely dry, the couple backed out of the rental agreement, claiming the house was not satisfactory.

In this crime the couple made a mistake. Over a blank sheet of paper bearing Fay's signature they typed a letter to the dead woman's stepdaughter, Mrs. Spencer, asking her to send on some personal belongings. Spencer found this request strange since Fay didn't own a typewriter and didn't know how to type. Spencer took the letter to the police.

Near the end of January that year, Beck and Fernandez traveled to Grand Rapids, Michigan, where Ray worked his charm on 28-year-old widow Delphine Downing. Delphine had a two-year-old daughter named Rainelle.

Ray quickly ingratiated himself with Downing, and he and Martha moved into the widow's home. Downing reassured Beck she was welcome and explained that Fernandez moving in "on his own might have caused a bit of scandal with the local folks. You know what it's like in those close-knit communities" [1].

For the next month Ray busied himself in separating Delphine from her assets by having her sell off property in preparation for marrying him and moving to Long Island. He had sex with the widow which aroused Martha's jealousy. When Delphine told her guests she thought she might be pregnant, nurse Martha took over and fed her a large dose of sleeping pills under the pretense that it was medication to induce an abortion. As Downing lay unconscious Fernandez pumped a bullet into her, and they placed Downing's body in the cellar.

Beck and Fernandez were left with the disconsolate, weeping Rainelle, who kept asking where her mother had gone. A neighbor was told that Delphine had gone away unexpectedly for a long time. Suspicious of this and leery of the couple, this neighbor went to the police. Two or three days after the murder Rainelle had gotten on Fernandez's nerves. "You'll just have to do something about her," he said to Martha. Beck didn't like the child and needed little encouragement; she calmly drowned the screaming child in a washtub.

Rainelle's body was buried with her mother's in the basement and the hole was cemented over. That evening the couple went to the movies, intending to leave Grand Rapids the following morning. However, when they returned home that evening, March 1, 1949, they found the police awaiting them. Initially they claimed the Downings had gone away for an indefinite period of time. In answer to further questions, Fernandez told the police to search the house if they wanted to. They took him up on his suggestion and quickly found the patch of fresh cement in the basement.

Under arrest, Fernandez readily admitted to the way in which he made his living. He and Beck quickly confessed to three murders, the Downings and Fay, but would admit to no others. Michigan had no death penalty at the time but New York did, so the couple were extradicted to New York, a move they fought, where they stood trial for Fay's murder.

The trial revolved around the issue of sanity more than that of guilt. To that end, the details of their degenerate sex life were brought out in detail. Fernandez was painted as having gone sex-mad after his accident, while Martha was characterized as insane and also sex-mad since her childhood rape. By turns, Ray sometimes claimed Martha was the sole culprit and deserved to die, sometimes that he alone was the killer and Martha should be freed. He also alternated pleas of not guilty and not guilty by reason of insanity. The jury believed the prosecution's evidence that they were sane and deliberated for one day before finding them guilty of murder in the first degree.

The passion between the pair continued during their incarceration. They corresponded regularly; Martha treasured a letter from Ray which said, "I would like to shout my love for you to the world." If they caught a glimpse of each other across the exercise yard they would wave and sort of wiggle their bodies at each other. Ray boasted about his sex life with Martha to other prisoners. To get his goat, some of them started a story that Martha was having an affair with somebody in the women's wing. This caused much rage and jealousy for Ray. Once during their trial when they were being led into court separately, Beck broke away and rushed over to Ray, smothering him in kisses until she was pulled off him. "I love him, and I always will," she yelled.

Known as the Lonely Hearts Killers, the pair marked time on Sing Sing's death row until March 8, 1951, when all their appeals were exhausted. They were put to death in the electric chair that evening shortly before midnight. Four people were executed that night. Two other murderers went first, Fernandez third, and Beck fourth. Martha was slated last because it was felt that she was the most likely to break down as the end neared and perhaps hold everybody else up. They needn't have worried. Martha showed no evidence of remorse or any sign of mental or physical breakdown.

For her last request Martha had her hair meticulously curled and knocked off two chicken dinners for her final meal. On that last day she sent yet another love note to Ray that made him "want to burst with joy."

In her last statement Martha Beck said, "What does it matter who is to blame? My story is a love story, but only those tortured with love can understand what I mean. I was pictured as a fat, unfeeling woman. True, I am fat, but, if that is a crime, how many of my sex are guilty? I am not unfeeling, stupid or moronic. The prison and the death house have only strengthened my feeling for Raymond, and in the history of the world how many crimes have been attributed to love? My last words and my last thoughts will be: Let him who is without sin cast the first stone" [1].

Sources

1. *Crimes and Punishment,* vol. 5. New York: Marshall Cavendish, 1985, pp. 693–98.

2. Gaute, J. H. H. *The Murderers' Who's Who.* London: Harrap, 1979, p. 38.

3. Green, Jonathon. *The Greatest Criminals of All Time.* New York: Stein & Day, 1980, p. 183.

4. Hyde, H. Montgomery. *United in Crime.* New York: Roy, 1955, pp. 139–43.

5. "Lucky, Says Survivor." *New York Times,* March 2, 1949, p. 29.

6. Nash, Jay Robert. *Look for the Woman.* New York: M. Evans, 1981, pp. 21–22.

7. Scott, Harold. *The Concise Encyclopedia of Crime and Criminals.* London: Deutsch, 1961, p. 22.

8. Seigal, Kalman. "3 Lonely Hearts Murders Trap Pair." *New York Times,* March 2, 1949, p. 1, 29.

9. Sifakis, Carl. *The Encyclopedia of American Crime.* New York: Facts on File, 1982, p. 60.

10. "2 Lonely Hearts Pay Death Penalty." *New York Times,* March 9, 1951, p. 52.

11. Wilson, Colin. *A Criminal History of Mankind.* London: Granada, 1984, pp. 19–20.

12. Wilson, Colin. *Encyclopedia of Murder.* New York: Putnam, 1962, pp. 205–06.

Marie Becker

(1877–?). *Place:* Liège, Belgium. *Time:* 1932–1936. *Age:* 55–59. *Victims:* 12. *Method:* Digitalin poisoning.

For more than half a century Marie Becker led a quiet and exemplary life in Liège, Belgium, until lust and greed got the better of her. She went on a murdering spree that extended over several years and claimed 12 victims. In addition, Marie attempted to murder three others and committed various other crimes such as fraud and theft.

Marie was born in a working-class district of Liège around 1877. She married a cabinetmaker and became a bookkeeper in her father-in-law's sawmill. The years and decades flew by uneventfully. Even at that time Marie was fond of spending money. She went out a lot and liked to buy expensive clothes, habits that would one day run out of control.

A neighbor who knew Becker in her law-abiding days recalled her as "a most pleasant little person. Always ready to lend a helping hand and as kindly a soul as ever lived" [4]. A severe transition in her character took place in 1932 when Marie was a 55-year-old, white-haired matron. No reason for this drastic change is known. Her husband Charles may have been bland and colorless, but there is no record of marital strife.

In that year, Marie met 46-year-old Lambert Beyer. The pair became lovers. For inexplicable reasons Becker decided that this turn of events necessitated the complete removal of Charles from the scene. In the fall of 1932 she slipped some of the poison digitalin into her husband's food; Charles quickly died. Only years later would his body be exhumed and the poisoning confirmed.

At the time of his demise no suspicion was cast Marie's way. However, the sympathy extended to her by neighbors soon turned to disgust. Not only did the widow recover from her grief with inordinate speed, but she lived a wild life, frequenting bars and dance halls. She took many lovers, most of whom were in their twenties and thirties. It appears that Marie attracted these men by pretending to be wealthy. She had got some money upon her husband's death, but it wasn't a great sum. To hold her young men Marie was forced to spend lavishly on them. What resources she had diminished rapidly.

To earn extra money Becker took up dressmaking; she was efficient enough to develop a clientele who could afford to have clothes made to order. By supplying attractive dresses and using flattery, Marie formed close associations with some of her customers, most of whom were elderly widows.

Mme. Doupagne was one of these customers who turned to Marie for comfort when she was ill. Marie offered solace and suggested that Doupagne move into her home for nursing, saying, "I shall be able to give you more attention and look after you better if I have you under my eye" [4]. The delighted Mme. Doupagne moved into Becker's home in January of 1933. She then insisted on making out her will in favor of her devoted new friend. Just two months later, in March, Becker dispatched her houseguest with a dose of digitalin.

The money from this murder kept Marie flush enough to finance her lovers for over a year. By the end of 1934 Beyer was still in the picture but only one of many. Unhappy with that situation, Beyer became an annoyance to Marie with his constant complaining. She marked his account paid, with digitalin, in November of that year.

The period from March 1935 to September 1936 was a murderous peak for Marie, who murdered nine elderly women over that span of time, bringing her total to 12. In each case, she ingratiated herself into the woman's trust and then killed her. Besides receiving legacies from some of these women, Marie openly engaged in stealing from them and, on occasion, attempted to forge a will. Between murders she kept up her carousing and spending money on young lovers.

Becker slipped up with a woman named Mme. Guichner, who told Marie she would like to get rid of her husband permanently. When Guichner refused Marie's offer of a powder to do the job, she found herself the victim of stomach pains. Becoming suspicious and worried, she reported Becker to the police. At about the same time authorities received an anonymous letter accusing Becker of murder in the case of a Mme. Castadot. These two events prompted a police investigation.

As it turned out, the anonymous letter was from M. Castadot, who was on the staff of the police at Liège. After the death of his wife he became one of Becker's lovers. However, when she found him with another woman Marie quickly dumped him. Sending the letter was Castadot's way of taking revenge.

Bodies were exhumed and found to contain digitalin. When the police moved to arrest Marie, they found a quantity of digitalin in her purse. It was for her heart condition and prescribed by a doctor, she explained. When the doctor she named was questioned on this matter, he denied even knowing Becker.

In a courtroom jammed with spectators, Marie went on trial in 1938 for numerous counts of murder, attempted murder, and fabricating false wills. The indictment was 12,000 words long and took a full three hours to read in court. Initially Becker was cool and calm. She denied everything and said to the judge, "You are mistaken. Think it over and you will agree with me" [1]. The witnesses all lied, she claimed.

When asked in court about why she had bought so much digitalin Marie replied that it was for a Dutch friend whose address she couldn't remember. A check for this woman turned up no such person. In answer to the question as to how Mme. Lambert had died, Becker said, "Like an angel choked by sauerkraut." To the same question about Mme. Castadot, the poisoner said, "Beautifully, she lay flat out on her back" [4]. The only item that made Becker emotional was the charge that she had affairs with many men. Marie emphatically denied this.

At the end of the three-week trial, Marie was pale and trembling but still defiant; just before the jury retired she said to them in a weak voice, "I declare to you that I am innocent" [2]. The jury disagreed; it took just three hours to find her guilty. Marie was sentenced to death, but since the death penalty didn't apply in Belgium at that time, it meant a sentence of life in prison. According to unconfirmed reports, Becker died in prison during World War II.

Sources

1. "Belgian Poison Trial." *The Times* [London], June 14, 1938, p. 15.
2. "Belgian Poison Trial." *The Times* [London], July 9, 1938, p. 11.
3. Nash, Jay Robert. *Look for the Woman.* New York: M. Evans, 1981, pp. 22–23.
4. O'Donnell, Bernard. *The World's Worst Women.* London: Allen, 1953, pp. 163–72.
5. "Poison Trial in Belgium." *The Times* [London], June 8, 1938, p. 11.

Kate Bender

(1849–1873?). *Place:* Cherryvale, Kansas. *Time:* 1871–1873. *Age:* 22–24. *Victims:* 10–12. *Method:* Bludgeoning, knifing.

The reward poster issued for Kate Bender by the state of Kansas in 1873 described her as "about 24 years of age, dark hair and eyes, good looking, well formed, rather bold in appearance, fluent talker, speaks good English with very little German accent" [1]. When the Bender family arrived in Kansas, it consisted of father John, 60 years old; his wife, who was about 50; their son John, Jr., 25; and the daughter Kate. All of the family members had a German accent, but nothing of their background is known.

The Benders settled in Cherryvale, Kansas, in March 1871, in a one-room log cabin that measured 20 by 16 feet. Cherryvale was a small railway town about 14 miles east of Independence. A canvas curtain was installed in the cabin that divided it into two equal parts. One side functioned as both living and sleeping quarters for the Benders and contained a trapdoor which led to a small pit. This door was discreetly hidden by furnishings.

The other side of the cabin served as a general store, restaurant, and hotel with a sign marked "Grocery" over the door. Travelers, and others, could have a meal there, spend the night, or just buy groceries off the shelf. The business was poorly situated and probably wasn't much of a money maker. That was all right with the Benders, since the business was only a front for the more lucrative trade of murdering and robbing their guests.

Of all the Benders, Kate was the most important and pivotal member of the family. John, Jr., was described as a "moron," while Mrs. Bender made so little impact that her first name goes unrecorded. Mr. Bender kept a low profile. Only Kate went out and about. One of her tasks was to attract guests to the family business; as a young, buxom, sensual woman she was equal to the task.

Kate passed herself off as a psychic and healer and toured small towns in the area to hold seances or to give lectures. She called herself Professor Miss Katie Bender; one of her handbills claimed she "can heal all sorts of Diseases; can cure Blindness, Fits, Deafness and all such diseases, also Deaf and Dumbness" [1].

35

Presumably some of the people who attended her lectures later went to her restaurant for a meal. Some were simply travelers passing through. Once a suitable guest arrived at the Benders' restaurant Kate would serve him the food, cooked by Mrs. Bender, and stay and talk to him as he was set up. It was Kate's job to get him to sit against the curtain with his back to it. Thus the man's head could be clearly seen from the other side. At an appropriate moment one of the Bender men, on the other side of the curtain, would cave in the diner's skull with a sledgehammer. Kate would then finish the job by slashing the victim's throat with a knife. The body was hurriedly thrown down the pit in case other guests should stumble in; then, the Benders would strip the victim of any valuables at their leisure and bury him during the night somewhere in the back part of their property.

Dr. William York ended a visit to his brother, Colonel York, on March 9, 1873, and set off for his home at Independence. He had a fair amount of money with him and told friends he would be stopping at the Benders for a midday meal. Dr. York never made it home. A few weeks later Colonel York was leading a search party and traced his brother as far as the Cherryvale area. The posse stopped at the Benders, but the family denied any knowledge of William or that he had stopped there. Although the group left to continue the search, the Benders became nervous.

Rumors and unease over Bender hospitality had already circulated to a minor degree, fueled by a number of suspicious incidents. One man, believing in Kate's power as a healer, journeyed to the café with a friend in the hopes the woman could cure his neuralgia. Kate, friendly and solicitous, told him she could. First, though, she suggested the men have a meal. She sat them close to the curtain as expected. The men had both noticed the hard scrutiny they had received earlier from the Bender men. As soon as they sat down, the Bender men disappeared. Feeling uneasy, the men took their meals to a nearby counter and ate there. When they did this Kate suddenly became abusive, calling them names. This added to the pair's growing suspicions, and they left. Another guest was reported to have fled the restaurant after a gust of wind blew Kate's apron aside to reveal a knife in her hand.

The Benders were sufficiently rattled from Colonel York's visit that they fled the town on May 5, 1873, taking everything with them and leaving the cabin stripped bare. A lone rider noted their disappearance and alerted the posse, which returned en masse to the Bender cabin a few days after their departure.

Their first discovery was the pit, which gave off a powerful stench—the smell of the blood from which it was saturated. Satisfied there were no bodies in this cellar, Colonel York looked around and remarked, "Boys, I see graves yonder in the orchard" [7]. And there were. Digging in the area yielded 10 to 12 bodies—accounts vary. All the victims were men, except for one woman and one child. One victim was William York. Some of the bodies were so badly decomposed that they could not be identified.

The Benders had left after enriching themselves to the tune of $5,000 to $10,000 from their victims, a large sum in those days. Several rewards were offered for the Benders' capture, particularly Kate's, who was credited with being "the leading spirit of her murderous family" [1]. Although the Benders were sought for decades, no trace of them was ever found.

When news of the family's exploits spread, souvenir hunters descended on the area and trashed the cabin, carting it off piece by piece to be sold for souvenirs. False identifications of the family abounded. In 1889 a pair of women in Michigan were identified as Kate and her mother. They were extradicted to Kansas but released when they produced proof that they could not be the Benders.

Old man Bender was said to have been captured in Montana in 1884 and to have died in custody. There was no ice house in the town, and by the time people arrived from Kansas to identify the body it had decomposed too much. Nevertheless, the skull was put on display as Bender's in a local bar, where it remained a tourist attraction until it disappeared in the 1920s. Today a historical marker, put up by the Kansas Historical Society and the State Highway Commission, marks the spot of the Bender cabin.

In Cherryvale the Benders had been friendly with a man named Brockman, another German store owner. When the posse had uncovered the bodies, they suspected Brockman as an accomplice and hung him from a beam for a few minutes to make him confess. This process was repeated twice more, but the crowd let him off when no confession was forthcoming. It is now thought that Brockman may have been using his store to fence some of the booty stolen from the victims.

Brockman was also one of the many of Kate's suitors and hoped she would marry him. Brockman had several fistfights with John, Jr., which were later explained by the report that Kate admitted to having an incestuous relationship with her brother and that they both had gonorrhea.

It seems most probable that the Bender family was killed in 1873. When Colonel York found the Benders gone, he immediately sent a posse after them. Later the wagon they escaped in was found abandoned and bullet-ridden. It is said that the posse put them to death in a particularly brutal way, perhaps torturing them or burning them alive. They then helped themselves to whatever money the Benders had with them and swore themselves to secrecy.

George Downer was a member of that posse; in 1909 he made a deathbed confession to that effect in Chicago. They buried the remains, he said, in a 20-foot well. The following year, 1910, another posse member by the name of Harker lay dying in New Mexico. He made substantially the same confession and specifically mentioned the 20-foot well. He had no knowledge of Downer's confession. A search was made of the area indicated by these men, but it had long since been planted over by corn and nothing was found.

Sources

1. *Crimes and Punishment,* vol. 5. New York: Marshall Cavendish, 1985, pp. 773–79.

2. Gaute, J. H. H. *The Murderers' Who's Who.* London: Harrap, 1979, p. 43.

3. Green, Jonathon. *The Greatest Criminals of All Time.* New York: Stein & Day, 1980, p. 148.

4. Nash, Jay Robert. *Bloodletters and Badmen.* New York: M. Evans, 1973, pp. 53–54.

5. Nash, Jay Robert. *Look for the Woman.* New York: M. Evans, 1981, pp. 25–27.

6. Sifakis, Carl. *The Encyclopedia of American Crime.* New York: Facts on File, 1982, pp. 64–65.

7. Wilson, Colin. *Encyclopedia of Murder.* New York: Putnam, 1962, pp. 74–75.

Patricia Bolin

(1936–1976). *Place:* Upper Arlington, Ohio. *Time:* December 8, 1976. *Age:* 40. *Victims:* 4. *Method:* Firearm.

A newspaper account of these homicides said that Patricia Bolin went "berserk." And that's as close as anyone ever got to explaining why it happened. Patricia, 40, and her 43-year-old husband Ronald had no financial problems. They lived in an impressive ranch-style home in Upper Arlington, Ohio, a wealthy suburb of Columbus. Ronald had designed the house for Patricia and had it built for her. The couple had three children and had lived in Upper Arlington for six years. In the early 1960s Mr. Bolin had founded his own company, Riverside Design, a mechanical and machine-design business he was still president of in 1976. He also had three children by a previous marriage.

If the homicides were inexplicable, they were also planned. On October 25, 1976, Patricia bought a 22-caliber pistol and 50 shells in a store for $51.50. She hid them away in her sewing basket; no one in the house knew of their existence. The Bolins never kept guns at home. After the tragedy, Ronald's mother said, "My son never liked guns. He never went hunting and never wanted a gun in the house" [2]. Following the shootings, the police couldn't account for seven shells; they speculated Patricia had used them at some time for practicing.

At 5:30 P.M. on the evening of December 8, 1976, Patricia and Ronald were home alone. Apparently Patricia threatened her husband with the gun and Ronald tried to run out the front door. He was shot numerous times in the head, neck, and chest, collapsing just inside the front door.

A few minutes later their daughter Tamela Jean, 12, arrived home from school. Tamela entered the garage first to enter the house by a connecting door. Waiting for her was Patricia, who shot her in the garage and then, judging by the trail of blood, dragged her daughter's body into the house. The girl was found still wearing her winter clothes.

Next Patricia called her nine-year-old son Todd Matthew home from playing outside. No sooner had he gone in than he ran back outside yelling, "She's shooting everyone" [1]. Patricia called him in again and he complied. Todd was shot before he could take his coat off.

39

The couple's last child was 15-year-old Alicia Ann, who arrived home at about 6:00 P.M. As she was about to enter the house through the connecting garage door, Alicia spotted her sister's body and ran to the back door, yelling for her mother. As she entered, Patricia confronted her with the gun, pointed it at her, and pulled the trigger three times; by this time the pistol was empty. Patricia ordered her daughter to go to her room. Alicia started to go but came across her brother's body and fled the house by the back door. She ran to a neighbor's and the police were summoned. In the meantime, Patricia had reloaded.

Officer Thomas French was first on the scene. He tried to enter through the front door but found it blocked by what later turned out to be Ronald's body. The officer walked around the house shining his flashlight into the darkened house. As he peered in one window he saw Patricia, who pointed the gun at him. He ducked away. Patricia by then was wearing a winter coat apparently preparing to go outside after Alicia. When French looked back into the room he saw the woman pointing the gun at herself. He and a second officer who had by then arrived on the scene forced the front door, but they heard a single shot as they did so. Patricia killed herself with a shot to the temple. In all, she fired 18 times.

Neighbors all expressed shock and surprise, describing the family as being a loving and close-knit one. Police could uncover no evidence of marital or financial troubles. The Bolins were very active members of the Upper Arlington Lutheran Church. On the Sunday before the shootings, the couple had participated in the Advent candle-lighting ceremony. Patricia worked with the local Girl Scout organization.

Ronald and his wife went out frequently together. An outing was planned for the night of the killings; a freshly pressed suit and a formal gown were laid out on the couple's bed. One of Ronald's employees described his boss as easy to work for and liked by everyone.

Patricia was described as a social drinker who was for years in the habit of having a cocktail before dinner. Only in recent times had she begun to drink more heavily. During their investigation the police found two empty pints of vodka, apparently consumed the afternoon of the shootings by Patricia.

Police Captain Kenneth Borror acknowledged that even if she were drunk, "There had to be something else that triggered her. You would normally think a mother would be unable to shoot as many times as she did. There is nothing to indicate that she had any mental problems. Her brothers know of no drinking or mental problems in the family. There is no family history of suicide or murder, her brothers told me" [2]. No motive was found.

Sources

1. Smith, Jim. "Mother Kills Two Children, Husband; Commits Suicide." *Columbus Citizen-Journal,* December 9, 1976, pp. 1, 8.

2. Smith, Jim. "No Reason Known for Area Murder-Suicide." *Columbus Citizen-Journal,* December 10, 1976, p. 5.

Harjit Kaur Bhuller Brar

(1947–1979). *Place:* Calgary, Canada. *Time:* May 1, 1979. *Age:* 32. *Victims:* 5. *Method:* Drowning.

Harjit Brar was a Sikh from the Punjab who emigrated to Canada in 1967. She first settled in Montreal, where she married her husband Santokh. Later the family moved west to Calgary, Alberta, where they seemed to adjust well to Canadian life. Santokh had a business in India; he owned six taxis and was co-owner of the Plaza Theatre in Calgary. The couple had relatives in Calgary and other Canadian cities.

Described as slim and good-looking, Harjit had, in May 1979, recently joined a sewing class and was planning to take a trip to India later that month. On May 1 the day passed uneventfully, according to first reports. Harjit was in good spirits, not depressed, or lonely, or having any fights or quarrels with family members. She took her children swimming for a couple of hours in the early evening.

The Brars were accustomed to going to bed at 9 P.M. On the night of May 1 Santokh did just that, but Harjit told her husband she would stay up to look after an ill child. Soon after she drove away from the family home with the children, parked in a lot, and walked to the middle of a bridge over the Bow River, which cuts through the city.

At about 10 P.M. witnesses saw Harjit throw her three oldest daughters, six-year-old Ravinder, four-year-old Savinder, and 18-month-old Sukhjit, into the water and then jump in herself, clutching her infant daughter Amrit, two months old. All five died. It was the worst murder-suicide in Calgary's history.

Witnesses said the children offered no resistance. Police Sargeant Roy Evans commented, "I don't know why it happened. I don't know why they didn't resist. I can only think it was because they trusted their mother" [3].

An ambulance arrived at the Brar house at 11 P.M. that evening; its presence was at first inexplicable. It turned out that the woman who "never had any complaints about her kids or her husband" was not free from depression. An hour before her death, Harjit had made an emotional call to a relative. According to Police Inspector Cec Byers, "There was nothing said at that time that she might jump into the river, although there was some indication she might commit suicide" [1]. This relative tried to phone Harjit later, but getting no response, called for an ambulance whose crew awakened the sleeping Santokh.

Several years earlier, Harjit's only son had died of cancer at the age of five after suffering for two years. A friend, Rajinder Sidhu, said, "She used to think about him a lot. She was always crying for him. She wanted a son very badly. Actually she was expecting the fourth child to be a boy. ... Most of the time she was in bad shape. She would listen to his tapes, and then cry the whole day. Her friends would say to her she should not think of him so much. But she would say, 'I satisfy myself because I can listen to his voice on the tapes'" [2].

Sidhu felt that Harjit, although not pressured by other people, was under internal pressure to produce a son; it was common for Sikhs to prefer a son in the family even if they had been out of the Punjab for years. Comments from other Sikhs who didn't know the Brars indicated that it was significant that all her children were female and that she took all of them with her on her suicidal leap.

Some Sikhs came forward to speak to authorities in case the Punjab cultural bias in favor of male children might be overlooked by Canadian investigators. One such person was a Sikh medical doctor, unknown to the Brars, who said, "Prejudice against girls is very, very common in our country. Sometimes women who produce only daughters are mistreated. There's beating, abusing and even people committing suicide. This is common even among educated people. This is our tradition. There is happiness when you have a boy, and misery when you have a girl" [2].

Traditionally Sikh males have the middle name Singh, which means lion, while Sikh females have the middle name Kaur, which roughly translates to "second in command." Harjit and all four of her daughters had Kaur as their middle name.

Sources

1. Hallman, Mark. "Woman Phoned Relative Before Murder-Suicide." *Calgary Herald,* May 3, 1979, p. A1.

2. Warden, Kathryn. "Young Son's Death May Have Led to Drowning Tragedy." *Calgary Herald,* May 3, 1979, pp. A1–2.

3. West, Ken. "Mother Kills Family, Self." *Calgary Herald,* May 2, 1979, pp. A1–2.

Marie de Brinvilliers

(1630–1676). *Place:* Paris, France. *Time:* 1664–1672. *Age:* 34–42. *Victims:* 50 or more. *Method:* Arsenic poisoning.

She was described as small and thin, with unusually large blue eyes noted for their "profound expression." Marie was rich and beautiful, but she wanted even more. She killed family members and total strangers. She killed for money, for lust, and probably just for the sake of killing as well. Beneath her beauty lay arrogance and indifference as she routinely tried out her poison brews on the down-and-out class of Paris to make sure the potions worked as she wanted them to.

Marie Madeleine d'Aubray was born in Paris, France, on July 22, 1630, the eldest of four children of Antoine Dreux d'Aubray. M. d'Aubray held a number of important posts, including that of Civil Lieutenant of the City of Paris. The family was well connected both politically and socially and financially well off. Growing up in such circumstances, Marie matured into a willful and self-indulgent person. By the time she was in her teens she had had sexual intercourse with both of her brothers, and prior to that had been first seduced, by her own account, at the age of seven. She was the aggressor in her affairs with her brothers. Marie would devote much of her future to taking a long string of lovers.

As was to be expected for a man in his position, M. d'Aubray was able to arrange a good marriage for his daughter. In 1651 Marie married Antoine Gobelin de Brinvilliers, the son of another well-connected Frenchman. The couple had an enormous annual income for the time of perhaps $250,000 a year. However, their life-style was more than equal to the task of spending it.

The Brinvillers' maintained elaborate housing and numerous servants, and Marie spent a lot on clothing, jewelry, and other luxuries. Their greatest extravagance was gambling. Both of them gambled to excess and both lost heavily. Both partners took a series of lovers rather openly and often spent time away from home in pursuit of these liaisons. Each knew of the affairs of the other and raised no objections. For the most part, each went his or her own way.

This attitude was not shared by M. d'Aubray, who kept a close watch on his daughter even after she was married and out of his house. Well aware of his daughter's life-style and vehemently opposed to it, d'Aubray often chastised and upbraided her. Marie had no intention of changing her habits and grew to dislike her father more and more; she found his endless criticisms intolerable. If the willful daughter didn't lash out at the criticizing father, it was only because of the large inheritance she would come into upon her father's death, which was especially important in light of her gambling losses.

Antoine de Brinvilliers made the acquaintance of Gaudin de Sainte-Croix, a cavalry officer, in 1659. Sainte-Croix was as dissolute as Brinvilliers and shared his interests: gambling, womanizing, and drinking. However, Sainte-Croix did not have the money that Brinvilliers had. The two men soon became fast friends, with Brinvilliers picking up most of the bills. Inevitably Marie met this new friend of her husband's, and the pair soon became lovers. Sainte-Croix openly escorted Marie to functions. Brinvilliers raised no objections to this flagrant affair, but M. d'Aubray did.

Things came to a head when Sainte-Croix suggested that Marie separate her fortune from that of her husband; when the couple married, they had pooled their money. Sainte-Croix, hoping to ensure Marie could afford to support him, suggested separating the money because, he argued, Brinvilliers spent more money on his gambling and his lovers than Marie did on hers. Marie agreed and initiated proceedings. M. d'Aubray and both of her brothers intervened this time. They worried that somehow Marie might lose everything. The headstrong Marie told them all to mind their own business.

The enraged father warned her that a man in his position could put an end to his daughter's wanton ways. The openness of the affair, the fact that Sainte-Croix was already married, and the matter of the money all proved too much for d'Aubray, who made good on his threat.

He got a *lettre de cachet* against his daughter's lover. This was an arrest warrant issued under the king's private seal that could be obtained by well-connected people. Such a document ordered the arrest of the named individual for no stated reason and for an unstated length of time. People obtained such documents to get rid of those who were regarded as nuisances. On March 19, 1663, Sainte-Croix was tossed into the Bastille. While there, he made the acquaintance of an Italian known only as Exili who had a reputation of being Europe's master poisoner. Sainte-Croix learned something about arsenic and poisoning during his stay in prison.

After just ten weeks, Sainte-Croix was released from the Bastille on June 2, 1663. It is unknown whether d'Aubray arranged the release or whether Marie came up with enough money for a substantial bribe. Once released, Sainte-Croix came straight to his lover's side. Marie was smouldering with hatred toward her father and her family in general. She was also short of money as her gambling debts mounted. The couple must have planned to murder d'Aubray then, spurred on by the information from Exili.

The two continued their affair but kept it much more discreet in an attempt to not antagonize d'Aubray further. Sainte-Croix set up a lab of sorts in a rented room and he experimented with poison concoctions, including "aqua toffania [sic]," named for the infamous Italian poisoner, and thought to be a combination of arsenic, vitriol, and toad venom. Whatever he had picked up from Exili wasn't enough, for he recruited Christopher Glaser, a well-known chemist, for more advice.

All of this required money and put a further strain on Marie's resources. She worried that if her father died mysteriously, suspicion would automatically fall on her. It was necessary, she felt, that Sainte-Croix's recipes be tested to make sure they would work to her satisfaction and would allow her to escape detection. She suggested, and her lover readily agreed, that she test the poisons at the Hôtel Dieu, the Paris hospital that catered to the poor and downtrodden of that city. Even one hundred years after Marie's time, patients at the Hôtel Dieu could still be found crowded six and even more to one bed.

Although Marie had never shown any charitable impulses before, she suddenly did—at least on the surface. She would often set out from her home laden with a basket of food on her arm to minister to the poor and the sick. Most people of her class would normally have dispatched a servant with their charity, but no one found it unusual that Marie went herself. She gave the patients wine into which arsenic had been stirred and food sprinkled with powder supplied by Sainte-Croix. Acting methodically, Marie always made sure the target ate or drank the offerings in her presence, anxiously inquiring if the patient enjoyed it and if the flavor was good.

On her next visit, she would note which persons had died and which had merely gotten sicker. She would request to visit the morgue for a last look at so-and-so, but in reality she wanted to note the condition of the body. Once in a while she would dose one of her servants to test a concoction, but she devoted most of her experimenting to hospital patients. If the death rate rose at the hospital, it was not noticed. In the scheme of things, patients there were held to be of no consequence.

More than two years passed between Sainte-Croix's release from jail and the murder of d'Aubray. How many people died at Marie's hands is unknown, but some sources estimate it at between 50 and 100, numbers that seem plausible. During this period of time d'Aubray became totally reconciled with his daughter. He thought Sainte-Croix was out of the picture and was proud of Marie's charity work. While she appeared to be a devoted daughter, her hatred for her father—and lust for his money—burned.

Early in 1666, Marie moved into her father's home for a visit.

D'Aubray began to experience periods of illness. Deciding he needed a rest at his country estate, he left Paris, requesting that his daughter accompany him. When she did join him his health continued on a downhill course, and by the end of summer he felt himself near death. Returning to the capital, he died almost immediately, on September 10, 1666.

The death of a prominent person in those days automatically brought up the possibility of poison, and an autopsy was performed on d'Aubray. However, since forensic science was very crude, the death was ruled to be the result of natural causes. Much later Marie admitted poisoning her father. It was a process that required the administration of 27 doses over an eight-month period. Daughter and lover received a shock when the will was read. D'Aubray had left most of his fortune to his other three children, two sons and a daughter. Marie's financial problems remained.

She and Sainte-Croix were not faithful to each other, and both actively sought out other lovers. Marie continued a carousing life-style, usually going to bed at dawn and then rising in the afternoon. Over the years this non-maternal woman gave birth to five children, two thought to be by Sainte-Croix, to whom she was totally indifferent. One of her daughters was regarded by Marie as stupid and a particular nuisance. Fed up with her, Marie once gave the child a dose of poison only to have second thoughts and administer an antidote in time to save her. She would repeat the process with this daughter once or twice more over the years.

One day Brinvillier's main mistress stopped by the house to see her lover. Hit by a sudden fury, Marie tried to stab the woman with a knife, even though she cared little for either party. Her money problems worsened as she refused to pay tradesmen. Some servants had not been paid for months. A house owned by Brinvilliers, a favorite of Marie's, was seized by creditors. Taken by another fury, Marie tried unsuccessfully to burn the house down.

Whatever money had been left her by her father was by this time gone; the solution in Marie's mind was to kill her two brothers, who had inherited the bulk of the estate. Their money would then come to her. Her lover readily agreed with the idea. The couple first installed one of Sainte-Croix's own servants, Jean Hamelin, known as La Chaussée, in the domestic staff at the house shared by the brothers. Chaussée agreed to administer the poison for a fee, but since Marie then had little money, he had to settle for a promissory note to be paid after she inherited her brothers' money.

Sainte-Croix also charged for his services and also received a promise to pay. His love of money exceeded his love for Marie; he had already blackmailed her on occasion and would do so in the future. He had several very incriminating letters from her in his possession.

In the spring of 1670, Chaussée fixed a special pigeon pie for one of the brothers and his dinner guests. The brother took ill and died off slowly, after an agonizing few months of illness. The other brother was poisoned to death in the fall of that year. So well had Chaussée worked his way into the brothers' confidence that one of them left him a small sum of money in his will as a reward for all the care he tendered.

Doctors examined the bodies of both brothers and found, in both cases, that the stomach and duodenum had gone black and fallen to pieces and that the liver was parched and gangrenous. Everything pointed to death by poisoning but they couldn't be positive, so they ruled death due to natural causes — a "malignant humour."

The emboldened Marie determined to next poison her sister but felt she should wait for some time to pass first. She took Chaussée as a lover, followed by a man named Briancourt whom she had hired to tutor her children. Perhaps overconfident from her successes, Marie told Briancourt much of her past. He had also picked up some unpleasant rumors from servants in the house who served M. Brinvilliers. Briancourt went so far as to send a warning letter to the sister.

Becoming aware that she had told too much to Briancourt, Marie and Sainte-Croix made a few unsuccessful attempts to kill him. By then Briancourt had some idea of what to expect and managed to escape the house alive. He didn't report anything to the authorities.

Marie was anxious to marry Sainte-Croix; the first step should be, she decided, to murder her husband. Brinvilliers's food was soon laced with arsenic by Marie, and he began to ail. The urge to marry was not reciprocated by Sainte-Croix, who had no wish to be united with his lover. Unbeknownst to Marie, Sainte-Croix administered antidotes to Brinvilliers; the health of Marie's husband waxed and waned in seemingly inexplicable fashion. All this came to an end in July 1672, when Sainte-Croix suddenly died.

It is thought that from the time the second brother died in November 1670 until Sainte-Croix died, Marie and her lover killed an unknown number of victims just to keep in practice and because by then poisoning had become an evil lust with them.

Sainte-Croix died in his lab, apparently at work on some of his poisonous brews. Some believe that he simply died of natural causes. Others believe that an accident occurred in which the mask he habitually wore in the lab somehow broke and fell from his face, causing him to expire from inhaling noxious fumes. He was interested in developing poisons that could kill from contact or inhalation rather than having to be ingested.

This death put Marie into a panic, for she knew her late lover had incriminating material on her in a box he kept at home. Marie's feverish attempts to get the box failed. The authorities opened it and immediately set out to arrest her and Chaussée, who was also implicated by the contents of the box. Marie barely managed to escape her pursuers and fled to England. Chaussée was arrested.

Initially Chaussée denied everything but confessed after being tortured; early in 1673 he was put to death by being broken alive on the wheel. Extradition procedures were started but, staying one step ahead of the law, Marie headed for the European mainland. She moved from one city to another until settling in Liège, where she boarded in a convent. Since authorities couldn't enter a convent to effect an arrest, Marie felt she was safe. While she was in the convent, she wrote a confession in which she admitted to poisoning her father, two brothers, attempting to poison her daughter and husband, and planning to poison her sister.

Marie remained at large for several years until she was arrested on March 25, 1676. The French dispatched an agent to Liège, who entered the convent disguised as a visiting abbé. He convinced the bored Marie to go outside the convent for a walk along a nearby river. It would do her good, he told her. Once outside, he arrested the furious Marie and bundled her back to Paris.

At her trial Marie defiantly repudiated her confession and denied all the charges. However, the evidence was overwhelming and she was sentenced to death. She did confess before the sentence was carried out. Before her execution, Marie was subjected to water torture in which the body was tied in a painful position, a funnel inserted into the mouth, and a large amount of water poured directly into the stomach.

On July 16, 1676, Marie, barefoot, with a white cap on her head, wearing only a thin white chemise, was driven in a rough cart to an area in front of Notre Dame Cathedral. The crowd roared its approval as she stood before them; with the light shining through her thin garments, she was practically naked. The humiliation was complete when she was forced to make a public confession: "I admit that wickedly and for vengeance I poisoned my father and my brothers. I attempted to poison my sister-in-law. I did this in order to possess myself of their property, and for it I ask pardon of God, of the King, and of Justice" [5]. Marie was then beheaded, her body burned on a fire, and her ashes scattered.

Sources

1. Dumas, Alexandre. *Celebrated Crimes,* vol. 7. Philadelphia: Rittenhouse, 1895, pp. 6–7, 12–29, 44–45.

2. Green, Jonathon. *The Greatest Criminals of All Time.* New York: Stein & Day, 1980, p. 223.

3. Gribble, Leonard. *Sisters of Cain.* London: John Long, 1972, pp. 27–41.

4. Nash, Jay Robert. *Look for the Woman.* New York: M. Evans, 1981, pp. 58–59.

5. Plaidy, Jean. *A Triptych of Poisoners.* London: Robert Hale, 1958, pp. 75–130.

6. "Poison as the Weapon of Women Criminals." *New York Times,* April 26, 1925, sec. 9, p. 12.

7. Wilson, Colin. *A Criminal History of Mankind.* London: Granada, 1984, pp. 390–92.

8. Wilson, Colin. *Encyclopedia of Murder.* New York: Putnam, 1962, pp. 102–05.

Inez Campbell

(1921–1945). *Place:* Glasgow, Montana. *Time:* May 25, 1945. *Age:* 24. *Victims:* 5. *Method:* Drowning, bludgeoning.

Inez Ethel Kapphann was born in Plentywood, Montana, on April 17, 1921. She would live only a little more than one month past her twenty-fourth birthday, but by then would be the mother of six children. Inez married Andrew Campbell, an employee of the Montana-Dakota Utilities Company, around 1939. At that time Inez was the mother of a one-year-old boy. Andrew was not the father. The couple settled in the rural community of Glasgow, Montana, and had babies at the rate of one per year.

On May 25, 1945, Inez gathered five of her children—three-year-old Bud was visiting relatives—and took them over a bridge across the Milk River, supposedly to visit a friend of the family named Clarence. Clarence had agreed to let the Campbells plant a small garden for themselves on his farm.

This trip was cut short when Inez stopped in the middle of the bridge. Taking out a hammer, Inez clubbed Johnny, seven, over the head with it and then threw him off the bridge into the river. Mrs. Campbell then meted out the same treatment to her other children, five-year-old Janet, four-year-old Jerry, one-year-old Larry and three-month-old Howard. When she was finished, Inez jumped into the river herself. All died except Johnny, who never lost consciousness and witnessed his mother killing his siblings. Johnny swam ashore and went to his aunt's house, from whence the police were summoned.

At the Campbell house a note from Inez was found. It was addressed to "Dear brother" and signed "From your crazy sister." Part of it read, "I know I was going crazy over it and cannot stand it any longer" [2]. Police described the rest of the note as incoherent.

Sources

1. "Drowns Her Four Children." *New York Times,* May 26, 1945, p. 17.
2. "Report Mother Drowns Four Children, Self." *The Billings Gazette,* May 26, 1945, pp. 1, 2.

Patty Cannon

(1783?–1829). *Place:* Delaware. *Time:* 1802–1829. *Age:* 19–46. *Victims:* 25 or more. *Method:* Firearm, stabbing, bludgeoning, poisoning.

The anonymous author who outlined the crimes of Patty Cannon a dozen years after her death fumed indignantly, "It has probably never fallen to the lot of man to record a list of more cruel, heart-rending, atrocious, cold-blooded and horrible crimes and murders. ... And it seems doubly shocking and atrocious, when we find them committed by one of the female sex, which sex, have always been esteemed, as having a higher regard for virtue and a far greater aversion to acts of barbarity, even in the most abandoned of the sex, than is generally found in men of the same class" [1].

The subject of such hyperbole was born Lucretia P. Hanly near Montreal, Canada, around 1783. Her father, Mr. Hanly, was described as the son of a wealthy English nobleman. After destroying his life by abandoning himself to "intemperence," Hanly left England for Canada, where he engaged in a life of smuggling and petty crime. One of those criminal escapades resulted in Hanly murdering a man; he was tried for the crime, convicted, and executed. Mrs. Hanly opened a boarding house to make enough money to feed her family, which numbered five children. Lucretia, known as Patty, was the youngest daughter.

Alonzo Cannon was a wheelwright from Delaware who chanced to stay at Hanly's establishment while in the area. Mrs. Hanly considered him to be a good catch because he was presentable and had a little money. A minor illness kept Alonzo at the house longer than expected, and Mrs. Hanly had Patty serve as his constant attendant. Patty was described as "being an uncommonly agreeable person and by no means bad looking, although rather large. She was extravagantly fond of music, and dancing, a great talker, very witty and fascinating in her conversation" [1]. The matchmaking worked, and when Alonzo recovered he married the 16-year-old Patty, taking her back with him to his home near the southern end of Delaware. They settled close to the Maryland state line, near the town of Reliance.

After three years of marriage, Alonzo died of what were thought to be natural causes. It was then about 1802. Patty was 19. Years later Cannon confessed that she had murdered her husband by slowly poisoning him. Freed from whatever moderating influence Alonzo may have had, Patty became, according to one account, "one of the most abandoned and notorious of women, giving loose to every species of licentious [sic] and extravagance" [1]. She moved a few miles down the road where she constructed a "low tavern" which became the headquarters for her various criminal pursuits. Principal among them were robbing and murdering travelers and dealing in slaves. She had several men accomplices who formed her gang, but Patty was always the leader. It was she who planned and masterminded those pursuits. Rough, tough, and always ready to fight, it was said that she could lift 300-pound sacks of grain with ease.

Trade was never lacking at the tavern, since Patty was considered a very hospitable woman. The fact that she rarely charged visitors anything tended to increase clientele. A traveler from Richmond, Virginia, on his way to New York stopped for a meal and to feed his horse. When Cannon learned he had a large quantity of money on him she placed him at a table with his back near an open window. One of her accomplices then shot him to death as he ate. After Patty stripped him of valuables she hid his body until nightfall, when it was buried on the grounds near the house.

Another time, two travelers with money stopped for a meal. Patty entertained them until it got dark, at which time they finally left for their destination. Immediately Cannon got a couple of her gang members together. By taking a shortcut they got in front of the two travelers and ambushed them, killing one and wounding the other. Another traveler was eating his supper at the tavern when Patty came up behind him and stabbed him to death. In the middle of the night his body was taken out to the middle of the river and dropped in, weighted down with a stone.

Among the people who stopped at the tavern were a number of slave dealers going back and forth between the north and the south. Cannon must have determined that there was money to be made, for she soon entered the business herself. Members of her gang, together with a couple of blacks recruited just for this purpose, worked the streets and bars of Philadelphia, enticing or waylaying unsuspecting blacks onto a slaver ship that Cannon operated. When full, it would sail to a convenient point near the tavern, where Patty would load the captives onto somebody else's slaver which was sailing south.

Aboard the first slaver, if the gang decided any of those picked up were too old or decrepit, they were thrown overboard to drown. When Cannon inspected the prisoners, if she determined that any of the children the women had might make themselves too noticeable or troublesome by crying and fussing, she beat them to death with a club she had especially for that purpose. Deep in the cellar of her tavern was a special area where she buried some of her victims, both children and travelers. One five-year-old black child so enraged Cannon by its crying that Patty grabbed it, ripped its clothes off, beat it senseless, and then held it face first in a fire until it burned to death.

Fellow slave dealers got no special treatment from Cannon. One such dealer stopped overnight at the tavern with two slaves. During the night Patty entered his room and beat him to death. He was robbed of his valuables and buried on the grounds. The two slaves were held for a week until a slaver heading south came by, at which time Patty sold the pair.

One of Cannon's servants was a 15-year-old black boy who, after witnessing a particularly gruesome bit of violence by his mistress, threatened to report her. An angry Patty beat him half to death with a shovel and then locked him in the cellar with the remains of previous victims to reconsider his position. After a couple of days there without food or water, Cannon asked him if he still felt inclined to report her. When he said he did she picked up the closest weapon, a large stone, and beat him to death.

Neighbors had grown more and more suspicious of Cannon over the years: too many people entered the tavern never to be seen again. One day early in 1829, a group of them paid her a visit determined to find out what was going on. They asked permission to tour the house, claiming that one of their number wished to build one just like it. Patty let them look around, but denied them access to the cellar. The neighbors managed to talk to a servant alone. Pressed about what was in the cellar, the servant refused to talk, saying only that it was something terrible and she couldn't tell since Patty would kill her. Thinking they had enough evidence, these neighbors went to the local sheriff. Early the next day the sheriff, armed with a warrant and a dozen men, arrived at the house to arrest Patty. Several members of her gang were also taken into custody. One of these men told the authorities everything he knew. He directed the sheriff where to dig in the garden. Numerous skeletons were unearthed. At the time of her arrest, Cannon had 21 black people confined in the house awaiting transportation to the south to be sold into slavery. They were all set free.

At the trial, Cannon and two of her gang were convicted and sentenced to death. Three others, fairly new to the gang, were each sentenced to seven years in prison. A few weeks before her scheduled execution, Patty somehow got hold of some poison and poisoned herself. In agony from the poison, Patty raved like a maniac, tearing the clothes from her body, ripping the hair from her head in handfuls, and trying to bite anything within reach.

About an hour before her death, Patty became calm. Calling for a priest, she expressed a desire to confess. When one arrived, she told him she had poisoned her husband, murdered her own infant when it was three days old, killed 11 other people with her own hands, and been involved with her gang in the murder of over a dozen others. When arrested, she and her gang were planning to murder two neighbors whom they considered to be wealthy. Patty Cannon died in jail in April 1829.

After her death, a respected but unnamed phrenologist sought and obtained possession of Cannon's skull for the purpose of conducting a phrenological examination. What he determined apparently went unreported. A dozen years after she died, Cannon's skull was in the possession of a Mr. O. S. Fowler of Philadelphia.

Sources

1. *Narrative and Confession of Lucretia P. Cannon.* New York, 1841.
2. "Sale of Maryland Home Recalls Murder Legend." *New York Times,* September 17, 1967, p. 43.
3. Wilder, Martha. "Cannon House Being Restored." Unidentified clipping.

Opal Juanita Collins

(1931–?). *Place:* Hammond, Indiana. *Time:* May 26, 1956. *Age:* 25. *Victims:* 4. *Method:* Firearm.

The marriage between 25-year-old Opal Collins and Ben Collins, Jr., was a violent and short-lived union. Less than one month after the wedding ceremony, after much acrimony, Opal took a rifle and shot and killed four members of the Collins family.

In December 1955 the Collins family had moved to Hammond, Indiana, from Louisa, Kentucky, into a new three-bedroom ranch home owned by Ben Collins, Jr., 28 years old. Aside from Ben, the family included his parents, Julia, 48, and Ben, Sr., 50; his sisters Mary Sue, 11, and Martha Ann, 14; and his six-year-old brother, Bobby.

Ben, Jr., was a World War II veteran who had been involved in an auto accident in 1947 while still in military service. As a result of the accident he was paralyzed frm the shoulders down but still had the use of his arms. Bars and chains on his bed enabled him to pull himself up, and he got around in a wheelchair.

Opal had been married and divorced twice; the first wedding took place when she was just 14 years old. Two children had been born from these unions, but the young woman did not appear to have custody of them. She first became acquainted with Ben, Jr., around 1953 in Kentucky. From the beginning it was a stormy relationship. In mid–1955 Opal locked Ben, Jr., in his car after throwing in his wheelchair cushion, which she had set on fire. After knocking out a window Ben was able to open the door, fall to the ground, and use his arms to pull himself clear of the burning vehicle. Opal then helped put the fire out.

After the incident Ben, Jr., stayed clear of his friend for a while. However, the persistent Opal drove past the Collins home repeatedly, blowing the horn to get his attention. In mid–April of the following year, Opal arrived at the Collins' new home in Hammond. She claimed she had stopped to visit Ben, Jr., while passing through on her way to Columbus, Ohio, where she intended to look for work. The Collinses let her stay with them and on May 1, she and Ben, Jr., eloped to Crown Point, Indiana, where they married.

During her time in Hammond, Opal got a job at a textile factory but quit after one week. From the beginning there was great animosity between Opal and her in-laws. Mr. Collins claimed that Opal "acted nice for three or four days after the marriage." Then she started "pouting and fussing" with her two new sisters-in-law [3]. Mrs. Collins had become particularly close to her son after his accident and didn't appreciate sharing his love with another woman.

Financial affairs were a major bone of contention, and the couple argued repeatedly as to whether Opal should be on the title deed to the house. Opal also wanted to be listed as beneficiary on Ben, Jr.'s, $10,000 insurance policy. Physical fights were common. About the middle of May Opal reportedly tried to strangle her husband. On May 23 she scratched Ben, Jr., pulled his hair, gave him a black eye, and clawed his face and chest so that she bloodied the paralyzed man's T-shirt.

Mrs. Collins disliked her new daughter-in-law intensely; prior to the marriage, she had threatened Opal with a beer bottle and a wrench. After the wedding Mrs. Collins antagonized Opal further by saying she had used the marriage certificate for toilet paper.

The fight on May 23 brought things to a head. Ben, Jr., decided he wanted a divorce. First he offered Opal $350 to return to Kentucky, but she declined the offer, saying, "It won't be that easy now" [3]. On May 25 Ben, Jr., filed for a divorce, claiming that his wife became violent after drinking excessively, slapped and beat the plaintiff on several occasions, did not love the plaintiff, and on May 23 slapped and beat the plaintiff until his nose bled and his face became scarred.

Only a couple of days previously, a box of shells for Ben, Jr.'s, 22-caliber rifle had become missing. Opal was considered to be a good shot and often practiced with the weapon. She had also asked Mr. Collins who the beneficiary of his son's life insurance policy was and complained bitterly when informed it was not she.

Ben, Jr., was worried about his wife and on May 25 he advised his family to sleep elsewhere that night. The three children slept with neighbors and relatives, and Mrs. Collins slept in a locked pick-up truck parked outside the family home. The next day, Saturday, May 26, at approximately 4:30 P.M. everybody was in the house except for Mr. Collins. A freshly baked cherry pie and a hot supper were almost ready for the table. Opal was in the couple's bedroom talking to Ben, Jr., who was in his wheelchair.

Mrs. Collins and her two daughters were in another room. Opal recalled, "I heard Mrs. Collins say that she had asked me to leave and if I didn't leave they would haul me out. I looked up and saw Mrs. Collins and the girls coming in the door of the bedroom. I remember going for the gun, but which one I shot first or how many times I don't know. The next thing

I remember is shooting my husband." The bride killed the three females first, chasing them into the living room, before turning the gun on her husband in the bedroom. He pleaded with her not to shoot him. "If I can't have you nobody can," responded Opal, and shot him [4]. One of the bodies was shot nine times.

The only person left alive in the house was six-year-old Bobby, who ran to a neighbor screaming, "Please call the police because Opal has a gun and shot Mary Sue." Opal was arrested at the home of another neighbor and readily confessed. "I did it and I'm ready to go," she told police. "They were trying to break us up. They told my husband I was trying to get all his money" [1].

In a written statement to the police Opal said, "I got that rifle out of the closet and walked to the kitchen and fired a shot at my mother-in-law, Julia. She ran to the living room, as did Martha Ann and Mary Sue. There I shot Julia. I don't know how many times. Then I shot the two girls. But I don't know which I shot first or how many times. Then I went to my husband's bedroom and he was in his wheelchair. . . . Then I shot him one time" [5].

Opal was tried for just one count of murder, that of Mary Sue Collins. Her defense was a plea of insanity. However, she was judged sane, found guilty, and on October 26, 1956, sentenced to die in the electric chair. During the trial the arresting officer, Howard Snyder, testified that Opal told him at the time of her arrest, "I'm the one that did it. I'm ready to go with you. . . . I just shot up the whole damn family" [5].

Sources

1. "Bride of Paralyzed Vet Held." *Hammond Times*, May 27, 1956, pp. 1, 2.
2. "File Murder Charges in Hammond Deaths." *Hammond Times*, May 28, 1956, pp, 1, 2.
3. "May Pick Opal Jury by Friday." *Hammond Times*, October 18, 1956, p. 1.
4. "Opal Recalls Killing Ben, No Others." *Hammond Times*, October 25, 1956, pp. 1, 2.
5. "Opal Sobs on Witness Stand." *Hammond Times*, October 23, 1956, pp. 1, 2.
6. "Opal Trial Underway." *Hammond Times*, October 22, 1956, p. 1.

Patricia Columbo

(1956–). *Place:* Elk Grove Village, Illinois. *Time:* May 4, 1976. *Age:* 19.
Victims: 3. *Method:* Firearm, stabbing, bludgeoning.

It started out as a series of disagreements between father and daughter
that any teen-aged girl might understand, but it soon escalated into something much more vicious and ended in a gruesome mass murder.

Just west of Chicago is the prosperous and normally peaceful bedroom
suburb of Elk Grove Village. Police were called there on May 7, 1976, to
check out the Columbo home, where no activity had been observed for
several days. When they arrived they found that three members of the family had all been murdered on May 4 in a bloody murder scene that shocked
even the most hardened cop. Frank Columbo, 43, had been shot four times
in the head. His skull was battered and bludgeoned almost beyond recogni-
tion. Burning cigarettes had been extinguished on his body. Mary Columbo,
41, was shot once in the head. Her throat was slit. Their son Michael, 13,
was shot once in the head. He had been stabbed a total of 97 times.
Daughter Patricia Columbo, 19, was the only member of the family still
alive. She lived in her own apartment.

Elk Grove Village was suddenly gripped with shock and fear — shock
at what had happened, and fear that crazed killers might be on the loose.
Both Columbo cars were missing, but a few thousand dollars in cash and
other valuables had not been touched, leading police to believe robbery was
not a motive. They feared they had a Charles Manson–like cult of deranged
killers and torturers on their hands. In Frank's safe, an address book with
the names of Mafia figures was found, leading to brief speculation that the
Mob was involved.

On learning of her family's deaths, an apparently grief-stricken Patricia speculated that the killers might have been young punks high on
drugs. She urged the police to find the killers who had wiped out her entire
family. A week later they obliged: they arrested and charged first Patricia
and then her boyfriend Frank DeLuca, with the slayings.

At Elk Grove Village High School teachers remembered Patricia as an
exceptionally poised, well-groomed student who did "nothing more, nothing less" than was required of her in class. While most of her fellow students

wore blue jeans, Columbo preferred to sport fancy dresses and costume jewelry. When she was still in high school Patricia got a part-time job in the cosmetics department of an Elk Grove drug store. The manager and pharmacist was Frank DeLuca. He was married, had five children, and was 18 years older than Columbo. They began an affair.

Instead of graduating from high school, the teenager dropped out in her senior year to work full-time in the drug store. Sometime in 1974 Patricia had a brush with the law and was placed on probation for the fraudulent use of a credit card. Until then the relationship between father and daughter had been described as close. After the credit card problem the relationship became strained, and Patricia moved into her own apartment in the suburb of Lombard. Frank Columbo paid his daughter's rent of $330 a month. Around this time, unknown to Frank Columbo, DeLuca left his wife and children and moved into Patricia's apartment.

Things between father and daughter deteriorated further in June 1975 when Columbo learned his daughter was living with the druggist. Enraged, he confronted DeLuca about this arrangement in the parking lot of the drug store he managed. What started out as a shouting match turned physical when Columbo, said DeLuca, "Knocked me in the face with the butt of a rifle. One tooth popped out, and it loosened three others" [1]. DeLuca reported the incident to the police and filed a charge of battery against Columbo.

At that point Columbo stopped paying his daughter's rent. To a large extent he also cut her out of his will. In a new will he drew up, Patricia's share of what was a substantial estate was reduced to a few thousand dollars. By the fall of 1975 Patricia Columbo harbored a burning rage toward her family in general and toward her father in particular.

In October Patricia met a man named Lanyon Mitchell, and within a week she asked Mitchell to kill her parents. Mitchell introduced her to his friend Roman Sobcynski. The two men pretended to be hit men with syndicate ties in order to impress her. Of course, they told her, there would have to be a fee. The subject of money was put off for a time when Patricia offered them sexual favors. According to Mitchell she said, "What do you want me to do, put my cunt on the table?" To which the men replied, "Yes. ... How about tonight" [1]? Numerous sexual encounters between the three then followed.

Columbo supplied her hit men with a dossier on her family that included photos, physical descriptions, floor plans of the family home, and their daily routines. In November a "dry run" was conducted. Mitchell and Columbo drove to the family home. Patricia entered while Mitchell waited outside in the car. Patricia's mother and aunt arrived unexpectedly and a quarrel ensued. When the girl left the aunt found that three exterior doors to the house, normally locked, were unlocked.

Both hit men said they never had any intention of murdering anyone and were just stringing Patricia along to get what they could out of her. They testified at the trial under a grant of immunity as unindicted co-conspirators. A lie detector test confirmed Mitchell's contention that he took no part in the killings.

Patricia wanted her family dead by Christmas; she felt it would be a nice present for her. When it didn't happen, she complained to the men, "I've been putting out sexwise for you two and you haven't done anything for me yet" [4]! As the early months of 1976 dragged by, Patricia became more impatient. The men asked for money. Columbo countered that there would be money after the family was dead. DeLuca finally told Patricia they were being jacked around and they would have to do the job themselves. The evidence indicates that on May 4, DeLuca and Columbo entered the family home and murdered the family.

When the police started their investigation they quickly found one of the missing Columbo automobiles. A bloody handprint belonging to a man with a missing finger was obtained from the vehicle. DeLuca had lost that very finger in an accident years previously. A girlfriend of Patricia's came forward to tell police that Columbo had told her of the plot and mentioned Mitchell by name, who was then picked up. Patricia was arrested about a week after the bodies were discovered.

When the police arrived at her apartment Patricia delayed opening the door for some 10 minutes. Fearing that she was getting rid of evidence by throwing it out the window, police dragged a lake that fronted the building, but found nothing. Patricia was unemployed and behind on the rent at the time. She told police she was a model for Frederick's of Hollywood, the maker of erotic lingerie. Police found the apartment to be in a deplorable condition. One source said, "It was filthy. Dishes were piled high in the sink. Clothes were strewn all over the place. There were dog feces all over the floor, and it really smelled." A Christmas tree was still standing [8].

DeLuca was soon picked up but not charged immediately. Held in "voluntary custody," he asked to take a lie detector test to back up his contention he was not involved in the triple slaying. He failed the test. Like Patricia, he soon stood indicted on three counts of murder.

After her arrest, Patricia told the police that she indeed wanted to kill her family and had discussed a murder plot with her hit men. She also acknowledged providing them with a dossier. However, she claimed to have changed her mind and backed out of the scheme. Patricia denied any involvement in the actual murders. Two days after her arrest she told a sheriff's investigator that she had a "vision." From there she went on to accurately describe the murder scene and said, "I think I see myself there" [1].

To another investigator, Ray Rose, Columbo related that DeLuca didn't know she was having sex with the other two men, although even if he knew she said he wouldn't have minded, since the couple had sent their pictures in to a "swingers" magazine because "we thought we would change partners in sex." Rose showed Patricia some photos the authorities had found in her apartment. They showed a nude Patricia apparently engaged in sexual activity with a dog. Rose said, "She told me that maybe her moral feelings were different than mine, but it didn't matter" [1].

The day after the murders DeLuca casually told two of the employees at his drug store what he had done. One of them was Joy Heysek, DeLuca's former mistress. The other was assistant store manager Bert Green who, on the morning of May 5, found DeLuca in the store's basement burning bloody clothes. According to Green, DeLuca confessed and took delight in telling how he had taken care to blow out several of Frank Columbo's teeth with a shot, gloating, "Now his teeth are like mine" [1]. When he confessed to Heysek and Green, he had threatened to kill them if they talked. DeLuca's cellmate before the trial claimed that Frank tried to hire him to kill the two people at the store.

Since both of the accused maintained their innocence, it is uncertain what happened in the house. It seems that both were present; perhaps DeLuca did the shooting and Patricia urged him on. All of the "tortures" took place after the shootings. Concerning the multiple stabbing of 13-year-old Michael, assistant state's attorney Ralph Berkowitz said it was the "kind of thing that only a hateful person could do." Another assistant state's attorney, Algis Baliunas, said that the stab wounds were "light puncture wounds" caused by a person with "some type of sick, twisted motivation." He maintained the lack of force behind the cuts was "consistent with a woman" [1, 6]. Michael had become the substantial beneficiary when Frank Columbo changed his will against Patricia.

During the trial Patricia Columbo showed little emotion. She and DeLuca remained devoted to each other. On July 1, 1977, after two hours of deliberations, the couple were found guilty on all three counts of murder. As they were taken out of the courtroom Patricia hugged DeLuca and started to cry on his shoulder. The sentences meted out were the same. Each got 200 to 300 years in prison. They have continued to maintain their innocence.

In September 1979, while incarcerated at Dwight Correctional Center, Columbo got into the news again when several female inmates accused her of recruiting them to have sexual relations with male prison officials. An investigation absolved Patricia of any wrongdoing. However, the institution's warden and Columbo's civilian boss both resigned. Patricia lost her valued job as resident clerk as a result of the scandal. In a separate incident that same year, she was placed in a maximum-security cottage for possessing beer.

A year later Columbo was in the middle of a two-year associate of arts degree program and was hoping to go on and take a four-year degree—then unavailable to female inmates at Dwight. She told a reporter, "I want to be a journalist. I want to show all of you how to do it right." Summing up her life to that point Patricia commented, "I had a great life. I had never been to a wake or a funeral. I never had anything happen to me. My father protected me from any hurt. ... My life was a bed of roses, but Daddy didn't tell me about the thorns" [9].

In December 1987, after having been turned down for parole on two occasions, Columbo's lawyer announced that for the first time Patricia was ready to publicly admit responsibility for the murders. This was in preparation for her third parole hearing. She was turned down a third time in February 1988. The report did not mention whether or not Columbo made such an admission at the hearing.

Sources

1. Branegan, Jay. "Columbo, DeLuca Guilty." *Chicago Tribune,* July 2, 1977, pp. A1, A2.

2. Griffin, William. "Daughter Charged in Slaying of Elk Grove Village Family." *Chicago Tribune,* May 16, 1976, pp. 1, 12.

3. Johnson, Steve. "Columbo to Admit Killing Her Family." *Chicago Tribune.* December 16, 1987, sec. 2, p. 13.

4. Nash, Jay Robert. *Look for the Woman.* New York: M. Evans, 1981, pp. 90–95.

5. O'Brien, John. "Daughter Charged in 3 Murders." *Chicago Tribune,* May 18, 1976, pp. 1, 11.

6. O'Connor, Meg. "Police Say Daughter Admits Plot, Denies Slaying Family." *Chicago Tribune,* May 17, 1976, pp, 1, 13.

7. "Patty Weeps on Lover's Shoulder." *Chicago Tribune,* July 2, 1977, p. A2.

8. Sneed, Michael. "Family Disputes Probed as Motive in 3 Killings." *Chicago Tribune,* May 18, 1976, p. 11.

9. Sneed, Michael. "Patty Columbo's Prison Life: College Courses and 'Growing.'" *Chicago Tribune,* September 7, 1980, p. 4.

Glenda Cooper

(1943–). *Place:* Watsonville, New York. *Time:* February 23, 1969. *Age:* 25. *Victims:* 3. *Method:* Hatchet.

The combination of an unhappy marriage and an unstable personality and background proved too much for Glenda Cooper to bear. The former Glenda Benson had married James Cooper while still a teenager. James was employed as a welder at the General Electric Company in Schenectady, New York, where the couple lived. Early in 1967 the family moved to the small community of Watsonville, about 30 miles from Schenectady. The Coopers then had three young children.

At that time, Glenda's mother had been confined to a mental institution for over a decade. Her father had had the marriage annulled and then remarried. Glenda disliked living in the country and worried constantly about prowlers in Watsonville. Normally a neat housekeeper, she began to neglect her duties. She also devoted less attention to the care of her children. These things did not pass unnoticed by either James or her father; finally, in March 1968 Glenda was admitted to a hospital because James believed she was acting strangely. Transferred from there to a mental facility, Mrs. Cooper spent a couple of weeks in a closed ward before being moved to an open ward and then released.

During her stay there Glenda told a psychiatrist, Dr. Funk, that she didn't want sex or pregnancies and had been in love only once in her life, when she was 15. She told the psychiatrist she still thought of that man. She was released even though Funk said she didn't initiate conversation, seldom answered questions, and expressed a desire to join her mother. Funk didn't consider her violent, but he did recommend that Glenda not continue living with her husband. Apparently this advice was not taken.

Less than a year after her release, on February 23, 1969, Glenda took a hatchet and killed her three children, James, eight; Joann, five; and Jeffrey, three; as they slept in their beds. Her husband James was at work that night. Mrs. Cooper then set fire to the house, slashed her wrists, and lay down on a bed to die. However, heat from the fire drove her out of the house, which burned to the ground. The bodies of the three children, along with the murder weapon, were found in the cellar.

After her arrest Dr. Funk examined Glenda again. She told him, "It was a terrible thing I did but better I did it than someone else." She wanted to be convicted, she told Funk. The psychiatrist added, "She knows she did it, but she was afraid her husband would commit her to a mental hospital" [5]. Glenda also told the doctor she had threatened her husband once.

To the police Glenda said she was worried about the custody of the children in the event she and James separated. She didn't want her husband to have them. Glenda told District Attorney Robert Ecker that she killed her children and set fire to the house "because she hated her husband" [4].

Glenda was tried on three counts of murder early in 1970. In February the jury found her guilty on all counts after five hours of deliberations. The defense contended that Mrs. Cooper was insane at the time. Judge Johnson said that since the jury found her guilty, he had no alternative but to impose a sentence. Glenda was sentenced to serve from 15 years to life, concurrently, on each of the three counts. It was the minimum sentence that the judge could impose.

Sources

1. "Gets 15 Years in Infanticide." *New York Times,* February 28, 1970, p. 17.
2. "Husband of Defendant Heard in Murder Trial." *The Knickerbocker News Union-Star,* February 4, 1970, p. 5B.
3. "Mother Guilty in Slayings of 3." *The Knickerbocker News Union-Star,* February 18, 1970, p. 5B.
4. "Mother Sentenced in Slayings." *The Knickerbocker News Union-Star,* February 28, 1970, p. 3A.
5. "Murder Trial Nearing Close." *The Knickerbocker News Union-Star,* February 9, 1970, p. 5B.
6. "Murder Trial Underway." *The Knickerbocker News Union-Star,* January 21, 1970, p. 3.

Mary Ann Cotton

(1832–1873). *Place:* England. *Time:* 1850s–1872. *Age:* 20s–40. *Victims:* 14–23. *Method:* Arsenic poisoning.

Economic considerations formed one motive for the murders committed by Mary Ann Cotton, even though the sums were small. Other factors were also involved. Sex was one; to clear the way for a new lover, Cotton sometimes murdered old husbands and children who got in the way. Mary Ann liked sex, it seems, but never really wanted children. In an age of little or no birth control, this was not a good combination. She remains one of Great Britain's worst mass murderers regardless of gender.

In October 1832, Mary Ann Robson was born in the small mining village of Low Moorsly in county Durham, England. Her parents were young, still in their teens. Her father, Michael, worked in the mines as a pitman, and the family moved around the area from time to time as his work dictated. Their little girl was described as a strikingly pretty child; throughout her life men would be drawn to her.

Michael Robson died in a mine accident in 1846. Soon thereafter Mary Ann's mother, Margaret, married a miner named George Stott. When Mary Ann was 16, she took a job as a nursemaid with a family in nearby South Hetton. While she was there Mary Ann taught at a Wesleyan Sunday school; she would be a religious person and regular churchgoer all her life.

After three years in South Hetton Mary Ann left and returned home, where she decided to take up dressmaking and served a short apprenticeship. This career was interrupted on July 18, 1852, when Mary Ann married William Mowbray, a 26-year-old laborer.

For about five years the Mowbrays traveled in a wide area around the country as William sought work. In 1857 the couple returned to Mary Ann's home area. With them was a one-year-old girl named Mary Ann. During their time away Mrs. Mowbray had borne five children, she told friends, and all but one died. The year she returned home Mary Ann gave birth to another child, who soon died. Isabella was born in September 1858, followed by Margaret June in October 1861 and John Robert in November 1863.

On June 24, 1860, the little girl Mary Ann, then four, died of what doctors called gastric fever. Somewhere during this period William Mowbray, perhaps worried by the fact that so many children were dying, insured the lives of those left as well as his own life. In September 1864, John Robert died. Diarrhea was certified as the cause of death. The next to die was William Mowbray himself. On January 18, 1864, he stayed home from work with an injured foot when he was taken with an attack of diarrhea so violent that he died that very day. Diarrhea was again listed as the cause of death. Margaret June was stricken just three months later and died after a two-day illness. Gastric fever was the reason given by the doctor. Listing gastric fever or diarrhea as the cause of death was a common practice in those days. Both terms were vague and tended to be freely used by physicians when they didn't know the real cause of death.

In April 1865, Mary Ann Mowbray was a widow with one surviving child, her daughter Isabella. The other eight children she had borne since 1852 or 1853 were all dead, not to mention her husband. Mary Ann seemed to take the deaths badly and grieved openly. She collected about £30 in insurance money upon the deaths of William and a couple of the children. Isabella was taken to her grandmother, Mrs. Stott, to live. Totally on her own, Mary Ann spent a short time working as a dressmaker. She met 28-year-old Joseph Nattrass, with whom she had an affair. Nattrass was engaged, however, and he went ahead with his wedding. Mary Ann then moved to Sunderland and got a job as a nurse at the Sunderland Infirmary, working on the 20-bed fever ward.

The job only lasted a few months, but it led her to her next husband. The doctor in charge of the fever ward praised her work and considered her to be one of his best nurses. Mary Ann seemed to be concerned about her patients. One of these was the 32-year-old George Ward. After he recovered and left the infirmary, the couple married on August 28, 1865. Ward was unable to find work; by November he was receiving parish relief.

Soon Ward was seeing a doctor with complaints of nosebleeds and a lack of strength. Remaining unwell for months, he began to display symptoms of paralysis of the limbs. Ward died in October 1866 of "fever." A month later one James Robinson's wife died, leaving him a widower with five children to care for. He advertised for a housekeeper. Mary Ann applied for the post, got it, and moved into the Robinson household before Christmas. Only a week after her arrival the youngest Robinson child, 10 months old, took sick and died within a day. Convulsions were prominent among the symptoms. Once again, doctors attributed death to gastric fever.

Early in March 1867, Mrs. Stott took sick and called for her daughter to come and nurse her. Mary Ann did so. While the illness was not considered serious, Mary Ann was curiously pessimistic and prophesied a speedy demise for her patient. While Mrs. Stott lay ill Mary Ann appropriated linen, clothes, and other household items for herself, storing them with neighbors and telling them her mother had made her a present of the items. In fact, Mrs. Stott did die quickly. She expired on March 18 at the age of 54, only nine days after her illness began. Neighbors were resentful and suspicious of her daughter's behavior.

There was no obvious rift between mother and daughter and no record of any insurance money passing to her. Mr. Stott didn't get along with his step-daughter and after his wife's death said he didn't want Mary Ann in his house again. The poisoner took her daughter Isabella, by then nine years old, and returned to the Robinson household.

She was back only a short time before illness struck the Robinsons again. James Robinson, Jr., aged six, and eight-year-old Eliza were soon bedridden. Mary Ann devoted herself to nursing the children. Worriedly she told neighbors she feared that her own Isabella would fall victim to the same malady; she did. All three of these children died during the last days of April 1867. All had the same symptoms; rolling around in bed, foaming at the mouth, and vomiting. Gastric fever was given as the cause of death.

James Robinson appeared to see nothing unusual in all these deaths. His new housekeeper seemed much grieved by the tragedies; she had the support, confidence, and affection of Robinson. Mary Ann admonished herself by criticizing her own behavior and saying she should have done better. If Robinson was fooled by this, his three sisters were not. They openly distrusted the housekeeper and were the first to strongly suspect that Mary Ann might be a poisoner. Robinson was clearly infatuated with Mary Ann and defended his housekeeper. Later he would say he couldn't let his mind dwell on some thoughts—he dare not.

With money in the bank and in the process of buying a house, Robinson was fairly well off. Over the objections of his sisters Robinson and Mary Ann married on August 11, 1867. On the marriage certificate she gave her name as Mowbray. Robinson was probably never told about Ward. The new Mrs. Robinson gave birth to a daughter on November 29, 1867, who subsequently died of gastric fever in February 1868. During 1869 Mary Ann gave birth to another child by Robinson.

From the time of their wedding Mary Ann urged her husband to insure the lives of his children, but he refused. It appears that on their deaths Robinson did get some money from some society, which he passed on to his wife. Mary Ann also got a bit of insurance money for Isabella. Robinson refused to have his own life insured; when Mary Ann tried to have him insured without his knowledge, he found out and put a stop to the effort.

So complete was his trust in Mary Ann that Robinson turned all his financial affairs over to her to manage. She repaid this trust by doctoring the entries in his bankbook and stealing his money. Eventually the discrepancies were brought to James's attention. The couple had a big fight over the matter which destroyed Robinson's faith in his wife. They agreed to separate after Mary Ann repaid the missing amount. However, Mary Ann simply skipped out, taking the baby with her. She would later try and make it up to James, but would find the door locked against her.

Robinson was left with debts and a depleted bank account. Mary Ann had not needed extra money; she had not lived in poverty with Robinson. In fact, her material circumstances with Robinson were better than with any other man she had or would know. She was also not personally extravagant. At the end of 1869 Mary Ann and her baby visited an acquaintance. On the pretense of mailing a letter she stepped out by herself for a minute. She never returned. In due course the acquaintance found Robinson and returned the baby to him.

After she skipped out on Robinson he never saw her again. When the reports of the murderous Mary Ann Cotton first became public, Robinson's sisters said, not knowing that Mary Ann Cotton and Mary Ann Robinson were one and the same person, "Thy Mary Ann could have done that" [1].

From the time she left Robinson, Mary Ann engaged in a spate of "loose living." For a while she lived with a sailor, whose possessions she stole when he went off to sea. Early in 1870 Mary Ann was introduced to Frederick Cotton by his sister Margaret Cotton, who was an old acquaintance of Mary Ann's. Frederick was about the same age as Mary Ann and a recent widower with three children.

As she had before, Mary Ann immediately became the family housekeeper. Within a couple of weeks, on January 29, 1870, the youngest Cotton child was dead. Two months after that Margaret Cotton died after experiencing severe stomach pains; she was 38. The motive for her death may have been Mary Ann's worry that Margaret knew too much about her past, for Frederick knew his new housekeeper only as Mary Ann Mowbray. By the time of Margaret's death, Mary Ann and Frederick were lovers. By April she was pregnant.

Some sort of break then took place between the couple. Mary Ann moved 20 miles away and got work as a household servant. When she left this job, her employer found some cash and some jewelry missing. The rift with Frederick was healed and Mary Ann returned to the Cotton family as housekeeper in July. On September 17, 1870, they married. On the certificate Mary Ann stated she was a widow, giving her name as Mowbray. Since Robinson was very much alive, this marriage was bigamous. Cotton had no idea he was husband number four. Mary Ann gave birth to a child in January 1871.

Soon Mary Ann was at loggerheads with most of the neighbors. They gossiped about the new Mrs. Cotton being pregnant before the wedding, and she gave neighbors so many conflicting accounts of her background that what remained of her reputation was lost. Mysteriously the village pigs died in a mass poisoning, which was attributed to Mrs. Cotton. The atmosphere became so strained that the Cotton family moved away to the hamlet of West Auckland, where Frederick found work in a mine as a pit-man. In West Auckland the family lived on the same street as Mary Ann's old lover, Joseph Nattrass, who then was living on his own. Presumably this relationship was reestablished.

Gastric fever struck again on September 19, 1871, when Frederick suffered severe pains and died suddenly. Neighbors initially extended sympathy to Mary Ann after her husband died. Money was collected on her behalf and the mine owners gave her free coal. Nevertheless, Mary Ann was in financial distress and took nursing jobs to stay afloat. Sympathy for Mary Ann declined sharply as a result of her subsequent behavior.

Three months after Frederick died, Nattrass moved into his home as a "lodger." He and Mary Ann intended, it seems, to marry. Before that could happen Mary Ann took a job as nurse to a Mr. Quick-Manning, who had smallpox. He was a customs official and higher on the social scale than any of Mary Ann's other men. They became lovers.

Nattrass and the children were now in the way. Between March 10 and April 1, 1872, Nattrass, Cotton's oldest surviving child, and Mary Ann's baby by Cotton all lay dead. Once again, gastric fever was blamed. Nattrass left what little money he had to Mary Ann; until the end he had faith in his lover. He told a visitor to his sickbed that she was the only person who cared for him. In the meantime, while he lay ill Mary Ann was sending out for things to bury him in.

Another visitor to see Joseph while he was sick was shocked to find the dead baby in a coffin in the house. When he told Mary Ann the child should be buried Mary Ann replied, "I am going to put it off till Joe dies. He has gone upstairs now, and, poor fellow, he will never come down till they carry him out feet first" [5]. It was cheaper to bury two at once. Within two weeks of Nattrass's death, Mary Ann was pregnant by Quick-Manning. She was living alone except for seven-year-old Charles Cotton.

In July she was offered another nursing job, but declined it because she had to look after Charles. This annoyed her greatly. She had tried with no luck to have an uncle take the boy off her hands. She had also tried to have the child taken into a workhouse, but they wouldn't take him unless Mary Ann also went in with the child.

Mary Ann complained to a storeowner named Thomas Riley that it was hard on her to keep the boy when he wasn't her own, especially since she had the chance to take in a respectable lodger. Since everyone knew of her affairs, Riley laughed and asked if this lodger was Quick-Manning. At this Mary Ann smiled and said, "It might be so. But the boy is in the way.

Perhaps it won't matter as I won't be troubled long. He'll go like all the rest of the Cotton family" [1].

On July 12, 1872, only a couple of days after speaking with Riley, Charles was dead. Riley was shocked, hostile, and suspicious when he learned of the boy's death. He went to the police with what he knew. The death certificate was delayed and a postmortem held. When she learned of this Mary Ann said, "People are saying I poisoned the child but I am in the clear. I've had a great deal of trouble with the Cotton family with so many of them dying in such a short time" [1]. At the trial it was stated by various witnesses that Charles had been ill treated by his stepmother. She often beat him and gave him insufficient food.

The results of this postmortem seemed to vindicate Mrs. Cotton. The physician had performed his examination in a cursory and hurried fashion only one hour before the results were due at the inquest. No chemical analysis was done—nor was one requested by the coroner or the jury. As a result, death was attributed to natural causes. However, the doctor had saved part of the stomach. When the community exploded with rumors that Mary Ann was a wholesale poisoner, the doctor did a more thorough examination of Charles's remains and found arsenic. On July 18, 1872, Mary Ann was arrested for the murder of Charles Cotton.

Six weeks before the boy died, Mary Ann had been doing some cleaning with the help of a neighbor, Mrs. Dodds. According to Dodds, Mary Ann sent Charles to the drugstore for two cents' worth of arsenic and soft soap to rub on the bedstead, which the poisoner said contained bugs. The druggist wouldn't serve Charles, so Mary Ann convinced Dodds to go and buy it for her. Half the arsenic was used on the bedstead, which Dodds claimed had no bugs.

In the summer of 1872, as Cotton was walked back and forth to the train station by the police on her trips between jail and court, mothers ran to hide their children from her. Her name was used to conjure up a bogeywoman to scare kids into obedience. Children responded by making up rhymes about her.

Investigation disclosed Mary Ann's background. Nattrass was exhumed and his body found to contain arsenic. The same poison was found in the bodies of two of Frederick Cotton's children, who were also exhumed. On a macabre note, police tried to exhume Frederick's body but couldn't find it. The graves were unmarked and close together. After some failures, the police brought in people who had attended his funeral in an effort to pinpoint the spot. After between one and two dozen of the wrong graves were opened, the authorities abandoned the search.

Mary Ann gave birth to her thirteenth and last child in January 1873, while in Durham jail. She was indicted on four counts of murder but tried in the spring of 1873 on only one count, that of murdering Charles Cotton.

Surprisingly she still elicited some sympathy; a committee was formed to raise money for a defense fund for the impoverished woman. Mary Ann seemed to be able to draw people toward her with her strong personality and sexual attractiveness, and people did her bidding.

When she did come to trial the room was jammed. Many of the spectators were fashionable and brought opera glasses for a better view. Witnesses told how she abused and starved Charles. A doctor said that before Charles's final illness, his body was wasted and his belly distended. Mrs. Cotton reportedly had told one person that the Cottons were weak-stomached children and couldn't abide too much food. The all-male jury deliberated for just 55 minutes before returning a guilty verdict on March 7, 1873. Mary Ann was sentenced to be hanged. The custom then was to let three Sundays intervene between sentencing and execution. Therefore, Monday, March 24, 1873, was scheduled as the day of her execution.

During that waiting period, the poisoner was cool and reserved. Jailers termed her cunning and intelligent. The baby was with her, and she was watched night and day by two guards. One of her visitors asked why she had done it, but the prisoner merely pointed to her cradle and said, "I am as innocent of the crime as that baby. The only crime I'm guilty of is bigamy, but what was I to do when that man Robinson drove me to the door?" From prison she wrote to Robinson asking him to visit with the children or send the children if he didn't want to come himself. She admonished him that "you are the cause of all my trouble." Robinson didn't respond [1].

On March 19, Mary Ann's baby was taken away and placed with a family. There had been no lack of interest; around 150 people, some well-to-do, had offered to adopt the baby. Some were even willing to pay large sums of money for the privilege. At 8 A.M. on the appointed day Mary Ann Cotton went calmly and quietly to her death, never having confessed.

During her adulthood, Mary Ann Cotton was close to or lived with 28 people over the years—23 of them died suddenly and in similar circumstances. The dead included Mowbray himself and nine children, Ward, three of Robinson's children by his prior wife and one by Mary Ann, three of Cotton's children by his prior wife and one by Mary Ann, Cotton himself, Margaret Cotton, Nattrass, and her own mother. The survivors were limited to the child born in jail, one child by Robinson, two of Robinson's children by his former wife, and Robinson himself. Some observers feel that some of these deaths, particularly the early children by Mowbray, may have been from natural causes, and that Mary Ann's death toll could be as low as 14 or 15. Whatever the count, many people died by her hand.

A child's rhyme about her went like this:

Mary Ann Cotton
She's dead and she's rotten
She lies in her bed
With her eyes wide oppen
Sing, sing, oh, what can I sing
Mary Ann Cotton is tied up with string.
Where, where? Up in the air.
Sellin' black puddens a penny a pair [1].

Sources

1. Appleton, Arthur. *Mary Ann Cotton: Her Story and Trial.* London: Joseph, 1973.

2. Dunbar, Dorothy. *Blood in the Parlor.* New York: Barnes, 1964, pp. 20–24.

3. Gaute, J. H. H. *The Murderers' Who's Who.* London: Harrap, 1979, pp. 73–75.

4. Green, Jonathon. *The Greatest Criminals of All Time.* New York: Stein & Day, 1980, pp. 148–49.

5. Lambert, Richard S. *When Justice Faltered.* London: Methuen, 1935, pp. 108–37.

7. Nash, Jay Robert. *Look for the Woman.* New York: M. Evans, 1981, pp. 106–08.

Anna Cunningham

(1878–?). *Place:* Valparaiso and Gary, Indiana. *Time:* 1918–1923. *Age:* 40–45. *Victims:* 5. *Method:* Arsenic poisoning.

In 1918 the Cunningham family of Valparaiso, Indiana, consisted of two parents and six children. In 1925 the family was reduced to one healthy daughter, one son almost dead, and the mother. The members of this family died with alarming regularity—all done in by Anna Cunningham, the mother, who was 40 years old in 1918.

Anna was apparently a normal wife and mother until 1918, when her 15-year-old son Charles accidentally shot and killed a neighbor's son. The whole family was traumatized; Anna took it especially hard. Described as unbalanced from that time on, Anna became violent at times and threatened to kill all those around her. A doctor examined her at the request of the family and said she should be hospitalized. When the same doctor was called some years later, he refused to come unless Mrs. Cunningham was committed. The family called in another doctor, who said that Anna was all right.

The first to die was her husband David, 51, who sickened and died two weeks later in July 1918. He was insured for $1,000. The family farm in Valparaiso was sold for $4,000, and the Cunninghams moved to Gary, Indiana. The 18-year-old daughter Isabelle died in December 1920 under the same circumstances as her father, enduring two weeks of searing pain and agony. Harry died in October 1921 at the age of 24, and Charles was the victim in the next year, expiring in September 1922. Walter, 13, died in September 1923. These three sons all died after 10 days to two weeks of illness. No one died in 1924, but the next year the last son, 24-year-old, David, became ill.

David took ill at work one day after eating a lunch prepared by his mother. He remained at death's door for two weeks, but then recovered and returned to work. Only two days later he became violently ill again, right after eating supper at home. He was taken to a Gary hospital where he deteriorated and became paralyzed—the same symptoms as the other Cunninghams had developed. Miraculously, David did not die even though he lost 40 pounds in six weeks.

None of the deaths had aroused any suspicions, except in one relative of the Cunninghams. In her hometown of Gary, Anna received much sympathy for the spate of bereavements she had suffered. Financially she was not well-off; she relied on her children's earnings and the proceeds of insurance policies. Each of the dead had been insured for $300 to $1,000.

George Arnold, a nephew of Anna's by marriage, told the authorities, "Whenever a member of her family was sick she would write to my mother, telling of the illness and predicting that the patient would die" [4]. When the Arnolds got a letter about David, they persuaded Anna to send him to Chicago for treatment, where arsenic was discovered in his system. They then told the police about their suspicions. Anna haunted the hospital where David was under treatment, trying in vain to be alone with her son, who was thought to be dying. At first Anna had resisted sending David to Chicago, saying, "Oh, what's the use of worrying about him? He'll soon die anyway."

A month or so before David's illness, Anna suffered a bad bout of mental instability. It was a continuation in her mental decline that dated from the shooting. Mrs. Williams, Arnold's sister, reported, "A month ago she had a particularly severe attack. She threatened with death everyone who came near her. She would shriek and collapse into uncontrollable hysteria. Only one person, the pastor of her church, could soothe her at such times" [5].

Hospital personnel in Chicago called in the police after they discovered arsenic in David's body. An investigation turned up poison in the Cunningham home — enough to kill a whole town of people — and Anna readily admitted ownership: "Why certainly. I've always kept arsenic in my house — lots of it. Why, only a short time ago I got a half-gallon of arsenic from a Gary drug store" [4]. Her one remaining child, 17-year-old Mae, claimed she also bought arsenic. Mae said it was used to kill rats, while Anna stated she used to "spray my plants with it every spring."

From his hospital bed David made a statement regarding his mother's instability and that the other members of the family had all developed the same symptoms as he had before they died. "But mother always loved them and was very sad when they died," he added [4]. David didn't know his mother was then suspected of murder. The bodies of three Cunninghams were exhumed.

During the preliminary investigation Anna was held in the hospital, where she tried to commit suicide. Tearing the hem from a sheet she twisted it around her neck to choke herself to death. When a policewoman tore it away from her, she wailed, "Oh, I'm sick — and I wanted to end it all." After the doctors and an alienist questioned her for the rest of that day, the latter pronounced that Anna was suffering from "epileptic psychosis, a dangerous mental condition" [9]. She was transferred to jail, but her sanity hearing was delayed a day while Anna lay in some sort of comatose state, lips drawn tight, eyes squeezed shut, and limbs stiffened. Some physicians felt she was faking, some thought her coma state was real. Anna was pronounced sane.

Daughter Mae later changed her story and denied buying arsenic. Mrs. Cunningham maintained her innocence and angrily repeated to her accusers, "How dare you insinuate I gave my children poison. I loved them all too dearly for that." The next day Anna complained of pains in her head and nausea. She then collapsed to the floor in a coma after having some type of attack, which was reported as epilepsy.

On April 15, 1925, Anna broke down and confessed to poisoning three of her children by giving them arsenic. She denied poisoning her husband David and son Harry, although Harry's body was one of those found to contain arsenic, as did the others that were exhumed. Her son David wasn't mentioned at all.

Mae was on hand to hear the confession, which Anna prefaced by saying, "Now Mae, I've done with the whole bunch of you. I'm done with you, too, and I'm coming clean" [10]. The police and a reporter for a newspaper were also present. Mae urged her mother not to talk, as lawyers had advised, but Anna insisted, telling Mae, "Shut up. I want to get this off my conscience. . . . I killed them and I want to get it over with. I'm tired. I've been tired a long while. . . . I don't want to see you any more Mae, and I don't care what becomes of me" [6]. The hysterically weeping Mae fled from the room. Anna was upset with her daughter because she felt Mae didn't spend enough time with her and spent too much time out carousing in dance halls.

According to Anna, after her husband died she wanted to join him in heaven but the thought of the children alone grieved her. Accordingly, each time she decided to poison herself Anna gave poison to her best-loved child to share her fate. Isabelle was first. She lingered for weeks, and while constantly nursing her daughter, Anna just didn't think to take any more arsenic herself. "There was something the matter with me," she explained. "I just took as much as they, but I couldn't die" [6].

Cunningham admitted poisoning Charles and Walter in the same fashion. The arsenic was spread on bread and butter. Always she took poison herself as well, she maintained. "I took just as much poison myself and I got sick, but I did not die. Eight weeks little Walter was sick. All the time in between I was taking arsenic off and on myself. I would decide to do it when I got those terrible blue spells. All the time I thought about dying" [6].

Another reason she gave for killing was that "something seemed to draw in my head and told me I had to get rid of them. I thought I was going to die and wanted to take them with me. I only poisoned the ones I liked best in turn because I wanted them with me" [9]. Mae was the only family member to escape alive and healthy and that was because Anna loved her the least.

After the confession, Sheriff Strong left her cell proclaiming, "The woman is either an arch fiend or a maniac. A second Belle Gunness." The person who stood watch over Anna that night in jail reported that she stayed up all night talking nonstop about how she administered the poison, about the funerals, and other things.

The money from the insurance policies had all slipped through her fingers. "The money from the insurance is all gone, every nickel of it. First I spent money on doctors' bills. More money went on funeral expenses. The rest I gave to the children when they asked for it" [6].

A few months later, in July 1925, Mrs. Cunningham was found guilty of murdering her son Walter and sentenced to life in prison.

Sources

1. "Arsenic Is Found in Bodies." *Chicago Tribune,* April 15, 1925, p. 3.

2. "Cunningham Bodies Exhumed for Tests." *New York Times,* April 14, 1925, p. 25.

3. "Discovers Arsenic in Cunningham Boys." *New York Times,* April 15, 1925, p. 21.

4. "Find Poison in Home Where Five Had Died." *New York Times,* April 12, 1925, pp. 1, 7.

5. "Had Arsenic, Widow Admits in Death Quiz." *Chicago Tribune,* April 12, 1925, pp. 1, 2.

6. M'Kernan, Maureen. "Poison Widow Confesses in Indiana Jail." *Chicago Tribune,* April 16, 1925, pp. 1, 2.

7. "Mother Found Guilty of Slaying Her Child." *New York Times,* July 26, 1925, p. 19.

8. "Mrs. Cunningham Held for Next Grand Jury." *New York Times,* April 19, 1925, pp. 1, 8.

9. "Poison Widow Tries Suicide." *Chicago Tribune,* April 13, 1925, p. 1.

10. "Poisoning Confessed by Mrs. Cunningham." *New York Times,* April 16, 1925, pp. 1, 8.

11. "Sixth Ill in Family After Death of Five." *New York Times,* April 11, 1925, p. 4.

Lillie May Curtis

(1900–?). *Place:* Center, Texas. *Time:* March 16, 1938. *Age:* 38. *Victims:* 7. *Method:* Firearm.

Lillie May Curtis was born, raised, and spent all her life in and around the small community of Center, Texas. Center is in the far-eastern portion of the state, 20 miles from the Louisiana border and almost 200 miles north of Houston. In 1919, when Lillie was a young married woman of 19, she had her first child; her ninth child was born in 1933.

Curtis's mental difficulties surfaced in June 1935, when she shot and killed her husband Robert with a pistol while he lay asleep in bed. One account states that at that trial, Lillie said Robert was involved in illegal liquor activities, and she decided she had to sacrifice him or the children. A second version has it that Lillie killed Robert because he ran around on her and "mistreated" her in various ways. Found guilty of murdering Robert, Lillie received a five-year suspended sentence. The presiding judge advised the woman to exercise self-control and to accept life's burdens in the future. There was some question at the time of Lillie's sanity.

On March 15, 1938, Lillie went to a hardware store and purchased a 22-caliber pistol for $9.50. The reason she gave for wanting the gun was to scare thieves out of the cornfield. The next evening, she was in a worse state than usual. The seven youngest of her children were home; a 19-year-old married daughter had her own home, and a 17-year-old boy was visiting his grandfather.

In a statement given to the police on March 17, Curtis recounted the tragic events of the previous evening. "About two or three days ago is the first time I began thinking about killing my children. I was studying about trouble and how I was going to take care of the children and was in bad health and was unable to do nothing. About 9 o'clock last night they, the children, all went to bed about the same time. Then I went to bed and stayed there about an hour and was just studying trouble, that fact that I was unable to take care of them; that is that I was not physically able and not able in way of money. I had not undressed when I went to bed and I was thinking kinda about killing them when I went to bed. . . . The gun was under the bed and I got it and went to T. O. and he was laying on his left

78

side and I put the gun to his breast and it was in front and I pulled the trigger. He just hollered — he did not get up, but hollered. That did not wake up the others" [1].

Lillie killed six of the seven children in the same fashion. Travis, 16, was not murdered because his mother felt "he could take care of himself" [2]. Those killed were T. O., 13; Gloria Jean, 11; Billie Burke, 10; Robert, 9; Margie Ree, 7; and Marcie Jack, 5.

Curtis shot them in the left side because it was near the heart and they would die quicker. The woman's statement added, "After I had shot them all I went back to see if they were dead. They all died pretty fast. None of them said anything at all. I could see most of them struggling. I did not say anything to them. I just kissed them all before I shot any of them. After I had kissed them all I began to shoot them and then after I had shot all of them I felt of them to see if they were dead and after they had all quit breathing I kissed them again." A note left by Curtis that was found in the house with the bodies said, "I couldn't stand to see them starve to death and I didn't know what else to do with them" [1].

Travis fled the house and alerted the authorities, who apprehended Lillie in the woods about 400 yards from the house. She told the police she hid the gun under the steps of the house. An estimated 5,000 people attended the funeral for the six Curtis children. Authorities denied Lillie permission to attend, for her own safety, because feelings against her were running very high in the community.

Lillie completed her statement by saying, "I knew that it was wrong to kill these children. I killed the father of these children about three years ago. I am sorry now that I killed them and if I had it back I would not do it now" [1].

At her trial held the month following the slayings, Lillie's sister testified that the family had plenty of food on hand and was in no danger of destitution. The poverty was, apparently, all in Lillie's mind. A panel of four doctors agreed that Curtis was suffering from paranoia — delusions of persecution often accompanied by violence — and that "there is no recovery for a paranoic." At her trial Lillie said, "The court ought not to try me for killing my six children. My children had not done anything to me to make me want to kill them. I guess my children would not have wanted me to kill them. ... I don't think the courts ought to do anything with me or try me for I think my mind is bad. I don't feel right all the time. Over there when I was being tried for killing my husband they said my mind was not right and I don't think it is right" [1].

Despite the evidence to support an insanity plea, none was used. Instead, a deal was struck. The state agreed not to demand the death penalty if the defense agreed to plead guilty to five counts of murder and not introduce any evidence of insanity as a defense. A sixth count of murder was left pending. Under this deal, Lillie was sentenced to 99 years on each count plus the imposition of the five-year suspended sentence for murdering her husband. Curtis was taken away to the state penitentiary to serve a sentence of 500 years.

Sources

1. Grimes, Roy. "Paranoia Plea Saves Children's Slayer from Chair." *Houston Post,* April 7, 1938, pp. 1, 3.

2. "Poverty Claim in Mother's Mass Killing of Six Probed; Husband's Slaying Cited." *Houston Post,* March 18, 1938, p. 6.

3. "Six Slain Children Buried Together." *Houston Post,* March 19, 1938. p. 2.

Rachal David

(1939–1978). *Place:* Salt Lake City, Utah. *Time:* August 3, 1978. *Age:* 38. *Victims:* 7. *Method:* Throwing from tall building.

On August 2, 1978, a religious fanatic and loner named Immanuel David, 39, was found dead from carbon monoxide poisoning in a van. It was suicide. The next day, pedestrians in downtown Salt Lake City, Utah, were horrified to see his wife, 38-year-old Rachal David, throw herself and her seven children from the eleventh floor of the International Dunes Hotel. One child survived. It marked the end of a bizarre family saga.

Immanuel was born Charles Bruce Longo on November 9, 1938, in Yonkers, New York. His father was a prominent doctor in the area, and Charles grew up prosperous, handsome, and the type of boy neighbors categorized as "commanding your attention." The family held no strong religious beliefs. After graduation from high school in 1956, the boy served in the U.S. Marine Corps. Around that time he had his first contact with the Church of Jesus Christ of Latter-Day Saints, or Mormons. Back home in Yonkers in 1958, Charles converted to the Mormon religion and became active in youth work, where he was considered a "strong influence on the young people."

Becoming more involved with the Mormons, Longo left the United States in March 1960 for Uruguay, where he worked as a Mormon missionary. A companion of the time recalled that Longo had virtually memorized the Book of Mormon. This stay in Uruguay was cut short in February 1961, when Longo returned to the States. One reason given for this early return was hepatitis. By that time, however, Longo was displaying signs of mental instability; he was planning to become an apostle and was hearing voices. According to Charles's brother, Dean Longo, when Charles returned from Uruguay Mormon officials suggested that he seek mental help, a suggestion that he did not follow. A second account has it that Longo did in fact receive some type of psychiatric care when he got back to Yonkers.

In the fall of 1961 Longo went to Utah, where he enrolled at Brigham Young University, majored in Spanish and continued his church work. Longo's superior, Bishop James B. Winterton, recalled, "He was an extremely devout man. I've never met anyone with a stronger testimony in my life. But people began to wonder about him when he blessed his first son to be a prophet" [7].

While attending B.Y.U., Longo met and married Margit Birgitta Ericsson (later Rachal David), who was born on November 4, 1939, in Sweden. Margit was not a student at B.Y.U. and how or why she came to Utah is unknown. Before leaving B.Y.U., the couple had two children. A neighbor of that period remembered them as a "lovely, strong family." When Charles graduated in 1965 the Longos settled in Salt Lake City.

His mental problems intensified as he clashed repeatedly with Mormon officials. One point of contention was an unspecified dispute over the Book of Mormon. Longo was convinced he was going to be a key figure in the church very soon, and then began to demand that the church turn the tithing over to him, claiming he was the rightful prophet of the Church of Jesus Christ of Latter-Day Saints. This conflict came to a head on June 18, 1969, when Longo was excommunicated from the church. It was feared then that he would be violent, but he was not.

Some time shortly after this break with the church, the Longos officially changed their names to Immanuel and Rachal David. Their children were also renamed with religious monikers. Immanuel established his own small religious cult, and the Davids and their small band of followers lived for the next few years in Manti and then Duchesne, small communities in Utah. In Manti, where they lived from 1969 to 1971, the group was remembered by a former judge, Forest Washburn. He said that 12 adults and 31 children lived in a one-bedroom house that also served as a knife-sharpening business, the only apparent source of income for the group. Washburn recalled that David threatened him several times and was partial to carrying a three-foot sword around with him. Those who even saw this sword unsheathed would die, David had claimed. He often threatened to "lop off thousands of heads" if necessary.

Although he was long gone from the Mormons, David was distraught when that group didn't name him their president when the incumbent died in January 1970. The cult leader always urged his followers to consider him the Messiah.

In Duchesne, the Davids and at least three other families occupied a small two-bedroom house. Their neighbor Porter Merrill said that David told him he was waiting for a shipment of gold to arrive, which would put his group in "clover." David also told Merrill that he would soon take over the universe and was in communication with people in the state of Washington to achieve that end. Reportedly the Davids received food stamps while living in Duchesne. David had a series of loans which he couldn't pay; at the height of these financial difficulties, the Davids skipped out and headed for Salt Lake City.

David was said to be an expert knife thrower and a karate expert, perhaps a black-belt holder. From the mid–1970s the David family lived alone in Salt Lake City, although David still presided over a small number of cult followers. He was definitely the leader. Where he got money to finance the expensive life-style he led in Salt Lake City is unknown. However, a few of his associates were either in jail or being investigated by the FBI. David himself had been known to the police for years and was under investigation by the FBI just before his suicide; an unspecified "wire fraud" case against him was coming to a head. Toward the end of 1976, a gun was fired into the family's hotel room from the outside, and their car was burned in the parking lot.

The Davids spent some time living in the Hotel Utah before moving to the Ramada Inn in May 1976. One year later they moved into the International Dunes Hotel. The family's three-room suite at the Dunes cost $90 a day. Each morning David paid the bill in cash, usually with a $100 bill. During their 14 months at the Dunes, the Davids paid more than $38,000 in rent. By that time David characterized himself as the Holy Ghost, Jesus Christ, and God, all three at once. Police estimated that in the two years prior to the deaths he paid over $75,000 in rent alone.

One source claimed that followers of David paid him large sums of money; one follower paid $21,000 in a lump sum, another $11,000, and a third paid $25,000 to join the cult. One of the followers, who had been renamed Matthias David, was undergoing psychiatric examination before beginning a prison sentence for fraud. The number of David's followers was always small, and was never more than a handful during his years in Salt Lake City.

Besides the enormous expense for rent, David was partial to expensive clothes; in the month before his suicide he had ordered about $3,000 worth of clothing. The entire family was always well dressed and neat. David ate lunch every day near his hotel at a pricey French restaurant, La Fleur de Lys, where the staff described him as fussy about his food, something of a braggart, and always accompanied by two "bodyguards." Sometimes David and Rachal had dinner for two at the restaurant — at $35. Once a month all nine members of the family ate at the restaurant — at $150. Ordinarily all meals were sent in to the family at the hotel. Just before his death, David ordered two $47,000 pianos.

During that last year, David weighed about 300 pounds. He had a long beard and long hair that he wore braided down his back. All the children wore their hair in an identical fashion. When the family emerged from their room the children followed behind David "like ducklings," according to observers. Rachal and the children confined themselves to their suite almost continuously. They emerged into the outside world only once every week or two.

The David children didn't attend school and apparently hadn't for years. Some, or perhaps all, had never attended a school. Once a month David went to a local bookstore, where he purchased grammar books, dictionaries, reference books, and the like, usually spending $100 each trip. David kept his children out of school as far back as when he was in Manti. School board officials there had discussed the situation with him and tested the children; their progress was found to be satisfactory. Manti officials planned to study the situation again when the children reached high school age, but by then the family was gone. In Salt Lake City school officials had no knowledge of the David children or their nonattendance at school.

When the family made one of their infrequent public appearances, the children were not even allowed to acknowledge a "hello" from someone without permission from their father. The hotel manager admitted that he would not recognize the children, so infrequently were they about, if it were not for their unusual appearance. All reports stated that the children were quiet and obedient in the extreme. When a maid came in to clean the family's suite, the children were shut away in one room while the maid worked in another. At no time in any of the hotels they stayed at was any noise ever heard from their suite.

In that final year David had decided he wanted to destroy the state of California, that he had the power to do so, and that he was "concentrating" to do just that. After their deaths, notebooks kept by the children were found that indicated they believed their father could destroy California and hoped that he would do it.

On Tuesday, August 1, 1978, David borrowed a van and drove to a spot outside the city, where he connected a hose to the vehicle's exhaust pipe, ran it into the window, and gassed himself to death. Detective Sgt. Brent Davis speculated that he committed suicide because "there was no way he was willing to go to jail, and I think he must have been aware of the wire fraud investigation and how close he was to being locked up. His ego just wouldn't allow him to face jail, he just couldn't let that happen" [5].

It was not until the next day, Wednesday, August 2, that the body was discovered and Rachal informed of her husband's death. Most of the staff at the Dunes couldn't recognize Rachal; the period after her husband's death marked the first and only time she engaged anyone at the hotel in conversation. Rachal told people her husband often expressed a disgust with life and said he was ready for the next world; she had feared that he might kill himself. Repeatedly she asked hotel employees to try and understand what David had done. Described as shaken and nervous, Rachal was still able to converse normally. The woman worried about money, claiming she had no access to any and could no longer pay bills.

The Dunes's manager, James Bradley, called the family "extremely strange. They were loners—complete loners." That Wednesday around noon, Rachal called Bradley and asked if she would be forced to leave the hotel if she was unable to pay the bill. Bradley told her not to worry then and that they would discuss it later when her present problems were over. She kept saying, "I must get myself together; there's nothing you can do" [5]. That evening Bradley bought the family a bucket of chicken, which Mrs. Bradley delivered to Rachal's suite. Rachal took the food and thanked Mrs. Bradley, but wouldn't let the woman into the room.

The next morning, Thursday, August 3, Rachal took her seven children out onto the balcony of their eleventh floor suite, some 250 feet above the street. Chairs were stacked on the balcony so the youngest children could reach over the side. It was about 7:20 A.M. At a loss over the death of her autocratic husband, Rachal apparently decided that the only solution was for her and the children to join David in the next world.

Rachal threw the youngest child over the balcony; the older ones may have been pushed, but seemed to jump voluntarily. Obedient to the end, the children did not struggle or make any noise. An examination of the bodies revealed that only one child may have resisted by trying to keep a grip on the balcony railing. When all the children were over the side, Rachal jumped to her own death.

A crowd of about 50 witnesses, helpless to do anything, watched the horrifying scene as the bodies came crashing down one by one. Many in the crowd screamed at Rachal to stop. After the last child was gone some in the crowd yelled obscenities at the mother and chanted for her to jump as well. One witness related, "There was no emotion in the thing. They didn't scream and they didn't seem to fight" [9]. The children were: Eva Longo, 15 (renamed Rachal David); Elizabeth Longo, 14; Frank Longo, 13 (Joshua David); Deborah Longo, 12 (Deborah David); Joseph Longo, 9 (Joseph David); Bruce Longo, 8 (David David); and Rebecca David, 6, the only child born after the family assumed the name David. Officially the police classified the tragedy as six homicides, one attempted homicide, and one suicide.

Miraculously the oldest child, Rachal, survived. She spent almost a full year in the hospital and was released into the care of a foster family in Salt Lake City in July 1979. Rachal comprehended the death of the members of her family and often cried over it, but had no personal recollection of the events of that day. Doctors said it was too soon to determine if Rachal would lead a normal life.

Sources

1. Bauman, Joe. "Davids Had Money, Expensive Tastes." *Deseret News,* August 4, 1978, p. 6A.

2. Bauman, Joe. "Plunge from 11th Floor Kills Mother, 6 Children in Salt Lake." *Deseret News,* August 3, 1978, pp. 1A, 3A.

3. Bernick, Bob, Jr. "Longos Say David Changed in 1950s." *Deseret News,* August 5, 1978, pp. 1A, 8A.

4. Bernick, Bob, Jr. "Rachal Saw No Alternative to Death." *Deseret News,* August 5, 1978, p. 13A.

5. Croft, David. "Fear of Jail Drove Cultist to Suicide." *Deseret News,* August 4, 1978, pp. 1A, 6A.

6. "Girl in Plunge with Family Cannot Recall the Incident." *New York Times,* July 8, 1979, p. 18.

7. Hancock, Janetha. "From Bruce Longo to Immanuel David." *Deseret News,* August 4, 1978, p. 6A.

8. Hancock, Janetha. "Husband and Wife Were Quiet, Polite." *Deseret News,* August 3, 1978, pp. 2A, 6A.

9. Hicks, Christopher. "Family Was Obedient to the Last." *Deseret News,* August 4, 1978, pp. 1A, 9A.

10. "Immanuel David Successful as Teacher to His Children, Sanprete School Officials Say." *Deseret News,* August 3, 1978, p. 8A.

11. "Police Sort Names." *Deseret News,* August 5, 1978, p. 8A.

12. "Stop! Witnesses Plead." *Deseret News,* August 3, 1978, p. 2A.

Nellie Dcyzheski

(1899–?). *Place:* Saxonville, Massachusetts. *Time:* May 25, 1933. *Age:* 34.
Victims: 3. *Method:* Bludgeoning.

Paul Dcyzheski, 37, was severely stabbed in a neighborhood fight on
December 31, 1931. As a result he lost his job at the Roxbury Carpet Company. It was the height of the Depression, and Paul was still without work
almost a year and half later in May 1933. Paul, his 34-year-old wife Nellie,
and their four children—Irene, 11; Paul, Jr., 8; Chester, 7; and Eugene,
5—lived in a cramped two-bedroom tenement. Enduring the financial
difficulties due to her husband's unemployment, Nellie was tired of assum-
ing the entire financial burden of the family's support.

Nellie worked intermittently for the Roxbury Carpet Company as a
rug-loom operator. The company considered her an intelligent and valued
employee, and she was offered steady work. The company wanted her to
run a three-loom unit, but Nellie objected to this, saying she couldn't stand
the work. Since neither she nor her husband had worked for the company
in recent months, the Dcyzheskis were served an eviction notice on May 23.
Their tenement was owned by the company and reserved for employees.
Nellie then had the added worry of having no place for the family to go.
She decided "to get rid of the kids."

Paul, Jr., had recently turned eight. A belated birthday party was held
for him on May 24, when his parents gave him 30 cents' worth of candy.
That day Nellie sent him off to the grocery store with his wagon to bring
back three gallons of kerosene, which Nellie said she wanted for fuel. Mr.
Dcyzheski went to see his mother-in-law that day to ask her to come and
visit the family on the following Sunday. He stayed overnight.

At 10 o'clock that evening, the family was all in bed. Paul, Jr., awoke
with stomach pains—probably from too much birthday candy. Nellie
tended him but couldn't get back to sleep when she returned to bed. She
was tortured mentally, she told police, by the family's money troubles and
the eviction notice. Getting up some time later, Nellie took a hammer and
bludgeoned all four of her children in the head while they slept. Fortunately
for Paul, Jr., he was still awake with a sore stomach and struggled with his
mother. He took refuge in the cellar. Nellie then doused the tenement with

the kerosene and set it on fire, apparently to try and cover up the hammer attack. All the children died except Paul, Jr., who was rescued in critical condition from the cellar.

Doctors quickly determined that the children had been bludgeoned, and Nellie was arrested. She told the police that even going to the electric chair would be preferable to the suffering she had been through during the past two years that her husband had been out of work.

A couple of days later, she was arraigned and charged with three counts of murder. A preliminary examination by alienists found Nellie to be deeply depressed and subject to profound feelings of unworthiness. Nellie expressed no desire to attend the funeral of her children. She was committed to a psychiatric facility for observation. By then she claimed a complete loss of memory from 9 P.M. on May 24 until 7 or 8 the next morning.

Mrs. Dcyzheski was described by those who knew her as "personable," formerly beautiful, and a woman who "expresses herself well." District Attorney Warren Bishop interviewed Nellie in jail and said, "She seems a woman of culture and refinement. . . . She asks for no sympathy or mercy, but rather begs for immediate punishment. In the most pitiful way she begged me to send her to the electric chair as soon as possible. She said, 'Why all this trouble? Why all this fuss? Why all this procedure? There is no problem here. There is no difficulty. I must be guilty, and I want to be punished. I don't know why I did it. I loved my children'" [1].

Sources

1. "Saxonville Wife Pleads for Electric Chair." *Boston Globe,* May 27, 1933, p. 13.
2. "Say Mother Killed Three, Fired Home." *New York Times,* May 26, 1933, p. 42.
3. "Triple Murder Laid to Mother." *Boston Globe,* May 26, 1933, p. 17.

Catherine Deshayes

(1640s–1680). *Place:* Paris, France. *Time:* 1669–1679. *Age:* 30s? *Victims:* c. 2,500. *Method:* Poison, stabbing.

As a self-styled witch, Catherine Deshayes, known as La Voisin, was much in demand in Paris in the 1670s. Her clients, drawn from the elite of the French aristocracy, sought her out to obtain potions to attract lovers or poison to eliminate unwanted spouses. This woman's fortune-telling, crafty prophecies, and dabbling in the occult made her very wealthy. Her influence reached into the highest levels of the French government.

Little is known about her early life except that she was of low birth. Described as being in her thirties in the late 1670s, she must have been born some time in the 1640s. Catherine married a man named Antoine Monvoisin, who sold cheap jewelry in the squares of Paris. Catherine encouraged Monvoisin to open a shop, but the business venture failed, leaving the couple close to abject poverty. To generate income Catherine turned to the occult, starting with face-reading. Her psychological manner must have been effective, for by giving customers the standard prophecies in regard to sex, love, and money, her business flourished. The time was around 1667.

Financial success enabled Catherine to buy a large and comfortable home. From face-reading she expanded into telling the future through cards, a crystal ball, reading the coffee grounds in a customer's cup, and on occasion killing a small animal to read its entrails for signs of the future. Some customers weren't content with such passive glimpses of the future; they wanted more direct intervention and control. For a large fee La Voisin was willing to oblige by supplying love potions, by performing abortions, and by supplying poison to get rid of an unwanted person or to speed up the collection of an inheritance.

Fortune-tellers such as La Voisin abounded in Paris at the time, in response to a huge demand for such services. None approached Catherine's popularity. One client wrote, "La Voisin could make a lady's bosom more bountiful or her mouth more diminutive, and she knew just what to do for a nice girl who had gotten herself into trouble " [1].

The first documented murder by Catherine seems to be that of Judge Leferon, whose wife Marguerite approached La Voisin complaining that

89

her husband bored her and was "insufficient" in bed. The judge died in agony on September 8, 1669, after La Voisin obligingly supplied Marguerite with a vial of poison. Word of the sorceress's prowess spread, and soon other nobles such as the Duchesse de Bouillon, the Duke of Buckingham, the Duc de Luxembourg and the Duchesse de Vivonne were among her growing client list. By then La Voisin was conducting black masses for those of her clients who wished to devote themselves to the Devil.

At one of her black masses, the celebrant lay naked on the altar while various rituals were performed by Catherine and her helpers. La Voisin was decked out in what she called her "Emperor's robe," a red cloak embroidered with 205 double-headed, wing-spread golden eagles. One ritual of the mass involved holding an infant over the woman's body, slashing its throat and allowing its blood to drip onto the woman below. When that was done Catherine casually threw the infant's corpse into a nearby oven kept red-hot to receive it. Reportedly, the infants they used were bought cheaply from starving French people eager to sell their children to buy a little bread.

Catherine took numerous lovers and was usually in a state of drunkenness. One of her lovers urged her to murder her husband. Catherine made several attempts but never succeeded. Their maid saved his life once by accidentally bumping his elbow while he was raising a deadly bowl of soup to his mouth. On another occasion La Voisin had an apparent change of heart, for she gave her husband a counterpoison. The man recovered, although "he hiccupped for eighteen months thereafter. . . .and suffered constant nosebleeds" [1].

Perhaps the most illustrious of La Voisin's clients was the Marquise de Montespan, the main mistress of King Louis XIV. Rumor has it that she may have participated in Catherine's black masses. She may have wanted Louis XIV murdered—she was concerned about being replaced by another mistress—for at the time of her arrest, La Voisin had placed one of her people in service as a maid to Montespan and was in the process of planting a second accomplice. Both would have had access to the King, putting him at risk.

The poisoning of nobles had reached such epidemic proportions, not only as a result of La Voisin's handiwork, that Louis XIV ordered a full investigation to put an end to it all. This resulted in La Voisin's arrest on December 27, 1679. In the end over 200 people were imprisoned. Thirty-six were executed, none of them nobles. Twenty-six people, some nobles, were banished.

Catherine was subjected to several days of torture but refused to reveal any of her secrets, neither her crimes nor her client list. One form of torture was having the Spanish Boots applied to her. The person's feet were placed into tight-fitting iron boots. A number of wedges were then pounded in one by one, crushing the bones in the feet.

On February 22, 1680, in a public ceremony in front of Notre Dame in Paris, La Voisin was burned to death at the stake. As she was driven to the execution site in a cart through the streets of Paris, Catherine repulsed the priest, fought against being removed from the cart, refused to make a public confession, and had to be dragged to the stake, cursing her captors every step of the way. Commented one observer, "She was roaring drunk the day of her death just as she had been almost every day of her life" [1].

The number of murders she committed is unknown. One source states 2,500 infants were slaughtered, a figure claimed to have been obtained from a confession Catherine made at her trial. However, Catherine never confessed to anything. Given the way poor people and peasants were treated by the ruling class in those times, a number in the hundreds or thousands would certainly be possible.

Sources

1. Mossiker, Frances. *The Affair of the Poisons.* New York: Knopf, 1969.
2. Nash, Jay Robert. *Look for the Woman.* New York: M. Evans, 1981, pp. 118–25.

Nannie Doss

(1905–1965). *Place:* Alabama, North Carolina, Kansas, Oklahoma. *Time:* 1924–1954. *Age:* 19–49. *Victims:* 10. *Method:* Arsenic poisoning.

When she was finally caught, Nannie Doss struck everyone as a plump, very ordinary grandmotherly type of woman. Friendly and eager to please, she seemed far removed from the profile of a mass-murderer. Yet over a period of three decades, Nannie had systematically poisoned to death 10 people by dosing them with arsenic-laced rat poison. Victims included four of her five husbands, two of her children, two children related to her husbands, one of her sisters, and her mother.

Motivation for her crimes is unclear. While she did collect insurance money in one case, the amount was small. Her husbands may have been murdered mainly because Nannie didn't like them. Since she never admitted to more than killing her four husbands, the reasons for the other deaths are unknown. Although she was judged sane in the end, the courts still considered her to be mentally "defective."

She was born Nancy Hazle in 1905 in Blue Mountain, Alabama, near Anniston. The family had four daughters and one son. By the time of Nannie's arrest, only one sister and the brother were still alive. At the age of seven, Nannie was in a train wreck in Alabama and suffered a fractured skull. "I remember it very well," she recalled. "I was in a buggy. The train hit it and it overturned. I'll never forget crawling out from under it and running to my father, who was with me." Doss said she suffered all her life from headaches" [8].

When she was just 15, Nannie had already been working for several years in a cotton mill at Jacksonville, Alabama. She married for the first time at that age, in 1921, to railway worker Charles Braggs. The couple became the parents of four daughters. Braggs recalled coming home one night, around 1924, to find two daughters, one-and-a-half and two-and-a-half years old, lying unconscious on the floor. They died before a doctor arrived and "turned black." The symptoms were consistent with arsenic poisoning, but the children were buried without an inquest.

Braggs continued to live with Nannie for several more years. However, he and his relatives became increasingly afraid of the woman, and he divorced her in 1928. Nannie stated that she divorced Charles that year because he brought home another woman to live with him and she "couldn't stand for that." Braggs was the only one of Nannie's five husbands whom she didn't murder.

Nannie married her second husband, Frank Harrelson, in Jacksonville, Alabama, early in 1945, although she also insisted the year was 1929. In July 1945, Robert Lee Higgins, Harrelson's two-and-a-half-year-old grandson, who lived with the couple, died mysteriously and suddenly. Just two months later, in September, Harrelson himself died under similar circumstances. Doctors attributed both deaths to food poisoning. Speaking of those deaths, Frank's brother Ernest said, "I didn't like the looks of it at the time and was going to ask for an autopsy but my younger brother didn't approve of it and I just let it go. But I never was satisfied about it." Once when Frank and Ernest were walking to the cemetery to visit the child's grave, Frank turned to his brother and said, "I'll be the next one" [3].

When Nannie confessed to killing Frank, she claimed to have done it because he was "a jailbird and a drunkard, and he beat and mistreated me." Frank had been drinking one Saturday night and Nannie was summoned on Sunday morning to drive her passed-out husband home. By the time they got home Frank was awake and wanted to have sex with Nannie, who refused. Frank said, "My God, woman, I may not be here next Sunday to go to bed with." His wife got to thinking about that and decided, "I'll just teach him." She got up from bed and poured some rat poison into Frank's pint jar of corn liquor. Later that day he emptied the jar and sure enough, he wasn't around by the following Sunday [2].

Husband number three was Harley Lanning, whom Nannie married in 1947 at York, North Carolina. Harley was about 49 at the time. After the marriage the couple moved to Lexington, North Carolina. A young nephew of Lanning's who lived with them, died under mysterious circumstances in 1952. Just a few months after that Lanning died suddenly, murdered by Nannie. According to his murderer, Harley had brought it on himself because he had been running around.

Nannie returned to Lanning after a brief visit with relatives only to be informed by his sister that a drunken party of men and women had taken place in her absence at their home. That was the first trouble, from Nannie's point of view and for the next six months he continued to run around with other women. Said Nannie, "We kept on arguing until it brought on serious trouble and then I put rat poison in his food" [2]. Harley was dead within a couple of days.

Following Lanning's death, Nannie's mother, Sue Hazle, moved from Jacksonville to Lexington to be with her daughter. She died in January 1953, just one day before Nannie moved on to husband number four. In

1953 Nannie's sister, Mrs. Sula Barttee, also died. Her father, Jim Hazle, died in that year as well; he had been in a mental institution for a year or more. While Nannie never admitted it, she is generally credited with the murder of her mother and sister. Both women died suddenly, mysteriously, and in pain, with all the symptoms of arsenic poisoning. Of the 10 victims attributed to Nannie, the woman "nursed" every one of them through their final illness. Many sources list a second sister, Mrs. Dovie Weaver, who died in 1951, as Nannie's eleventh victim, but she passed away after a long bout with cancer.

The same month that her mother died Nannie journeyed to Emporia, Kansas, and she married 69-year-old Richard Morton. She had met him through a lonely hearts club, although Nannie always denied they met that way. She insisted she made his acquaintance when they both passed through a bus terminal in Birmingham, Alabama.

The club was called The Diamond Circle and was operated out of St. Louis, Missouri, by Frank Finley. Nannie joined in June 1952 by paying a five dollar fee which entitled her to receive lists of lonely men once a month for a year. Morton joined the same club in September 1952. Finley received a letter from Morton dated January 21, 1953, which read, "Will you please take our names off your list — R. L. Morton, Sr., Emporia Kans., and Mrs. Nannie Lanning, Jacksonville, Ala. For we have met and are very happily married. She is a sweet and wonderful woman. I could not have met her had it not been for your club" [8]. Four months later, on May 19, Morton was dead thanks to his wife's rat poison.

She did him in because of jealousy. It seems Nannie returned to Morton's house after a short visit with relatives only to be told by one of Morton's daughters that he had bought some rings and probably given them to Virginia. Virginia was a sister of Morton's former wife, and Nannie had heard stories that her husband was running around with her.

That was enough for Nannie, who poured one to one-and-a-half inches of rat poison into Richard's coffee. At the pool hall that evening, Richard was feeling unwell and told friends, "I guess I shouldn't have had that second cup of coffee." He was dead the next day. After Richard's death his widow stayed in Emporia only long enough — ten days — to collect about $1,400 from life insurance policies before departing for Tulsa, Oklahoma, and husband number five.

Morton's pet dog was found dead in the yard a day after his master's demise and poisoning was suspected. However, Nannie declared, "I couldn't have. I used all the poison in the bottle in the cup of coffee" [2].

Samuel Doss, 58 when he died, proved to be Nannie's last husband. Apparently Nannie had begun to correspond with him around January 1954. She had gotten his name from the lonely hearts club; she never denied this connection in the case of Doss. Their correspondence culminated in

Nannie going to Tulsa in July 1954 to marry the highway department employee.

The new Mrs. Doss poisoned her husband on two separate occasions. The first time was early in September, when Nannie dosed up a bowl of prunes with rat poison. "He sure did like prunes," said Mrs. Doss. "I fixed him a whole box and he ate them all." However, the dose was too large, and Doss vomited most of them up, saving his life. Nevertheless he was confined to the hospital for 23 days. In October Nannie tried again. This time she added the rat poison to his coffee and this time she succeeded. Samuel Doss died on October 10, 1954.

She did it "because he got on my nerves." Elaborating on that point Mrs. Doss added there were a lot of little things. She said "he refused to allow a radio in the home; wouldn't let her visit neighbors to watch television; wouldn't let her use a fan in summer to keep cool; and made her go to bed each night when he did, at nightfall. He said he had been a Christian man all his life, and that I would be a Christian woman. He told me I didn't need radio or television" [2].

Dr. W. Hidy had treated Samuel during his illnesses and was suspicious of the cause of death. He went to the county attorney prepared to order an autopsy if Mrs. Doss refused permission. However, when Dr. Hidy asked her if it was all right to perform one, saying that he was unable to determine the cause of death, the woman readily agreed. Nannie told him she also wanted to find out what killed Samuel because "it might kill someone else" [4].

When the autopsy was completed Doss's body was found to contain enough arsenic "to kill a horse." The police then began an investigation into Nannie's background. By checking her mail they learned she still used the name Morton in corresponding with that dead man's survivors in Kansas. She had neglected to inform them of her remarriage. Nannie Doss was arrested by the police on Friday, November 26, 1954.

Initially Doss denied any part in Samuel's death, claiming she neither bought nor possessed poison and telling the police, "You can't prove I ever did." In those days prisoners were often questioned without a lawyer present, and Nannie was grilled almost nonstop over the weekend. Questioning went on until 3 A.M. on Saturday morning and resumed again at 10 A.M., continuing until midnight. Sunday's session lasted about 15 hours, terminating again around midnight. When the police showed her Morton's insurance policies, Doss relented and admitted, "Well, you got me trapped. I guess I did know him" [3].

When stories about the woman were picked up around the country by the media, relatives of some of her other victims, unknown then to the police, came forward with more information. The police were then able to piece together her past. A store clerk in Tulsa, Dorothy Jones, remembered selling Nannie a 50-cent bottle of rat poison early in September. When she jokingly asked Mrs. Doss what she planned to do with it, she replied, "I'm going to feed it to my husband."

Over the course of that weekend's questioning, Doss admitted to poisoning her four husbands to death and signed separate statements to that effect. At the end she informed the police that "my conscience is still clear." When the questioning ended police were unsure if they would be able to obtain any information about her other victims for, as homicide chief Harry Stege said, "When we start talking about relatives she gets touchy" [2].

Despite the long hours of questioning Nannie found the time to hold a press conference for reporters; she agreed when such a session was proposed. She was genial and smiling and told the media representatives that the police had not mistreated her. They had "been very nice to me," she stated. Regarding her questioners, Doss smiled. "I feel like we're old friends now" [2].

Investigators found the woman to be an enigma. Stege commented, "She defies description. She is just about as nondescript as anyone I've ever met. She answers just about all of our questions in a straightforward manner. She laughs when something funny is said. She looks you straight in the eye when telling you that she poisoned this husband or that. A strange woman" [5].

Before her press conference took place Nannie applied cosmetics and put on earrings, saying, "I want to look my best." Near the end of the Sunday night questioning, Doss told her interrogators, "I feel awful bad about keeping you fellows up this way. I'm sorry to be so much trouble" [5]. Any chance of getting more information from Doss ended Monday morning, when her newly acquired lawyer advised her not to submit to any more such sessions.

Nannie even found time to give an exclusive jail-house interview to a reporter on the *Tulsa Daily World*. Doss explained to this woman that her favorite reading material was *True Love* magazine. The murderess ducked her head and giggled like a schoolgirl when she commented that "my favorite television programs are stories of amour." Elaborating, Nannie said, "I like to read. Mr. Doss wouldn't let me. He didn't believe in magazines. I've done a lot of reading lately. I like romantic, happy stories." The seriousness of her situation didn't bother Doss, for she said, "I'm not the type to take things serious," although she later admitted to finding "the whole thing upsetting." The reporter, Joanne Gordon, found Nannie was possessed of a sly sense of humor, pathetically eager to please, and had a disarming friendliness. For Gordon the best adjective to describe her was "child-like" [6].

In May 1955 Doss stood trial for the murder of Samuel Doss. All her other victims were murdered in other states, and no charges were pursued in those cases. A jury took only 15 minutes to decide Nannie was sane and could stand trial. The prosecution sought the death penalty. At the trial it came out that in the six weeks between Doss's death and Nannie's arrest she had already made contact with her next husband-to-be.

On June 2, 1955, Nannie Doss was sentenced to life in prison; she had pleaded guilty. Presiding Judge Elmer Adams declared that the state of Oklahoma never contemplated the assessment of the death penalty against a "mental defective." Adams had sided with the experts who considered her defective as opposed to those who termed her a "selfish, scheming woman." Nannie hoped she would be sent from the state penitentiary to the Eastern State Hospital where she had previously spent 90 days undergoing a psychiatric examination. Nannie described the hospital as "the nicest home I ever had." She felt the superintendent of the facility was "like a father to me." Her wish then was to spend the rest of her life there [9]. She did. Nannie Doss died of leukemia in 1965.

Sources

1. "Chronology of 12 Deaths." *Tulsa Daily World,* November 29, 1954, p. 1.

2. Clayton, John. "Widow Admits Poisoning 4 Mates." *Tulsa Daily World,* November 29, 1954, pp. 1, 2.

3. Clayton, John. "Woman Admits Feeding Husband Rat Poison." *Tulsa Sunday World,* November 28, 1954, pp. 1, 6.

4. Curtis, Gene. "Woman Set Off Own Quiz by Signing Autopsy." *Tulsa Daily World,* November 29, 1954, pp. 1, 2.

5. "Emotionless Doss Woman Proves Enigma to Probers." *Tulsa Daily World,* November 29, 1954, p. 5.

6. Gordon, Joanne. "Mrs. Doss Recalls Life's Search for Perfect Love." *Tulsa Daily World,* November 30, 1954, pp. 1, 4.

7. Gordon, Troy. "Judge Holds Up Sentence in Doss Case." *Tulsa Daily World,* June 1, 1955, pp. 1, 4.

8. Gordon, Troy. "Mrs. Doss Refuses to Give More Details on Poisoning of 4 Mates." *Tulsa Daily World,* November 30, 1954, pp. 1, 4.

9. Gordon, Troy. "Nannie Given Life Term for Poison Death." *Tulsa Daily World,* June 3, 1955, pp. 1, 4.

10. "Kansas Hubby Called Nannie 'Sweet, Wonderful Woman.'" *Tulsa Daily World,* November 30, 1954, p. 4.

11. "No Link Seen in 2 Deaths." *Tulsa Daily World,* November 30, 1954, p. 1.

Amelia Dyer

(1839–1896). *Place:* Bristol and Reading, England. *Time:* 1880–1896. *Age:* 41–57. *Victims:* 11 or more. *Method:* Strangulation.

When she was on trial in England in 1896, 57-year-old Amelia Elizabeth Dyer looked like a typical grandmother. She stood just five feet tall and wore her white hair pulled back tightly into a bun. Behind her "vicious mouth" lay the mind of a murderer. Amelia's method was simple. She "adopted" babies, for a fee, from women who couldn't look after them — and there were many such women in poverty-stricken Victorian England. Then she murdered the infants, pocketing the money as mostly pure profit. The woman had been, or was, a member of the Salvation Army. Invariably she trotted out this fact as a reference to impress women who were considering placing their babies with her.

Amelia was born around 1839 to respectable parents in Bristol, England. She grew up there and married William Dyer, but by 1896 had separated from him. Sometime before 1880 Amelia began her business of adopting unwanted children or taking them in for shorter stays from parents who paid a few shillings a month board. Inevitably some of these children disappeared. Dyer moved frequently, which she found the most convenient way of avoiding correspondence and inquiries from parents who had left a child with her.

Over the years, the Bristol police developed a sizeable file on the woman. In 1880 Amelia was sent to prison for six weeks for running a baby farm. She was admitted to the Gloucester Asylum in November 1891 with a superficial throat wound, said to be self-inflicted. Released after one month, Dyer was admitted to Wells Asylum in December 1893, after supposedly trying to drown herself, for another one-month stay.

In December 1894, Amelia was readmitted to Gloucester Asylum. Four children found in her home were packed off to a workhouse. A doctor who examined her at this time said she was violent and suffering from delusions. According to this physician, Dyer charged at him with a poker, threatening to break his skull; she said she heard voices telling her to kill herself and claimed the birds talked to her. At the 1896 trial this doctor testified he may have been wrong about Dyer and that she may have been faking her symptoms as a possible defense in case she was discovered. Just before this second admission to Gloucester, a woman who had placed her illegitimate child with Amelia subsequently married the child's father and wanted the child back. This child had disappeared, and the authorities later thought that the urgent nature of the letters from the mother may have sparked Amelia to feign madness.

After a two-month stay at Gloucester, Amelia was transferred to a workhouse where she stayed until June 1895. While at the workhouse, Dyer became friends with another inmate, 70-year-old "Granny" Smith. On the day of Dyer's release Granny asked for a day's leave and never returned. Granny stayed with Amelia until the end, functioning perhaps as a servant or companion. For the first time in her life Amelia left Bristol to settle in the Reading area of England for the last year of her life. Her daughter Mary Ann and her husband, Arthur Palmer, followed her to Reading but had their own home. No sooner had Amelia settled into the first of what would be several different Reading addresses than she inserted her usual ad in the local papers: "Couple having no child would like to take care of one or would adopt one. Terms £10" [3]. Dyer used a variety of aliases and passed herself off as the wife of a wealthy farmer or something similar.

Dyer operated in Reading for less than a year, during which she took in an unknown number of children. Most were infants under two years of age, but occasionally one was older. One was the 10-month-old daughter of a barmaid. Two infant arrivals were the illegitimate children of women who worked as live-in servants in Reading. A few of the children were lucky; the mother of one removed her child after growing suspicious of Amelia. One child was sent away by Amelia after its mother fell behind in paying the board fee.

Somehow officials with the National Society for the Prevention of Cruelty to Children became aware of the crowd of children housed by Amelia and told her she would have to register as a baby farmer. They also told her the older ones would have to be sent to school. Amelia managed to talk her way out of the situation in some fashion.

On March 30, 1896, a bargeman on the Thames River fished a brown-paper parcel out of the water. He discovered it contained the body of a baby girl; she had been strangled with a piece of tape, which was still wrapped around the neck. The parcel had been weighted with a brick. One of the sheets of paper wrapping the body bore the address and name that Dyer was then using as an alias. Although she had already left that address, she was easy to trace. Early in April the police arrested Amelia. Granny Smith implicated Dyer, as did one of the older children in her home. Granny identified the body as being of a child who was formerly in Dyer's care. Mrs. Palmer gave damaging evidence against her mother, reporting that on two successive nights she had arrived at the Palmer residence, strangled a baby out of sight there, and then stashed it under the sofa to be disposed of the next day. Each time Amelia told her daughter the infant was sleeping. Palmer had not challenged the statement.

Dyer's usual method involved strangling the child with tape and then hiding it in a cupboard at her house until it was convenient to wrap it up, carry it to the Thames in a large carpetbag, and throw it in. The house still contained the stench of decomposing bodies when the police investigated.

All this information led the police to search the Thames. They found a total of seven dead infants, all of whom had been strangled in identical fashion, with the tape knotted under the left ear. All of them were wrapped in similar parcels. Mr. and Mrs. Palmer were both involved to some extent. Mary Ann had once picked up a new child for delivery to her mother. Arthur had sometimes accompanied Amelia to a pick-up. Both were arrested, but Arthur was released for lack of evidence, and Mary Ann was acquitted on the one count of murder she faced.

Shortly after her arrest Amelia tried to stab herself with a pair of scissors, but was prevented by a policeman. Later she tried and failed to strangle herself with her bootlaces. They were tied around her neck in exactly the same way as the tape found around the necks of the dead children.

In mid–April Amelia gave a statement to the police in which she swore her daughter and son-in-law had nothing to do with the murders and had no idea what she was doing. The statement added, "I do know I shall have to answer before my Maker in Heaven for the awful crimes I have committed." When she finished her statement and handed it over to prison officials Amelia said, "Now I've eased my mind." A matron asked her if she was pleading guilty to everything by the letter, to which Amelia responded, "I wish to. They can't charge me with anything worse than what I have done" [3].

Amelia came to trial in May charged with two counts of murder. Of the seven infants found, only two could be positively identified enough to proceed in court. Her lawyer didn't deny her guilt, but rather relied on a defense of insanity. A doctor who examined her while she was awaiting trial testified she was suffering from melancholia and delusional insanity. Amelia told this doctor that her bed was sinking through the floor, that she had visions, and that she had the right to kill because she had been ill-treated at Gloucester and placed in a padded cell. Other doctors argued that Amelia was faking symptoms of mental illness. The jury found her guilty of murder after only five minutes of deliberations. Amelia never said how many children she had murdered, commenting only, "You'll know all mine by the tape around their necks" [3]. Amelia Dyer was executed on June 10, 1896.

Only five children were alive in the house at the time of Dyer's arrest. When they searched her house, the police found a large amount of children's clothing. Much more was found to have been pledged to various pawnbrokers in the area. Many letters came to the police from parents who had left children. Four years after Dyer's execution some digging took place in the garden of one of the many homes Amelia had once lived in at Bristol and revealed human remains. More excavation yielded the remains of about four children's bodies. This matter was not pursued. No accurate body count exists for Amelia, although 11 would seem to be the minimum number of children murdered. Given that she was engaged in baby farming for over 15 years, the total could be very high.

Two years after the execution the Palmers, then living in Oxfordshire, were arrested and charged with abandoning a baby. They had placed a "baby wanted" ad in the paper. After agreeing to take one from Plymouth for £14, Mary Ann picked up the child. Returning home on the train she stripped the child naked and hid it under the seat in a carriage that was being shunted off the train at a stop. The screaming infant wasn't found until the next morning. The Palmers were found guilty and each received a sentence of two years' hard labor.

Sources

1. Gaute, J. H. H. *The Murderers' Who's Who*. London: Harrap, 1979, p. 92.
2. Green, Jonathon. *The Greatest Criminals of All Time*. New York: Stein & Day, 1980, p. 207.
3. Wilson, Patrick. *Murderess*. London: Joseph, 1971, pp. 233–42.
4. Wood, Walter, ed. *Survivors' Tales of Famous Crimes*. London: Cassell, 1916, pp. 174–90.

Lillian Edwards

(1906–). *Place:* Fresno, California. *Time:* December 11, 1940. *Age:* 34.
Victims: 3. *Method:* Strangulation.

After the birth of her third child, Lillian Edwards's mental health went
into a rapid decline. She spent many months in mental hospitals before being released at her own wish to resume caring for her children. Since she
had never made any threats against her children's lives, the doctors felt she
posed no threat of violence. A misunderstanding between her husband,
away on a business trip, and the housekeeper left Lillian home alone one
night with the children a week after her release from the hospital. She
strangled all three of her children to death that night.

Lillian Ralston was the daughter of a minister. She grew up in San
Jose, California, graduated from San Jose State College, and then taught
school in Monterey County for three years. Her career ended when she
married Kenneth Edwards, a former star athlete at San Jose High and student body president. The couple settled in San Francisco, where one child
was born. Around 1933 the family moved to Fresno, where they had two
more children. The last was born in January 1940.

Shortly after the birth of her third child Lillian was admitted to a
private hospital in San Francisco for treatment of what was termed a nervous disorder. Following several months there, she was committed by a
judge to the Stockton State Hospital for the Insane in September. The staff
at that institution diagnosed Lillian as suffering from a manic-depressive
psychosis. This 1940 episode was the woman's first bout of mental instability.

Upon her admission to Stockton, Lillian was found to be deeply
depressed but made a rapid recovery over the following few months. As she
improved, Lillian kept asking the staff to let her go home so she could
care for her kids. She could do it better, Lillian reasoned, than anybody
else.

Finally Lillian got her wish. She was "paroled" on December 5, 1940.
Such releases were for a trial period of one month. Hospital superintendent
Dr. Margaret Smyth said of the release, "She always talked quite rationally.
. . . There was never any indication of any violent element in her nature" [3].

102

During Lillian's stay in the hospitals, Kenneth employed Fay Reuter as a housekeeper to look after the children. Fay stayed overnight when Mr. Edwards's work as a salesman took him on the road. On December 11, Kenneth left on one such business trip. When he left, he recalled, "My wife seemed to be in pretty good shape. I felt more cheerful about her condition than I had in a long time" [3]. Reuter was with Lillian during the day but left in the evening. After Lillian washed and put the kids to bed on the night of December 11, she used bedsheets to strangle nine-year-old Veryl Ann, six-year-old Donald, and 11-month-old Susan to death.

When Reuter arrived for work the next morning she was met by a wild-eyed Lillian dressed in a blood-spattered slip. Mrs. Edwards had inflicted very minor scratches on her neck and both wrists with a knife. Lillian chased Reuter out of the house. The police were summoned and the dazed mother was taken into custody. The bodies of the three children were found with pieces of sheets wound tightly around their necks, apparently strangled while they slept.

Lillian had no recollection of the murders and told authorities that after she put the children to bed, "Then they came, the man and woman in white, and unlocked the front door. They had lots of keys and a big black car. I don't care about myself, but I love my babies and they took them away to operate on them just like they did to me. Why wasn't Kenny there—he loved us all and didn't want us to go away forever" [5].

Doctor Smyth said the Stockton hospital was assured by Kenneth that someone could always be in attendance with Lillian after her release. Mr. Edwards claimed to have no recollection of giving such an assurance to the hospital. However, he added that he was under the impression that Reuter understood she would go home in the evenings when he was in town but would stay overnight when he was away overnight. Reuter claimed she had arrangements with Kenneth whereby she would not have to stay in the house overnight at any time.

Reuter left at 7 P.M. on the night of the murders, since Lillian seemed "perfectly rational at that time." Of the tragedy Mr. Edwards said, "Since the birth of our last baby, my wife had not been in good health and I feel her mental condition was brought about by the childbirth" [3]. Doctors felt Lillian might never know what happened that night. Authorities agreed she was insane, and she was quickly recommitted to the Stockton State Hospital from which she had so recently been paroled.

Sources

1. "Father Told of Tragedy by Business Companion." *Fresno Bee,* December 12, 1940, p. 1.

2. "Mother Kills Her Three Children Then Slashes Herself." *San Francisco Chronicle,* December 13, 1940, p. 14.

3. "Mother Who Killed 3 Children Was Paroled from Insane Asylum." *Fresno Bee,* December 13, 1940, pp. 1, 6.

4. "Police Find Bodies of Youngsters in Bed at Poplar Avenue Home." *Fresno Bee,* December 12, 1940, pp. 1, 12.

5. "They Took My Babies Sobs Slayer Mother." *Fresno Bee,* December 12, 1940, p. 1.

Christine Falling

(1963–). *Place:* Blountstown, Perry and Lakeland, Florida. *Time:* 1980–1982. *Age:* 17–19. *Victims:* 5–6. *Method:* Strangulation.

Born to a teen-aged mother unable to care for her, with little education and limited intelligence, Christine Falling lived a nomadic existence, moving from one relative to another. Only by doing bits of housekeeping, baby-sitting, and taking handouts was she able to keep a step ahead of complete poverty. Over a two-year period she strangled five infants to death while they were in her care. Authorities passed them all off as a terrible coincidence, thinking that since Falling and her charges all came from impoverished backgrounds, diseases connected with poverty must have done the damage. After the fifth death, however, even they found the coincidence theory difficult to believe any longer.

She was born Christine Slaughter in March 1963 in Perry, Florida, to a 16-year-old known variously as Ann Moore, Ann Odom, Ann Slaughter, and Ann Adkins. An older sister Carol and Christine were both given the surname of Tom Slaughter, a one-time husband of Ann's. At the time of Christine's birth Tom was 65 years old. At least six other children were born to Ann, most of whom were sent off to foster homes.

Home for Christine over the years would be a series of run-down trailers, dilapidated shacks, jail cells, motels, foster homes, church missions, and detention centers. In 1967 the two sisters were adopted by Jessie and Dolly Falling of Perry. It afforded a few years of relative stability for the girls. Mrs. Falling saw the girls for the first time in church and recalled, "They literally tore this Sunday School class all to pieces. They hadn't never been taught anything right." When her husband asked her if she was sure she wanted them Dolly said, "Well, somebody has to take them" [10].

For the most part Christine would not discuss her adoptive parents in later years but did at one point claim Jessie had abused her. It was a claim denied by Mrs. Falling. As a youngster Christine was raised in a strict environment. "I made her behave," said Dolly. "When she was bad, I put a paddle on her. But I didn't treat Christine bad. I brought her up right. . . . I taught her to go to church and school and worship the Lord Jesus Christ. I've done the best I could. I don't feel guilty" [10].

Dolly remembered Christine as being a kind-hearted, intelligent child who made mostly As and Bs in school and who had many friends. She also remembered boating trips on a nearby river, as well as family gatherings at Christmas and Easter. Christine had a different childhood remembrance; she termed that period as "miserable," marred by stuttering and epileptic fits. Christine did have epilepsy and was on medication for that condition when she was arrested, although Dolly stated, "She never had epilepsy when she was with me. I told her she better not have epilepsy around me—I went too many miles for that girl. She knows the ground I stand on." Mrs. Falling's only worry about the upbringing she gave Christine was that she might have spoiled the girl too much [10].

As a young girl Christine preferred playmates much younger than herself. From early on she was preoccupied with babies. By the time she was 12 she was in the habit of telling people she might be pregnant. Then later she worried she might not be able to get pregnant. Sometimes she told friends she had a child of her own. In an interview given shortly before her formal arrest, she told a reporter she had been pregnant twice and miscarried twice. None of these stories were true. Talking of her childhood, Christine said, "When I was growing up, I wanted parents, but when I got to a certain age, I found out it wasn't going to happen. . . . I know I've got stepparents, but they're not like a stable family" [7].

The financial fortunes of the Fallings began to decline in 1972 when Jessie became disabled and unable to work at his normal trade of carpentry. Seeking lighter work, the family moved from one Florida community to another before settling back in the Perry area. Sometimes the family worked on chicken farms in exchange for expenses. The girls helped gather the eggs. Friction between the parents and their two adopted daughters became intense in 1975, when Christine and Carol rebelled at family discipline. According to Dolly, "Christine started skipping school and staying with rotten dirty people. . . . She became a big heavy-set girl—a sensible girl, but a mean little girl—a girl who went with other men" [10]. Christine left the Fallings to live in Blountstown, Florida, with her natural mother. Between November 1975 and March 1976 a social worker reported the girl had five different addresses.

The year 1977 saw both girls marry: first Carol, then Christine. Both were only 14 or 15 years old. Christine married Bobby Joe Adkins, her stepbrother. Soon after the wedding the couple, with a baby, visited friends around Perry. Falling told everybody it was her child. It really belonged to a friend. The couple split up after six weeks of marriage.

Falling dropped out of school after the seventh grade. Relatives drove her to school, but nobody could make her stay. "I just never could get into school," Christine said. "I was constantly in fusses or fighting." When arrested her IQ was established to be just 69.

Around the time of her marriage another strange incident took place. Falling was looking after one of her natural mother's husbands, an elderly man, when he died. Christine telephoned Dolly to announce that one of her mother's babies had died.

When she and her husband split up, Christine turned to a life of traveling and drifting around, staying briefly in a host of Florida cities as well as venturing farther afield to other states such as Georgia, West Virginia, Ohio, and Colorado. She always returned to one of three Florida cities: Perry and Blountstown in the Panhandle area, and Lakeland in the central part of the state. She had relatives—most of them distant ones—in these cities. Speaking of her constant traveling, the teenager commented, "I'm the type, if there's nothing holding me down, I just go" [7].

She had many scrapes with the law during her travels. After a suicide attempt in 1978 the court termed her a danger to herself because of the attempt and a lack of parental supervision. A year later the courts adjudged her to be delinquent. The temporary homes she resided in were described by officials who had dealings with her as unsanitary and impoverished. In these homes she committed her murders, making it easy for authorities to blame the deaths on an inadequate environment.

Charges that brought Christine before the courts were all minor; they included fighting, grand larceny, delinquency, passing bad checks, and public drunkenness. At the time of her arrest for murder Falling faced six counts of check forgery. From time to time Christine phoned Dolly, who said she despaired of being able to help her. "I began to wonder about her travel program in life. Where does she want to go? What does she have in mind? What does she aim to gain by this? I didn't live that way. ... I couldn't understand it" [10]. Just before her formal murder arrest Christine phoned Dolly, who would only talk to her very briefly, claiming she couldn't afford the long distance charges.

In February 1980, Christine was living with two unrelated families in Blountstown. The whole group was crammed into a tiny shack. Falling was alone baby-sitting two-year-old Cassidy Marie Johnson while everyone else was away from the house collecting fishing bait, which they sold to make a living. The child lapsed into a coma and was rushed to a hospital, where she died two days later on February 22. An autopsy was performed. While the signs for encephalitis were inconclusive, this was listed as the cause of death. Not long after that, three-year-old Kyle Summerlin suddenly became critically ill while being baby-sat by Falling. He recovered.

Moving on, Christine was in Lakeland in February 1981. Among the people she lived with were Betty Daniels and Betty's sister Geneva Burnette. Both were distantly related to Christine. Betty remarked, "She was quiet. She never bothered nobody. When she stayed with us, we could ask her to wash the dishes, clean the floor, mind the kids—she'd do it" [10]. That month Christine's four-year-old nephew Jeffrey Michael Davis died suddenly when Falling was taking care of him, on February 23. Jeffrey simply didn't wake up from his nap. Only three days after that two-year-old Joseph Spring, Jeffrey's cousin, awoke with a scream from his nap. Falling claimed the infant was dead by the time she got to the bedroom. Autopsies were done, with death in both cases being ascribed to myocarditis, an infection of the sac enclosing the heart.

While staying with other Lakeland relatives, Falling was baby-sitting Charles Heil, three, and his 14-month-old brother Jeffrey. They were neighborhood friends of the Spring child. Both were suddenly taken ill and hospitalized, but both recovered. Falling would always deny any involvement in the cases of the three children who sickened in her care but recovered.

On July 14, 1981, in Perry, Falling was watching eight-month-old Jennifer Daniels while her mother Geneva Burnette went to the grocery store. Suddenly the child died. This time the cause of death was listed, after an autopsy, as sudden infant death syndrome (SIDS), commonly known as crib death. Listing SIDS as a cause of death can be just a way of saying that the cause of death couldn't be determined.

By then publicity was catching up with Christine. Medical officials tested her to see if she might be harboring a mysterious lethal virus. She wasn't. Before receiving this clean bill of health Falling swore to stay away from children, but changed her mind after getting the medical green light saying, "The way I look at it there's some reason God is letting me go through this. If God hadn't wanted me to go through this, he wouldn't have let it happen" [1].

People in Florida still had their suspicions. According to family members, Christine became the butt of public torment. Restaurants and motels turned her out. She wasn't able to get a job. Passers-by moved away from her on the street. Early in 1982 Christine turned up at the City Mission in Huntington, West Virginia, run by the Rev. James Funderburk. Falling told him she left Florida because she was an outcast, because people called her a witch.

During her short stay there Christine suffered several seizures. Police also arrested her three different times on minor charges. When she told the minister about the deaths of the children, she then "directly, unequivocably" denied any responsibility for their deaths. Funderburk added, "But there were times when she would say things like, 'Well, I just don't know what happened to those babies,' and she'd act very strange. . . . Then she would say the thing that bothered her the most was the way people reacted to her" [10].

The minister found her to be a driven and troubled girl who always had something violent happening around her no matter where she was. Finally

Funderburk asked her to leave the mission because of her dating and drinking. "Christine wasn't that pretty to look at her," he said, "but men seemed to flock to her, you know what I mean" [10]. A few weeks after she left his mission Christine phoned the reverend from a Huntington motel. She needed help, she told him, because she had a nine-month-old baby in Florida who had just died there. She explained that she had once dropped the baby during an epileptic seizure, causing the courts to award custody of the child to her sister. When mission workers checked into the story and found it totally false, Funderburk refused to give Falling any money.

By spring 1982, the teenager was back in Florida. In May she moved into a rundown trailer in Blountstown with her boyfriend Robert Johnson. He was the uncle of the first child to die—Cassidy Johnson. Lisa Coleman brought her 10-week-old son Travis to this trailer on July 3, 1982, to be taken care of overnight by Christine. Travis died suddenly that day of what was at first listed as crib death.

Many authorities were willing to put even this fifth death into the category of grim coincidence. One who was not willing was Joseph Sapala, the district's newly arrived medical examiner. He performed a more thorough examination than is usually done for a routine autopsy. Results showed severe external ruptures and other signs consistent with death by foul play, not natural causes. These results would not be available until the end of July.

Between the time of the Coleman child's death and the end of July, Christine was not arrested but underwent extensive questioning. Many people leaped to her defense. Dr. Flora Wellings of Tampa had studied tissues from earlier victims and stated, "I think this is a girl who is a victim of circumstances. I have no scientific reason to think otherwise" [5]. In cases of strangulation, she said, a medical examiner would usually see external and internal bruising. A support group of local citizens was organized to try and help Falling, whom they believed was being railroaded. Ironically, its first meeting was scheduled for the day after Christine was finally charged with murder. Falling claimed to be puzzled by all the deaths but convinced she wasn't to blame. She told one reporter, "It's an awful weird coincidence that it always happens to me, but there's really not much I can do or say about it" [6].

Just after the Coleman death, a psychiatrist interviewed Christine and recommended her hospitalization because he thought her to be suicidal. County sheriff W. G. Smith asked Falling to submit to a hospital stay and more psychiatric tests. By law, Smith could not force her to go; however, Christine agreed to go voluntarily to help solve the mystery of the deaths. She spent a week or so at a psychiatric facility at Tallahassee.

During her stay at that facility, Falling made a full confession to a psychiatrist that she murdered all five children who died in her care. She also told her sister Carol the same thing at the same time. On July 24, as soon as she was released from the Tallahassee hospital, Falling was arrested and charged with two counts of murder—the ones in Blountstown. There was a question at the time as to whether or not the confession could be used in court. Some considered that it could not, since it would violate the principle of doctor-patient confidentiality. The psychiatrist and others thought it could, since the psychiatrist considered himself a consultant and not the woman's official psychiatrist. The two counts with which she was charged were felt by the state to be strong enough to stand alone without need of the confession. The trial was set for December 1982. Shortly before the trial was to start, a sixth suspicious death came to light. On January 4, 1982, 77-year-old Wilburn Swindle of Perry died on the very day Falling started work as his housekeeper. Police regarded this death as possibly linked to Falling but apparently pursued no vigorous investigation of it. Since they were unaware of it when Falling confessed, she was obviously not quizzed about it.

Falling passed her time in jail awaiting trial by working puzzles, coloring pictures, and playing canasta with the matron. Psychiatrists deemed her fit to stand trial, however, just days before her trial was to commence, Falling pleaded guilty to three counts of first-degree murder—the Blountstown and Perry children—in a plea-bargaining deal. She was sentenced to life in prison with the possibility of parole in 25 years. In exchange, the state agreed not to prosecute Christine in the deaths of the two Lakeland children or that of Swindle. Her defense lawyer Baya Harrison felt it was a deal they couldn't refuse and commented, "You have to understand that she was facing potentially six death sentences. Three of the cases were relatively strong. The question became: Should she risk her life under those circumstances" [9]? The decision was made by Falling.

Back in July when she confessed, Falling made numerous confessions to nurses, doctors, other hospital aides, and law officers. About her first murder, Johnson, she said, "Well, it was about, I'd say about 8:30, she got kinda rowdy or something. Anyway I choked her until she quit breathing and she had turned purple. Her heart had stopped beating and her pulse had stopped and she wasn't breathing." About Jeffrey Davis she said, "Well, he had come in from outside playing, and he had got ahold of some kind of spray, white-looking—I don't know if it was paint or what. And he had made me mad or something. What it was he had made me mad, and I was already kind of mad that morning, and I just took it out on him. I started choking him until he was dead." About Joseph Spring she related, "He had laid down for a nap, and he was asleep. And I don't know, I just got the urge I wanted to kill him, so I went down and choked him, and that's when I called the ambulance." About Jennifer Daniels's death, Falling stated, "Well, her mama had went in the grocery store to buy groceries and was continually crying and crying and crying, and it made me mad, so I just put my hands around her neck and choked her until she shut up." On the death of Travis Coleman, Falling remarked, "I just choked him—no apparent reason, I guess. I just picked him up off of his pallet and choked him to death and laid him back down." When asked about the three children who became critically ill while in her care the teenager said, "The ones that took sick, I don't know what happened to them, other than they took sick." At the end of her confession Christine became tearful, saying, "I don't know why I did none of this" [4].

Many questions were raised by people as to why the state hadn't acted much earlier. State Attorney Jerry Blair said, "If nothing else, this case indicates how incredibly easy it is to murder a child without leaving a trace. I think that's why it took five children. A baby can be killed with a slight pressure to a certain artery and the marks disappear shortly after death" [9]. Hospital personnel had reported seeing red and blue marks on the throat of Jennifer Daniels.

Sources

1. "Baby Sitter Arrest Came After 5 Deaths in 2 Years." *New York Times,* July 26, 1982, p. 12.

2. Baby-sitter, 19, Admits 5 Slayings, Officials Say. *Chicago Tribune,* July 28, 1982, sec. 1, p. 2.

3. Chandler, David. "Real Life Dr. Quincy." *People,* October 11, 1982, pp. 139–40.

4. "Christine Falling's Confession." *Tallahassee Democrat,* December 5, 1982, p. 7A.

5. DeFord, Susan. "Mysterious Death Just a Coincidence, Officials Suspect." *Tallahassee Democrat,* July 7, 1982, pp. 1A, 2A.

6. "5 Children Die in 2 Years in Case of Sitter, 19." *New York Times,* July 17, 1982, p. 10.

7. Olson, Karen. "After Her Years of Wandering, She Has a Place." *Tallahassee Democrat,* December 5, 1982, pp. 1A, 7A.

8. Olson, Karen. "Baby-sitter Charged in Two Child Deaths." *Tallahassee Democrat,* July 23, 1982, pp. 1A, 3A.

9. Olson, Karen. "Falling Pleads Guilty." *Tallahassee Democrat,* December 4, 1982, pp. 1A, 2A.

10. Olson, Karen. "Falling Wanted a Baby of Her Own." *Tallahassee Democrat,* July 25, 1982, pp. 1A, 12A.

11. "One Question Left in Sitter's Killings." *Chicago Tribune,* December 5, 1982, sec. 1, p. 18.

12. Robertson, Betsy. "Autopsy Results Withheld in Falling Case." *Tallahassee Democrat,* July 24, 1982, pp. 1A, 2A.

13. "Sitter Pleads Guilty to Slayings, Gets Life." *Chicago Tribune,* December 4, 1982, sec. 1, p. 2.

14. "Witness Says Baby Sitter Told Sister She Killed 5." *New York Times,*, November 13, 1982, p. 8.

Susanna Fazekas

(c. 1865–1929). *Place:* Nagyrev and Tiszakurt, Hungary. *Time:* 1911?–1929. *Age:* 46?–64. *Victims:* 100 or more. *Method:* Arsenic poisoning.

The Hungarian hamlets of Nagyrev and Tiszakurt nestle beside the Theiss River 60 miles from Budapest. The population of the area was about 1,400 at the time of World War I. Twenty-five miles from the nearest railroad station, the hamlets were isolated from the world and completely cut off in the winters.

Poor peasants scratched out a living, or tried to, on land that was ever being sliced up into smaller and smaller pieces as sons took over from their fathers. Huge estates ringed the area, curtailing expansion. The main industry was the growing of grapes and the manufacture of wine. Village men were fond of consuming the final product and were said, in general, to be brutal to their women.

The area had no hospital, doctor, or trained nurse, nor did it have any teachers. The most influential position in the community, at least for women, was that of midwife—a post filled in these hamlets by the sinister figure of Susanna Fazekas, a widow, who was also known as Susanna Olah or simply as Aunt Susie.

Other than the fact she was born around 1865, nothing has been reported of her early life and background. She was not from the area but had settled in Nagyrev by 1910, perhaps earlier. Described as a "fat, smiling, Buddhalike figure" [7] Fazekas had learned her trade in big cities; she soon came to know all the cares and problems of the villagers. Soon she was doctor, midwife, and father-confessor to the women of the area. Her influence over the peasants was strong.

During her early days in Nagyrev, the town's only other midwife disappeared without a trace. That woman's son, convinced of foul play by Susie, took a couple of shots at her but missed and was duly sent to jail. Villagers came to think of Fazekas as having a charmed life. Her eyes were very bright and black and, some said, glowed red in the dark of night. To heighten her mystique Susie kept snakes and lizards at home, which was taken as a sign of her powers. Not surprisingly, this woman came to be called "white witch."

Nominally her profession was life, but death soon took precedence. Between 1911 and 1921 Fazekas performed abortions — illegal — and found herself charged in court on at least 10 separate occasions. Each time she was acquitted, which probably did little to detract from her reputation. At the same time, Fazekas was building a poison ring that claimed untold numbers of lives.

The year of her first murder is unclear, perhaps 1911. The first few may have been children. A poverty-ridden mother with one too many mouths to feed sought advice from Fazekas and came away with one of her potions; soon there was one less mouth to feed.

All victims died from arsenic poisoning. Susie obtained the poison from flypaper, which had a coating of arsenic. Susie boiled it off the flypaper. These small hamlets would soon order more flypaper in a given period of time than all the rest of Hungary combined as the murder business picked up.

All of the murderers were women; they purchased their poison from Fazekas at prices ranging from $8 to $40, depending on what they could afford. Some of the victims were women and some children, but the majority were men. Women dispatched husbands because they didn't like them or so that they could take on lovers. They dispatched old lovers for new ones. They killed second husbands for thirds. And they killed anyone if it meant an economic improvement.

Murders continued for close to 20 years, and it wasn't until 1929 that mass arrests were made and the ring broken. The number of victims is unknown, but estimates of at least 100 do not seem to be exaggerated. Scores of women stood trial. Incredibly, the men of the area did not get suspicious as their friends died off at a prodigious rate. The women of the area, even those not directly involved, all seemed to know what was happening. It was in a way a war on men and was quite successful for a long time.

Long before Fazekas's ring was broken up, the area became nicknamed the "poison villages" in the district and its women the "angel-makers of Nagyrev." The authorities displayed little interest despite the area's reputation and the fact that, over the years, they had received anonymous tips that all was not right in the two hamlets.

Fazekas herself gradually became known as the "widow-maker" of the area as discontented women learned of her unique service. Her fame as a disposer of unwanted people spread by word of mouth. Her murder business apparently got a boost during World War I, when most of the able-bodied men left for service with the military.

Some of the wives left behind took lovers from among the remaining males, many of them too young to enter the military. They didn't especially welcome their husbands' return. A couple used Susie's special potion to become what they jokingly referred to as "war-widows." Then, said a contemporary report, "Apparently envious of the facility in exchanging old mates for new, other women from time to time followed their example with great success" [10]. Susie's business boomed.

Officials did occasionally look into the situation in the hamlets when they received tips. Each time, the police found a death certificate that was properly filled out. That was the extent of their checking. Only later was it discovered that the position in the village corresponding to coroner was held by a man who was Susie's cousin. Each time he was called to certify a death he held a feather over the face of the victim—if it didn't move the person was dead—and then listed the cause of death as pneumonia, heart trouble, or whatever came into his mind as appropriate.

One of Fazekas's clients had poisoned her mother in 1924 and then, just to be sure, dumped the body into the river. It was discovered by the authorities to contain arsenic, but a lax investigation again produced nothing.

The murder ring was broken up in the summer of 1929 when the police, still receiving tips, questioned the Szabo family about the death of Mrs. Szabo's father and uncle. It was Mr. Szabo who finally cracked under pressure and admitted, "Yes, we killed my father-in-law four years ago and last autumn my wife's uncle. All on account of land. My wife incited me to do it" [7].

The Szabos pointed directly to Fazekas and "Aunt Susie's Inheritance Powders." Questioned by the police, she denied everything. The prosecutor, feeling Susie would never crack, got an idea. He released her from custody but told the police to watch her closely. Fazekas fell into the trap and immediately went from house to house in Nagyrev, apparently alerting clients, without noticing the trailing police. All she spoke to were picked up by the law and many confessed. Armed now with a mountain of evidence, the police went to pick up Susie again. As they entered her home Fazekas sensed all was lost and she downed one of her own potions in front of the police, dying within an hour.

Many of the confessions were later retracted as the villagers worked to obstruct the authorities. The police systematically exhumed bodies from the cemetery for examination. Just as systematically, unknown hands tried to remove or deface names and inscriptions on tombstones. Bodies of people who had died naturally were taken out of their graves and exchanged with those who had been murdered.

Victims who were exhumed were found to contain enough arsenic to kill 10 people. Usually the container from which the arsenic was drunk had been buried with the victim. Susie's house was found to be full of flypaper.

At one point the police were holding over 100 women—so many that they had room for no more in their cells. Due to problems in the cemetery the authorities could never put a final figure on the number of murders committed, although they estimated it might be 100 or more.

Four of the women arrested followed their mentor's example and committed suicide. Ultimately 34 women were put on trial for murder; 18 of them received prison sentences, eight were executed, and the remainder were acquitted. The defendants ranged in age from 44 to 71 years of age. The defense lawyers were, in some cases, able to get relatively light sentences by pleading the low cultural level of the two villages. Illiteracy was said to be 28 percent.

One of those tried was Maria Kardos who, after marrying and divorcing two husbands, found herself at the age of 40 with a 23-year-old son. The son was in bad health and a burden to his mother. He also interfered with Maria's pleasures, since she didn't want to be reminded of her age, particularly since she had taken a young lover. She killed him with one of Susie's potions after asking him to sing one of her favorite songs just minutes before he died. Kardos married again but was threatened with divorce by her third husband when he found she was being unfaithful to him. A trip to Susie put an end to his complaints permanently. That dose was on the house, courtesy of Susie, who had once had the man as her lover and had never forgiven his defection. Kardos was executed.

One villager had been blinded in the war and sent home from a military hospital to his wife. She didn't want to look after him, especially since she had taken on a young lover. The wife brought her lover into the house and the couple had sex in the presence of her husband, who could only stand by helplessly. Finally she dosed the husband with arsenic; when the first attempt failed, Susie showed up herself the next night to expertly administer dose number two.

Juliana Foldvari poisoned her mother to inherit property, and went on to erase husbands one and two the same way. Rosalie Sebestyen and Rosa Holyba each murdered a husband because the men "bored" them. They each drew sentences of life in prison. Mrs. Csaba eliminated her husband as she found him "always drunk and brutal." She received an eight-year sentence. Maria Szendi, who also poisoned her husband, said she did it because "He always had his own way. It's terrible the way men have all the power" [9].

Susie's steadiest customer over the years was Juliana Lipka, 66 years old at the time of her trial. Lipka disposed of her mother first, around 1912, to inherit. Over the years she returned to Susie six more times to get rid of an aunt, an uncle, a husband, and three other relatives. The motive was usually financial gain.

Blackmail was another of Susie's occupations; she had no hesitation in visiting one of the area's numerous widows for a few dollars. Apparently

Lipka was approached often in this way, and it is possible that a vicious circle formed where Lipka killed to get more money only to be blackmailed out of some of it by Susie, which caused her to kill again, and so on.

The mother had been killed only a couple of days after Lipka had had her make a will in her favor. The uncle made over all his property to Lipka in return for life care, which for him was seven more days. At the time of her arrest, this pock-marked, squat senior citizen told the police she had her eye on a 24-year-old man she hoped to make her husband by means of enticing him with her wealth. She was executed.

Few of the defendants got any sympathy from courtroom observers. They showed no remorse or moral sense and exhibited mostly sullen and defiant faces. One 70-year-old woman who had murdered her husband said, "We are not assassins! We did not stab our husbands. We did not hang or drown them either. They died from poison, and this was a pleasant death for them." The judge asked one defendant if she had heard of the Ten Commandments and about the one against killing. "I never heard of the Ten Commandments. I never hear anything about 'Thou shalt not kill.' ... I have never heard of it" came the surly reply, after which she sat down angrily [6].

On the surface the communities professed to be religious, yet murder had become a way of life. Almost no inhabitant of the area was not involved directly or indirectly in some way. Ladislas Tots, a Calvinist clergyman at Nagyrev, attributed the murders to a hunger for land and a postwar laxity which he thought was leading women to consider husbands solely as sources of income. He added, "The peasants hereabouts are mean and grasping and think only of money and comfort. All the women, who somehow seem stronger than the men, are married two or three times. Spiritually they have no existence, nor yearning for spirituality. My church is empty, although I must admit that among the accused are several of my few faithful—women who have been active in all kinds of parish work" [10].

Sources

1. "Admits Poisoning Son and Husband." *New York Times,* January 18, 1930, p. 6.
2. "Five Hungarians Held for Slaying Husbands." *New York Times,* February 7, 1930, p. 23.
3. "4 Women Sentenced in Mass Murders." *New York Times,* December 15, 1929, p. 10.
4. Gribble, Leonard. *Sisters of Cain.* London: John Long, 1972, pp. 140–53.
5. "Hungary Opens Grim Trials of Fifty Women for Poisoning Husbands and Other Relatives." *New York Times,* December 14, 1929, p. 6.

6. "Hungary's Poison Villages." *Literary Digest,* 104: 16–17 January 25, 1930.

7. "Murder by Wholesale: A Tale from Hungary." *New York Times,* March 16, 1930, sec. 10, p. 3.

8. "More Held in Poisonings." *New York Times,* August 24, 1929, p. 3.

9. Nash, Jay Robert. *Look for the Woman.* New York: M. Evans, 1981, pp. 157–60.

10. "100 Husbands Dead in Poison Plots." *New York Times,* September 15, 1929, sec. 3, p. 6.

11. "Reveal Poisoners as Widow Makers." *New York Times,* August 13, 1929, p. 6.

12. "Thirty-one Women Facing Trial in Hungary." *New York Times,* December 29, 1929, sec. 3, p. 3.

13. "Two Nagyrev Babies Poisoned by Arsenic." *New York Times,* September 13, 1929, p. 22.

14. "Woman Prisoner Must Die." *New York Times,* October 19, 1930, p. 16.

Elizabeth Fiederer

(1898–?). *Place:* Passaic, New Jersey. *Time:* January 21, 1936. *Age:* 38. *Victims:* 4. *Method:* Asphyxiation from gas.

For the last three months of 1935 and into the first month of 1936, 38-year-old Elizabeth Fiederer was an almost daily visitor to the General Hospital in Passaic, New Jersey. Mrs. Fiederer was convinced that she was suffering from incurable cancer and that members of her family already had, or soon would, contract the disease from her. Physicians from the hospital assured the woman again and again that she had no symptoms of cancer and treated her in various ways, but the woman refused to believe them.

Sometime in the early hours of January 21, 1936, Elizabeth wadded up the keyholes in her apartment and turned on all the gas jets of her stove. At 7:30 A.M. three men arrived at the tavern operated by Elizabeth's husband, Hans. The tavern was always open by that hour, and the surprised men went upstairs to the Fiederer's second-floor apartment over the bar. When they forced the door they found Hans dead, along with the couple's three children, Elsie, 4; Tessie, 13; and John, 11. Ironically Elizabeth, although coming close to death, was the lone survivor.

It was six days before she recovered enough to be told by the police that her family had all died. "If they died, why did you let me live," she wailed [1]. Indicted on four counts of murder, Fiederer readily confessed to the police and chanted frequently, "I did it, I did it." She had read about mercy killings and decided this was the best way out so that the family could avoid suffering from the cancer she was convinced they all had.

On February 14, 1936, Elizabeth appeared in court on the four murder charges. Her attorney stated, "The prisoner is unable to coherently comprehend her position and stands mute." The judge then directed the jury to "determine whether the prisoner stands mute through obstinacy or by providence or by an act of God" [4]. The jury took just seven minutes to declare her insane. Elizabeth Fiederer was immediately committed to a state hospital.

118

Sources

1. "Says Woman Admits Murdering Family." *Newark Evening News,* January 27, 1936, p. 1.

2. "Three Die of Gas in Home." *Newark Evening News,* January 21, 1936, p. 7.

3. "Woman Confesses 4 Mercy Slayings." *New York Times,* January 28, 1936, p. 40.

4. "Woman Killer Held Insane." *Newark Evening News,* February 11, 1936, p. 2.

Priscilla Ford

(1929–   ). *Place:* Reno, Nevada. *Time:* November 27, 1980. *Age:* 51.
Victims: 6. *Method:* Automobile.

Thursday, November 27, was the date of Thanksgiving in 1980.
Virginia Street in downtown Reno, Nevada's, casino district was always
busy. It was the home to casinos such as Harrah's, Harold's, and the Cal-
Neva Club. At 3 P.M. that day it was especially busy.

A 1974 blue Lincoln Continental automobile was moving along
Virginia Street at a high rate of speed when it suddenly lurched onto the
sidewalk; it traveled at an estimated 50 miles per hour for two blocks, running down pedestrians. The Lincoln then veered back onto the street and
stopped behind traffic at a stop light. By then, six people were dead or dying
and 23 others injured, many seriously. One person had a leg torn off. An
estimated 1,000 people were on the street at the time.

Virginia Street was left looking like a battlefield. Coins, purses, shoes,
eyeglasses, and other personal effects littered the two-block area. A blond
wig turning crimson lay in a pool of blood. Bodies were sprawled everywhere. The injured screamed for help. People frantically dove into casinos
and behind parked cars as they tried to avoid the vehicle. One witness said,
"It looked as though someone had gone through the streets with a lawn-
mower, mowing people down. It looked like a battlefield—there were
bodies all over the place" [9].

Bodies draped over the hood and windshield were swept off as the Lincoln sideswiped parked cars and knocked over street signs, only to be
replaced as more pedestrians were hit. At one point the windshield was
completely covered with people. The car stopped suddenly, the people fell
off, and then it continued. Witness Marty Edmondson sobbed, "She came
right at us, she came right at us with a body still on the hood of the car and
she looked like she was looking for somebody else to hit" [1].

One of the problems police had on the scene was in controlling spectators, some of whom were stealing wallets and purses from the victims as
they lay on the street. The police officer who made the arrest was already
on the street and was one of those who had to dodge the car. The driver,
51-year-old Priscilla Ford was arrested without incident; she was unhurt.

120

The rampage was deliberate on the part of Ford, who was trying to kill as many people as she could. On her way to the police station she reportedly uttered "vulgarities."

Ford told investigators, "I deliberately planned to get as many as possible. A Lincoln Continental can do a lot of damage, can't it? In June I was in Boston. A voice told me to drive through a crowd at a theater and kill as many as possible, but another voice said she's too much of a lady to do that. I had wine today specifically to blame it on the accident. The more dead the better. That will keep the mortuaries busy. That's the American way." When asked if she had any concern for her victims or felt it was wrong to kill Ford said, "No, I could care less. They were like pigs to me. . . . It's not wrong for me to kill because I deserve vengeance. Vengeance is mine" [6].

The only other explanation the woman offered to the police for her actions was that she was upset because her daughter, Wynter, had been taken away from her in 1973 by Nevada's Washoe County welfare authorities and placed in a juvenile facility. The girl was then 11 years old.

Priscilla Ford was born in 1929 in Berrien Springs, Michigan, where she grew up in a family of nine girls and two boys. Both parents were devout members of the Seventh-Day Adventist Church, raising their children in that faith. Considered the smartest of the siblings, Priscilla went on to earn a degree and a teaching certificate. An early marriage produced two sons but ended in divorce. This was followed by a marriage to William Scott, which produced Wynter before it also failed. In later years Ford would marry a few more times.

She worked as a teacher in Cass County, Michigan, from 1957 to 1964. Mrs. John Keller, an acquaintance from that period, recalled her as "brilliant, outstanding in music or art or anything she tried—an all-A student. She was always very pleasant and was a very good teacher" [5]. Ford ran unsuccessfully in a 1963 election for a local junior college board of trustees. An incident took place in 1957 between Priscilla and her then-husband William Scott, in which both were wounded from gunshots. Apparently she wounded him and then shot herself. Police in Niles, Michigan, investigated the shooting but no charges were filed.

Around 1966 Ford left Michigan, taking Wynter with her. For years she drifted around the country, never staying long in any one place or any one state. She supported herself by taking a variety of low-paying, unskilled jobs. By 1971 Priscilla was consuming a lot of marijuana. It was a religious sacrament, she explained to her daughter. Around the same time she told Wynter she was receiving revelations from Ellen G. White, a Seventh-Day Adventist prophet from the previous century. Then she informed her daughter that she, Priscilla, was the reincarnation of White. Later she became convinced that she was Jesus Christ and also told the confused Wynter that she would soon find someone to artificially inseminate Wynter so that the girl would have a virgin birth. Ford took to calling herself the Rev. Dr. Priscilla Ford.

The pair dropped in to spend some time in Illinois with Franklin, Ford's grown son. Franklin was appalled to find his mother intoxicated much of the time or stoned on marijuana, which she also gave to his half-sister. Patricia once tried suicide at Franklin's house. In 1972 Ford journeyed to Miami, convinced she was invited to speak on White's prophecies at that year's Republican Convention. Security officials threw her out of the convention center. The Devil had prevented her from speaking, thought Ford. Letters sent to old friends in Michigan around this time baffled the recipients; the correspondence was filled with rambling jargon that made no sense.

After she arrived in Reno in 1973, Priscilla had several minor brushes with the law. Each time Wynter was taken away from her, only to be quickly returned by county officials after the scrapes were resolved. One job she had in Reno was working in a rest home in exchange for room and board for herself and her daughter. Ford always contended that her daughter was "stolen" from her at that time by the authorities after the operator of the rest home had Ford arrested for trespassing. Joan Austin ran the home then and remembered that Priscilla was employed as a cook. When Austin fired Priscilla, the woman later returned and tried to physically assault her former employer. Austin then had her arrested. Police records confirmed that Ford was arrested on misdemeanor charges of trespassing and assault and battery. Both charges were dismissed.

This time Wynter was not immediately returned to Priscilla's custody. Officials told her they would not return the child until Priscilla could prove she was working and could provide for the child. An angry Ford decamped the city, threatening legal action. Before leaving Nevada, Ford told Wynter she was going to Chicago to find a lawyer who would bring them together. One year later, Priscilla wrote a letter to welfare officials in Nevada threatening to murder the caseworker if Wynter wasn't immediately returned to her. During that year welfare workers had unsuccessfully tried to find Priscilla to see if her circumstances were such as to return her daughter. After that one letter they never heard from the woman again. From the time she left Reno in 1973, Ford made no attempt to contact Wynter until she sent her a letter in 1980. The letter asked how the girl had been, as if all the intervening years had not gone by. Wynter was then living in Los Angeles with one of her half-brothers. During her final stay in Reno, Ford knew the whereabouts of her daughter.

From Reno Priscilla went back to her nomadic existence, this time alone. During a stay in Boise, Idaho, in 1978, as the Rev. Dr. Priscilla Ford, she launched a civil lawsuit against the Mormon Church and Joseph

Califano, the Secretary of the Department of Health, Education and Welfare. Demanding $500 million in damages for suffering mental and physical anguish, this incomprehensible suit was, of course, quickly thrown out of court. In Buffalo, New York, in 1979, Priscilla ran afoul of the law again with a total of eight charges against her for passing bad checks, possession of marijuana, and theft of services. All of this got her a short stay at the Buffalo Psychiatric Center, where she was diagnosed as a paranoid schizophrenic.

Priscilla arrived in Jackman, Maine, in May 1980. She arrived alone and knew no one in the town of 850 people. Jackman sits near the border of the Canadian province of Quebec and is popular with hunters and fishermen. Curiosity was aroused in the town over what Ford was doing there. She stayed in several different motels during her stay of about six weeks.

Patricia Thomas owned one of the lodges where Ford stayed and said, "It was very mysterious. She came here, and she said she was a writer, but she was very vague about it. Everybody in town wondered what she was doing here." Town manager Elsie Crawford remembered that Ford had as much money as she needed. For the most part she stayed in her room. Priscilla also spent time at the Jackman Motel, where owner Irene Gagne found her constantly depressed. "I would tell her, 'Why don't you erase the pain and start out fresh again?'" Irene said. "I tried to get to know her — she seemed like a very nice woman. But I could never get the real story behind her. ... She was writing all the time, up in her room, always writing" [5].

To these three women, and a few other town residents, Priscilla told the story of her daughter being kidnapped. Ford even expressed an interest in settling permanently in Jackman and once met with a real estate agent to discuss houses. However, she left just as quickly as she had arrived moving on to Bangor, Maine, in June. In that city she occasionally chatted with Arline Robinson, a neighbor in the apartment building in which Ford was renting. Robinson said, "She's a strange person. She never caused any trouble, and she never bothered a soul." According to Robinson, Ford asked her to read a handwritten manuscript of 200 to 300 pages, which amounted to Priscilla's autobiography. The book was laden with religious allusions [5].

While in New England, Ford phoned a U.S. attorney in Portland, Maine, demanding he bring both civil and criminal actions against the people who kidnapped her daughter seven years earlier. She threatened to drive her car from Jackman to Portland, killing everybody she saw on the way by running over them, if she didn't get action.

At the beginning of November, Ford left Bangor and moved to Reno. The first job she applied for didn't pan out, but the man she spoke to felt

sorry for Ford, who told him she had no money and was living in her car.
He let her have an apartment he was remodeling rent-free since it had no
working bathroom. It was on Virginia Street. Ford did get a job at Macy's
department store as a gift wrapper for the Christmas season. She worked
there for two weeks before going on her rampage.

Coworkers found her to be a pleasant and efficient worker. They were
told by Ford that she was a retired teacher and unpublished writer. Priscilla
also told them her daughter had been kidnapped in 1973 in Reno, that she
hadn't seen her since, and that she had recently returned from Maine to try
and find the girl. To one employee, Ford said she felt she wasn't getting
enough help from authorities in finding her daughter and that a couple of
years previously she had received a letter from someone in Los Angeles
claiming to be her daughter but she could never find the sender. All these
fellow employees were shocked at Ford's Thanksgiving Day actions.

Priscilla came to trial late in 1981 on six counts or murder and 23 counts
of attempted murder. The trial lasted five months and was the longest one
in northern Nevada history. Priscilla's lawyer pleaded not guilty by reason
of insanity. Priscilla's sister testified about Ford wanting to artificially inseminate Wynter so the girl could give virgin birth to the next Jesus Christ.
Wynter and her half-brother both took the stand to say their mother began
to claim that she was Jesus Christ around 1971. Wynter added that her
mother knew she was living in Los Angeles for at least six months before
the murders.

Defense attorney Lew Carnahan called three psychiatrists, who all
diagnosed Ford as a paranoid schizophrenic with delusions. All said she
didn't know it was wrong to kill at the time of the murders. Two of them
said she had religious delusions which she felt gave her the "Godlike" right
to kill. A psychiatrist for the state testified that Ford was a paranoid
psychotic who did know it was wrong to kill.

During a search of Ford's apartment after she was arrested detectives
found a harsh and rambling letter to advice columnist Abigail Van Buren
correcting that woman's advice. Ford felt it to be her duty, since she was
America's "Only authorized divinity." They also found a grant application
to the U.S. Department of Education, in which Priscilla asked for three
million dollars to research the anatomy and physiology of the soul. As
director of the project, Ford planned to pay herself $60,000 a year.

Carnahan did not want Ford to take the stand, but she insisted. The
attorney went so far as to make an unsuccessful motion to prevent her from
testifying. Carnahan felt she was committing "public suicide" by taking the
stand.

On the stand the defendant was asked why she had written the name
Barbara Walters in the margin of her Bible so often: "Because she is a wild,
fierce beast," was the reply. As to why she had so many books about Hitler

and the Nazis in her room, Ford said, "Because I've always had a soft spot in my heart for Hitler." The defendant claimed to have no recollection of running anybody down in her car. The car wasn't steering well and had gone out of control into the crowd, she thought. On her last day on the stand, she said, "I am human and I am divine. I don't like it any more than anyone else does. I don't want to be divine" [6].

Apparently the thought of being labeled insane was more repugnant to her than the possibility of receiving the death penalty. Priscilla was adamant on the stand that the doctors were wrong, that she was not mentally ill, that she didn't think she had a Godlike right to kill, and that she did know it was wrong to kill. The jury believed her; after 13 hours of deliberations on March 19, 1982, they found her guilty on all counts. Ford remained emotionless throughout the trial, During the penalty phase of the trial the jury deliberated five days before reaching a decision. At the end of March, Priscilla Ford was sentenced to die.

Sources

1. Barber, Phil. "Car Rams Reno Crowd." *Reno Evening Gazette,* November 28, 1980, pp. 1, 5.

2. Barber, Phil. "Driver of Death Auto Woman of Many Faces." *Reno Evening Gazette,* November 28, 1980, pp. 1, 3.

3. "Car Hits Reno Pedestrians, Killing 5 and Hurting 27." *New York Times,* November 28, 1980, p. 20.

4. "5 Killed by Car on Reno Sidewalk, Driver Held." *Los Angeles Times,* November 28, 1980, pp. 1, 4.

5. Foo, Rodney. "Ford Profile Emerges in Autobiography." *Reno Evening Gazette,* November 29, 1980, pp. 1A, 6A.

6. Kuncl, Tom. *Ladies Who Kill.* New York: Pinnacle, 1985, pp. 70–95.

7. Phillis, Michael. "Ford Defense Rests." *Reno Evening Gazette,* March 6, 1982, pp. 1A, 12A.

8. Phillis, Michael. "Ford's Future: Execution or Prison." *Reno Evening Gazette,* March 20, 1982, pp. 1A, 12A.

9. Phillis, Michael. "I'm Thankful I'm Alive." *Reno Evening Gazette,* November 28, 1980, p. 3.

10. "Reno Woman Who Killed Six with Auto Sentenced to Die." *New York Times,* March 30, 1982, p. B13.

11. Voyles, Susan. "6th Person Dies in Holiday Rampage." *Reno Evening Gazette,* November 29, 1980, pp. 1A, 6A.

Lafonda Fay Foster and Tina Marie Hickey Powell

(Foster, 1963– ; Powell, 1958–). *Place:* Lexington, Kentucky. *Time:* April 23, 1986. *Age:* Foster, 22; Powell, 27. *Victims:* 5. *Method:* Firearm, stabbing, automobile.

At 9 P.M. on the evening of April 23, 1986, police discovered the body of 59-year-old Trudy Harrell in the parking lot of a shopping center in Lexington, Kentucky. She had been shot in the back of the head, stabbed five times, and run over and dragged over 100 feet by a car. An hour and a half later, police found the body of Virginia Kearns, 45. She was shot in the back of the head. Numerous stab wounds were inflicted on the body, including 16 on the neck alone. Virginia was also run over by a car. Just past midnight, authorities were called to a burning car parked on a service road. Three more bodies were discovered. Roger Keene, 47, was under the car. He was shot twice, stabbed five times in the chest and 12 times in the back, and run over. His body was partly charred. Theodore Sweet, 52, was also found outside the car, where he had been stabbed many times in the face, chest and back, and shot twice in the head, once in each ear. Inside the car was 73-year-old Carlos Kearns, Virginia's husband, who was shot twice in the head, twice in the neck, stabbed in the neck, and run over. He also suffered burns on his body. When police found him he was still alive, but died a short time later. After being run over, Carlos was placed back in the car by his killers, who then set fire to the vehicle. The car was owned by Carlos. All the victims except Harrell and Carlos had extremely high blood-alcohol levels in their systems.

Around the time that the authorities discovered the automobile, the two killers, 22-year-old Lafonda Fay Foster and 27-year-old Tina Hickey (also known as Tina Powell), walked into a nearby hospital. Having torched the car, they were without transportation. Growing impatient when a nurse was slow to fill Foster's request to call a taxi, Foster pushed her aside to dial the number herself. Staff at the hospital could tell the pair had been drinking. This, coupled with their belligerence and the fact the pair wore clothing saturated with blood, caused the staff to alert several

126

police officers who were in the hospital on an unrelated matter. Suspicious police took the women into custody on public drunkenness charges, which soon changed to five counts of murder as they quickly connected Foster and Powell with the five murders. The pair tried to explain the blood to the police by saying they had fought with each other. It was the worst mass murder in Lexington's history. It also surpassed all other murders in the city for its brutality. When taken into custody, blood samples were taken from both women for alcohol analysis. The insides of their elbows were so heavily scarred from drug injections that the nurse had to take the samples from the wrists.

All the victims except Sweet lived in the same apartment building. Sweet was a friend of the others and a regular visitor to the building. Carlos, described as a feeble man who got around with the aid of a cane, walked through the neighborhood with a pistol strapped to his waist. Estranged from his grown children, he had had no contact with any of them for several years. He and Virginia had been married around six years, although one son thought they weren't officially married. In 1979 and again in 1983 Carlos was convicted of carrying a concealed deadly weapon; in 1974 he was convicted of assault; in 1981 a conviction was registered against him for public intoxication. Virginia was often found knocking on doors in the apartment complex in hopes of getting a free beer or cigarettes. She was also prone to going door-to-door trying to sell household items such as shoes, makeup, and coffee from her own apartment in order to raise some cash. Mrs. Kearns had many convictions for public intoxication in 1981, 1982, and 1985, as well as a 1981 conviction for theft. Neighbors thought Carlos married her because he felt sorry for her after she was released from a hospital. On one occasion she went on a wild spree, which ended when Carlos called in the sheriff.

Apartment manager Mary Martin said of the couple, "She was really pitiful. She needed help, but never got it." Ray Musick, a neighbor, said, "He was a good man, but his wife was crazier than hell. She would come to the door and ask for a beer, but I told her to get the hell away. . . . One day, she tried to sell me an $8 can of coffee for $3, but I knew she stole it from her husband" [12]. Virginia had been seen walking the streets in her nightclothes trying to sell clothes Carlos had bought her to get beer money. The couple spent most of their time in Roger Keene's apartment, where Roger and Virginia drank heavily. Apparently Carlos drank less or perhaps not at all, trying to keep Virginia out of trouble.

Keene arrived in Lexington in 1984 after spending all his life in Pikeville. His departure from Pikeville was the result of getting into some sort of trouble with somebody in that community. A lifelong addiction to booze kept Roger from holding down a steady job. Numerous convictions for public intoxication were on his record. His personality bounced from nice to nasty. Upset when the local basketball team once lost a game, Keene went on a tear and broke all except one of the windows in his apartment.

Trudy Harrell had shared the Kearns's apartment for the previous four years. She did the cooking and cleaning, since Virginia could do neither, as well as chauffeuring Carlos around. In exchange she got room and board. A booze problem had dogged Trudy for years. Since 1981 she had around 10 convictions for public intoxication. In October 1985, Trudy spent three days in jail for disorderly conduct. In the July prior to that she spent seven days in jail for intoxication. Neighbors thought of Trudy as a street person Carlos took in. One of them, Charles Cowan, said, "Carlos took in about everything that came along. She was one of them. ... Evidently she'd get on binges. She'd be found lying out in the alley, or in the street. Then she'd stay off of it for three or four months" [12]. Theodore Sweet was twice convicted for driving while intoxicated, in 1985 and 1986. His license was suspended. Both Sweet and Keene had lived with the Kearns off and on in the past.

Lafonda Fay Foster was born in 1963 in Anderson, Indiana, to a teen-aged mother named Glenda Adams. Much of her youth was spent being shifted between foster homes and the homes of relatives. At one such home Foster was sexually abused by a great-uncle. When Fay complained, this man held her feet to a hot furnace. By the time she was nine Foster was using drugs. On three occasions, when she was 12, 14, and 19, Fay attempted suicide. Frequently truant from school, Foster quit after the ninth grade. In her early teens she was abusing alcohol and drugs, inhaling solvents, and was sexually promiscuous. At 18 she was engaged in prostitution to support her expensive drug habits.

Between 1978 and 1982 Foster was sent to at least five different youth homes. Her first brush with the law came on a shoplifting charge when she was 13. Over the years, numerous convictions were registered against Foster for public intoxication, driving while intoxicated, and disorderly conduct. At 18 she was convicted of second-degree robbery; Foster and two other women broke into the home of a woman they thought was a prostitute, threatened to kill her, tied her up, and robbed her. At the time Fay was using Quaaludes, Valium, and taking LSD almost daily. Sentenced to 10 years in prison for robbery, she was released within a month on five years' probation. Arrested again in 1983 for parole violation, Foster was released from custody soon afterward due largely to the efforts of a Lexington business-man named Oaklie May, 65, who promised to give Foster a job in his super-market and to rent her an apartment. Friends considered Foster to be May's girlfriend. He committed suicide in 1983.

It was through May that Foster met his friend Carlos Kearns. The latter took a liking to Foster, whom he allowed to stay at his place on occasion. Carlos gave her money and often loaned her his car, even though she once wrecked it. Margie Barbee, a friend of Carlos's, claimed he told her that Foster hit him when he didn't give her what she wanted and had taken money from him. To another friend Carlos said Foster once deliberately put shampoo in his eyes while she bathed him. Then she fled the apartment with $450 of his money.

Tina Powell was the mother of an uncertain number of children by 1986, perhaps four. Born in 1958 in Youngstown, Ohio, she had lived in Lexington most of her life. Her alcoholic father left the family when Tina was four. Tina left high school before graduation. Powell was briefly married in 1979 in what was described as "a destructive relationship." By 1980 she had a long string of arrests behind her, most on charges of public intoxication. Other convictions included endangering the welfare of a minor, carrying a concealed deadly weapon, and obtaining a controlled substance by fraud—altering a prescription for 21 Quaaludes to read 30. When she failed to show up for her trial on the last charge, authorities arrested her. An anonymous phone caller to the jail said Powell had drugs in her cell. A search disclosed 10 Valiums and a quantity of marijuana. Tina was sentenced to probation.

Rod Planck, Powell's parole officer, said of Tina, "I arrested her in my office one day for being real high on drugs. She came in that way, which is a violation of parole. ... She was hostile. She had terribly vulgar language. She had a very low self-esteem and was on a very self-destructive thing. Everything she did was for herself. She was out to have a good time and what she thought was a good time was getting high on alcohol and drugs. She was very promiscuous and would go with any guy who supported her with drugs and alcohol" [11].

Powell and Foster had been friends for several years by 1986. They were regulars in many of Lexington's bars. At noon on the day of the murders Virginia Kearns was knocking on doors in the apartment building, trying to sell makeup for $3. Two hours later, Powell and Foster showed up at the building. They were observed banging on the doors of the Kearns and Keene apartments. Neighbor Darlene Allen reported, "They were hollering and carrying on and going back and forth between the two doors" [10]. Apparently getting no answer, they left and started hitchhiking. The man who picked them up took them to a liquor store, where they bought a bottle of whiskey. When he took them back to the apartment building, Tina asked the driver if he wanted to have sex for money. He declined.

This time Powell and Foster got into the Kearns apartment. Neighbors heard Carlos yelling. At 4 P.M. Virginia phoned the police to complain that two drunk women were in her apartment and refused to leave. She met the police a few blocks away. Around the same time, Roger Keene was released from jail. He had been arrested the night before for public intoxication.

When the police arrived at the mall, they found Virginia to be "very intoxicated." Her speech was slurred and she couldn't walk straight. The police drove her back to the apartment, where they met Powell and Foster outside. Virginia cursed and screamed, "Make them leave." Powell and Foster explained they had come to give Carlos a bath. They were concerned that Virginia and Trudy, both former mental patients, were not caring for Carlos properly. The two women agreed to leave the building. The police left satisfied reporting, "We considered Ms. Powell and Ms. Foster to be sincere in their concern for Mr. Kearns" [6].

The two women adjourned to a nearby parking lot, where they drank some whiskey before returning to the apartment. Sometime in the early evening, all seven people piled into Carlos's car and took off. During a stop at a drugstore, witnesses saw Foster grab Virginia and shake her hard. At 7 P.M. the group stopped at another store, where Carlos cashed a check for $25. Sometime after that Foster and Powell began the killing spree that left all five of their companions brutally murdered. Virginia and Trudy were murdered first. There was probably more than a small element of torture involved. It is also likely that the three men were forced to watch.

Around 8:30, Foster had pulled the car into a liquor store. She asked manager John Haggard if he had any bullets. "She said she was going to shoot some rats," he reported. Haggard gave her four bullets. He also told her she should clean the car after he noticed blood on the passenger-side door. A short time later Foster returned with a clean car and a request for more bullets. Haggard told her he had no more to give her [6].

At least some of the killings took place at a small one-room apartment in the city, which was vacant. Foster had been seen there a week before with the male tenant, who had vacated the unit by the time of the killings.

At the trial, which started in February 1987, lawyers for both Powell and Foster acknowledged their clients had killed the five people. Their defense rested on the idea the pair were not responsible for their actions because they were intoxicated on alcohol and high on other drugs. Cynthia Ellis, who knew both Foster and her father, testified that Fay would often turn to her father for cocaine. Ellis said she saw the pair injecting cocaine into each other's arms on several occasions. When Fay didn't have enough money to buy drugs, she would turn to prostitution. Her father would set up the trick.

Although Foster didn't testify at her trial, a taped interview given to a social worker after her arrest was aired during the penalty phase of the trial. Foster said that when her brief marriage in 1985 ended with her husband tearing up the marriage license and throwing it in her face, she increased her drug usage. In February 1986, she was arrested on a drug charge and sentenced to 60 days in jail. Released on April 14 — nine days before the murders — Foster claimed she took drugs heavily during those nine days, getting only 32 hours of sleep in total while doing 12 to 15 grams of cocaine a day.

Fay told the social worker, "I wasn't respnsible for my actions. If I had been straight, I know I wouldn't have touched any of those people, much less killed them. . . . I was mentally deranged. I couldn't distinguish between reality and fantasy. . . . If it hadn't been them, it would have probably been somebody else or myself. I was angry and I was hurt about my failures, and I took it out on those people." When asked if the victims reminded her of her family or herself Foster replied, "They were all alcoholics, and they were just pitiful. They were useless. They had no desire. No ambition to better their selves in any kind of way. Yeah, it scared me" [17].

At the time of the murders Powell and Foster were having a lesbian relationship. Powell's lawyer portrayed his client as a timid alcoholic who was afraid of her own shadow. He claimed she had been abused many times by Foster. He likened her to a battered wife who couldn't leave her husband no matter how much he beat her. In her testimony during the trial's penalty phase, Powell told of starting drug and alcohol use at an early age and of turning to prostitution to support her habits. She had had a long string of boyfriends over the years, many of whom beat her. When asked about the murders, Powell said, "I remember stabbing one of the women and I remember stabbing somebody else, but that's it. I'm not denying that I didn't stab them all. I just don't remember. . . . If I hadn't done it to them then it probably would have been me, so it was either them or me. . . . I mean if I hadn't stabbed those people and if I would have showed any weakness toward Fay, then she probably would have killed me, too" [19]. Witnesses testified that Foster hit Powell but that Tina would not hit back even though some of the beatings she suffered at Foster's hands were severe. In Tina's version of the story it was Fay's idea to commit the murders, with her doing most of the actual killing.

Ethel Kissic shared a jail cell with Fay Foster after the latter's arrest. According to Ethel, Fay planned to kill Tina the night of the murders for fear that she would go to the police. This plan was not carried out because the only bullets Fay had left over were the wrong size for her gun.

Both Powell and Foster were convicted on all five counts of murder. Powell was sentenced to life imprisonment with no possibility of parole for 25 years. Foster was sentenced to death. Within a day or two of sentencing, Tina signed an affidavit saying that she lied about Foster being the instigator in the murders. She lied because she was worried about getting the death penalty. Now Tina insisted it was she who brought up the idea to kill the five victims. The prosecutor's office was extremely skeptical of this affidavit. Based on this revelation, Foster asked for and got a new sentence hearing, which was held in July 1988. At that hearing Tina did another about-face, refusing to testify on Foster's behalf as she had been expected to do. Placed on the stand, Tina indicated she would invoke the Fifth Amendment for every question put to her. Foster's death sentence stood.

Just before her death sentence was handed down, Foster read a statement in court that said that Tina first made the suggestion to kill and that their sentences should be the same in the interests of fairness. Fay added, "I don't know why Tina and I killed those people. I don't understand it. I know it wasn't for money or any logical reason" [1]. Foster is still under sentence of death, in appeal process.

Sources

1. "Conviction Is Based on Lies, Foster Says." *Lexington Herald-Leader,* April 25, 1987, p. A5.

2. Duke, Jacqueline. "Foster Sentenced to Electric Chair; Powell Received Life Prison Term." *Lexington Herald-Leader,* April 25, 1987, pp. A1, A5.

3. Gaines, John. "Victim Had Lent Money, Car to One of Suspects." *Lexington Herald-Leader,* April 25, 1986, p. A14.

4. Gaines, John. "Woman Told Cell Mate of 5 Killings, Official Says." *Lexington Herald-Leader,* May 6, 1986, pp. A1, A5.

5. Honeycutt, Valarie. "Families of 5 Victims Remember and Care." *Lexington Herald-Leader,* February 28, 1987, pp. A1, A10.

6. Honeycutt, Valarie. "Powell-Foster Witnesses Describe Chain of Events." *Lexington Herald-Leader,* February 26, 1987, pp. A1, A7.

7. Johnson, Angela. "Four More Murder Charges Filed Against 2 Women." *Lexington Herald-Leader,* April 29, 1987, pp. A1, A10.

8. Johnson, Angela. "Police Probe Mysterious Deaths of 4." *Lexington Herald-Leader,* April 24, 1986, pp. A1, A16.

9. Johnson, Angela. "Two Plead Not Guilty to One Murder." *Lexington Herald-Leader,* April 26, 1986, pp. A1, A10.

10. Marx, Jeffrey. "Two Charged in 1 of 5 Slayings." *Lexington Herald-Leader,* April 25, 1986, pp. A1, A14.

11. Mead, Andy. "Murder Suspects' Lives: Broken Homes, Drugs, Alcohol." *Lexington Herald-Leader,* April 27, 1986, pp. A1, A14.

12. Swasy, Alecia. "A Look at Five People Who Were Killed in Lexington." *Lexington Herald-Leader,* April 25, 1986, p. A14.

13. Tolliver, Thomas. "Defendants' Intoxication Is Focus of Questioning." *Lexington Herald-Leader,* February 27, 1987, pp. A1, A16.

14. Tolliver, Thomas. "Foster Is Described as Victim of Abuse." *Lexington Herald-Leader,* March 4, 1987, pp. A1, A8.

15. Tolliver, Thomas. "Foster Likened Herself to Manson, Ex-cell Mate Testifies." *Lexington Herald-Leader,* March 3, 1987, pp. A1, A10.

16. Tolliver, Thomas. "Foster Loses Bid to Set Aside Death Sentence." *Lexington Herald-Leader,* July 16, 1988, pp. C1, C2.

17. Tolliver, Thomas. "Foster Says Drugs, Rage Clouded Judgment the Night She Killed 5." *Lexington Herald-Leader,* March 12, 1987, pp. A1, A16.

18. Tolliver, Thomas. "Lawyers Admit Foster, Powell Killed 5." *Lexington Herald-Leader,* February 25, 1987, pp. A1, A7.

19. Tolliver, Thomas. "Powell: Fear of Foster Led Her to Help Kill 5." *Lexington Herald-Leader,* March 17, 1987, pp. A1, A5.

20. Tolliver, Thomas. "Powell Says She, Not Foster, Incited Killings." *Lexington Herald-Leader,* April 27, 1987, pp. A1, A6.

21. Tolliver, Thomas. "Witnesses: Foster Wanted to Kill Powell." *Lexington Herald-Leader,* March 13, 1987, pp. A1, A11.

Edna Fuller

(1890–1926). *Place:* San Francisco, California. *Time:* August 30, 1926. *Age:* 36. *Victims:* 6. *Method:* Asphyxiation from gas.

By all accounts Edna Fuller seems to have been unstable. Her condition was perhaps exacerbated by a life of poverty spent in a cramped apartment with five children. On the morning of August 31, 1926, 40-year-old Otto Fuller returned home to his two-room basement apartment in San Francisco. It was just after seven in the morning, and Otto was coming off shift from his job as a night watchman. To his horror, he found gas pouring from the jets and his entire family dead. In one room was 36-year-old Edna with their two daughters, aged 10 and 2. The second room held the bodies of the three sons, aged 11, 9, and 4.

The Fullers had occupied the apartment for only six months after they had been evicted from an Oakland dwelling for failing to pay the rent. Their new landlord, C. J. Mauer, had already had problems with his new tenants. Mauer called Mrs. Fuller "demented" and said she didn't look after the children properly and let them disturb the neighbors.

The Society for the Prevention of Cruelty to Children had cited Edna to appear in court in early September to determine if she was a fit mother. The family's condition was investigated by a charitable organization. They reported Mrs. Fuller claimed the family had lots to eat at all times and money ahead. A police report found the family destitute, with some of the children virtually naked. Otto earned $140 a month and paid $34 for rent.

Two weeks before the murders Mauer reported, "The mother acted queerly. She would lock her three oldest children out of the house and they tore up shrubbery and kicked at doors. I don't think her two youngest ones ever saw the outdoors. The children whooped and yelled all day, and even past midnight at times" [1]. Mauer had had enough and complained to the police. A charge of disturbing the peace was laid against Otto but was later dismissed. Mauer also stopped taking rent and told the Fullers to move. A judge ordered them to do so.

When Otto left for work late on the evening of August 30, the Fullers had only a little more than 24 hours before they had to move but no place to go. As he left the apartment Edna said to him, "I have found a place for the children and me." Fuller replied, "All right," thinking she meant a place they might move to [1]. It was not until the next morning that Otto learned what she had meant.

Sources

1. "Mother Slays 5 Children, Self." *San Francisco Chronicle.* September 1, 1926, p. 13.

Janie Lou Gibbs

(1932–). *Place:* Cordele, Georgia. *Time:* 1966–1967. *Age:* 34–35. *Victims:* 5. *Method:* Arsenic poisoning.

In Cordele, Georgia, Janie Lou Gibbs was a liked and respected member of the community. A grandmother at age 33, Janie was known for her religious zeal. She taught Sunday school, served on every church committee and was considered a tireless and devoted worker for the Lord.

Born in 1932 in the Cordele area, Janie's father died while she was still a young girl. A childhood acquaintance said, "I can remember the days when she worked like a horse picking cotton out in the fields. She worked awfully hard to help her mother make a living for the family after her daddy died" [6]. Leaving the farm and her large family early, Janie married Charles Gibbs, 20, when she was just 15 years old. For almost two decades the family lived quietly and apparently harmoniously. Janie raised her three sons and did her church work while Charles worked as an appliance repairman. In the middle of 1965, the Gibbs family home was wiped out in a fire. The family moved into an apartment in Cordele.

Six months later, tragedy struck the Gibbs family, to come again and again. On January 21, 1966, Charles died. Heart attack was listed as the cause of death. Later that year, on August 29, Janie's son, Marvin, 13, died of what was thought to be virulent hepatitis. On January 23, 1967, another son, Melvin, 16, died of what was described as a rare muscular disease. Janie's 13-month-old grandson Ronnie died on October 7, 1967, of a heart infection. Exactly three weeks later, on October 28, Janie's last son, 19-year-old Roger—Ronnie's father—died.

A month or so after Melvin died Janie bought a house, moved into it, and operated a children's day nursery out of it with eight children in attendance. Janie and the kids got along fine. Apparently the money came from insurance proceeds after the death of her family members.

Despite so many deaths in such a short time, Gibbs bore up remarkably well. Neighbors remarked, "She never really seemed to lose her composure. All of us often wondered if we could bear up to the strain she had undergone during the past two years." Often Janie spoke of her situation to the neighbors but always in a calm and emotionless way. Frequently

136

she asked the question, "Why did all of this happen to me?" A few neighbors spread nasty rumors about the deaths. When confronted by this fact Gibbs said, "It's just some old busy-bodies talking; they'd better watch what they're saying" [6].

None of this had any effect on her ceaseless church work. She did volunteer work not only at her own church, but also for the 33 Baptist churches in the area. One church member said that in early December 1967, Janie "gave one of the most stirring testimonies a Christian could offer, and there were very few dry eyes among us when she had finished. She was kind, loving and up-standing in character and everything else, and seemed to be everything a person should be" [6].

That sentiment expressed how most people felt about Janie. When Gibbs was arrested for murder just after Christmas in 1967, the community was shocked. Disbelief was widespread.

When Roger died, a doctor, suspicious of the circumstances, requested an autopsy. Roger's wife agreed, and surprisingly, so did Janie. Arsenic was found. All the other bodies, except the infant's, were exhumed. Their remains also contained the deadly poison. Not long after her arrest, Janie confessed to police that she had poisoned the five members of her family to death by feeding them an arsenic-based rat poison. On February 7, 1968, a jury declared Gibbs mentally unfit to stand trial. She was incarcerated at the Central State Hospital in Georgia, where she was declared sane on June 13, 1974, and thus fit to stand trial. Various legal motions delayed the trial until 1976. Janie was found guilty and sentenced to serve five consecutive life terms in prison. The jury acknowledged that the woman had mental problems but decided she fit the legal definition of sanity.

Sources

1. Becker, Marjorie. "Court: Janie Gibbs Confessed Voluntarily." *Macon Telegraph and News,* January 3, 1979.

2. Becker, Marjorie. "Poisoning Confession Ruled Voluntary." *Macon Telegraph and News,* February 2, 1979, pp. A1, 2A.

3. Borg, Jim. "Poisoner Loses Appeal." *Macon Telegraph and News,* May 25, 1978.

4. Boyd, Bill. "7 Years Later." *Macon Telegraph and News,* July 21, 1975, pp. 1A, 2A.

5. "Cordele Woman Is Arrested in Arsenic Death of Son, 19." *Cordele Dispatch,* December 26, 1967, pp. 1, 2.

6. Simpson, Harvey. "Authorities Begin Exhuming Bodies of 3 in Gibbs Family." *Cordele Dispatch,* December 27, 1967, pp. 1, 2.

7. Simpson, Harvey. "Post-mortem Tests of 3 in Gibbs Family Begins to Seek Death Cause." *Cordele Dispatch,* December 28, 1967, pp. 1, 6.

8. Simpson, Harvey. "Visitors Restricted to Immediate Members of Family for Mrs. Gibbs." *Cordele Dispatch,* December 29, 1967, pp. 1, 6.

Sister Godfrida

(1934–). *Place:* Wetteren, Belgium. *Time:* 1977. *Age:* 43. *Victims:* 3 or more. *Method:* Insulin overdose.

Cecile Boombeek was born in the small farming village of Wichelen in Belgium. Wichelen is close to the marketing town of Wetteren in Belgian Flanders, near Ghent. In 1977 Cecile lived in Wetteren. She was then Sister Godfrida, a Roman Catholic nun of the Apostolic Congregation of Saint Joseph employed as a nurse at a home for chronically ill, incurable, geriatric cases called the Institute Marie-Felicité.

During 1977, three nurses who worked under Godfrida began keeping a diary of her activities at the home. Mysterious deaths were taking place, as well as cases of maltreatment of patients. Hospital authorities, independent of the nurses, were aware that all was not right with Godfrida. For one thing, she was addicted to morphine. The hospital suspended her in August 1977, dispatching her to a Ghent hospital for drug treatment. Back at her post in January of the next year, it became obvious the treatment had not been successful. A female roommate was suspected of smuggling drugs to Godfrida during her visits to the nun while she was undergoing treatment.

When the hospital administrators were unreceptive, the three nurses took their diary to Dr. Jean-Paul de Corte, a general practitioner who sat on the board of the institute. Dr. de Corte turned the evidence over to the police despite the fact that one member of the hospital board asked him not to. Initially Godfrida was accused of stealing $30,000 from patients at the home. The money was used to pay for her morphine habit as well as to support her opulent life-style; the nun enjoyed expensive wines and meats and often dined at pricey restaurants with her roommate, also a nun, who was her lover. Godfrida had sexual affairs with others, including men, one of whom was a retired missionary priest. Her apartment was lavishly and expensively furnished.

After being taken into custody Sister Godfrida confessed to killing three elderly patients at the home by injecting them with overdoses of insulin. She told the authorities she killed them "sweetly" and painlessly because they were difficult at night. In the summer of 1977 the three nurses had observed Godfrida leaving a patient's room with a syringe. They went into the room and were told by the woman that Godfrida had injected her. She was dead two hours later. Three empty vials of insulin were found. The nurses had also documented cases of patient abuse by the nun such as ripping catheter tubes out of patients' bladders.

Godfrida was suspected of more killing because 21 patients out of 38 had died over the course of one year. It was a number that de Corte felt was "too much." When questioned why something was not done earlier, de Corte thought there was a conspiracy of silence on the part of some hospital administrators. He added, "There was just no one who thought a nun could do such things" [1]. Apparently Godfrida never came to trial but was instead confined to a psychiatric facility.

Sources

1. "Drugs and Death in Home for Elderly." *The Washington Post,* March 15, 1978, p. A18.
2. "The Nun's Story." *Time,* 111:51, March 13, 1978.

Delfina Gonzales
and Maria Gonzales

(Delfina, 1908– ; Maria, 1925–). *Place:* San Juan de los Lagos and San Francisco del Rincon, Mexico. *Time:* 1954–1964. *Age:* Delfina, 46–56; Maria, 29–39. *Victims:* 91 or more. *Method:* Torture, beatings.

The Mexican sisters Delfina and Maria Gonzales operated a white-slavery business for a decade. Thanks to influential friends and bribery paid to some of the police, the sisters were not bothered by the authorities. Over the period they were in business, nearly 100 people, perhaps more, were murdered by the two women.

Delfina and Maria operated from a base in the small central Mexican town of San Francisco del Rincon where they had a ranch, Rancho El Angel, in a remote area. The nearest major city to the area is León. Their ranch was actually a brothel. One method the women had of recruiting women into prostitution was to place help-wanted ads in newspapers throughout Mexico. Ostensibly girls who responded to the ads were to work as maids to the sisters. If they were attractive enough they would be hired with the promise of good pay and working conditions, "a home away from home," they were told.

One such recruit was 16-year-old Maria Hernandez, who was hired at $16 a week as a maid. After accepting the job, Maria was packed off to the town of San Juan de los Lagos, the site of a second brothel run by the sisters. The woman who acted as an intermediary for the Gonzales' in checking Maria out was paid about $60 for recruiting Hernandez. Most of the girls who were picked up staffed the brothels run by Delfina and Maria. A few were sold to other madams for amounts ranging from $40 to $80 "according to the quality of the merchandise."

When these girls found out the real reason they were hired, many rebelled. Those that resisted were clubbed, thrown into freezing water, or flogged while they were forced to kneel and hold heavy bricks. If the initial tortures didn't have the desired effect, more were administered until the girl either agreed to cooperate or died. All were held prisoners in the brothels.

After five years or so, most of the girls lost their looks. Usually they

140

were then killed. If one fell sick from the scanty daily diet of tortillas and beans, she was clubbed to death. When one of the inmates became pregnant, she was hung by the hands from ceiling rings and then beaten until she miscarried. Each brothel had its own private cemetery. Girls were routinely made dependent on cocaine and heroin to make it less likely that they would try and escape. On her first night in the brothel, Hernandez had liquor forced down her throat. Then various customers were allowed to "break her in." The next day she was too ill to get up. She was beaten black and blue and forced to service more customers that night.

Three inmates did manage to escape early in 1964. They made it as far as León, where they told their story to the police chief. An investigation into activities at the ranch was launched. By then the sisters had been alerted to potential danger and had disappeared. Those who remained at the ranch cooperated with the authorities. Digging on the grounds of the brothels produced the remains of at least 80 women; the remains of an unknown number of new-born babies were also found.

As a sideline, the Gonzales sisters also preyed on migrant workers returning to Mexico from America with their season's pay. When one of these men stopped off at the brothels, he was fed knock-out drops. He would never be seen again. Eleven male bodies were unearthed during excavation.

Delfina and Maria were captured in a Mexican town where they were trying to arrange a sale of their properties and flee the country with the proceeds. At their trial in 1964, the sisters refused to admit any guilt. Delfina said, "The little dead ones died all by themselves. . . . Maybe the food didn't agree with them" [1].

Found guilty, they were both sentenced to 40 years in prison, the maximum under Mexican law. A lengthy police investigation into the corruption that permitted the sisters to stay in business resulted in long prison sentences handed out to a number of people. The money amassed by the sisters was distributed as compensation to victims still alive and relatives of those who were murdered.

Sources

1. "Murdering Madams." *Newsweek,* 64:60, November 2, 1964.
2. Wilson, Colin. *The Encyclopedia of Modern Murder 1962–1982.* New York: Putnam, 1983, pp. 83–85.

Gesina Gottfried

(c. 1798–1828). *Place:* Germany. *Time:* 1818?–1828. *Age:* 20–30. *Victims:* 16. *Method:* Arsenic poisoning.

She was without feeling and without a conscience. Her only love was for money and what it would buy—and those she loved with a passion. Being attractive, Gesina had plenty of suitors coming to call. With an unrelenting callousness she dispatched suitors, husbands, parents, and her own children—as well as anyone else she felt stood between her and money.

Born in northern Germany around 1798, Gesina grew to be beautiful, blonde, and buxom. Her parents were of humble means, but their headstrong daughter was indulged whenever possible, and she matured into a woman used to getting her own way. From an early age she declared to friends that she would only marry a man with money, someone who could provide the luxuries she craved.

By the time she was 15, Gesina was sexually active and was vetting many suitors. The field was narrowed down to a man named Mittenberg, who seemed a good choice. Reportedly he had his own busness, money in the bank, and a reputation as an ambitious man. With the approval of her parents, Gesina wed this man in 1815 when she was about 17 years old. Three years later the couple had two children, but Gesina found herself living not in the paradise she had envisioned, but in hell.

It turned out that Mittenberg had neither money nor ambition and was heavily in debt. He was also a heavy drinker. The couple took to fighting, and Mittenberg often struck his wife. Gesina took out her anger on the children by beating and starving them. She often put them naked into the backyard to play, their bodies covered with bruises.

Gesina denied her husband sex and took on a large number of lovers. These admirers provided the young woman with clothes, jewelry, and trinkets. That, aside from sexual gratification, was the only interest she had in these men until she met Hermann Gottfried, with whom she fell in love—or so she thought.

A casual afternoon visit to her mother's house, probably around 1818, started Gesina on her murderous trail. The mother's house was troubled by an infestation of mice, and the daughter watched the mother as she put a

GESINA GOTTFRIED   143

white powder on some cheese. A few questions elicited the fact that the powder was arsenic and that it was good for killing vermin. Bells must have gone off in the daughter's head for, when her mother was out of the room, Gesina appropriated some of the powder for herself and quickly adjourned to her own home.

That evening at dinner, the young wife dosed her husband's ever-present beer with the arsenic. Mittenberg was dead within a matter of hours. A doctor certified death by natural causes. Now free, Gesina turned her attention to Hermann, whom she had decided to marry next. Described as a docile and submissive man when in her presence, Gottfried was reluctant to rush into a marriage with the woman he had begun to see while her husband was still alive. His feelings toward her were highly ambivalent.

The young woman's parents disliked Hermann and also argued that their daughter should stay away from men and devote herself to looking after her children. Since Gesina was of age by then, these parental objections should not have been serious obstacles except that Hermann, in a display of ambiguity, declared he wouldn't marry Gesina unless her parents approved. "They don't like me, I know that," he said to her. "Very well, show them that they should like me. I don't want to feel they might hate me" [2].

A few arguments later, Gesina found she could not move either side. Affecting a conciliatory manner, she invited herself to an evening meal at her parents' home and even offered to prepare it for them. The parents hoped their newly submissive daughter had seen the light, and the meal passed happily. Within hours both parents were dead, thanks to their daughter's white powder.

After showing no tears or remorse at the funeral, Gesina looked up Hermann almost immediately to tell him the good news that they could now wed. An unnerved Hermann threw another roadblock in the way by saying that they could not marry because of the children, a fact he had not mentioned before. "They are another man's children," he said, "and as long as they claim a share of your affection you will always belong partly to him" [2].

Turning to her sweetheart Gesina said, "You don't object to me, I suppose?" Hermann replied he didn't. "Very well," she replied. "I will wait until the children are not a burden to anybody" [3].

Just two weeks later, she contacted Hermann and told him that her two children were dead. She had killed them in the same way she had her parents, and the doctors had again certified the deaths to be from natural causes. By then Hermann must have had some idea that things weren't right. However, when Gesina asked him to marry her he couldn't come up with any fresh excuses. He agreed to an engagement but wouldn't be pinned down to setting a wedding date.

The answer to this problem, she thought, lay in getting him dependent on her and in physically weakening him. Gesina spent much time with him and started to systematically poison him. The doses of arsenic were not lethal ones — just enough to make him ill and keep him in bed, where Gesina nursed him tenderly and solicitously.

Hermann did become more and more dependent on her. He cried on the occasions she was not at his bedside and in the end he brought up the idea that they should marry soon. After the wedding, the first postnuptial business was to draw a will in Gesina Gottfried's favor. Any desire Gesina had harbored for Hermann had long since changed to contempt, but she was determined to see the project through. People had sneered at her long engagement, and she was determined to show them. Less than a week after the marriage ceremony, Gesina gave her new husband one of her more standard doses of arsenic; he was dead in hours.

Her monetary gains were small, the equivalent of only a few hundred dollars. At her husband's funeral, Gesina met a prosperous merchant who quickly became her new lover. This relationship moved along smoothly until a brother who had been a soldier, whom Gesina had not seen for years, came home and moved in with his sister since he had no parents to take him in.

The brother was a drunk; and Gesina loathed him because he and his habits reminded her of her first husband. Wilhelm, the brother, got drunk at night, was rude, and insulted Gesina's lover. Interfering in love's progress, he had to go. Gesina got out her white powder and dosed her brother's dinner one night. By the next morning he had become his sister's seventh victim.

Relations with the merchant were restored to an even keel, and a wedding date was set. Gesina couldn't wait, however, and administered small doses of poison, sending her groom-to-be to his bed. He too grew dependent on Gesina's nursing and drew up a will in her favor. A day later, he was dead. A lawyer she hired overrode objections from the merchant's relatives, and Gottfried came into a tidy sum of money. Another suitor became a victim in exactly the same way as the merchant, about a year later.

For the first time, Gesina was fairly well off financially. She had a house, spent a good deal on clothes, acquired an extensive jewelry collection, saved gold coins, and was in the habit of carrying 500 pounds on her person in notes and gold. Despite this she would borrow money from the poorest of her acquaintances with no intention of repaying them.

One such acquaintance was Katrina, to whom Gesina owed five pounds. Hearing of her affluent circumstances, Katrina wrote to Gesina asking for the debt to be paid. Deciding she didn't want to live alone, Gesina wrote to Katrina to come to her; soon Katrina was sharing the house with Gesina. For unknown reasons this arrangement did not work out, and Katrina was shortly poisoned to death.

Gesina had lived in a number of towns in the north of Germany. After Katrina's death she settled in Bremen, where she bought a large house that she thought would be a good investment for her earnings. Living luxuriously, she went through all of her money and had to place a mortgage on her property.

When she couldn't pay the mortgage, she lost the house to a Herr Rumf, a wheelwright who held the note. Rumf, his wife, and their five children moved into the house, while Gottfried was allowed to stay on, a servant-housekeeper to the family.

These were circumstances that Gottfried would not accept kindly. Frau Rumf died first, and Gesina ingratiated herself with Herr Rumf. Gesina then took full charge of raising the children; soon all five had been poisoned to death. Incredibly, neither the doctors nor Rumf seemed to have any suspicions at all about so many mysterious deaths in one family in such a short period of time. Later Rumf would briefly be considered a suspect in the death of his wife and children.

After a few months of quiet, Gesina turned her attentions to Rumf and used the method so successful in the past—the administration of small, nonlethal doses of poison. For a couple of weeks, Rumf had stomach troubles and everything he ate seemed to disagree with him. One day Gesina was away and another servant prepared him a meal from a joint of pork. Rumf was elated when he had no stomach trouble. He stashed the remainder of the joint away for future use and looked in on it in the larder from time to time.

When Gesina came upon this meat she dosed it with her white powder, unaware of its meaning to her employer. The next time Rumf looked, he saw the meat had been moved; he noticed the strange powder and grew suspicious. He wrapped the meat up and took it to the police, who analyzed the powder and declared it to be arsenic.

Gesina was arrested on March 5, 1828, and charged with murdering the six Rumfs. Her attitude to the authorities was one of defiance. Showing no remorse, she readily and brazenly admitted to poisoning 30 people, of whom 16 had died.

Described as beautiful for so long, when she stood trial reporters termed her ugly and almost skeletal. One commented, "It was appropriate, though, that she should be physically as well as morally hideous" [4]. In prison Gesina was denied the corsets and make-up that she had apparently used to good effect.

Gottfried was convicted, sentenced, and beheaded in 1828. She once said, "I was born without a conscience, which allowed me to live without fear." She died that way as well, showing neither fear nor remorse. As the time of her execution neared, Gesina joked with her jailors, "When I'm dead everyone will know I had false teeth" [2].

Sources

1. Green, Jonathon. *The Greatest Criminals of All Time*. New York: Stein & Day, 1980, pp. 240–41.

2. Gribble, Leonard. *Sisters of Cain*. London: John Long, 1972, pp. 57–70.

3. Kingston, Charles. *Remarkable Rogues*. London: John Lane, 1921, pp. 17–30.

4. Nash, Jay Robert. *Look for the Woman*. New York: M. Evans, 1981, pp. 170–72.

5. Wilson, Colin. *A Casebook of Murder*. New York: Cowles, 1969, pp. 123–26.

Gwendolyn Graham

(1963–). *Place:* Grand Rapids, Michigan. *Time:* 1987. *Age:* 23. *Victims:*
5–6?. *Method:* Suffocation.

When Ken Wood's wife Catherine left him, he was upset. When he
learned she had left him for a woman, he became even more upset. As the
animosity and friction between the couple increased, Ken finally decided to
tell the police something Catherine had told him over a year previously. It
concerned Catherine and her lover, Gwendolyn Graham, being involved in
a series of grisly murders at the Alpine Manor Nursing Home in Walker,
Michigan, a suburb of Grand Rapids. The two women had been employed
there as nurse's aides. A number of other nurse's aides at the home knew
of the story but didn't bleieve it, putting it all down as a bad joke.

Gwen was born on August 6, 1963, in Santa Maria, California, and
was raised in a strict Bible-based environment. Mack Graham, Gwen's
father, worked at a variety of jobs, finally working as a truck driver when
the family settled in Tyler, Texas, in 1972. Tyler was "dry," with no bars
or liquor stores. All three of the Graham children attended a nondenomina-
tional Christian school. Their mother Linda said, "We tried to teach our
kids responsibility and to make their own way. We gave them a Christian
upbringing. That was what we tried to do" [2].

At her murder trial, Gwen said that Mack Graham sexually abused her
as a child. The few times she mentioned this to friends previously she never
went into details except to say that her father had "messed with her." Mack
and Linda Graham divorced in 1982. Linda said she knew nothing about
this charge until her daughter's trial. Mack denied the allegation, claiming
Gwen told him she made up the story to gain sympathy from the jury.

In high school Gwen kept mainly to herself. For the most part she wore
jeans and T-shirts, refusing to wear dresses, make-up, or to brush her hair.
As a 16-year-old Gwen left Tyler for Modesto, California, to live with her
father. After getting into fights with other girls at Modesto High School,
Graham dropped out in her senior year, hitchhiking to northern California
with friends. Passing back through Modesto a short while later, she told
her father—and later her mother—that she was a lesbian. Both parents
were disappointed.

In 1981, Gwen was back in Tyler working as a clerk in a convenience store. She began to live with a fellow employee, Fran Shadden, who was originally from Grand Rapids, Michigan. According to Shadden, during the five years they lived together Gwen beat her "probably 10 times" but never seriously injured her. "If she'd have beat me so bad, I wouldn't have stayed with her." Fran stated that Graham told her many wild stories about stabbing someone in California, robbing a convenience store in Tyler, and robbing an IRS office in Tyler. When police arrested Graham and ran a background check, the only prior record was a bad check charge in Tyler. About the stories, Shadden said, "Like I say, I didn't know whether to think it was just bragging 'cause she likes to portray herself as a little tough" [2]. Gwen had a number of self-inflicted cigarette burns on her forearm. She told Fran that some were for her father, some were for other lesbian lovers who had hurt her in some way, and some showed her strength, that she could stand pain. Fran watched her apply a lit cigarette to her arm at least once.

One of a series of jobs Graham held at this time was delivering the Dallas newspaper in the early morning hours. Early in 1986 Shadden returned to Grand Rapids. A few months later Gwen followed, moving in with her again. "She was going to make something of her life and really change instead of going from job to job," said Fran. In June 1986, Gwen applied for a job and was hired as a nurse's aide at Alpine Manor.

This home contained about 200 residents, most of whom were senior citizens who couldn't care for themselves. During 1987, 40 patients died at the home. No qualifications or experience was necessary to become a nurse's aide. Training was one week on the job; pay was around minimum wage to start. Duties included rolling patients over in bed every two hours to prevent bed sores, changing their underwear, helping them use the bathroom, and bringing them their meals. Gwen worked the third shift, which ran from late evening until the early morning hours. There she met Catherine Wood.

Wood was born Catherine Carpenter in 1962 in Soap Lake, Washington. Ten years later the family settled in Grand Rapids to be near relatives while Mr. Carpenter served in Vietnam. Catherine, in a presentence report, stated that her father physically abused his wife and three children. Mrs. Carpenter said of her husband, "He often teased Catherine about her weight. He swatted her around. He was always downgrading and belittling, not just to Cathy but to everybody." The Carpenters divorced in 1980. Mrs. Carpenter obtained a court order to prevent her husband from "beating, striking or harassing his wife and children." Mr. Carpenter denied all allegations of abuse [2].

At school, Catherine was remembered as a shy and quiet girl. Other students teased her about her weight. When she was 16 she met 20-year-old

Ken Wood, a General Motors plant worker. Half a year later she quit school to marry Wood. She was 17 and pregnant. A daughter, Jackie, was born in 1980. Catherine gained over 100 pounds during her pregnancy, but lost only 25 after giving birth. "I thought marrying him was an escape. I soon had Jackie, but I again was in a bad atmosphere. . . . I didn't know what to do, so I withdrew completely into myself, never leaving our home" [2]. Her weight increased as she ate more, eventually reaching 400 pounds. The only time she left the apartment was to go to the laundromat, which she did at 3 A.M. to avoid people.

The Woods fought often; they separated briefly in 1984 but got back together. Trying to pull herself together, Catherine resolved to get her life in shape. She got the equivalent of a high school degree and started a college program in marketing; however, she left in 1986 a few courses short of a degree. Cathy started working at Alpine Manor on the third shift as a nurse's aide in July 1985.

Toward the end of 1986, Catherine began a lesbian affair with another nurse's aide at the home, Dawn Male. As she spent more and more time with Male, the Woods' marriage ended. Upon seeing Male for the first time after Catherine asked him for a divorce, Ken screamed, "This is what we gave up eight years of marriage for? So that you could be with your little girlfriend?" [2] That affair was brief but, according to reports, seemed to trigger something that led to a number of women at Alpine Manor leaving their husbands for women. Reportedly, in 1986 and 1987 there were 14 homosexuals working at the home out of a staff of about 100. Many of the aides began to party together, drinking and smoking marijuana, often at Catherine's house. Among these women was Gwen, who didn't let on at first that she was lesbian. Fran couldn't keep up with Gwen's fast-paced life-style, so they split up in September 1986. Gwen moved in with Catherine. Gwen was five feet, one inch tall and weighed about 145 pounds, while Wood stood six feet tall and weighed 250 pounds. Nevertheless, Gwen was considered to be the dominant, intimidating partner of the couple.

Ken Wood was not completely out of the picture. Enraged at losing his wife to a woman, he asked a neighbor to watch Catherine's house. He would then call periodically for reports. In June 1987 Ken accused Catherine of not spending enough time with their daughter. He had custody; their divorce had become final that May. Catherine told Gwen, who phoned Ken and said, "If you ever come over here again, I'm going to take care of you." Ken responded by driving to the house, where he rammed his car into the back of Graham's Volkswagen. He blasted the horn to let her know he'd been there. An hour later, at 2 A.M. Ken returned, intending to slash Gwen's tires. He said, "By the time I confronted them, they were on the screen porch. We were yelling back and forth. And Gwen got a baseball bat. Cathy had showed up by that time. I stood in front of the screen, and I put my fist through the screen, and tried to grab her (Graham). Gwen's trying to hit my hand with the bat, and Cathy's trying to hold me back." Grand Rapids police arrested Ken on a charge of malicious destruction of property. In August 1987 Ken was sentenced to one year's probation, fined $170, and ordered to pay $70 restitution [2].

Fights often broke out between Catherine and Gwen. Tony Kubiak worked at Alpine Manor late in 1986. He lived with the women for a couple of weeks, during which period Wood discovered Graham had had sex with another woman. Wood dragged Gwen into the bedroom, where they kicked, scratched, screamed, and knocked a hole in the wall. After that, Kubiak couldn't wait to move out. Fights and jealousies spilled over to the nursing home. Robert Decker, a one-time licensed practical nurse there, described the scene: "That place was insane. It was a covey of lesbians. They just did bizarre things, like fist fights in the parking lots, slashing each other's tires. There was always some strange little war going on" [2].

Decker felt that Catherine was the biggest source of trouble. Several times he told people in administration that they should take her off the floor. One who agreed was Susan Davis, a registered nurse at the home, who said Wood verbally abused patients. Wood denied all these allegations; however, in 1987 she was given an administrative job at the home which did remove her from the floor. The third shift on which the two women worked was normally quiet and boring, since most patients were asleep. To pass the time, Graham, Wood, and other aides would sometimes play practical jokes. Hiding under beds, they grabbed the ankles of passing nurses; once they propped up a mannequin in a wheelchair, scaring a nurse; they poured water on the beds of sleeping patients to make it look as if they had wet themselves.

The stormy relationship between Wood and Graham ended in the spring of 1987 when Gwen left Catherine for Heather Baragar, another nurse's aide at the home. In June 1987 Gwen quit Alpine Manor. She and Heather moved to Tyler, where Gwen got a job as a nurse's aide in a private hospital. Two months later, in August, Catherine confessed to Ken that she and Gwen had murdered six "total care" patients at Alpine Manor. Ken thought she told him to get it off her chest. There was probably some animosity on her part toward Gwen for dumping her, which may have helped spur the confession. Apparently Catherine had some communication with Graham after she returned to Texas, because Catherine later said she cooperated with police because, "When she was killing the people (at Alpine Manor) and I didn't stop it, it was bad enough. But when she was in Texas she said she wanted to smash babies. She worked in a private hospital and told me she liked walking past the nursery and wanted to smash them" [9].

Ken Wood did nothing with the information he received from Cathy for 14 months, anguishing over it all the while, he reported. Finally, in October 1988 he went to the police and told them Catherine's story because, he said, Cathy was not going for the therapy he thought she needed and was also not spending enough time with their daughter. Animosity may have also played a part in Ken's decision to tell the police.

Questioned that month by the police, Catherine initially claimed the entire story was a joke played on Ken. Changing her story, Wood said she was a witness to the murders and was threatened by Graham if she ever told. Detectives were suspicious of this story, although Catherine maintained it for two weeks. Police then convinced their suspect to take a lie-detector test, which Wood failed, confirming their belief that she was more than a scared witness. Police also questioned Graham in Texas but got no confirmation. However, the hospital that employed her fired her immediately upon learning the nature of the investigation. Authorities continued to investigate, looking into a total of eight suspicious deaths. Two bodies were exhumed for examination. Two others had been cremated. Early in December 1988, Wood and Graham were arrested by the police. Wood had quit Alpine in October and was working at a fast food outlet. Graham was extradited to Michigan from Texas in January.

Catherine told the police in her confession, and later in court testimony, that Gwen had killed all but one of her victims because it gave her "emotional release." Ken Wood said Catherine told him she helped Gwen kill because "it was fun," and that the two women discussed killing people with certain initials in their first or last name to spell out "murder"—a plan that was later dropped [1]. Ultimately, Graham was charged with five counts of first-degree murder and one count of conspiracy to commit murder.

According to Catherine, the subject of murder first came up in October 1986, when Gwen said she wanted to kill Heather Baragar. It was thought by Wood to be just a joke. Early in January 1987, Gwen brought up the subject of murder again, this time suggesting killing a patient. Wood brushed it off. Several days later Graham mentioned it once more. Wood asked how she would do it. Gwen said it would be by suffocation. A pillow wouldn't do, since the victim could turn his or her head, but a washcloth would work. It also wouldn't leave bruises. Selected victims would have to be unable to talk in case they survived. They also couldn't have any teeth, since they would leave bruises on the lips.

Later that month Gwen approached Catherine in the home to tell her "Marguerite was dead." However, she was still alive. The women assumed she must have just passed out and that they would have to hold the washcloth over the face longer. On January 18, 1987, Gwen announced to Wood she "was going to do Marguerite." Marguerite Chambers, 60, suffered from Alzheimer's disease. A patient at the home for less than a year, she couldn't talk and spent much of her time in bed in a fetal position. Gwen entered her room around 7 or 8 P.M. while Wood stood watch at the door. Gwen suffocated the patient with a rolled-up washcloth held over the face. The pair took a small balloon from a potted plant in Chambers's room as a souvenir, which they put in their own bedroom. No autopsy was performed. The cause of death was listed as a myocardial infarction, or heart attack.

The couple had the next day off from work, and they spent it drinking. Due back to work the next day, both called in sick. Gwen wouldn't let Catherine out of her sight because she was afraid she would talk. To scare her, Gwen would carry a rolled-up washcloth in her back pocket or place one in the shower while Catherine was taking a shower.

On February 10, the pair were at work when Gwen suddenly announced, "I am going to do Myrtle." Myrtle Luce was 95 and couldn't talk. They took one of her socks as a souvenir. Death was listed as a result of cardiac failure. Back at home Wood, insecure in her relationship with Gwen, began to view the murders as a way of cementing the bond between them since either could inform the police on the other. Wood told Gwen she could never leave her now. Gwen said she wouldn't, but expected Wood to kill someone now as assurance Wood would not leave Gwen. Wood picked out a patient: "I went into the room, I was ready to, and I was going to, but when I touched her—touched her nose—she looked at me, and I couldn't" [2].

Wood did help Gwen select possible victims. They pinched the noses of various patients to see who struggled and who didn't. Victim number three was 79-year-old Mae Mason, who was killed on February 16. Belle Burkhard, 74, was murdered on February 26. Number five was 97-year-old Edith Cook, who was murdered on April 7, 1987. No autopsy was performed on any of the victims. The killings stopped after April 7, apparently because shortly after that date Catherine was promoted to an administrative position as supervisor of nurse's aides, working a shift different from Gwen's. The sixth death occurred after a patient had some sort of struggle with Gwen. The details went unreported, but it was because of this that Graham faced one count of conspiracy to commit murder. No attempt at secrecy was made by the women. Gwen told Heather, Dawn, and a number of other nurse's aides about the murders. In addition to Ken, Catherine told her sister in Florida.

Gwen was tried in September 1989. A week before the trial Catherine, as part of a deal with the state, pleaded guilty to one count of second-degree murder and one count of conspiracy to commit second-degree murder. Part of the deal was that Catherine would testify against Gwen. Her sentencing was delayed until Gwen's trial was over.

Nurse's aides from the home testified that Gwen and Catherine had a troubled relationship in which each was unfaithful to the other. Dawn Male said that both women told her of the murders. When she expressed disbelief, the pair took her to their bedroom and showed her the various souvenirs they had taken from each of their victims. Throughout the trial, Gwen maintained that the story of the murders was a "big joke" engineered by Catherine. Gwen went along with it because she loved Wood and wanted to please her. Under questioning by Gwen's attorney, Catherine denied she made up the story to get revenge on Graham for leaving her for Heather. Catherine did admit she threatened to break up the new twosome. For cooperating with the police, Catherine told the court, she believed she would be treated leniently: "I thought I would get two or three years" [9]. Among the several other nurse's aides who testified about being told of the murders by Wood, Graham, or both, was Heather Baragar. All said they thought it a joke.

Dr. John Campbell, medical director at Alpine Manor, testified that he stood by his original conclusion that Cook died from a heart attack. Campbell did not look at Cook's body either before or after he filled out the death certificate, claiming, "It is not normal practice" for physicians at Alpine Manor to view the bodies of deceased patients before determining the cause of death. Campbell added there was not an unusual number of deaths at Alpine in early 1987. He admitted he had no numbers on which to base that statement. Pathologist Stephen Cohle examined the exhumed remains of the two patients not cremated, Cook and Chambers, but could not find definite evidence of suffocation [7].

On September 21, 1989, Graham was found guilty on all counts. Members of the jury commented that they considered Wood's testimony to be more truthful and believable than Graham's. They were also swayed by the consistency of the testimony of the several nurse's aides as to the number of murders and the detail involved. Deliberations lasted five hours. In October, Wood was sentenced to a term of 20 to 40 years in prison; she will be eligible for parole after 10 years. The following month, Graham received a sentence of life in prison without the possibility of parole. By the end of 1989 the nursing home was in the process of being sold for $5.125 million, and relatives of two victims had initiated lawsuits against Alpine Manor.

Sources

1. Collins, Susan. "Suspect Relates Bizarre Tale of Killing." *The Grand Rapids Press,* December 8, 1988, pp. A1, A4.

2. Kolker, Ken. "Fatal Friendship." *The Grand Rapids Press,* January 28, 1990, pp. C1–C3.

   3. Kolker, Ken. "Friends, Co-workers Describe 2 Aides." *The Grand Rapids Press,* December 6, 1988, p. A4.
   4. Kolker, Ken. "Two Arrested in Nursing Home Death." *The Grand Rapids Press,* December 5, 1988, pp. A1, A4.
   5. Sypert, Tracy L. "Aides Felt Murder Tales Were a Joke." *The Grand Rapids Press,* September 19, 1989, pp. A1, A2.
   6. Sypert, Tracy L. "Alpine Death Tale a Joke, Attorney Says." *The Grand Rapids Press,* September 14, 1989, pp. A1, A4.
   7. Sypert, Tracy L. "Jury Mulls Fate of Graham in Deaths of Elderly." *The Grand Rapids Press,* September 20, 1989, pp. A1, A2.
   8. Sypert, Tracy L. "Killing Story Too Real to Be False: Jurors." *The Grand Rapids Press,* September 21, 1989, pp. A1, A4.
   9. Sypert, Tracy L. "Wood Says She Confessed to Keep Former Lover from Killing Babies." *The Grand Rapids Press,* September 15, 1989, pp. A1, A2.
   10. Weist, Jan. "Nursing Home Aide Guilty of Slayings." *Detroit News,* September 21, 1989, pp. 1A, 14A.

Belle Gunness

(1859–1908?). *Place:* La Porte, Indiana. *Time:* c. 1896–1908. *Age:* 37–49. *Victims:* 16–28 or more. *Method:* Hatchet or cleaver, strychnine poisoning.

Like so many other impoverished immigrants who left their homeland for the United States in the late nineteenth century, the young woman who would become known as the "female Bluebeard" anglicized her name when she arrived, hoping perhaps it would help her to settle in more quickly. Determined to make good, Belle Gunness got her feet wet in crime slowly at first, with an occasional murder and the odd arson job done to her own property. As the new century dawned, she turned to wholesale murder as she lured one man after another into her clutches.

Belle was born Brynhild Paulsdatter Storset on November 11, 1859, in the small hamlet of Selbu on Norway's west coast. Her father eked out a living as a sharecropper, with occasional work as a stonemason to supplement his income. Living in extreme poverty, Belle's family received relief from the state at least once when she was a child.

By the age of 14 Belle was working for other farmers as a cattle girl or dairy maid; she did this type of work in Norway for about 10 years. Some villagers of Selbu recalled Belle as hard-working and of exemplary character. Others remembered her as more malevolent. In 1908 a local newspaper editorialized about its former resident, "Here in Selbu she is remembered by many, and most they tell she was a very bad human being, capricious and extremely malicious. She had unpretty habits, always in the mood for dirty tricks, talked little and was a liar already as a child" [9].

Belle had an older sister, Olina (Nellie) Larson, who had emigrated to Chicago and married there. Nellie paid the passage money for Belle, who arrived in Chicago in 1883, with her occupation listed as servant girl. As soon as she arrived she anglicized her given name to Belle or sometimes Bella, and found work as a servant.

Things improved for Belle quickly, and in 1884 she married a fellow Norwegian by the name of Mads Sorenson. Some accounts of this union claim the couple were poverty-stricken, while other accounts state they were financially well-off. Mads was a department-store guard when the couple first wed, and it is probable that the pair had a steady working-class income.

155

A dozen years went by in which nothing noteworthy seemed to have happened. However, Belle was developing a strong urge for money and all that it could buy. Belle opened a confectionery store in Chicago around 1895, which burned down in 1896. A kerosene lamp exploded and set the store on fire, Belle said to the insurance investigators. Even though no lamp was found in the debris, the insurance money was paid over.

Some of the money was used by the couple to buy a house in the Chicago suburb of Austin. This house burned down in 1898, and Belle collected insurance money once again. Later another house burned down. In the years of the first two fires, Belle saw two of her four children die. The oldest child, a girl, died in 1896, and the oldest son in 1898. Both were infants and died of symptoms associated with either acute colitis or strychnine poisoning. The lives of these children were insured; Belle collected on both.

Near the end of the 1890s Belle was living well; a decade later a newspaper account would look back and say that Mads "provided with lavish hand for every want of his wife, dressing her handsomely, providing her with jewels, and in every way satisfying the little ambitions so inseparably linked with womanhood" [9]. Mads was then making $12 to $15 a week working for a railroad and couldn't afford such luxuries. It was more likely insurance money that provided the ostentatious life-style.

Nellie Larson said, "My sister was crazy for money. That was her great weakness. As a young woman she never seemed to care for a man for his own self, only for the money or luxury he was able to give her." Nellie recalled that her sister had "lots of money and property" but she didn't "know where she got all of her money" [9].

On July 30, 1900, Mads died suddenly. Fortunately for Belle, the day of his death was the one and only day on which two life insurance policies with different companies overlapped. A doctor called to the scene that day found Mads dying with all the classic symptoms of strychnine poisoning. Belle told the physician she had given her husband nothing except a powder to help his cold. Death by natural causes was duly certified, and Belle collected $8,500 from the insurance companies.

At the funeral for Mads, Nellie got a strange sensation. It would be the last time she would ever see her sister. "While I was there a terrible feeling came over me. I just felt like something terrible was going to happen and I could not stand up," she would later recall. "Now I see what it meant. There has been found a lot of dead people on my sister's land. I don't understand it" [9].

With the insurance settlement, Belle bought a farm on the outskirts of La Porte, Indiana. The community had a population of 10,000 people who observed the arrival of the widow with her two surviving children, Myrtle, born in 1897, and Lucy, born in 1899, and a foster daughter, Jennie.

Belle worked hard fixing up the place and adding improvements. Neighbors considered her a hard-working woman who kept mostly to herself. As far as they knew, Belle made her living by raising and slaughtering pigs. She did all the work herself, and it was not uncommon to see her with a one-hundred-pound pig under her arm. Belle appeared to love and enjoy children. She was also religious and regularly attended church. About the only time she mixed with her neighbors was at church.

Belle had been on the farm only a short time when she married Peter Gunness, a Norwegian farmer, in April 1902. Peter suffered a fatal accident in December 1902, when his head was split open by a heavy cleaver.

At the inquest Belle explained what happened. Peter bent over to pick up a shoe and accidentally banged against something which dislodged a heavy cleaver on a shelf over his head. The cleaver fell and killed him. Jennie agreed with this story. Even though one of Belle's daughters told a playmate that her mother had killed her father with a hatchet, the inquest jury was sympathetic to Belle's hard luck and ruled the death an accident. She collected several thousand dollars from the insurance company.

A last child, a son, was born to Belle a few months after her husband's death. In the future the formality of marriage would be ignored and the turnover in men would be more rapid. A series of hired hands came and went over the next few years. They tended to disappear unexpectedly. One left suddenly in the middle of digging a privy hole. Belle took most of the men, perhaps all, as lovers, for she had an enormous sexual appetite.

Other men came to Belle's farm as well. These were potential husbands who arrived in response to newspaper ads placed by Belle to attract suitors. One ad said: "Rich, good-looking woman, owner of a big farm, desires to correspond with a gentleman of wealth and refinement. Object matrimony." A second ad went: "Wanted—A woman who owns a beautifully located and valuable farm in first-class condition wants a good and reliable man as partner in the same. Some little cash is required for which will be furnished first-class security" [5].

Interested men would send a letter and, if the widow Gunness judged them suitable, would receive a reply urging them to come to her farm—with their money, of course. Many did. They were never seen again. After they were dead, Belle dismembered the bodies and buried the pieces in her basement or somewhere on her 40-acre property, usually under the hog pen. The bounty she reaped from these killings was money and, perhaps as a secondary consideration, sex.

In her 40s by then, Belle was an unlikely but nevertheless successful vamp. A contemporary account described her as "a coarse, fat, heavy-featured woman forty-eight years of age, with a big head covered with a mop of mud-colored hair, small eyes, huge hands and arms, and a gross body with difficulty supported on feet grotesquely small" [7].

Many of Belle's victims were of Scandinavian stock, for she liked to place ads in newspapers oriented to that community. Occasionally a man was able to escape alive. When George Busby arrived at Belle's place after answering one of her ads, Belle immediately asked him how much money he had with him. George explained that he had brought very little but that he had several hundred dollars in the bank and a well-stocked farm. Belle advised him strongly to sell his farm and stock and return with cash. Busby failed to take her advice.

Belle's foster daughter Jennie disappeared in 1906. Belle explained that she had sent her away to school in Los Angeles.

Belle liked to pick out applicants who lacked relatives and close friends. A typical reply to an applicant went as follows: "You are my king. ... I know from your letters you have a loving heart. ... Come to me. Your bride awaits you. We shall be as happy here as a king and queen in the most beautiful home in Northern Indiana." Another reply stated: "I feel sure you are the one man for me. I feel you will make me and my dear babies happy and that I can safely entrust you with all that I possess in the world. ... I have decided that every applicant I have considered favorably must make a satisfactory deposit of cash or security. I think that is the best way to keep away grafters who are always looking for an opportunity. I am worth at least twenty thousand dollars, and if you could bring five hundred just to show you are in earnest, we could talk things over" [17].

Ray Lamphere was a hired hand taken on by Belle in 1905 or 1906. He was the only one who lasted, claiming to be in love with Belle. According to Lamphere, Gunness had promised to marry him after he made a will out in her favor. He did so, but Belle continued to stall. The two were lovers, and Lamphere went into fits of jealousy when Belle slept with the various men who came to the farm.

Ray said he had been walking down the street in La Porte one day when he was confronted by a big woman with a smile who said to him, "I've been watching you. I want you to come and work for me." On his first night at Belle's ranch, he was asleep in the hired man's room when he was awakened by Belle, wearing a nightgown and liberally covered with perfume. "Move over," she said [5].

Among Belle's victims were John Moo, who turned up at the farm around Christmas in 1906. On December 26, accompanied by Belle, he went to the bank, drew out $1,100, and then vanished. Ole Budsberg arrived at Belle's in April 1907. On the sixth of that month he and Belle went to the bank, where he withdrew $1,800 and then disappeared. When relatives inquired about his whereabouts, Gunness told them he had departed for Oregon.

Abraham Phillips left West Virginia with a diamond ring and a wallet full of money. John Brewster of McKeesport, Pennsylvania, talked of marrying an Indiana widow. Tonnes Peter Lien sold his farm in Rushford, Minnesota, and departed with $1,000 sewn into his coat. Emil Tell left Osage City, Kansas, with $5,000.

C. J. Thiefland of Minneapolis, S. B. Smith, and Paul Ames were also among Belle's victims. George Berry, Christian Hinkley, Herman Konitzer, and Charles Neiburs all headed for La Porte with money in their pockets only to disappear. Another was Olaf Jenson, 23, who wrote his mother that he was on his way to La Porte to get married.

The last victim of the woman who would come to be known as, among other things, "The Mail Order Circe" and the mistress of "Murder Hill," was Andrew Helgelian, who arrived at Belle's early in 1908 and vanished soon thereafter. Like all the other victims, Andrew soon drew all his money out of the La Porte bank, where it had been lodged to his credit from his home bank, and turned it over to Belle. He then disappeared. To snag Andrew, the persistent Belle had written him a letter once a month for 16 months.

When Helgelian had arrived, Belle could stand Ray Lamphere's jealousy no more. She fired Ray, but he continued to hang around. She had him charged with trespassing. Lamphere knew a lot of secrets and began to talk around town. Law officers began to think about investigating.

Belle kept a special room in her house that no one was allowed to enter. It was there she dismembered the bodies, severing the four limbs and the head with an axe or saw, before burying the remains. When the grisly truth about Gunness came out, rumors circulated that the sausage she sold from her hog farm couldn't all be traced back to pigs. Belle may have either poisoned her victims, or axed them directly, or perhaps chloroformed them first and then axed them.

About the same time that Ray Lamphere was becoming a potential hazard to Belle, Andrew Helgelian's brother, Asle, wrote Belle asking about Andrew. To Asle's query Belle replied, "It is with tears flooding my eyes and a heart over-whelmed with grief that I write you about your dear brother, my sweetheart. He left my house seemingly happy and since that time I have not seen him. I will go to the end of the world to find him. I love him and will help you. Sell off everything he owns, get together as much of your own money as you can and come here. We will then go and seek him. Do not neglect to bring the money in cash" [5].

Asle did come, but not with money. And when he arrived it was too late. Apparently Belle was getting nervous about things. Ray was a problem, and Asle wasn't the only person inquiring about missing relatives. Some were persistent. On April 27, 1908, Belle told her lawyers that she was worried that Ray might burn down her house. It was the beginning of Belle's plan to set up Lamphere. That very night, April 27, 1908, Belle's house did in fact burn to the ground.

Investigators found Belle's three children dead in the fire and the headless body of a female adult. Gunness had worn dentures anchored to a single tooth, and these were also found in the fire debris. Lamphere was arrested. He insisted Belle was alive—that Belle had picked up a woman, killed and decapitated her, and left her as a substitute for herself. Gunness had weighed something over 200 pounds, while the headless corpse weighed not much over 100 pounds. Despite this discrepancy, the coroner declared the body was that of Gunness because, he said, roast meat shrinks.

By then Asle had arrived and urged a fuller investigation, convinced Andrew was dead but still on the farm. Authorities did start to dig under the hog pen and soon found at least 14 bodies; the total number couldn't be determined because they were in pieces. Only a small area of Belle's property was dug up, since the authorities considered combing the entire 40 acres to be too daunting a task. Among the identified bodies were Andrew Helgelian and Belle's daughter Jennie.

Belle Gunness is believed to have killed between 16 and 28 people, including two husbands, three children, three women, and from eight to 20 suitors. These numbers were good enough to have Belle included in the *Guinness Book of World Records* for most murders committed by a modern murderess [9]. Ray Lamphere claimed Belle killed about 49 times.

Lamphere was charged with murder and arson. He finally confessed to setting fire to the farm and was sentenced to jail for arson. No guilty verdict was returned for murder. In December 1909 he died in prison of tuberculosis. His final confession, made public by a minister after Ray's death, was that he helped Belle murder the three children but that Belle escaped alive. It was difficult for anyone to believe Lamphere, he had changed his story so many times.

The first victims were unearthed in Belle's farm on May 4, a week after the fire. The first Sunday after that, and for many more to follow, the Gunness farm was turned into a circus with crowds of curious spectators, estimated at 10,000 to 15,000, jamming the area. Special train cars were laid on from Indianapolis and other points. Spectators stole bricks from the ruins and even stripped leaves from trees—anything for a souvenir. Vendors sold food, picnics were held, and picture postcards of Andrew Helgelian's dismembered body were offered for sale.

A contemporary report of the Sunday, May 10, scene stated: "The Gunness farm to-day rang with the laughter of children, the jargon of postcard sellers, and streetmen, and the loud disruptions of souvenir hunters. At least 15,000 people poured into La Porte on special excursion trains, interurban cars, autos, and all sorts of vehicles, to attend an organized exploitation of the farm" [3].

Belle's takings from her victims are unknown, but they have been estimated at $20,000 or perhaps more. Most felt she did not die in the fire, but got away with her loot after setting Lamphere up. Reports of Gunness sightings flooded in over the years. The authorities never stopped looking and watching, but to no avail. In 1914 a large number of police closed in on "Belle" near Neville, Saskatchewan. In 1930 she was "caught" in Mississippi. A retired police officer even spent some time checking out a sighting in 1959—one hundred years after Belle's birth.

At the time of the discovery of the bodies on her farm, a Dr. Jones, who had attended Mads Sorenson, commented, "I can explain psychologically to my own satisfaction the causes that started her on her terrible work. I remember her well as a religious fanatic type" [7]. No trace of Belle Gunness was ever found.

Sources

1. "Bodies of Five Unearthed in Yard." *New York Times,* May 6, 1908, pp. 1, 2.

2. *Crimes and Punishment,* vol. 5. New York: Marshall Cavendish, 1985, pp. 686–88.

3. "Great Crowd Visits the Gunness Farm." *New York Times,* May 11, 1908, p. 2.

4. Green, Jonathon. *The Greatest Criminals of All Time.* New York: Stein & Day, 1980, p. 228.

5. Gribble, Leonard. *Such Women Are Deadly.* London: John Long, 1965, pp. 161–76.

6. Hynd, Alan. "Madame Bluebeard." *Good Housekeeping,* 119:43 + December, 1944.

7. "Indiana Murders Laid to Fanatic." *New York Times,* May 8, 1908, p. 1.

8. Jones, Ann. *Women Who Kill.* New York: Holt, Rinehart and Winston, 1980, pp. 129–39.

9. Langlois, Janet L. *Belle Gunness: The Lady Bluebeard.* Bloomington, Indiana: Indiana University Press, 1985.

10. "Mrs. Gunness May Have Gone to Europe." *New York Times,* May 17, 1908, pt. 2, p. 16.

11. Nash, Jay Robert. *Bloodletters and Badmen.* New York: M. Evans, 1973, pp. 235–37.

12. Nash, Jay Robert. *Look for the Woman.* New York: M. Evans, 1981, pp. 176–77.

13. Scott, Harold. *The Concise Encyclopedia of Crime and Criminals.* London: Deutsch, 1961, p. 160.

14. Sifakis, Carl. *The Encyclopedia of American Crime.* New York: Facts on File, 1982, pp. 304–05.

15. "Suspects Woman Is Belle Gunness." *New York Times,* July 18, 1930, p. 3.

16. "Trap Set in Canada for 'Belle Gunness.'" *New York Times,* March 27, 1914, p. 13.

17. Wilson, Colin. *Encyclopedia of Murder.* New York: Putnam, 1962, pp. 247–49.

Anna Hahn

(1906–1938). *Place:* Cincinnati, Ohio. *Time:* 1929–1937. *Age:* 23–31. *Victims:* 5–15(?). *Method:* Arsenic and strychnine poisoning.

Anna Hahn took advantage of her German background to strike up friendships with elderly male members of that ancestry in Cincinnati, Ohio. She gave them each a little comfort and a lot of poison. Her body count was at least five and most certainly more, perhaps as many as 15. Since Hahn was not cooperative with police, the final tally will never be known.

She was born around 1906 in Füssen, Germany, and gave birth to a son, Oscar, in 1925. Later she married Phillip Hahn, and the new family left Europe, resettling in the large German community in Cincinnati. The year was probably 1929. Anna often told people she had been a teacher in Munich, a statement she later denied. When she arrived in the United States she knew no English and had only a grammar school education.

Reportedly, she briefly operated a German bakery in Cincinnati the year of her arrival. That year Phillip also suffered a strange illness and, over Anna's protests, was taken to the hospital by his mother. The symptoms were consistent with having been poisoned. Perhaps it was Anna's first attempt. Phillip recovered, but the couple soon became permanently estranged.

Traveling through the beer gardens and shops in the German area, the young Anna, described as blonde and beautiful, had little trouble catching the fancy of lonely elderly men. She may have started her murderous ways as early as 1929, since she was substantially linked with deaths from that year until 1937. However, the first case with solid evidence took place in 1932, when Anna moved in with the over-80-year-old Ernest Kohler. He seemed to be in excellent health but died on May 6, 1932, very shortly after Hahn moved in. Kohler bequeathed his house to Anna.

She then moved on to caring for Albert Palmer, 72, a retired railroad worker, who also had a hasty demise. That time Anna had simply borrowed Palmer's money; she gave him an I.O.U. for the amount, which she then tore up after he died. Before making Anna's acquaintance, Palmer was described as a robust man in the best of health. That was in November 1936. The following year he was sick most of the time in February and March, and died on March 26. Palmer was bombarded with notes from Anna asking him for money. One was addressed to "My Dear Sweet Daddy." Another one read, "Honey, I have to have a hundred dollars in the bank for that check I gave that fellow. I hope you won't turn me down. I'll stop at your house at 9:30 A.M. And after I get there we go down to the bank together." A third note said, "I looked all over the place for your pocketbook and couldn't find it. This sure is terrible" [13].

Jacob Wagner, 78, left Anna $4,000 in his will after his speedy demise on June 3, 1937. In the middle of May, Hahn had been in Wagner's neighborhood asking if any old men lived there. An introduction to Wagner followed after she left a note under his door claiming he had received an inheritance.

Wagner's will naming Anna the beneficiary was dated January 10, 1936, over a year before he met the woman. On the day Jacob died, Anna went to his bank with a check for $1,000 made out to her and a note from Wagner authorizing the withdrawal. The bank refused the transaction because the amount wasn't legible on the document. Bank official Arthur Schmitt drew a new check for $1,000 and told Hahn to have Wagner sign it. She returned in an hour, but the bank was still suspicious. Hahn told Schmitt her "uncle"—a favorite term she used for all her elderly men friends—was in a certain hospital. Schmitt phoned the hospital, only to be told no Wagner was registered. When Hahn was told of this, she suddenly "remembered" the right hospital. When Schmitt called this one, he learned that Jacob had died several hours previously. Anna then admitted forging the check and pleaded with Schmitt not to prosecute her on account of her young son.

George Heis, 62, was one of her targets that didn't die. At the trial Heis testified from a wheelchair—paralyzed from the poisoning Anna administered to him. Before he became bedridden on October 11, 1936, he had also enjoyed good health. When they first met, Anna concocted various stories and managed to extract $2,000 from Heis. Some of it was for repairs on a mythical house Hahn owned in another city, while other sums were to pay equally mythical legal bills and inheritance taxes.

In September and October 1936, Anna brought meals to George's home. After eating each one, Heis became ill. The doctor who treated him suspected poisoning by arsenic. Becoming suspicious, George finally refused one of the meals, complaining that they didn't sit well with him. Confronting her about his illness, he charged, "You did this to me." Hahn replied, "No, I didn't." Heis then ordered the woman out of his house. After testifying at the trial, Heis mentioned to reporters outside the courtroom that Anna was his girl and commented, "I still love her" [5].

Another victim was 69-year-old George Gsellman, who died on July 6, 1937. George Obendoerfer, 67, was her last victim. He died on August

1, 1937, in Colorado Springs, Colorado, when Anna accompanied him on a trip to that city. Before the trip Hahn tried, and failed, to withdraw $1,000 from his Cincinnati bank account. A second attempt was made in Denver, where Anna posed as Obendoerfer's wife at a bank to try and cash a $1,000 check. She failed again. Heis was then pressing her to repay the "loans" she had obtained from him.

Later in August Anna was arrested in Cincinnati and charged with murder — specifically that of Wagner. All of Anna's victims had displayed the same symptoms: violent stomach pains and vomiting.

At the time of her arrest, Hahn was wearing a $75 ring that Heis reported she had stolen from him, along with $100 in cash. While in Colorado she had made off with $300 worth of jewelry from the hotel.

Mattie Monroe, who had lived in the same rooming house as Wagner, testified at the trial that she entered Jacob's private bathroom after his death to find two bottles of poison and a syringe. Only the deceased and Anna had keys to that room.

When arrested Anna said, "This is one case I'm going to win. I am not guilty. I can face anything there is to come." Detectives who questioned her asked if it wasn't strange that all the old people she became friendly with died suddenly, all from dysentery. She replied, "It looks bad for me, but I didn't do anything" [16]. A couple of druggists came forward to report that they had sold Anna poison at different times. In her eight years in the United States, police estimated she had received as much as $50,000 from her aged German victims.

The prosecutor, Dudley Outcalt, termed the case "one of the biggest mass murders in the country." He dispatched one of his assistants to Washington, D.C., to personally ask J. Edgar Hoover of the FBI for the help of handwriting experts.

Soon the police were investigating 11 mysterious deaths; one policeman stated they had learned Anna had "bought enough poison to kill half the town." Anna's estranged husband Phillip came forward with a bottle of poison which he said was hers. He also informed the authorities he had once had the same symptoms as his wife's victims. Another druggist reported that Hahn had sent 12-year-old Oscar to get some poison, but he refused to sell it due to the boy's age. Anna used a variety of poisons for her murders: arsenic, strychnine, and perhaps others. More poison turned up in Anna's home.

All the time, Hahn maintained her innocence. In an interview she claimed her one ambition was to have enough money to take care of "the poor unfortunates, the old people and the children." She protested again her innocence and complained, "Why don't they go out and find the real criminals. . . . All this is kind of hard to take. . . . But it doesn't take much to throw someone innocent into the gutter" [2].

Anna came to trial in October 1937. Handwriting experts testified that Jacob Wagner's will had been forged by Anna. Oscar testified for his mother but at one point admitted to the prosecutor that one of the stories he had told had been made up at the insistence of his mother. Hahn testified herself and denied all charges. "I don't remember" became her stock answer on the stand when the prosecution made her look bad. Evidence presented included the fact that on the day of her arrest, her pocketbook was found to be "poison-saturated"; the lint in the corners was 25 percent arsenic. Pots and pans found in Gsellman's room also had enough poison in them to kill 17 people.

In his summation, Outcalt described Hahn by saying, "She's sly. She's avaricious. She's avaricious because no act was too low for her if it meant slight gain. She's cold, cold-blooded beyond the conception of any one in this courtroom, because she has been sitting here for four weeks and displaying no human emotion. She is heartless. . . . I don't think I'm exaggerating when I say she is the most heartless, cruel, cold, greedy person any of us will find in the scope of our lifetime" [6].

The jury of 11 women and one man found Hahn guilty, after two hours of deliberations, with no recommendation for mercy, which meant the death penalty. The conviction was on one count of murdering Jacob Wagner. The other counts were not pursued. Five bodies had been exhumed. All contained poison, including Wagner's.

Until the time of her death, Anna remained calm and composed. She was confident almost to the very end she wouldn't be executed. However, all hope died on December 6, when Governor Martin L. Davey refused to intervene. When she learned this Anna moaned, "I had no idea he would do this to me," before she fainted. Governor Davey explained his decision not to spare her life by commenting, "Something inside of me has sort of rebelled against the idea of allowing a woman to go to the electric chair. I was brought up to respect womanhood and cannot escape the feeling that there is a little difference when a woman is involved in a tragedy of this kind. And yet the crimes committed by Mrs. Hahn were so cold blooded, so deliberately planned and executed, that they horrified the people who followed her trial. I feel sorry for her boy, but I think his mother has been most unfair to him. What could I say to the mothers whose sons have had to die in the chair for committing only one murder" [3].

Anna's son Oscar spent most of her last day with his mother. Phillip had not visited her once in all the time she was in jail. As she was led down the prison corridor she was calm, but at the door to the room housing the electric chair, she broke down.

Four guards were needed to forcibly carry her to the chair and strap her in. Then she screamed to the warden, "Don't do this to me. Think of my boy. Can't you think of my baby. Isn't there anybody who will help me?" [1] Finally she called for the chaplain, who was able to quiet her. On the evening of December 7, 1938, Anna Hahn was executed.

Sources

1. "Anna Hahn Dies in Electric Chair." *New York Times,* December 8, 1938, p. 3.

2. "11 Deaths Studied for Link to Woman." *New York Times,* August 16, 1937, p. 3.

3. "Execute Anna Hahn, Poisoner." *Chicago Tribune,* December 8, 1938, pp. 1, 14.

4. "Federal Aid Asked in 'Mass Murders.'" *New York Times,* August 15, 1937, p. 17.

5. Gardner, Virginia. "Anna Hahn Hears Self Accused by Poison Survivor." *Chicago Tribune,* October 27, 1937, p. 5.

6. Gardner, Virginia. "Anna's Poison Guilt in Jury's Hands." *Chicago Tribune,* November 6, 1937, pp. 1, 8.

7. Gardner, Virginia. "Jury Hears of Money Willed to Mrs. Hahn." *Chicago Tribune,* October 19, 1937, pp. 1, 6.

8. Gardner, Virginia. "No Angel, But Didn't Kill Is Plea for Anna." *Chicago Tribune,* November 5, 1937, pp. 1, 4.

9. "Jury Hears Anna's Denials." *Chicago Tribune,* November 2, 1937, pp. 1, 4.

10. "Mrs. Hahn Denies 4 Murder Charges." *New York Times,* November 2, 1937, p. 9.

11. "Mrs. Hahn Guilty; Faces Execution." *New York Times,* November 7, 1937, p. 25.

12. Nash, Jay Robert. *Look for the Woman.* New York: M. Evans, 1981, pp. 178–79.

13. "Poison Deaths of 2 More Told to Hahn Jurors." *Chicago Tribune,* October 23, 1937, pp. 1, 2.

14. "Poison Trial Nears Jury." *Chicago Tribune,* November 4, 1937, pp. 1, 4.

15. "She Wants to Tell Her Own Poison Story." *Chicago Tribune,* October 30, 1937, p. 1.

16. "Woman Is Accused; Five Deaths Sifted." *New York Times,* August 14, 1937, p. 30.

Violet Hultberg

(1909–1928). *Place:* Minneapolis, Minnesota. *Time:* November 5, 1928. *Age:* 19. *Victims:* 5. *Method:* Asphyxiation by gas.

At 33 years of age, Herbert Moreau had five sons ranging in age from eight years down to a baby. He and his wife had separated in the fall of 1927 while living in Long Lake, Minnesota. Mrs. Moreau had left her husband for unstated reasons. Herbert got custody of the four oldest boys, while his wife retained custody of the infant. After moving to Minneapolis in September 1928, Herbert was granted a divorce at the end of October.

While at Long Lake, Moreau had become acquainted with 19-year-old Violet Hultberg and began an affair with her. When he moved to Minneapolis Violet went with him, and the couple lived together. To the outside world Violet was passed off as the children's nurse. Neighbors spoke well of Violet. They said that the four young boys were devoted to her. Undoubtedly Violet hoped to marry Herbert, but her own parents were said to be vehemently opposed to the match.

On Monday morning, November 5, 1928, Herbert left the house for work at 6:30 A.M. as he always did. He was not expected home until 6:00 P.M. Sometime that morning Violet sealed up the house, turned on all four burners of the gas stove, and lay down in the bedroom with the boys: George, eight; Herbert, seven; Edward, five; and Robert, four.

Herbert was unable to unlock the front door when he came home because the keyhole was stuffed. After forcing the door he discovered the five bodies, by then dead for hours. During the day the window shades of the house were all drawn, but neighbors hadn't considered this strange because all the children were ill at the time, confined to the house under quarantine for scarlet fever. When he left for work that morning Herbert spoke to Violet and two of his sons, but all seemed normal.

Moreau admitted to the police that Violet was in love with him but that her parents objected to their marriage. Speculation by the authorities was that Violet also felt pity for Moreau after his wife left him alone with four young children. Feeling her own position to be hopeless, Violet carried out the murder-suicide as a way of helping Herbert by relieving him of the burden of looking after the children.

167

On the bedroom dresser the police found a note to Herbert (Hub) from Violet, which read, "Dear Hub — Please don't hate me or feel angry for what I am doing, but you needn't worry. I think God will forgive us. Hub, please forgive me and pray for me. The clock just struck 10. I wish I could have seen the folks, but I cannot wait a week. You have been so good to me; no one can blame you for what I am doing. Don't do any harm to yourself" [1].

Source

1. "Lovelorn Nurse Kills Self and Four Little Boys with Gas Fumes." *Minneapolis Morning Tribune,* November 6, 1928, p. 1.

Mary Jane Jackson

(1836–?). *Place:* New Orleans, Louisiana. *Time:* 1856–1861. *Age:* 20–25. *Victims:* 4. *Method:* Stabbing and bludgeoning.

Mary Jane Jackson, known as Bricktop because of her flaming red hair, was a well-known and much feared resident of New Orleans, Louisiana, in the late 1850s and early 1860s. One contemporary newspaper story described her as "one of the most reckless and lawless women of ill-fame that ever infested our city" [5]. Another account called her "one of the most incarnate fiends that was ever allowed to walk the earth in petticoats. . . . She has followed a course of shame and crime rarely equaled by the greatest criminals in the annals of jurisprudence" [4].

Born in New Orleans in 1836, Mary Jane took up with a bartender in 1853 and became a "public woman," or prostitute. Described as attractive and quiet in disposition, Mary Jane soon turned into a tigress. When the bartender tired of Jackson after a couple of years, he threw her out. An enraged Jackson returned to the bar and battered the man senseless, biting off one of his ears and part of his nose in the process. Over the years, in addition to murdering men, Mary Jane would send many a victim of one of her beatings to the hospital. In a knock-down, drag-out fight, Jackson was said to be a match for any man.

After parting company with the barman, Jackson got work in various brothels and dance halls in some of New Orleans's roughest areas. In every case the proprietors fired her when they found they couldn't control her. With her hair-trigger temper, Mary Jane fought with and terrified the other female employees of these establishments. Unable to work for anyone else, Jackson became a freelance prostitute and mugger.

The first murder she committed reportedly took place in 1856 when she clubbed a man to death after he insulted her in some fashion. Around 1857 she stabbed a man named Charles Reeves, known as Long Charley, to death on a street corner after getting into some kind of argument with him.

On the evening of November 7, 1859, Jackson, along with two of her tough street-women cronies, visited a bar for a few drinks. She was a heavy drinker and, if anything, became even more combative under the influence of alcohol. An altercation with some men ensued. When the owner intervened, he was stabbed several times by Mary Jane. Laurent Fleury, a 25-year-old blacksmith, tried to help out the owner. All three women jumped him and beat him up, almost strangling him to death. Jackson drove a knife into Laurent's skull, penetrating the brain. The blade broke off flush with the skull. Fleury went to the hospital, where he was treated for throat injuries and released because he said he felt strong enough to go home. Feeling worse the next day, he returned to the hospital, at which time the knife blade was discovered for the first time. The man died a couple of days later. Mary Jane was arrested. However, she was released in a short time when the coroner stated he couldn't say for sure Fleury's death was caused by the knife in his head and nothing else.

During that brief stay in prison, Mary Jane made the acquaintance of one John Miller. Born in 1830, he was a boozer, brawler, and notorious petty criminal. During a major gang fight in 1854, Miller had been chased down by a number of enemies. Knocked to the ground, he held up his left arm to shield his face while his pursuers slashed away at him. So badly damaged was the arm that it had to be amputated at the elbow. Miller had an iron hook attached to the stump which he delighted in using as a weapon. After he had just served a two-year prison sentence for some crime, the prison turned around and hired him as a turnkey. It was in this capacity that he met Mary Jane.

The couple started living together immediately. They led, said one account, "a strange life — turtle doves one day and tigers the next. It was said of them that they took their fights as regularly as they took their drinks and seemed to like the one about as well as the other . . . every one wishing them away, but no one bold enough to order them to remove" [6]. The couple had a particularly vicious battle in September 1861, during which Jackson stabbed Miller no less than nine times. Then she moved out on him. When Miller recovered from his wounds, he wooed her back to his shack.

On December 5, 1861, when they were both drunk, Miller pulled out a whip and informed Mary Jane he would now show her how he would tame her in the future. He managed to whip her just once or twice before she disarmed him. When Mary Jane began whipping him, Miller drew a knife. Mary Jane took it away from him and stabbed him five times. Miller died a few hours later. Jackson was arrested.

In June 1862 Jackson came to trial on the charge or murdering Miller. One newspaper snidely commented on the months she had spent in prison by saying, "Mary the Red looks much improved by her temporary imprisonment — the effects of shade and repose having bleached her countenance to a very agreeable lily white. Abstinence from the pipe and jug, too, to which she was devotedly attached, has contributed largely to the improvement of her personal appearance." The trial took a strange twist: "No one appeared to prosecute her, and she went on her way rejoicing" [1].

Later that year, in November, Jackson was arrested for severely stabbing a sailor named John Gray after the pair got into a fight. She avoided the police for a day until friends informed the police of her hiding place. Once again Jackson seems to have escaped punishment. From then on there are no more references to Jackson in New Orleans. She appears to have disappeared from sight.

Sources

1. "Charge of Murder." *The Daily Delta* [New Orleans], June 14, 1862, p. 5.

2. "Death of a Desperado." *New Orleans Daily Crescent,* December 9, 1861.

3. "Died of His Wounds." *Commercial Bulletin* [New Orleans], November 12, 1859, p. 2.

4. "A Fiendish Female." *Sunday Delta* [New Orleans], November 30, 1862.

5. "A Male Desperado Killed by a Female Desperado." *The New Orleans Bee,* December 7, 1861, p. 1.

6. "Murder in Freetown." *The Daily True Delta* [New Orleans], December 7, 1861.

7. Sifakis, Carl. *The Encyclopedia of American Crime.* New York: Facts on File, 1982, pp. 368–69.

Marie Jeanneret

(1836–1884). *Place:* Switzerland. *Time:* 1866–1867. *Age:* 30–31. *Victims:* 7–8. *Method:* Atropine, morphine, antimony poisoning.

With a strong affinity for medicine, Marie Jeanneret turned to nursing as an occupation. Over the course of a couple of years, she poisoned close to 30 people, of whom seven or eight died. Marie's personality combined elements of sadism, masochism, hypochondria, sexual repression, and misanthropy. There were no "traditional" motives involved in any of her poisonings—no greed, no revenge, only the apparent pleasure she received from the act of poisoning.

Marie was born in Locle, Switzerland, in 1836, to a family described as respectable. Orphaned in childhood, she was raised by an uncle until she was 18. A fever was said to have retarded her development.

Her family background was studded with mental instability. A great-grandmother was "deranged" during a pregnancy and termed, in general, ill humored and malicious, characteristics that would later be seen in her great-granddaughter. Marie's mother was said to be nervous. A great-aunt was a hypochondriac and committed suicide, and a daughter of this woman was also a hypochondriac and had to be watched constantly. Marie's maternal grandfather, a hypochondriac, died in unexplained circumstances, a suspected suicide. Yet another near relative was also considered to be a hypochondriac.

Not considered to be a pretty woman, Marie seems to have had only one close brush with marriage. A young man "without fortune" once proposed to her but was rejected by Marie even though she loved him, or thought she did. She had, according to a friend, yielded "to the suggestions of her companions who saw in the young man's addresses a motive other than love. She possessed a fortune of about 30,000 francs" [1].

An apparent lifelong virgin, Marie had had her hymen ruptured around 1859 by a physician so he could conduct an examination with a speculum. Seven years later she wrote a letter to this doctor, worried that the absence of a hymen would be misinterpreted by any doctor who might have a need to examine her. Her honor was at stake; Jeanneret asked the doctor to supply her with a statement as to the cause of her defloration.

As a girl, Marie showed clear signs of being a problem child. She was described as being changeable in her tastes, lacking in judgment, stubborn, emotional, and tending to lie and cheat. Marie's physical problems, whether real or imagined, dated from the onset of menstruation, when she developed a passion for consulting doctors and dosing herself with self-prescribed medicines. All of these visits to doctors allowed Marie to accumulate a certain amount of medical knowledge in which she took great pride. It made her, she thought, suited to look after the sick; therefore, in 1866 at the age of 30 Jeanneret decided she would become a nurse.

That year she was admitted to a nurses' school in Lausanne directed by Dr. Reymond. Complaining that she had vision problems in both eyes, Marie went to Dr. Dor at Vevey, who had examined her in the past for similar complaints. This time he satisfied himself that she was faking eye trouble. A second physician at Vevey, Dr. Murat, examined her for uterine complaints. He found her to be hysterical, unstable, excitable, and intent on ingratiating herself with people, especially doctors.

At this time she was discovered to have atropine in her possession. Dr. Dor felt she used this deadly poison—a derivative of belladonna, also known as deadly nightshade—on herself to fake eye trouble. Atropine had never been prescribed for Marie, but Dr. Dor thought she may have stolen some from his clinic.

While staying at Vevey in the spring of 1866, Marie became friends with Mlle. Berthet. One evening after dinner Berthet asked for a glass of water. Jeanneret told her water might disagree with her and insisted she drink a mixture of wine and sweetened water, prepared by Marie. Shortly after drinking this Berthet became ill. The solicitous Jeanneret urged her to come to her room, where she hunted through her stock of medicine and gave her friend something else to drink. Berthet became more ill and didn't recover for three days. This apparently marked Marie's debut as a poisoner.

Dr. Reymond found his student nurse to be restless, excitable, and talkative. After only two months at the school Marie took her leave, of her own accord, pleading she was almost blind. During her brief time as a student nurse Marie had, like the other students, been sent out to care for the ill in their homes once in a while. One of Marie's patients was Mme. Eichenberg of Lausanne whose mother, Mme. Chabloz, was ill and needed watching at night.

After Jeanneret was called in Chabloz got worse; she became delirious, had dilated pupils, and was subject to vomiting fits. Later she said Marie had made her drink several times. Confronted with this the nurse denied it, saying, "What the devil should I have given her to drink" [1]. One evening she came home to find the Eichenberg family having supper and insisted they all eat some bonbons she had that she called "princesses." Soon after all were stricken with bouts of vomiting.

In the presence of doctors, Marie usually gave the appearance of being solicitous, intelligent, and skillful in tending the sick. Behind their backs she often called the doctors "damn fools," claimed she didn't "care a hang," and referred to a patient as "a piece of carrion, a poison" [1]. Often questioned about the very large supply of medicines she carted around with her, Marie claimed she just used them on herself.

She did not neglect her hypochondria during this time; she sought treatment from Dr. Goudet in Geneva for neuralgia, uterine complaints, and the inability to pass urine. She insisted on being subjected to the most painful treatment available. Goudet obliged and burned her with a hot iron, noting that she seemed to take pleasure in it and, by the marks on her spine, had had this treatment many times before. Later her papers would reveal several letters she had forged in her aunt's name as letters of introduction to various doctors so she could be treated by these physicians.

In 1866 a private hospital was established by Mme. Juvet. Marie applied for a position as nurse and was accepted after stating she would work for "board, lodging, and laundry, without asking any salary" [1]. Soon after starting work at the home, three of the patients attended by her died suddenly.

One was Mlle. Junod, who entered the home in September 1867. The next month Jeanneret told Junod's brother that his sister "would probably have a congestion of the brain." She knew this, she said, from her experience working with the sick. Sure enough, Junod became violently ill a few days later with the symptoms all Marie's victims would display: dilated pupils, bouts of vomiting, and delirium. Two days later, Junod died.

M. and Mme. Juvet heard noises coming from the room of their young daughter Julie one evening. Investigating, they found Marie, who had taken a dislike to Julie, beating the girl. Showing repentance, Jeanneret escaped any discipline from her employer; she then set about poisoning the clan. Mother and daughter were fed bonbons laced with poison, while the son Emil was fed poisoned cocoa that Marie prepared. Julie got worse and died on December 27, 1866, while her mother lingered longer, expiring a month later.

While Mme. Juvet lay ill Marie used to say, "No consultation would be of any use for her." A Juvet servant later testified that Marie "had predicted her mistress's illness three or four days beforehand" while Mme. Juvet was in apparent good health [1]. The body of Mme. Juvet was found to contain a small amount of copper, some antimony, and a lot of morphine.

The death of the hospital's founder and owner caused the establishment to close; Marie was between jobs for six weeks before she was called in to nurse a Mlle. Lenoir, who died about three weeks after Jeanneret took charge. Next she cared for a Mlle. Bourcart, who lived near Geneva. She brought along a basket full of medicines. This time, when a Bourcart servant inquired about them Marie said, "If Madame has need of drugs, I have some here, in my basket." To another query she replied that they were "for the treatment of my eyes and of my spine" [1].

Within three days of Marie's arrival, Bourcart was violently ill. She recovered, but Marie was dismissed. By then suspicions had been aroused in at least one quarter. Dr. Binet, who had tended the Juvet family, advised a patient who was thinking of employing Marie, "Don't have anything to do with her. All her patients die" [2].

Before and after her brief stay with Bourcart, Marie rented a room in a house owned by M. Gros. As soon as she returned to the Gros house another roomer, Mme. Bouvier, became ill and died after a few days, on May 22, 1867. Just two weeks later Gros became extremely ill. One day before he was stricken Marie told one of his relatives, "I am sure he is going to have the same attack as Mrs. Bouvier" [1]. Indeed he did, and died a few days later. The bodies of Gros and Bouvier would later be found to contain atropine and morphine, with antimony also present in Bouvier's organs.

A visitor to the Gros house had also been dosed and became ill. She recovered, but the doctor recognized the signs of belladonna poisoning — Jeanneret's time was nearly up. Still, she moved on to another boarding house and in June committed the last crime attributed to her. Another boarder there became friendly with Marie and was promptly dosed. The woman was hospitalized but survived. Two other poisonings were made at that house but were not fatal. The authorities were alerted and finally arrested Marie, after she had poisoned an estimated 30 people in various parts of Switzerland. Many, however, were unwilling to give evidence.

Jeanneret was brought to trial charged with six counts of murder and 11 counts of poisoning. The prison physician, Dr. Badan, examined Marie at the time of her arrest and noticed no abnormal symptoms except dilated pupils, which disappeared in time.

A report drafted by Badan and two other physicians two months later noted a wide variety of physical symptoms that Marie claimed to be suffering from and stated that many of these had manifested themselves since her arrest; they included nervous attacks, vomiting, menstrual disorders, and disturbances of vision, digestion, and sensation. The report declared Jeanneret to be of a hysterical temperament but found her sane and responsible.

A pivotal event in her life was said to be her near-marriage. This break added hate and distrust to her "already far from sympathetic feelings" and thereafter she thought herself surrounded by people who only wanted her money. She came to hate even her relatives and "took pleasure in placing obstacles, wherever it was possible, in the way of the peace and happiness of her associates." Soon she was unable, she said, "to endure the sight of happy people" [1].

Dr. Dor testified at Marie's trial that he thought of her as "unbalanced, ill and hysterical ... untruthful, perverse, and malicious." He added that Marie knew her complaints were fictitious but still demanded very painful treatments—burning with a hot iron. Dor considered her to be a drug abuser who had used atropine for three years. "We can recognize as a symptom of intoxication," he said, "a retention of the urine which occurred during that time—a fact perhaps sufficient to have kept the accused in a state of overexcitement similar to that of eaters of opium and hashish" [1].

Dr. Goudet testified that Marie liked medical treatments rather than remedies and that she preferred treatments that gave her pain. He did not think her character was wholly hysterical, nor did he agree that her nervous attacks were faked.

During her trial Marie stood, impassive, as she cooly and calmly admitted to surreptitiously administering atropine or morphine to the six people she was charged with murdering. She also admitted giving poison to three others. Claiming that in all cases she had no criminal intent, Marie explained she had yielded to the desire to perform medical experiments or to enable patients to rest after they had taken doctors' medication that had irritated them.

Only once did Marie break on the stand; she said to a judge, weeping, "I was in the wrong, I forgot myself, I tried to give remedies that were not in the doctor's prescription, and that's my fault" [1]. When a judge asked her why she continued to give out medicine when she saw the results of her work, Jeanneret replied that she "had always believed the remedies that she gave ought to do good, to calm the patient." Only since she had been imprisoned had she started to think otherwise [1].

The court decided that Marie's mental condition was evidently defective but felt that factor, along with her low moral standards and capacities, weren't enough to move her from the criminal class into the insane group. Jeanneret was convicted on all six counts of murder and sentenced to 20 years at hard labor. Her sentence was not considered especially light for the time and place and crime. Thirty offenses were punishable by death, but capital punishment was exercised on less than one in eight possible occasions. Less than a life sentence for murder was also not uncommon. Marie Jeanneret died in prison in 1884.

Sources

1. Folsom, Charles. *Studies of Criminal Responsibility and Limited Responsibility.* Privately published, 1909, pp. 68–87.
2. Nash, Jay Robert. *Look for the Woman.* New York: M. Evans, 1981, p. 210.

Hélène Jegado

(c. 1803–1851). *Place:* Brittany, France. *Time:* Late 1820s?–1851. *Age:* c. 25–48. *Victims:* 27 or more. *Method:* Arsenic poisoning.

Hélène Jegado was known as bad-tempered and taciturn, with a propensity for robbing her employers. Unable to read or write, she readily nursed grievances and imagined wrongs done to her at the drop of a hat. If an employer reprimanded her for stealing a trinket, or if someone in the family contradicted her in an argument, deaths would surely follow: Hélène would lace one or more items of food with arsenic.

Jegado never seemed to lack for work as a domestic servant, moving from one town in Brittany, France, to another. She left behind her a string of corpses of people who had died an often slow and agonizingly painful death. Aware of her reputation, some citizens shunned her in the street or tossed insults her way. However, employers tended to overlook her petty thievery, to not prosecute her, and to give her a good reference, perhaps because they were being kind to her. Hélène had a reputation of being very pious. This was enhanced by the fact that she worked mostly for clergymen.

No logical motive existed for any of the murders. For the most part, Hélène didn't like the person targeted or had decided that person had slighted or upbraided her in some way. Jegado enjoyed nursing her victims when they became sick, and when death inevitably came, she grieved and lamented long and loudly, just like the family. Apparently autopsies made on some of her early victims showed the cause of death to be poison, but the authorities never made a connection with the servant.

Jegado was born in Brittany around 1803 and orphaned at the age of seven. She was then taken into a pastor's house where two of her aunts were employed as servants. It seems that Hélène started working as a servant at that young age. After a stay of 17 years there, Jegado went off on her own and began her string of grisly poisonings, probably in the late 1820s.

Her reputation was known as early as June 1831, when she entered the employ of Mlle. Keraly at Hennebont. Keraly was warned of Hélène's "fatal influence" but nevertheless employed the woman, only to have her father and another household servant die [4]. In the village of Guern, using

177

arsenic, Jegado poisoned a group of seven to death. One of the victims was her own sister.

Her victims included men, women, and children, and deaths took place in a dozen or so towns in Brittany. Working as a combination cook-housekeeper, Hélène had ready access to the household food and could lace soups, cakes, tea, chocolate, and other items with arsenic.

After her sister's death, Hélène took over her post as a servant and promptly dispatched three more people. Sometimes she was dismissed from a position for stealing some small item — and sometimes she managed to murder before taking her leave. At the town of Locmine two people died; a third escaped because he hated Jegado and refused to take any food from her.

Later Jegado coldly denied any involvement in the murders when a judge questioned her. The judge asked her if she was the cook at one household where several had died and whether she had also nursed the sick there. Replied Hélène, "Yes. I always nursed the sick — that has been my misfortune. That's the cause of my trouble today" [4].

At a house where the mother had died and the daughter was ill, Hélène said to the child before her mother expired, "I fear your mother will die. I carry death with me." While in Locmine, Jegado was insulted in the streets because of the number of deaths in her background, and she was called the "white-livered woman."

She fled Locmine and briefly entered a convent, perhaps to try and remove herself from murderous situations since she had no access to the kitchen. However, she was expelled from there in short order after it was determined that she had cut all the bed linen to pieces. Hélène always denied this and claimed she left the convent because the superintendent told her she was too old to learn to read and write.

After leaving a few more bodies behind her, she was employed by Mme. Etain but was soon thrown out of the house along with everything she had prepared, by Etain's son-in-law after the mistress of the house had dined with some clergymen who warned her that Jegado was dangerous.

Hippolyte Roussel employed Hélène and chastised her one morning for stealing an umbrella from another servant. Later that day Mme. Roussel was stricken with severe vomiting after eating Jegado's soup. When a judge asked her about this episode the servant replied, "She would have vomited whether she had taken the soup or not." Asked whether Roussel then got worse and could scarcely walk, Hélène said, "She could scarcely walk before" [4].

In Lorient the young daughter in a family died and all the adults sickened. None of the adults died although for years afterward two of them were said to suffer from body numbness, recurrent pains in the extremities, and partial paralysis. Suspicion fell on their servant, Jegado, who was fired.

She moved on to Port Louis 15 miles away and promptly got another job, but was quickly fired after being caught stealing a sheet.

The year was then 1841. Jegado appears to have abruptly stopped poisoning for the next eight years. At least, none were attributed to her by authorities during this period. One account claims that she declared God had forgiven her all her sins and then turned over a new leaf. This new leaf was relative; during the 1840s, Hélène still stole and drank to excess [2].

For the period from 1833 to 1841, authorities attributed 23 murders, five poisonings, and numerous thefts to Jegado. Considering that she had a "fatal" reputation as early as 1831, the actual toll is almost certainly higher. However, since Jegado was not brought to trial until 1851, a 10-year statute of limitations prevented her from being tried for any of these crimes. The authorities could only act on the second series of murders.

Jegado resumed her old ways in 1848 when five members of the Rabot family all fell ill after the family had given their servant notice for drinking their wine. The next year a young child died in a house in Rennes where Hélène was employed. The day before, Jegado had been reprimanded by her employer for stealing some brandy.

Staying in Rennes, Hélène next got employment at an inn called the World's End. Another servant at the establishment was a young woman named Perrotte Mace. First, the owner's mother became ill after reprimanding Jegado for insolence. Then Jegado took a dislike to Mace, perhaps because she was younger and better looking; Mace took to her bed with vomiting, pains in the stomach and limbs, distention of the abdomen, and swelling of the feet. Mace complained that Jegado, whom she disliked, gave her things to eat and drink that burned her.

At first the doctor thought Mace's condition was not serious. Hélène told him that she was mortally ill—and she was. Described as a healthy and strapping girl, she died on September 1, 1850. The doctors were suspicious and wanted to perform an autopsy, but Mace's parents refused permission. Soon afterward, Jegado was caught stealing liquor and was fired.

Never long between jobs, she took a position with a university professor named Theophile Bidard, also in Rennes. Surprisingly she came to him with excellent references and a reputation for filial piety; she always claimed that out of her wages she sent home money to support her aged mother and two little girls. The mother had been dead for 40 years, and the girls were nonexistent.

Bidard at first thought his new servant was intelligent, although endowed with a malicious sense of humor. A second servant in the house was Rose Tessier. Jegado took a dislike to Rose. One evening, she had stood outside Rose's door several times and called out "Rose, Rose" in a ghostlike voice. On Sunday, November 3, 1850, Rose was described as in good health. That day, after eating a noon meal prepared by Jegado, Rose became ill and died four days later. She had been tended during her illness, solicitously, only by Jegado.

Bidard called in the doctors during the sickness but Hélène said to him, "The doctors do not understand what is wrong with Rose. I can see she will die." Her employer thought it odd, since Tessier then had no fever and a normal pulse. Rose's death was slow and extremely painful.

After the death Jegado vied with Rose's mother in her grief and she repeated constantly, "Poor Rose . . . I loved her as I did that poor girl who died at the World's End." Bidard thought Hélène was sincere in her grief but had some doubts, saying, "Her body shook. I wondered whether it was with sorrow or glee" [2].

When Bidard suggested hiring a new servant Hélène said no: "I will do the extra work myself. I could not bear to see another taking Rose's place. I loved her too much." The professor yielded to Jegado for a time but then hired a second servant, Françoise Huriaux, to whom Hélène took an instant dislike. She cowed and dominated the newcomer, and Françoise then refused to eat the soups Jegado made, which prompted her to say, "Do you think I want to poison you?" [4] Françoise survived because she left the Bidard household.

Rosalie Sarrazin was then hired, and for a short time the two servants seemed to have been on friendly terms. This ended when Bidard, unhappy with the way Hélène accounted to him for expenditures, put Rosalie in charge of the books. The illiterate poisoner found this too much to bear and her friendship turned to hate.

Fighting between the pair became so rancorous that Bidard gave Jegado two weeks' notice; unfortunately he took pity on her and kept her on. Rosalie took to her bed with the usual symptoms and died July 1, 1851, after suffering extreme agony for three weeks.

Toward the end, Bidard began to suspect poisoning and ordered that the material Rosalie vomited should be kept for later examination. However, each time she was sick Hélène emptied the container and cleaned it. This strengthened her employer's suspicions. Doctors agreed that the deaths of two servants in the same house were suspicious and called in the law.

When the authorities arrived one said they were there because poisoning was suspected, to which a nervous Jegado replied, "I am innocent." The authorities said, "Of what? Nobody has accused you." She was then taken away [2]. Autopsies done on Sarrazin, Tessier, and Mace revealed that all had received a massive dose of arsenic.

Jegado stood trial late in 1851, charged with three counts or murder, three other charges of poisoning, and 11 thefts. Standing in the dock at the age of 48, she was described as having coarse features that gave her a repugnant air, "which was perhaps slightly relieved by her Breton accent. She took snuff and was dirty" [4].

Testimony at the trial revealed that people at the convent felt Jegado didn't have enough intelligence to learn to read. One witness said, "Hélène's conversation ran on deaths. She was full of jeremiads, complained of her lot, and would sit for a long time silent and thoughtful. When she left the convent she said, 'I am going out. I have no happiness'" [4]. Another witness, Huriaux, told about once drying a dress in her room. Hélène went to the room above it, bored a hole in the floor, and then poured vitriol through the hole onto the dress and burned it.

Late in her career Jegado remarked, "Wherever I go, people die" [1]. But at her trial she admitted nothing. She said, "I am innocent. I don't know any poisons. God will be merciful enough to keep me ignorant of them" [4]. Jegado was found guilty, sentenced to death, and guillotined in 1851.

Sources

1. Green, Jonathon. *The Greatest Criminals of All Time.* New York: Stein & Day, 1980, p. 151.

2. Heppenstall, Rayner. *French Crime in the Romantic Age.* London: Hamish Hamilton, 1970, pp. 210–11, 256–58, 261–64, 268.

3. Nash, Jay Robert. *Look for the Woman.* New York: M. Evans, 1981, p. 212.

4. Williamson, W. H. *Annals of Crime: Some Extraordinary Women.* London: Routledge, 1930, pp. 141–62.

Annie Jones

(1904–1936). *Place:* Madison, Maine. *Time:* June 21, 1936. *Age:* 32. *Victims:* 4. *Method:* Firearm.

Born in Woodstock, New Brunswick, 32-year-old Annie Jones lived with her husband Erwin a few miles across the Canadian border near the town of Madison, Maine. The couple had five children: Charles, 14; Shirley, 12; twins Robert and Edward, four; and Norman, two. Erwin Jones had an automobile repair shop that he operated across the road from the home.

While there was reportedly no discord in the family, Annie had not been well for about two years, during which time she had been under the care of a doctor. Family members and neighbors described her as despondent. Previously she had threatened to kill her children and commit suicide, but she had never made any actual attempts. Around the middle of June 1936, Annie bought some bullets for the family rifle. When Charles found out about the purchase, Annie threatened to kill him if he told.

Early on the morning of June 21, Annie took the three youngest children with her to the woods behind the house, an area that could not be seen from the road or the house. She told the kids she was taking them for a picnic, showing them cookies she had packed in a bag. In the bag she also had rope and rags. When the family reached the area where Annie had previously hidden the rifle, she tied the twins up hand and foot together and blindfolded them. Norman was tied around the waist to the other two but not blindfolded. Then Annie shot each one once in the back or side of the head at close range, killing them instantly. The bodies were then neatly arranged by her on a blanket, face up. Annie then held the rifle's muzzle under her chin, pulled the trigger, and killed herself. When the family didn't return home as expected Shirley called her father, who started a search. It was Erwin who came upon the grisly scene.

Sources

1. "Madison Woman, 32, Kills Three Children and Self." *Portland Press Herald,* June 22, 1936, pp. 1, 4.
2. "Mother Kills Three and Takes Own Life." *New York Times,* June 22, 1936, p. 40.

Roxanne Jones

(1958–). *Place:* Reseda, California. *Time:* March 20, 1990. *Age:* 32. *Victims:* 4. *Method:* Firearm.

When Roxanne Jones's second marriage broke up at the end of 1989, she began having a harder and harder time both financially and psychologically. She turned to religion for solace, but it didn't seem to help enough. Then she turned to murder.

Roxanne had three children: two daughters, Brandy Fernandez, 15, and Leticia Fernandez, 13; and a son, Jeremiah Jones, nine. Her marriage to Joachim Fernandez ended around 1979. This was followed by a nine-year marriage to Jeff Jones. Jones moved out of the house they lived in in Reseda, California, at the end of 1989. Jeff said of the split only that their problems were "nothing major." Since the separation the couple had kept in touch regularly.

Neighbors described Roxanne as "unusual," a woman who dressed in the styles of the late '60s and raised goats and chickens in her backyard, a Woodstock type. One neighbor said, "They were just kind of strange people and we kept away from them" [1]. Many thought of her as a lenient, permissive parent, perhaps overly so. One neighbor speculated that one of the problems with the marriage was that Jeff Jones felt his wife was too lenient with her daughters.

During the marriage to Jones, Roxanne had worked as a bookkeeper for her house-painter husband. After the separation Roxanne was unemployed. Unable to find steady work, she did baby-sitting and whatever odd jobs she could find. Brandy contributed her pay from a part-time job at a pizzeria to the household kitty, but was laid off in the middle of March 1990. Roxanne approached the pizzeria manager to see if he would pay her $80 to deliver advertising flyers.

Newspaper accounts say Roxanne was receiving welfare. A television report stated the woman was rejected for welfare one week before the killings. Welfare officials cited confidentiality requirements in refusing to discuss the case except to say that they did have a file on Roxanne. The same television report claimed that Roxanne was reduced at the end to selling her blood to get money for food. She did ask neighbors for small amounts of

183

money. Some accounts claim the Jones's marriage was a close and happy one until the separation. Others termed it stormy and difficult.

Religion became very important in Roxanne's life. She went for counseling to the Covenant Faith Center in Northridge, a church that practices faith healing. Jeff Jones said his wife was religious but "didn't quite interpret the Bible the way it should have been." Crystal Erickson, a friend of the two daughters, said that after the separation Roxanne "got pretty heavy into God. She would start reading Scripture to everyone when we were around" [3].

During that final month or so, Roxanne often spoke of suicide. If she did it she planned to take the children with her. Many of her friends and neighbors were aware of these threats but nobody took them seriously. Jeremiah told his first-grade teacher at school that his mother was going to take him to "a good place, where God is, and there are no worries" [3]. The teacher took the remark to mean a religious retreat. When Roxanne talked to others of having to "get out of here," they thought she meant she wanted to move out of the area.

On the evening of Monday, March 19, 1990, the two daughters went bowling with friends and did not arrive home until around 4 A.M. Tuesday morning. Roxanne saw Jeff for the last time on that Monday morning. He thought she seemed all right at the time. Roxanne told him she was leaving the state for "a couple of months," gave him a hug, and said good-bye.

Some time during those early morning hours on Tuesday, Roxanne took a 22-caliber rifle and shot and killed her three children while they slept. Each was shot once in the head and once in the chest. Then she shot herself to death with one shot to the head. When Crystal could not reach her friends Brandy and Leticia on Tuesday or Wednesday, she got worried. In the afternoon she entered the house through a dog door and found the bodies.

Scrawled on the wall of the dining room with a black marker was, "God please forgive me. My loved ones please forget me." A note on the desk said, "If we are not dead, then don't call an ambulance" [2]. A lengthy suicide note outlined her problems and asked God's forgiveness. It went on to say that she loved her children and hated to put them through living in a world full of strife.

News of the killings caused pedestrians to crowd the sidewalk and gawking drivers to turn the usually quiet street into a rush-hour traffic jam. Three cars collided in the street outside the murder home, injuring two people.

Sources

1. Chandler, Carmen. "4 in Family Found Slain in Reseda." *Daily News,* March 22, 1990, pp. 3, 22.

2. Curtiss, Aaron. "Despondent Mother Kills Her 3 Children and Herself." *Los Angeles Times,* March 22, 1990, pp. B1, B4.

3. Curtiss, Aaron. "Mother Had Long Talked of Suicide." *Los Angeles Times,* March 23, 1990, pp. 4, 8.

4. McDonald, Kathy. "4 Victims of Shooting Are Mourned." *Daily News,* March 23, 1990, pp. 4, 8.

Charlotte Juenemann

(1910–1935). *Place:* Berlin, Germany. *Time:* January 1935. *Age:* 24. *Victims:* 3. *Method:* Starvation.

By January 1935, 24-year-old Charlotte Juenemann was certainly down on her luck. By then her husband had been committed to an insane asylum and she was left with three small sons to raise. The boys were four months, 18 months, and four years old. Charlotte was unemployed and relied on welfare benefits to survive.

That month, she became enamored of a musician and spent what little money she had on booze, night life, and on her new boyfriend. She often stayed out all night and began to ignore the children, finding them an inconvenience.

Charlotte gave away milk cards intended for her children; welfare workers apparently became aware of the problem, because it was reported that she refused to allow them to care for her children during the day. The result was that Mrs. Juenemann locked her kids up for eight days in a rear room of her basement apartment, described as a "hovel." This left her free to go out to bars; she was rarely home during those days, saying later, "I had no time to give the children food and water" [2].

A couple of times she did come home but only for a few moments—just long enough to throw a few "dole potatoes into the room and hurry away in order not to hear the children's cries" [1]. Those few potatoes weren't enough, and after eight days the children were discovered, all dead of starvation.

Juenemann was charged with murder and convicted on March 30, 1935. Psychiatrists testified they found Charlotte to have limited intelligence but enough to be held responsible for her actions. Charlotte said at her trial, "I did not want the children to die" [3]. She was sentenced to be beheaded.

The next day it was announced that Juenemann was expecting a child. Speculation centered around whether or not she would get a reprieve, since women were not usually executed in such condition. However, public feeling ran strong against the woman and her "callous" crimes, making a reprieve less likely. The prosecuting attorney had been flooded with angry letters from German mothers demanding death for the accused. Also, Nazi ideas about not allowing a possibly "tainted" offspring to survive were at work.

Since Charlotte was described as "slim" at her trial, she must have been in the early stages of pregnancy. On August 27, 1935, the sentence was carried out with no mention made of her condition. She was either executed at six or seven months pregnant or, what is more likely, had never been pregnant at all.

Sources

1. "Doomed Reich Woman Is Expectant Mother." *New York Times,* April 1, 1935, p. 10.
2. "Nazis Behead Woman for Starving 3 Sons." *New York Times,* August 28, 1935, p. 4.
3. "Reich Sentences Mother, 24, to Be Beheaded." *New York Times,* March 31, 1935, p. 1.

Kathleen King

(1922–). *Place:* Xenia, Ohio. *Time:* April 12, 1958. *Age:* 36. *Victims:* 3. *Method:* Bludgeoning.

A tense, nervous woman was how neighbors described 36-year-old Kathleen King. Even prior to her marriage, she had received psychiatric care. After the birth of each of her three children Kathleen suffered mental problems. Kathleen and her husband Charles were longtime residents of Dayton, Ohio, until November 1956, when the family moved to the nearby community of Xenia where they occupied a modest one-story home. In April 1958, they had the house up for sale, planning to move back to Dayton where Charles worked for the post office as a letter carrier.

The first week or so of April was a particularly bad time for Kathleen, who was worried about bills and was under the care of a physician. Approximately one year earlier she had been placed in a private mental hospital, where she received electric shock treatments. At that time Kathleen already had a history of emotional instability.

During a trip to California in 1945, the trunk lid of a car had struck Kathleen on the head. Following that accident she received electric shock treatments back in Dayton. She took an overdose of sleeping pills in 1954 in an apparent suicide attempt and was confined to a mental institution for a time. She twice tried to jump from a window at that hospital. A dozen more electric shock treatments were administered. Kathleen believed they did her some good.

On April 8, 1958, Kathleen received a prescription for 30 tranquilizers from her physician. She was so depressed and nervous that she took 16 of the pills on April 9. She was ill most of the day. When Charles came home that night, he had trouble rousing his wife. The next day Charles stayed home from work to look after the children and to keep an eye on his wife. He had hidden the pills away by then. Kathleen nagged him all day for the pills.

When he left for work on Friday and Saturday, Charles gave his wife two pills on each day.

He left home that Saturday a little after 6 A.M. Kathleen was up with him pleading, "Don't go to work today, don't leave me. If you do, I'll kill the children and myself" [13]. It was a threat Charles had often heard his wife utter in the past, and he discounted it that day.

After Charles left for work, Kathleen took the two tranquilizers and went back to bed. At 8:30 A.M. she got up again to fix breakfast for the children. The family debts preyed on her mind again. They worried her and she didn't know what to do. Kathleen decided to kill the children because of the heavy debts. She put two-year-old Brian back in his crib. Charleen, five, was lying next to it on the rug in the bedroom. Donald, three and a half, was in the living room on the couch.

Taking a hammer, Kathleen struck Donald on the head. After that she went into the bedroom where she said to her daughter, "I'm going to send you to heaven and I'm going to hell." Charleen, thinking her mother was playing a game, sat up with her back to her mother and laughed, "OK" [6]. Kathleen bludgeoned Charleen twice with the hammer. Then she struck Brian in the crib. Returning to the living room, Mrs. King found Donald had somehow managed to stagger into the kitchen. She struck him down again and then stabbed him in the back of the head with an eight-inch butcher knife. By then the house was covered with blood and gore. Picking Donald up, she carried her son to the couch, where she lay down, holding his body, to watch television. When the police asked her if Donald spoke, Kathleen said, "No. He probably didn't like the program and he had his eyes closed" [6].

Over the course of the day Kathleen blacked out intermittently. At some point she proceeded to put the house in a state of great disorder by emptying out drawers and strewing clothes around. She washed the blood-stained pajamas she was wearing at the time of the murders. Around 3 P.M. she looked in the bedroom to see how Brian and Charleen were, later telling police she "found them both quiet and all right" [6].

Kathleen tried to commit suicide by taking a fuse out of the fuse box in the kitchen and sticking her finger in the socket. She also slashed her wrists and both upper arms with a razor blade and a knife. Around 7:30 that evening she thought about making supper for Charles, but when he didn't come home she drank some oven cleaner. Then she tried to choke herself by wrapping a cloth belt around her neck and tying it to a bed post.

Charles King got off work at the Dayton post office a little after 3 P.M. that day. He had a few beers with friends at a lodge, went for a pizza, and then went back to the lodge. He didn't arrive home until just past midnight, when he found his wife semiconscious. Kathleen was rushed to the hospital. All of her wounds were superficial except for the oven cleaner, which had burned her throat and tongue. Because of this she was unable to talk for a few days.

When the police asked Charles why he hadn't gone straight home from work on Saturday, he said he had reached the point where he didn't want to go home because of his wife's constant nagging. They had an argument the night before about being in debt. The police asked him if his wife's threat had crossed his mind at work that day. Charles replied, "One time, around noon, while on my route I looked down and saw something shiny. I thought it was a coin. I picked it up and found it to be a medallion broken off a chain. On it was written 'Sixth—Thou Shalt Not Kill.' The name of Kathleen flashed across my mind, but I didn't think any more of it" [6].

Dorothy Hartmann, Charles's aunt, said Kathleen was a good cook and a good mother. The couple, she claimed, never had any trouble. Next-door neighbors Mr. and Mrs. Hill never heard a sound even though their bedroom was just across the drive from the King home. Recalling Kathleen a few days before the murders, the Hills said, "She seemed awfully tense and talked about the bags under her eyes and how she'd been up with the kids all night. She was very quiet, but awfully nervous. More than anything else, she seemed despondent over bills and not being able to pay what they owed. She acted as if she were under terrific pressure. We were the only ones she'd ever visit. She used to come over here two or three times a week and tell us all about the terrible time she was having making ends meet." Another neighbor described Kathleen as "nice, but very withdrawn" [2].

On April 15 Kathleen became violent and almost escaped from the hospital where she was being treated for her injuries. She recovered her voice that day and told police she had killed the children because "I thought they would be better off dead" [16]. She readily admitted to killing them with a hammer, saying she was worried about debts. When she was released from the hospital Kathleen said she hoped to get some more shock treatments. Describing her husband to the police, she said he was "good . . . a good provider."

On the following day her lawyer pleaded not guilty by reason of insanity to the three counts of murder. Then she was transferred to a psychiatric facility, the Lima State Hospital, for observation. At the end of the 30-day observation period Kathleen was declared insane by officials there. In another court session a judge agreed with the hospital findings, declared Kathleen insane, and ordered her returned to Lima State Hospital for an indefinite period. Psychiatrists had diagnosed her as schizophrenic.

In October 1960, doctors at the hospital sent word to the court that Mrs. King had regained her sanity and could stand trial, The trial took place in December of that year before a panel of three judges instead of a judge and jury, at the request of Kathleen's lawyer. The judges founded Kathleen not guilty by reason of insanity on the three murder counts. By the end of December Kathleen had been returned to Lima State Hospital for an indefinite period.

Seven years after that Kathleen filed an application, under provisions of a new state law, for release. A hearing was held in which it was determined that she had been restored to sanity. Kathleen was given her release in December 1967.

Sources

1. "Asks Release in Slayings 9 Years Ago." *Journal Herald* [Dayton], December 8, 1967.

2. Eckert, Allan. "Neighbors Stunned by Tragedy." *Journal Herald* [Dayton], April 14, 1958, p. 3.

3. "1st Degree Murder Charges Filed Against Xenia Mother of Three." *Journal Herald* [Dayton], April 15, 1958.

4. "Former Xenia Woman Gets Freedom." *Journal Herald* [Dayton], December 29, 1967.

5. Heck, William A. "Relative Says Father 'in State of Shock.'" *Journal Herald* [Dayton], April 14, 1958, p. 3.

6. "'I'm Going to Send You to Heaven,' Mother Told Child." *Journal Herald* [Dayton], April 16, 1958, p. 3.

7. "Insanity Ruled in Slaying of Three." *Dayton Daily News,* December 23, 1960.

8. "Judges Free Xenian of Slaying." *Journal Herald* [Dayton], December 24, 1960.

9. "King's Home Tells Story of Horror." *Journal Herald* [Dayton], April 14, 1958, p. 3.

10. Lawson, Fred. "Fate Now in Hands of Judicial Panel." *Journal Herald* [Dayton], December 23, 1960.

11. "Mother Kills Three Children with Hammer, Police Say." *Dayton Daily News,* April 15, 1958.

12. "Mother to Face Trial in Xenia for 3 Killings." *Journal Herald* [Dayton], October 26, 1960.

13. "3 Children Beaten to Death with Hammer in Xenia Home." *Journal Herald* [Dayton], April 14, 1958, p. 1.

14. "Xenia Mother Is Adjudged Insane." *Journal Herald* [Dayton], May 20, 1958.

15. "Xenia Mother Is Returned to Hospital." *Journal Herald* [Dayton], May 24, 1958.

16. "Xenia Mother Pleads Innocent." *Dayton Daily News,* April 16, 1958, p. 10.

17. "Xenia Sanity Hearing Set for Today." *Journal Herald* [Dayton], May 23, 1958.

Tillie Klimek

(1876–1936). *Place:* Chicago, Illinois. *Time:* 1912–1921. *Age:* 36–45. *Victims:* c. 9. *Method:* Arsenic poisoning.

As a dumpy, middle-aged Polish woman Tillie Klimek wasn't much to look at, but all agreed she sure could cook. The authorities speculated that this ability drew men to her, for Tillie had many husbands; when she had had enough of them, she added a special white powder to the food she prepared. After that, it was time to look for another husband. Others besides husbands also fell victim to Tillie's murderous ways.

Born in Europe around 1876, Tillie Gburek came to the United States from Poland before she was five years old. The family settled in Chicago's Polish area and apparently eked out a precarious living. Neither of Tillie's parents would ever learn to speak English. Both were alive when their daughter was apprehended. At an early age, Tillie was sent out to work in the sweatshops of Chicago.

A plain-looking woman, her prospects for marriage did not seem good. After saving a little money, she gambled it all by spending it on the services of a matrimonial agency. The agency introduced her to Joseph Mitkiewicz, and the couple married around 1896. The financial status of the family remained low; Tillie continued to work long hours at back-breaking jobs—as all laborers did then. The couple had one son. In 1914 Tillie had been married for 18 years; suddenly, without apparent reason, she turned into a serial killer.

Mitkiewicz died suddenly on January 13, 1914, leaving his widow Tillie about $1,000 in life insurance proceeds. Just one month later, on February 17, Tillie married Joseph Ruszkakski. Three months later, Ruszkakski died in the same fashion that Mitkiewicz had—by ingesting rat poison in the food Tillie prepared for him. This time Tillie got $722 from a life insurance policy. When the bodies were later exhumed, both were found to be loaded with arsenic.

By the fall of 1914, Tillie was romancing John Guszkowski. John declined Tillie's offer of marriage after she told him she had poisoned her two previous husbands. The couple was traveling together, and Tillie was more than a little annoyed to have Guszkowski lose interest in her after her revelation. An angry Tillie told John she would have him charged under the Mann Act — a law that held it illegal to transport females across state lines for sexual purposes. John replied that he would turn her in to the police for murder. Before 1914 was over, Guszkowski was dead. Before John's death, one of his sisters became very ill after eating candy Tillie had given her after the two women had quarreled.

For the next few years, Tillie's activities remain a mystery. Before she married Frank Kupczyk in March 1919, Tillie went under the name of Meyers. She had utility bills mailed to her as Mrs. Meyers. Although the police searched for Mr. Meyers, no trace was ever found, and the authorities believe that Meyers was either a husband or live-in companion whom Tillie murdered. Frank Kupczyk died on April 20, 1921. He was another of Tillie's victims and his body would also be found to contain arsenic when it was later exhumed. One of Tillie's neighbors recalled, "Frank used to leave for work every day at 6 and I'd often see John Koski come over there to visit Tillie. Once I seen him kiss her." When asked what happened then, the neighbor went on, "Why, then Tillie put up some newspapers in front of the window, so I couldn't see in" [4].

Mrs. Wesolek, Tillie's landlady, remembered that when Frank lay dying Tillie came to see her, telling her about a bargain price of $30 for a coffin advertised in a paper. Tillie wanted to buy it and store it in her landlady's basement. Wesolek objected because Frank was only sick, not dead. During a visit to Frank, Wesolek saw Tillie sitting a few feet from her husband, busily engaged in sewing a mourning veil onto a hat. Wesolek recounted how her tenant played "o, so jolly music" on a record player while Frank lay dead in the same room. Tillie had often told Frank that his illness was fatal and that he would not live long. Another witness said Tillie grabbed the corpse by the ear and yelled, "You devil, you won't get up any more." The widow pocketed $675 in life insurance proceeds this time [6].

The next husband was 51-year-old Joseph Klimek, whom Tillie married in 1921. Klimek was a widower introduced to Tillie by friends only a few weeks after Frank's death. One year later, Tillie would poison him. Klimek came close to dying but survived.

Describing his wife, Klimek related, "As soon as we were married she burned up all the photographs of her husbands and her man friends. And she tore up all her letters. She had my picture over the mantel, that was all. . . . She didn't dance very much. She went to the movies occasionally with me; she never raised her voice at me; she never quarreled. . . . She gadded around a lot in the daytime. I don't know where she went, but she was always there to get my supper. She was never late. And she could cook! . . . Sure we were happy. . . . I got $26 a week and I brought home my pay envelope to her every Saturday. She kept it and gave me a dollar each morning when I started to work. That was my money" [18].

Suspicion finally fell on Tillie during Klimek's illness at home. His brother John noticed that two of Klimek's pet dogs had died mysteriously just before their master got ill. Over Tillie's objections, John called in another physician to attend his brother. This doctor diagnosed the problem as arsenic poisoning and removed Klimek to a hospital. At the hospital Tillie was visiting her husband when the stricken man asked a nurse for a glass of water. Tillie shouted at the nurse, "If he makes any trouble for you take a two-by-four board and hit him over the head with it." When the doctor informed Tillie that her husband had been poisoned she took the news, said the doctor, "with a merry twinkle in her eyes" [4].

In November 1922, Tillie was arrested. She went to trial the following year charged with one count of murder—that of Frank Kupczyk. Aside from the five dead husbands or boyfriends and Klimek's attempted murder, the authorities suspected Tillie in four other deaths. One was Rose Chudzinski, a cousin of the murderess. She died in 1919 soon after a quarrel with Tillie. During the period from 1912 to 1915, three more of Tillie's cousins died. They were Stanley Zakrzewski, 16; Stella Zakrzewski, 23; and Helen Zakrzewski, 15. They were the children of Francis Zakrzewski, and their family and Tillie had lived at the same address during the time of their deaths. Tillie had fought with their mother and attended all three of the children when they were ill. Authorities did not pursue these deaths to any extent.

After her arrest Tillie steadfastly denied all charges of murder. She was calm and emotionless. Referring to her cellmates with disdain, Tillie recalled her own strict youth and said, "Me, I came to this country when I was a year old. No foolishness with us. We work. ... Ugh, they smoke these cigarettes. Me, I don't smoke. No, they make me sick, those women. Ugh" [8].

As she went to trial she was termed "no beauty in the dock," "the squat, gruesomely cruel Polish woman," or a woman with "a greasy complexion and a lumpy figure, growls instead or murmurs, and knows a crochet needle better than a lipstick" [7]. Much of jury selection was taken up with ascertaining whether prospective jurors were prepared to punish a woman as severely as a man if she were guilty.

During her trial one witness recounted how she advised Tillie to get a divorce from Klimek after hearing about Tillie's marital troubles. However, Tillie responded, "No, I will get rid of him some other way." When Tillie took the stand in her own defense she proved to be unshakable in her denials. After three hours of intense questioning, the state could not make her waver in her denials or trap her in any way. She denied the suggestion that she had shown Frank a picture of his coffin the day before he died. When asked how long she waited after Kupczyk was dead to call in an undertaker, Tillie replied, "I went thirty minutes after he stopped breathing." When asked if she had any troubles with any of her husbands she said, "I did not. I loved them; they loved me. They just died same as other people. I not responsible for that. I could no help if they wanted to die." Witnesses spoke against her and lied, she said, because "they got it in for me. They no like me" [20].

Lieutenant Willard Malone was the police officer who had arrested her and was responsible for developing the case against her. During a break in the questioning one time, Tillie showed her own sense of black humor by shaking her finger at Malone and saying, "The next one I want to cook a dinner for is you. You made all my trouble." Another time, at the end of a long day's session in court the woman commented, "Isn't it a shame to keep the poor judge and jury working overtime. They won't get no dinner. Isn't it a shame" [9].

On March 13, 1923, Tillie was found guilty of murdering Frank Kupczyk and sentenced to life in prison. The prosecution had been seeking the death penalty. Tillie's only comment as she was led out of the courtroom was, "It was warm in there." The jury took one hour and 20 minutes to reach its verdict.

At the time the idea seemed to exist that women got off easier than men when charged with similar crimes. The prosecutor brought out the fact that in recent years 28 women were acquitted of murder in Chicago's Cook County. For the most part they had murdered their husbands. Of the four who were convicted, one was insane, one was "more than middle aged," and the other two were termed "no beauties." Beautiful women were very likely to be acquitted.

Prosecutor McLaughlin said after the Klimek verdict, "This will put a pausing hand on the hands of those fiends who, in the future, may think of sprinkling poison on their husbands' food." Thomas Peden, assistant state attorney, commented that the verdict was "a lesson to the women of this county that sob stuff where a woman is involved in a crime has come to an end. It is time that the chain of immunity for women be broken, and I hope this will be a lesson to the women that in Cook County they will be treated the same as the men" [7].

Tillie Klimek died in custody in 1936.

Sources

1. "Ask Indictments Today in Klimek Poisoning Cases." *Chicago Tribune,* November 20, 1922, p. 6.

2. "Death Called Mere Routine in Poison Home." *Chicago Tribune,* November 15, 1922, p. 1.

3. Forbes, Genevieve. "Arsenic Cousins Go to Trial with Air of Peasants." *Chicago Tribune,* March 7, 1923, p. 3.

4. Forbes, Genevieve. "Grave Digger Tells of Goings On at Klimek's." *Chicago Tribune,* March 10, 1923, p. 3.

5. Forbes, Genevieve. "Her Parents Loyal." *Chicago Tribune,* November 17, 1922, p. 3.

6. Forbes, Genevieve. "How Mrs. Klimek Jested of Death of Husband Told." *Chicago Tribune,* March 9, 1923, p. 7.

7. Forbes, Genevieve. "Life in Prison for Woman as Arch Poisoner." *Chicago Tribune,* March 14, 1923, pp. 1, 6.

8. Forbes, Genevieve. "Mrs. Klimek — A Study." *Chicago Tribune,* November 15, 1922, pp. 1, 14.

9. Forbes, Genevieve. "Poison Evidence Robs Mrs. Klimek of Indifference." *Chicago Tribune,* March 11, 1923, p. 7.

10. "K Cousins' Circle Haunted by Affliction and Death." *Chicago Tribune,* March 14, 1923, p. 6.

11. "Klimek Poison Charges Ready for Grand Jury." *Chicago Tribune,* November 18, 1922, p. 3.

12. "Klimek Poison List Is Twenty; Arrest 1 More." *Chicago Tribune,* November 19, 1922, pp. 1, 2.

13. "List to Date of Supposed Victims in Poison Sowing." *Chicago Tribune,* November 14, 1922, p. 3.

14. "Mrs. Klimek Is Formally Held in Poison Death." *Chicago Tribune,* November 11, 1922, p. 5.

15. "Mystery Deaths in Poison Case May Reach 20." *Chicago Tribune,* November 14, 1922, p. 3.

16. Nash, Jay Robert. *Look for the Woman.* New York: M. Evans, 1981, pp. 226–27.

17. "Poison Deaths May Total 12; Babes Victims?" *Chicago Tribune,* November 12, 1922, pp. 1, 6.

18. "Police to Delve Anew for Clues to Poisonings." *Chicago Tribune,* November 16, 1922, p. 3.

19. "Relatives Shun Two Women Held in Poison Cases." *Chicago Tribune,* November 13, 1922, p. 2.

20. "Tillie Klimek Is Strong Witness in Own Defense." *Chicago Tribune,* March 13, 1923, p. 7.

21. "Two Poisoned by Candy Given by Mrs. Klimek." *Chicago Tribune,* November 17, 1922, p. 3.

Christa Lehmann

(1922–). *Place:* Worms, Germany. *Time:* 1952–1954. *Age:* 30–32. *Victims:* 3. *Method:* Phosphorus poisoning.

Growing up in an unstable family in Worms, Germany, apparently left its mark on Christa Lehmann. Her mother was confined to an asylum by the time her daughter reached her teens, while her father completely ignored Christa. A series of petty thefts committed as a girl led to a jail sentence for Christa, which was suspended to a term of probation.

Her marriage in 1944 to Karl Lehmann proved no solution. Karl, a tilesetter, was a chronic drunk. The young woman engaged in several affairs but only grew more depressed and embittered by what she felt was a hopeless situation.

On September 17, 1952, Karl died suddenly in convulsive agony. A doctor attributed death to a stomach rupture. A little over a year later, on October 14, 1953, Valentin Lehmann, Christa's father-in-law, fell from his bicycle, collapsed, and died in convulsions in the street only 20 minutes after leaving the house where he lived with Christa. No one suspected Christa.

The woman's one close friend was Annie Hamann, who lived with her aged mother, Eva Ruth. Ruth had often criticized her daughter for associating with Lehmann, whom she disliked. On February 15, 1954, Christa bought some chocolate truffles filled with cream and passed them out among her neighbors. One was given to Ruth, who put it away in the refrigerator. When Annie came home that day, she found the treat and took a bite. Finding it bitter, she dropped the rest to the floor. An hour later she was in extreme agony with stomach pains; minutes after that, she was dead.

The police were called. They arrived to find the family dog also dead. He had eaten the rest of the truffle from the floor. Forensic scientists could at first find no trace of any known poison. A university scientist finally detected a new organic phosphorus compound known as E-605, used as a chemical insecticide, in Hamann's body.

At her friend's funeral Lehmann wept copiously. She was at that time under surveillance by the police, who suspected her but could see no motive. The other truffles dispensed had produced no ill effects. After checking Christa's background and coming across the now suspicious deaths of her husband and father-in-law, the police finally moved to take her into custody.

The case broke on February 23, 1954, when Lehmann called a priest to her cell and confessed to delivering the poison truffle. Christa intended, she said, to kill Ruth and not her friend Annie. She casually added, "By the way, I also poisoned my father-in-law, and I killed my husband, too" [1]. Christa had bought the new insecticide from a pharmacy in Worms.

On September 24, 1954, Lehamnn was convicted and sentenced to life in prison.

Sources

1. Nash, Jay Robert. *Look for the Woman*. New York: M. Evans, 1981, pp. 249–51.

Anjette Lyles

(1925–1977). *Place:* Macon, Georgia. *Time:* 1952–1958. *Age:* 27–33. *Victims:* 4. *Method:* Arsenic poisoning.

Anjette Lyles was a popular and well-liked restaurant owner in Macon, Georgia, during the 1950s. The restaurant was well patronized, and some of Macon's most powerful people often stopped in for a meal. When it was determined that Anjette had murdered four times over a six-year period, no one wanted to believe it. The chief investigating officer recalled his quarry as "a nice woman. She had black, graying hair, a nice smile and a good personality" [1]. Lyles was then twice widowed and just over 30.

By 1952, Anjette had been married to Ben F. Lyles, Jr., for several years and was the mother of two small daughters. Lyles's father was a prominent Macon restaurant operator for years. On his death in 1945, Ben took over the establishment and ran it until the middle of 1951, when he sold the café. On January 25, 1952, Ben Lyles died suddenly. Anjette bought the business back and operated it as "Anjette's Restaurant." A man by the name of Joe Neal Gabbert, a pilot with Capitol Airways, soon became Anjette's second husband. Joe died suddenly on December 2, 1955. Anjette reverted to using the name Lyles after his death. Anjette's mother-in-law, Julia Lyles, who lived with her, died suddenly on September 29, 1957.

Victim number four was the woman's eldest daughter, Marcia Elaine, who was nine years old when she was hospitalized in March 1958. On April 4 of that year, Marcia died. This time the authorities were warned about what was to happen but decided not to act. About three weeks before Marcia died, two of Anjette's aunts—sisters of Julia—who lived in nearby Cochran, Georgia, received a couple of anonymous letters. One read, in part, "Please come at once. She's [Marcia] getting the same dose as the others. Please come at once" [10]. Nothing was done, due to the "sketchiness" of the information.

One aunt went to the authorities about the letter but was shunted from coroner to police to sheriff. After the child's death, one of the waitresses at the restaurant began to get sick. She believed it was related to cups of coffee Lyles was giving her; every time she had a coffee from her employer she felt worse. When this woman went to the authorities, a full investigation was launched. The police never revealed who wrote the anonymous letters but speculated that it was a restaurant employee who had become fond of the child from her visits to the restaurant and who was suspicious of Anjette's behavior.

On April 25, 1958, all four bodies were exhumed and all four were found to contain arsenic. Anjette was soon arrested after a motive was established. Chief investigator Harry Harris said, "The telephone never stopped ringing when we arrested her. We got several calls telling us to lay off the case. The public was really interested in it" [2].

The arrest itself created a stir when Sheriff James Wood announced that they had taken four bottles of an arsenic-based ant poison, plus a load of paraphernalia Wood described as "voodoo equipment," from Anjette's house. Three of the four bottles of poison were empty, and the fourth was half empty. Discovered in the bedroom were several small containers labeled "Egyptian Love Powder Incense," "Lucky Sweetheart," "Good Luck," "Sweet Spirit of Nitre," "Love Potion," "Adam and Eve Root in Oil," and "Highly Perfumed Sprinkle Salt." Burnt and unburnt candles were also found, as well as a handwritten recipe that read, in part, "Dragon blood on top of heat, then put in pan. . . . As a cupid shoots his arrow . . . into the heart into the one he loves I am shooting this arrow into your heart." Wood found a man's picture in a blue sock pinned under Lyles's bed. A second picture of this same man was contained in one of Anjette's stockings in her dresser. Wood said he knew who the man was, and it wasn't one of the woman's husbands [10].

This man's identity was never revealed, but it may have been Bob Franks, a Capitol pilot, who came forward after Anjette's arrest. Franks was dating Lyles, whom he found "very attractive and affectionate. At pretty well every hotel I stayed as I flew around she would telephone me, even overseas," he said. "But I never accepted any of her calls. . . . I got the idea she was looking for another husband. In fact, it was pretty obvious. But I don't know if she picked me. We never discussed matrimony" [3].

Anjette's only comment after her arrest was, "I have committed no crime." The break came when police found a person who had helped Lyles forge several documents to gain her victims' money. Lyles's finances were jumbled, to say the least. Her home had been purchased in April 1957 for $20,000, with Anjette assuming a $10,000 mortgage. Immediately she issued a woman a mortgage of $9,000 more on the home. The next month she mortgaged her restaurant property and equipment for $10,500. According to police Lyles benefitted financially from the four murders to the tune of $40,000 to $50,000.

Witnesses reported that on numerous occasions Anjette had been observed carrying ant poison in her purse. While Lyles claimed the poison was for use in her restaurant, employees could not recall it ever being used for that purpose. Carrie Jackson, an employee of the restaurant, testified that when Marcia was in the hospital she had observed Lyles prepare lemonade for her child and then carry it into the restaurant washroom with something in a brown paper bag before she left for the hospital. A second employee reported the same thing. Jackson also reported seeing Anjette take buttermilk and something in a brown paper bag to Julia Lyles while Julia was in the hospital. According to Jackson, Lyles told her Marcia would die a day or two after the child entered the hospital.

A former waitress at Anjette's Restaurant, Cleo Hutchinson, testified that two or three months before Marcia's death, she and her husband had seen Lyles grab Marcia, shake and curse her, compare her to her dead grandmother, and tell the child that she hated her and would kill her "if it's the last thing I do." The provocation for that outburst was Marcia asking her mother for some money to buy something. When her second husband Gabbert was in the hospital, Lyles told Cleo he was going to die. She said the same thing to Cleo when the waitress visited Marcia in the hospital. By then Anjette had packed up all the girl's clothes and removed flowers from the room, even though the child was still alive [7]. Anjette purchased a casket for Marcia a few days before her death.

Lyles went on trial in October 1958 on one count of murder—that of her daughter Marcia. She never confessed, although an investigator said, "The first thing she said to us was that she knew nothing about it. She wavered several times but would never come across that thin line. A couple of times she came to the edge. She said she might be able to talk, but she would have to see her attorney first. Naturally, he told her not to talk" [2].

It took the jury just 90 minutes to convict Lyles of murder. Since she was sentenced to die in the electric chair, the other three murder indictments were left pending and never pursued. After the trial, an insanity hearing was held. Lyles was ruled insane and transferred from death row to Central State Hospital in Milledgeville in 1960. Anjette Lyles died in that institution in December 1977, from natural causes at the age of 52. This ended a case considered "the most sensational in Macon since World War II" [1].

Sources

1. Bolton, Philip. "Poisoner of Child Is Dead." *Macon Telegraph and News,* December 5, 1977.

2. Freeman, Scott. "Chain of Coincidences Broke Infamous Poison Caper." *Macon Telegraph and News,* July 12, 1958, pp. 1A, 6A.

3. Landry, George. "State Can Show Intent to Kill in Arsenic Deaths, Wood Says." *Macon Telegraph and News,* May 11, 1958, p. 1.

4. "Mrs. Lyles' Cafe, Home Mortaged." *Macon Telegraph and News,* May 9, 1958, p. 1.

5. Poisoning Given as Cause of Marcia Lyles Death." *Macon Telegraph and News,* June 17, 1958, p. 1A.

6. Tribble, Bill. "Court Is Told Arsenic Found in Four Bodies." *Macon Telegraph and News,* May 15, 1958, p. 1A.

7. Tribble, Bill. "Judge Defers Final Ruling on 3 Counts." *Macon Telegraph and News,* May 16, 1958, pp. 1A, 16A.

8. Tribble, Bill. "Mrs. Anjette Lyles Faces Hearings Today in Court on Four Murder Charges." *Macon Telegraph and News,* May 14, 1958, p. 1A.

9. Tribble, Bill. "Mrs. Lyles Held in Deaths." *Macon Telegraph and News,* May 7, 1958, p. 1A.

10. Tribble, Bill. "Voodoo Material Is Found in Lyles Home, Sheriff Says." *Macon Telegraph and News,* May 9, 1958, p. 1A.

Alma May McAninch

(1902–1937). *Place:* Norwalk, Iowa. *Time:* October 30, 1937. *Age:* 35. *Victims:* 6. *Method:* Firearm.

Growing up in the American heartland, Alma May followed the traditional path of marrying young and having many children. Poverty was ever present in her life, and her husband had scrapes with the law. Alma grew more worried and more depressed. It all ended in a bloody spree of murder.

In Spring Hill, Iowa, where Alma May was born, they remembered her as a happy, pretty girl who "took up with" Gurness McAninch when she was very young. The couple married in 1920. Gurness was about seven years older than his wife. McAninch worked for a farmer for a couple of years after the wedding and then left to work a farm of his own in northern Iowa. Apparently this didn't work out, since Gurness turned to a variety of semiskilled jobs in various parts of the state. Often he was out of work. The family lived in Des Moines around 1935, then moved on to Jamaica, Iowa, and then in December 1936, they moved into a tumble-down five-room shack in Norwalk. By then Alma May had seven children to look after. She was also pregnant with her eighth.

Pressures had become too much for Alma May. She worried about money constantly; there was never enough. Although the house they lived in was wired for electricity, the McAninchs used kerosene lamps, probably to save a little money. Scarcely a month after the family moved to Norwalk, Alma slipped on some ice and fell. She lost the baby. A neighbor, Mrs. Wendell Anderson, said, "After that Mrs. McAninch seemed to give up. She just sat and stared. Her children had to look after themselves. Often, when I would speak to her, Mrs. McAninch didn't seem to hear me. She wouldn't answer" [2].

Alma's family also noticed her despondency. According to her oldest son, 15-year-old Ray, his mother had threatened to kill herself on several occasions "if it wasn't for you kids." In the summer of 1937 Gurness was arrested on minor charges. He told the sheriff that he was worried his wife would commit suicide. The sheriff went to the McAninch home and took away the family's shotgun. Gurness was in jail only a short time.

203

Early in October 1937, the next oldest son, 11-year-old Gail, went to a neighbor to borrow a single-shot shotgun and some shells. He and Ray were planning to do some hunting at the end of the month. Alma used up all the shells shooting at tin cans in the backyard. Neighbors described her as an excellent shot.

On the morning of October 30, 1937, Ray borrowed six shotgun shells from neighbors because he and Gail planned to go hunting the next day. That afternoon Gurness was arrested again and jailed. He was booked on charges on breaking and entering. Alma protested little at this turn of events. In fact, after her husband was taken away, neighbors said Alma seemed happier than she had been in a long time. Ray and Gail had been watchful of their mother because of her suicide threats, but went out to visit friends that evening, convinced she was feeling better. They checked in to see her at 8 P.M. and left again when all seemed fine.

If Alma had seemed happier, it must have been only because she had decided what she was going to do. Just before midnight, she went to her children's beds and killed them one by one with the shotgun. Each was killed with a single shot at close range between the eyes. Then Alma killed herself with a similar shot. Neighbors heard nothing, and authorities speculated that the close-up shots into the beds somehow had a silencing effect.

Ray and Gail returned home at midnight to discover the bodies. They found their mother still holding the shotgun in her arms. They survived only because Alma had just six shells. The dead children were daughters Cora Belle, 13; and Geraldine, 10; and sons Morris, 6; Max, 4; and Dickie, 2.

A contemporary newspaper account said, "The wound in each case was almost exactly similar — a hole just above the bridge of the nose, between the eyes, about the size of a silver dollar. The brain of each was blown to bits" [2]. There was no sign of a struggle. It appeared that the children didn't know what was happening. With the exception of a rope swing on the front porch and a battered red coaster wagon, they had had no toys.

On a table in the house, next to a Bible opened to a passage from Exodus, Alma left a suicide note addressed to Ray and Gail. It gave them specific instructions about which neighbor to go and stay with temporarily and to inform the doctor, undertaker, grandparents, and so on. The note read, in part, "You will find us dead. Don't get excited. . . . Tell Dad I sure want him to go straight for you boys' sake. I have stood all I can take and best to take the kids along. All that saves you boys is no more shells" [3].

A grief-stricken Gurness was released from jail long enough to attend the funeral. "I was afraid something like this would happen," he said. "My wife hasn't been right for some time" [2]. A grave seven feet long and 20 feet wide was dug so that the family could be buried together. Mourners numbered about 500—more than the population of Norwalk. The mourners were allowed to view the open caskets and, in single file, they took over an hour to file past the six biers.

Sources

1. "500 Mourners Attend Rites." *Des Moines Register,* November 3, 1937, p. 6.

2. Grant, Donald. "Had a Feeling Mate Would Kill Children." *Des Moines Register,* November 1, 1937, pp. 1, 4.

3. "2 Sons Watch Woman Blast Own Life Out." *Des Moines Sunday Register,* October 31, 1937, pp. 1, 5.

Carol MacDonald

(1923–). *Place:* Mahwah, New Jersey. *Time:* May 3, 1953. *Age:* 29. *Victims:* 4. *Method:* Asphyxiation from auto exhaust.

Carol Tiedeman grew up in a socially prominent family in Mahwah, New Jersey. She graduated from Barnard College and then married Kenneth MacDonald, a star football player for Rutgers University in the early 1940s. The couple prospered financially. By 1953 they owned an expensive house with an attached two-car garage on one acre of land in a fashionable area of Mahwah. They also had four young children: Sharon, seven; Bruce, five; Katherine, three; and Thomas, two.

The marriage, however, was rocky. For several years before 1953 the couple had from time to time consulted Dr. Charles Taylor, a New York psychiatrist, in an effort to save the marriage. On February 3, 1953, Carol and Kenneth finally separated when Kenneth accused his wife of having an affair with a man in a New York hotel. Carol denied the charge. Kenneth was devoted to his children; he visited them regularly and often took them out. Friction developed over visitation rights because Carol objected to Kenneth visiting them at her home. She was also very despondent over the pending divorce.

Late on the evening of May 2, 1953, Carol made several phone calls: to her husband, her brother, her parents, and a New York newspaper. It is unclear how many of these calls got through. When she phoned the paper, Carol asked how to "give a story." She was told that a caller had only to ask for the city desk. Near midnight Carol woke up her four sleeping children, put warm clothes on over their pajamas, and loaded them into the family station wagon, which was parked in the garage. Noticing that the vehicle was almost out of gas, she drove to a nearby gas station, filled the tank, and returned to the garage. Parking the car with the children still inside and the motor running, Carol closed the garage doors and entered the house.

Once inside, Carol wrote six suicide notes, the contents of which were not divulged except to say the notes expressed a desire to "protect the children from disgrace." Sometime near 3 A.M. Carol returned to the garage to sit for an unknown length of time on the car's running board. Suddenly she changed her mind about killing the children. She dragged all the bodies out of the car and lay them on the garage floor, except for Thomas, whom she carried back into the house and put in his crib. It was too late; all four children were dead. Carol reached her brother on the telephone at 6 A.M., and he then alerted the police.

Police described Carol as "distraught" when they took her into custody. Carol told the authorities that she planned to take her own life as well but had failed in the attempt. The reason she gave for killing her children was the same one contained in her notes — to "save them from the disgrace" of the divorce suit Kenneth was bringing.

Sources

1. "Jersey Mother Kills Four Young Children." *New York Times,* May 4, 1953, pp. 1, 44.

2. "Mother Held in Killing of 4 Faces Mental Test." *New York Herald-Tribune,* May 5, 1953, p. 25.

Sarah Malcolm

(1711–1733). *Place:* London, England. *Time:* February 4, 1733. *Age:* 22.
Victims: 3. *Method:* Strangulation, stabbing.

Born in 1711 in Durham, England, Sarah Malcolm had a financially
more secure childhood than most. Her father had a small income from an
estate. When she was a young girl the family moved to Dublin, where Mr.
Malcolm was financially successful. Sarah received an education superior
to that which most young women received at the time. Some years later the
Malcolms moved to London, where Mrs. Malcolm died. When Mr. Malcolm remarried, Sarah and her new stepmother didn't get along, resulting
in Sarah leaving home, permanently estranged from her father.

Without financial resources, Sarah was suddenly forced to support
herself. She turned to work as a domestic servant; she comported herself
well and was commended for her diligence and sobriety by many of her
employers. One place she worked as a servant was a bar called the Black
Horse, where she made the acquaintance of Mary Tracey and two young
men who were brothers, Thomas and James Alexander. Among Malcolm's
employers early in 1733 was a Mr. Kerril; she took care of his laundry and
looked after his chambers. Lydia Duncomb, 80, also employed Sarah as a
laundress. Duncomb had two live-in servants, Elizabeth Harrison, 60, and
Ann Price, 17, as well. Apparently Sarah was not a live-in servant, but
worked for a number of different people at the same time.

On the evening of February 3, 1733, Sarah called at Mrs. Duncomb's
rooms ostensibly to visit Harrison, who was recovering from a bout of sickness. The real reason was to steal a key to the door or to alter the lock for
easier admittance later that night. Duncomb was rumored to be very
wealthy; it was thought that by robbing Duncomb, Sarah hoped to attract
one of the Alexanders as a husband by using her newly acquired wealth.

Early the next day, friends of Duncomb became worried when they got
no answer after repeatedly knocking on her door. When they finally entered
by breaking a window they found all the occupants in their beds: Duncomb
and Harrison were strangled to death, and Price's throat was cut from ear
to ear. The box in which Duncomb kept her valuables lay open and empty
on the floor.

Soon all the neighbors were discussing the murders. One of them was Kerril. When he returned home that morning from a coffeehouse, he found Sarah at work lighting a fire. During their discussion, Kerril and his friends had decided the killer must have been known to the victims, perhaps a servant. With that in mind Kerril said to Malcolm, "Nobody who was acquainted with Mrs. Duncomb shall be in my chambers, till the murderer is discovered; and therefore look up your things and be gone" [1].

As Malcolm was preparing to leave, Kerril discovered that two of his waistcoats were missing. When he asked Malcolm about them, she admitted she had taken them and pawned them. Begging for forgiveness, she promised she would redeem them. Observing a bundle on the floor, Kerril asked what it was. Sarah told him it was her gown and some linen tied up, and she hoped he would have the decency not to open it. Kerril let the incident pass. When he was gone, however, he found more of his clothes missing. Immediately she sent two watchmen out to secure her. A further search turned up strange linen in his apartment that wasn't his, as well as an unknown silver tankard with blood on it.

By then, Sarah was arrested. She explained that the objects were hers, left to her by her mother. The blood was the result of a cut she sustained on her finger. Put in prison, Sarah was searched by turnkey Roger Johnson who found a bag containing money concealed in her hair. Admitting to Johnson that the money was Duncomb's, Sarah said, "But Mr. Johnson, I'll make you a present of it, if you will but keep it to yourself, and let nobody know any thing of the matter; for the other things against me are nothing but circumstances, and I shall come off well enough" [1]. She also told Johnson she paid a couple of men a small amount of money to say that the tankard belonged to her mother. Later she told the turnkey that she had contrived the robbery but had three accomplices who committed the robbery and murders while she just watched from the stairs.

During her trial, Sarah insisted that it was Mary Tracey along with the Alexander brothers who were responsible. The jury didn't believe her. After deliberating for just 15 minutes, they returned a verdict of guilty for all three murders. Malcolm never admitted guilt for the murders. On March 7, 1733, Sarah Malcolm was publicly executed in London's Fleet Street. For the most part she was resigned and composed as the cart drove her to the execution site, although she did faint once. As she stepped from the cart she looked skyward and cried out, "Oh my master, my master! I wish I could see him" [1]. Then she called upon Christ to receive her soul.

Sources

1. Hogg, Alexander. *The Malefactor's Register*, vol. 2. London, 1779, pp. 251–64.

Martha Marek

(1904–1938). *Place:* Vienna, Austria. *Time:* 1932–1936. *Age:* 28–32. *Victims:* 4. *Method:* Thallium poisoning.

Martha enjoyed the good things in life and was determined to have them. When her money ran out, she coldly turned to mass poisoning to feed her greed and elaborate life-style. She was born Martha Lowenstein in Vienna, Austria, in 1904 to unknown parents. As a young foundling, Martha was adopted by a poor family in Vienna and raised in apparent poverty. She began to work in a dress shop at the age of 15 and was considered quite beautiful. One day an old man entered the store, and Martha's life changed forever.

The old man, Moritz Fritsch, was very rich. Smitten with the young clerk, he soon invited Martha to be his ward, a euphemism of the time for mistress. Lowenstein quickly accepted and just as quickly came to enjoy a life of luxury. The best of clothes came her way; Fritsch even sent her to a finishing school in London where she mingled with the elite and further strengthed her taste for luxury.

Moritz died in 1923 or 1924 at the age of 74. The young ward was his chief beneficiary, inheriting his money and house. This enraged Fritsch's relatives, but Martha prevailed. Before the old man died, Martha had been having an affair with a young engineering student by the name of Emil Marek. The couple married in 1924. They rapidly spent all of her inheritance and then ran up debts. They sold the house and used up those proceeds.

Desperate and broke, the couple hatched a bizarre scheme. Emil insured himself for the equivalent of about $30,000 in case of accident. Soon after he did have an accident. Emil was chopping down a tree with an axe and was later found with one leg almost severed. It was an accident, said Emil; the axe slipped. The leg had to be amputated below the knee.

When doctors examined him, they found three separate wounds at angles that could not have been self-inflicted. It was Martha who had wielded the axe. To make matters worse, Martha bribed a hospital orderly to say he had seen a doctor altering the state of the wounds. The Mareks were charged with fraud and bribery. Found not guilty on the former, they were convicted on the latter charge and sentenced to four months in prison. They settled with the insurance company and received about $9,000.

Over the next few years, the couple struggled along. They moved to Algiers, where they tried and failed in a business venture. When they returned to Vienna they were destitute. By this time they also had two children. For a time Martha had to sell vegetables from a cart in the street.

Suddenly, in the summer of 1932, Emil died of what was said to be tuberculosis. About a month later the couple's youngest child, a daughter, also died. Both yielded insurance money to Martha. Neither death aroused any suspicion. Within a year or so Martha had accepted a position as a companion to Susanne Lowenstein, an elderly relative. This woman died in short order after experiencing difficulty in swallowing and numbness in her legs. The same symptoms had appeared in Emil and the daughter.

Martha inherited Susanne's money and went on another spending spree; her son was then in boarding school. The money ran out within a couple of years, and Martha rented out rooms to make some extra cash. One of her boarders, Frau Kittenberger, died suddenly. She had been insured before her death, with Marek as the beneficiary. However, the amount was a paltry $900.

Still needing money, Martha tired another scam in 1937. She took some of the paintings out of her house and hid them. Then she reported these "valuable" paintings to the police as stolen, hoping for insurance money. Such a thin ruse failed completely, and there was no insurance settlement. In fact, Martha was thrown in jail.

Frau Kittenberger's son had been complaining to the police that his mother had died of foul play at Martha's hands. Coupled with her shady background, which came out during the painting scam, this caused the police to dig deeper. Kittenberger's body was exhumed, and then those of Susanne, Emil, and the daughter. All contained thallium, a deadly, tasteless, odorless form of rat poison. It was later shown that Martha had bought the poison from a local druggist.

A check was made of the son at boarding school. He was sick and slowly dying from thallium poisoning from food Martha had prepared for him during his visits. He later recovered. Martha was tried and convicted of all the murders except that of her daughter. Her lawyer said she was insane, but a court psychiatrist declared that "although the woman was hysterical and morally subnormal, she was fully responsible for her actions" [4]. On December 6, 1938, she was executed, beheaded by an axe.

Sources

1. Green, Jonathon. *The Greatest Criminals of All Time.* New York: Stein & Day, 1980, pp. 230–31.

2. Nash, Jay Robert. *Look for the Woman*. New York: M. Evans, 1981, pp. 275–77.

3. Wilson, Colin. *Encyclopedia of Murder*. New York: Putnam, 1962, pp. 376–78.

4. "Vienna Murderess Convicted." *The Times* [London], May 21, 1938, p. 16.

Rhonda Belle Martin

(1907–1957). *Place:* Montgomery and Mobile, Alabama. *Time:* c. 1934–1951. *Age:* 27–44. *Victims:* c. 6–8. *Method:* Arsenic poisoning.

When Rhonda Belle Martin was arrested on Friday, March 9, 1956, a little after 3 P.M., she was coming off her shift as a waitress at the Seabreeze Restaurant in Mobile, Alabama. As a part-time waitress working from 11 A.M. to 3 P.M., Rhonda made $9 a week plus about $2 a day in tips. After a long investigation, the police wished to talk to her about a series of eight suspicious deaths in Mobile and Montgomery that had occurred from 1934 to 1951. All of these victims had suffered searing abdominal pains and acute diarrhea before death—classic signs of arsenic poisoning.

Just hours after her arrest, the city editor of the *Montgomery Advertiser,* Joe Azbell, spent a few hours interviewing her—the first civilian to do so, he said. He found the suspect wearing wedding bands on both hands, her own on the left, and her fifth husband's on her right. It was the protracted illness of husband number five—one of her victims—which started the investigation that led to Martin's arrest. Rhonda told the editor that she never dated a man she didn't marry.

Azbell described the 49-year-old as "a plain woman with a rather kindly appearance. Four large moles stand out on her face, three on the cheek and one above the eye, and there is a circle of pock marks from pimples to her mouth line. She wears false uppers, modern brown-rimmed glasses. Her 170 pounds is shaped well for a woman of her age. Her fingernails are painted a fire-engine red and her eyebrows are streaked with black shade lines. The rouge on her face was light against a faint, pasty powder. Dime-store earrings, three clusters of flower buds, hung from her pierced ears. She had a hard stare in her dark eyes but her voice was tired and sugar-coated" [3].

Rhonda was born in Lucedale, Mississippi, in 1907, the daughter of a sawmill worker who deserted his family when Rhonda was 12. Prior to that the family had moved to Mobile, Alabama. Martin lived there or in Montgomery, Alabama, for the rest of her life. School ended for the girl when she dropped out at the age of 15. At the time her mother operated a Mobile boarding home. One of the lodgers made eyes at the teenager, and soon she

213

was married to W. R. Alderman, an upholsterer by trade. Four years later, when she was 19, Rhonda got a divorce. Two years later she dated and then married a next-door neighbor who worked for the railroad, George Garrett. After a 12-year union, George died. The couple had five children, all of whom were either dead at the time of George's demise, or would be soon after. Her next husband was Talmadge Gibson, an attendant at a V.A. hospital. Five months after the wedding, Rhonda divorced him.

Over the years Martin worked at a variety of jobs, usually as a waitress in coffee shops. She had also been a sheet-metal worker during World War II and a factory hand at Hazel-Atlas Glass Company. While working at the glass factory Rhonda met and married fellow employee Claude Martin, a widower with four children. The wedding took place after just a few dates, in 1949. About 18 months later, in February 1951, Claude became seriously ill. According to Rhonda, "I never had an argument with him" during the marriage. Claude was so ill that his son Ronald was called home from the U.S. Navy in which he was then serving. Claude died in April. A few years earlier Rhonda's 60-year-old mother had also died.

In December 1951, Ronald Martin, 21, married his step-mother Rhonda, then 44, after a courtship of a few months. Such a union is considered incest in Alabama and is a violation of state law. Claude's other three children were girls in their late teens. All of them were irate at the marriage and moved out of the family home in protest. Over four years later Lorraine, one of the daughters said, "We didn't like it when they got married and we don't like it now" [5]. She added that "she didn't blame him for the marriage," for Rhonda "could do almost anything with him" [4].

Around the middle of 1955 Ronald became seriously ill. Doctors couldn't determine what was wrong. Ronald continued to worsen, and eventually was confined to a hospital because of partial paralysis—a classic symptom of arsenic poisoning—a condition from which he would never recover. Finally a physician sent off a few strands of Ronald's hair for analysis. The results indicated arsenic in his body. Authorities began an investigation which led to the exhumation of Claude Martin's remains. There was enough arsenic in him to kill several men. Rhonda was taken into custody.

During that interview with Azbell, the suspect maintained her complete innocence. The first death was that of four-year-old Mary Garrett, in 1934, whom Rhonda said died of pneumonia. She was an "afflicted" child who never talked or walked, claimed the mother. Emogene Garrett, three, died on July 19, 1937, of what her mother said was a heart attack. The death certificate listed cause of death as "accidental poisoning." During 1939 one-year-old daughter Judith and 35-year-old George Garrett both expired of, according to Rhonda, jaundice and pneumonia respectively. Ann, six, died in 1940 of a throat disorder. Ellyn, 11, died on August 1, 1943, of a stomach disorder. Rhonda's mother died in 1944 of what she said were "infirmities."

Rhonda explained that Ronald, whom she sometimes called Bud, first got sick in June with "ulcers." He worked off and on until October, when he had several X-rays taken during a short hospital stay. Following this he had a "nervous breakdown" and was nursed at home by Rhonda. In December he returned to the hospital. Ronald told his wife about doctors taking strands of his hair, but they told him it was to test for a nervous disorder. No mention was made of testing for arsenic.

Speaking of her arrest, Rhonda said, "I know Bud will be heart-broken when he finds out what happened to me. I went to see him Thursday night at the hospital and he was glad to see me and hated to see me go. . . . I love him so much. He's a good-looking man. He's young: five foot seven, 135 pounds and has blond hair. We've been so happy together. My three step-daughters were mad when we told them we were getting married but they got over that. . . . If Bud ever thought I did anything to him, he never mentioned it. He is so sweet and good, my Bud. . . . You know what I regret. It's that Ronald and I couldn't have children. We both wanted children but we couldn't have any. I regret that so much" [3]. Explaining why she was wearing her husband's wedding band in addition to her own, Martin said it was because Ronald's hand was paralyzed and he wanted it this way.

Maintaining her innocence, Rhonda said, "If they say I poisoned anyone, they're wrong. I have never had a touch of poison in my hand in my life. There has never been any in my home. . . . Everybody always said I spoiled my husbands and everybody always said I spoiled my children. That's the way I am. I always spoil anybody I love" [3].

The reason she married Ronald, she said, was that on his deathbed Claude asked Ronald to take care of her. Money was not a factor in any of the deaths. George Garrett and the children only had burial policies in place. Rhonda did get $2,000 in insurance money on Claude's death. However, she immediately spent $400 of it to move Claude's first wife from her resting place to a spot beside Claude because he would have wanted it that way. When arrested she had $34 in her purse, which she said was all the money she had in the world.

The woman's favorite reading material was pulp romance and detective magazines. It was in one of these that she read of a movie star's marriage to a step-child being annulled, which gave her pause to think that her own union to Ronald might not be legitimate. The only times she had been in jail in her life were on two occasions in 1956; once for reckless driving, and once for being drunk. Her own health was not what it could be. "I still have a weak heart, very weak, and I can't stand excitement" [3].

Musing over her tragedies and the future, Martin told the newsman, "I'm a poor woman. I've had more than my share of tragedy. Somebody

I loved dying almost every year. I always thought if Bud didn't come through his sickness, I would never marry again. I always wanted a home but it looks like every time I get married, there's some tragedy. . . . I always tried to be a good Christian but I haven't been to church in a long time. I think I will start going again regular when all of this is over" [3].

Three days after her arrest, Rhonda confessed to poisoning six of the dead, as well as Ronald. She purchased arsenic-based ant poison at grocery and drug stores from "time to time." This she placed in liquids such as coffee, milk, and whiskey. Rhonda would always deny any involvement in the deaths of her daughters Mary and Judith, claiming they both expired from natural causes. Authorities exhumed the bodies of George Garrett and Ellyn. Both contained arsenic. When Lorraine learned of this development, her only comment was, "She's just crazy. That's all" [5].

The first murder Rhonda admitted to was that of Emogene. The poisoner told authorities her daughter was playing in the yard with her toys. She came to her mother to ask for a drink of water. On the spur of the moment Rhonda poured poison into milk and gave the drink to her daughter. The child died in short order. Her second husband George had arsenic fed to him in his whiskey over a period of several days. When he came home ill from work one day, Rhonda allowed him to stagger around in the yard before she soothed him. Then she took him inside to feed him another shot of arsenic-laced whiskey. George died the next day.

The daughter Ann got her poison mixed into milk; she too expired quickly. Ellyn lasted much longer; Rhonda fed her poisoned milk for almost a year. Before she finally died, Ellyn became crippled. Prior to administering the final, lethal dose, Rhonda expressed much grief to neighbors that Ellyn had lost the use of her limbs. Rhonda's mother was fed poisoned coffee over the space of a year. She also became a helpless invalid before she died. Claude Martin received arsenic in his coffee at every meal over a three-month period. Ronald got poisoned coffee for two months.

Investigators asked their poisoner how she was able to escape detection over such a long period of time. Rhonda explained that she never used the same doctor twice. While money was not a factor in the killings, the authorities did uncover the fact that Rhonda had set up a couple of mailbox addresses in Mobile. At one she received a Social Security check as Claude's widow even though she wasn't entitled to it, since she had remarried. The other box was set up in the hopes of collecting a check when Ronald died.

Perplexed by the apparent lack of a motive, the authorities speculated that Rhonda suffered from a "severe complex that no one wanted her around and this led to the poison murders." She was emotionally insecure resulting from her father deserting the family. Lingering methods of poisoning were employed, they thought, because Rhonda was "fascinated by the effects of the poison." The investigators all agreed the woman had a superior intelligence [1].

At the end of her confession, Rhonda requested a minister. When he arrived the pair prayed for "some time." After confessing Rhonda told the police, "I feel like a cloud of fear has been lifted now that I have been caught." In the police station corridors, reporters asked if she had any motive for the murders to which Rhonda replied, "No . . . no" [1].

Sentenced to death for the murder of Claude Martin, Rhonda was electrocuted early in the morning of October 11, 1957. For her final meal she had hamburger, mashed potatoes, cinnamon rolls, and coffee. She went to her death calmly and quietly.

Some time before her execution Rhonda left a note requesting, "At my death, whether it be a natural death or otherwise, I want my body to be given to some scientific institution to be used as they see fit, but especially to see if someone can find out why I committed the crimes I have committed. I can't understand it, for I had no reason whatsoever. There is definitely something wrong. Can't someone find it and save someone else the agony I have been through" [8]. The request was not honored. Rhonda was buried in an unmarked grave in the same cemetery that housed her victims.

Sources

1. Azbell, Joe. "Grand Jury to Review Waitress' Case in May." *Montgomery Advertiser,* March 15, 1956, pp. 1A, 2A.

2. Azbell, Joe. "Graves of Martin Family Due to Be Opened Today." *Montgomery Advertiser,* March 12, 1956, pp. 1A, 2A.

3. Azbell, Joe. "Jailed Waitress Vows Innocence in Mate's Death." *Montgomery Advertiser,* March 11, 1956, pp. 1A, 5A.

4. Azbell, Joe. "2 Bodies Exhumed Here to Test Cause of Death." *Montgomery Advertiser,* March 13, 1956, pp. 1A, 2A.

5. Azbell, Joe. "Waitress Admits Guilt in Seven Poison Cases." *Montgomery Advertiser,* March 14, 1956, pp. 1A, 2A.

6. "Governor Holds Murderess' Fate." *Montgomery Advertiser,* October 10, 1957, pp. 1A, 2A.

7. Swietnicki, Ed. "Mrs. Martin's Life Ends in Kilby's Electric Chair." *Montgomery Advertiser,* October 11, 1957, pp. 1A, 6A.

8. "Waitress' Final Wish Rejected by Relatives." *Montgomery Advertiser,* October 12, 1957, pp. 1A, 10A.

Daisy Louisa de Melker

(1886–1932). *Place:* Johannesburg, South Africa. *Time:* 1923–1932. *Age:* 37–46. *Victims:* 3. *Method:* Strychnine and arsenic poisoning.

Lust for money seems the only possible reason for Daisy de Melker to have poisoned two of her husbands, for she admitted they were not bad men. They did not abuse her. "Honest, thrifty, hard-working husbands" was how she described them [1]. Money may also partly explain her decision to murder her son; however, that relationship was marked by much animosity. Since she never admitted her guilt, her motives remain a source of speculation. Like other female mass murderers, she waited a long time — 14 years in her first marriage — before she struck for the first time.

Born on June 1, 1886, near Grahamstown, South Africa, Daisy Hancorn-Smith grew into an attractive girl who never had any trouble making friends. At the age of 12 she moved with her family to live in Bulawayo, Rhodesia. A few years later she was sent to a boarding school at Cape Town. After a couple of years there, Daisy returned to Bulawayo for another year and then left for Durban, where she entered the Berea Nursing School there. In 1907 she qualified as a nurse.

Prior to her graduation from nursing school, Daisy had met and fallen in love with a civil servant named Bert Fuller. The marriage was scheduled for October 1907, but had to be postponed when Fuller couldn't get leave from his job. Daisy went on to Johannesburg alone and settled into her aunt's boarding house in the suburb of Troyeville to await the wedding, which was rescheduled for March 3, 1908. Unfortunately, Fuller contracted a disease; Daisy attended him at his deathbed instead of the altar on that March day. Bert left a will bequeathing £236 to Daisy.

When Daisy was boarding at her aunt's she became friends with another boarder, William Cowle, a 36-year-old plumber who worked for the city of Johannesburg. They married on March 3, 1909. Five boys were born to the couple. The first were twins. Four died in infancy, and all exhibited symptoms of convulsions. Only Rhodes Cowle, born in June 1911, survived infancy.

Once Daisy came to trial, the authorities were flooded with anonymous letters accusing Daisy of poisoning her children. Beyond the convulsions —

218

a symptom of poisoning but also of other afflictions — there was no evidence to support the allegations. One woman did come forward to tell the police that one day after she complained to Daisy about what a burden her own retarded child was, the poisoner said, "Bring the child to me. I'll give you some white powder that will make it die" [1].

None of this was brought out at the trial, since the authorities feared it might prejudice their case. The police apparently made no investigation into the deaths of Daisy's children. From the three people Daisy is known to have killed, she got money after each death. It has not been recorded whether or not Daisy received any insurance money on the deaths of her offspring.

Cowle was described as a sober, industrious man and a devoted husband. He was greatly grieved by the deaths of his children. He lived quietly, did his work, pottered around his garden, and worked on the house in his spare time.

Three months after the wedding Cowle made a will in his wife's favor. Five years later a codicil was added whereby the proceeds from a life insurance policy were bequeathed to her. In September 1922, Daisy insured the life of Rhodes for £100. It was an endowment policy that matured on September 2, 1933, just after he turned 21, or at death. Daisy paid the weekly premiums herself. William Cowle didn't know it then, but he had only four months left to live.

Why Daisy waited so long to take up murder remains a mystery. However, on the morning of January 11, 1923, William drank a dose of Epsom salts prepared by Daisy just before he left the house for work. She had laced it with the poison strychnine. Soon he was doubled up in pain. Daisy quickly got a doctor and called in neighbors to comfort her. To one she cried, "Come over, my husband is dying." William lay in agony, sometimes lying rigid and sometimes wracked by convulsions. He foamed at the mouth. After arriving and hearing Cowle blame his illness on the salts, Dr. Pakes raced away for a stomach pump. It was too late, since Cowle died before his return.

The doctor refused to issue a death certificate; he told Daisy to inform the police and hand the salts over to them for analysis. Needless to say, Mrs. Cowle did not do this. Years later, at Daisy's trial, Dr. Pakes would testify that he suspected strychnine poison as the cause of death at the time. However, when the results of the postmortem were released a couple of days later he thought he had been mistaken, not realizing that no test was done for poisoning. A death certificate was issued listing the cause of death as chronic nephritis. Cowle had been in excellent health except for a minor kidney problem.

Daisy received about £1,800 from Cowle's estate. From 1923 to 1926 Daisy worked as a portress at the Johannesburg Children's Hospital for a wage between £8 and £10 a month. On January 1, 1926, Daisy married for the second time. The groom was a 46-year-old bachelor named Robert Sproat. He too was a plumber who worked for the city. Sproat was termed prudent and hard-working. In excellent health, he never missed a day of work until he hooked up with Daisy.

Not long after the marriage ceremony Daisy learned Robert's will was made out in favor of his mother. The new bride kept bringing up the matter of changing the will, but Robert never saw any immediate need to do it and kept putting it off. A little persuasion was in order.

One Sunday morning in October 1927, Sproat was in the garden talking to a neighbor, seemingly in good health. Just a few hours later he was in bed ripped by violent spasms and convulsions. A doctor was called in, who feared the worst. Robert's brother, William, came from Pretoria the next day since his death seemed imminent.

Daisy pestered William to speak to Robert about making out a new will. At first he refused because his brother was so ill, but finally he relented. He then informed his sister-in-law that her husband was going to write a new will. Daisy was prepared, though, and told William, "I've got a will here. He only needs to sign it" [1]. A neighbor was brought in to be the second witness. This woman suggested waiting, since Robert was so ill. Daisy insisted they get the will signed right then. William and the neighbor had to hold Robert up in bed so that he could scrawl his name on the document. Robert recovered slowly and was back at work after a week's absence.

He had no idea when he changed his will that he had signed his own death warrant. Three weeks later, on November 6, 1927, a doctor made an emergency call to the Sproat home to find Robert sprawled on the sofa only minutes from death. The physician thought death was due to a cerebral hemorrhage. In fact, Daisy had slipped her husband a dose of strychnine, probably in a glass of beer which, like the salts, would help to mask the bitter taste of the poison.

Daisy was so tight with money that when William Sproat suggested a postmortem his sister-in-law refused, saying, "Oh, not that! It will cost £7" [1]. Another sign of her miserliness was said to be that she never employed servants throughout her life. In South Africa, even working-class whites of modest means were expected to employ black servants, and usually did.

The day after Robert's death Daisy was in a lawyer's office to claim her inheritance which amounted to around £4,700 plus some real property. Apparently not satisfied, Daisy wrote to Robert's mother, Jane, in England, pleading poverty. She asked the elderly Mrs. Sproat for money because, she said, Robert's illness and funeral were expensive. Robert had also planned to take Rhodes on a trip to England. Would Mrs. Sproat pay for this? When Robert was ill visitors to his bedside had to be offered tea; "In these days every cup of tea counts," Daisy brazenly wrote to Jane.

As it happened, William had also been writing to his mother, and Jane knew that her daughter-in-law was well-off financially. Mrs. Sproat sent no money but passed Daisy's letter to William. An angry William confronted Daisy with the facts, which she denied, pleading misunderstanding on Mrs. Sproat's part, until William produced the letter. They parted bitterly that day, with William telling her he never wanted to see her again and to not put her foot in his house again. "Why?" puzzled Daisy.

Sixteen years old when Robert Sproat died, Rhodes was a problem. He had been spoiled by his mother, and it showed. Most of his education took place at boarding schools, where he did poorly academically. Sports were his only interest at such institutions. Daisy bought her son a motorcycle for his seventeenth birthday. It wasn't fancy enough, so Rhodes persuaded his mother to buy a more expensive one. She also bought him a car. A year later he wanted a fancier one. Mother complied.

Rhodes started work as a plumber's apprentice but quit after a few months because he didn't like the work. Other jobs ended similarly. The young man got into fights with coworkers, caroused at night, and refused to work in the daytime. It was reported that Rhodes hit his mother — frequently. Daisy never initiated physical violence against Rhodes, but she retaliated in kind when struck.

In an effort to remove him from his friends, whom she considered to be a bad influence, Daisy took Rhodes to Swaziland, where he got a job with the railroad. During one of Daisy's visits there, in June 1930, Daisy had Rhodes sign a will in her favor. His only assets were the £100 insurance policy which his mother had placed on him.

Daisy's third marriage took place on January 21, 1931, to Sydney de Melker, who was famous in South Africa in the early 1900s as a member of the Springbok rugby team. De Melker was also a plumber by trade. Rhodes quit his job in March of that year and returned to live with his mother and her new husband in the Johannesburg area. Rhodes started working at a garage in November 1931. It would be his last job. While there, he told his boss he expected an inheritance when he turned 21 and asked about the terms for a car. He was referring to the £100 that he would then receive. Early in 1932 Daisy wrote to her sister, "Rhodes's one ambition seems to be to see how nasty he can be towards me." She remarked to a neighbor that Rhodes had an insurance policy but she would see he didn't get it "because he would not work and did not seem to be playing the game" [1].

On February 25, 1932, Daisy journeyed to a pharmacy far from where she lived to buy some poison for a "cat." The pharmacist supplied her with arsenic. He knew her as Mrs. Cowle and was surprised to see her sign the register as D. L. Sproat. Daisy explained that she had remarried. Later, when the story of her murders hit the papers, the puzzled druggist stepped forward to identify Mrs. de Melker as Mrs. Sproat/Cowle.

Rhodes left for work as usual on March 2, 1932, taking with him the coffee and sandwiches customarily made for him by his mother. The coffee was laced with arsenic, and Rhodes was in distress within hours. He rallied and seemed to be on the road to recovery until Daisy sat up with him on the night of March 4, when she apparently gave him a second dose of arsenic. Amid much pain and convulsions, Rhodes expired on March 5 around noon. Malaria, which Rhodes had contracted while in Swaziland, was initially felt to be the cause of death.

Daisy at first resisted the idea of having a postmortem performed but then agreed, realizing that too much protesting might put her under suspicion. She had beaten the doctors twice before and was probably confident. And she succeeded a third time; cerebral malaria was certified as the cause of death. Rhodes was buried on March 6. On March 7 Daisy went to her son's employer and collected the half week's wages due him. On March 8 she claimed the £100 insurance money.

However, somebody in authority remained suspicious of Daisy's past; the following month, the three bodies were exhumed and examined. Rhodes's body was found to contain arsenic, while the bodies of the two husbands held pink strychnine. Pink strychnine, not its natural color, was available only in Rhodesia, where its use was common and widespread to kill wild animals. This use was so common, in fact, that it was colored pink to easily distinguish it, presumably as a safety precaution. Daisy had not been in Rhodesia since her late teens, and she must have obtained some then and saved it for years. Why she would have done that is unknown. Presumably when Rhodes's time came, Daisy was out of strychnine. Her unfamiliarity with a different poison may explain why she had to administer two doses to her son.

Arrested in April, Daisy was brought to trial in October on three counts of murder. She pleaded not guilty. Aggressive and confident at the beginning, over the course of her trial she turned slowly into a wan and scared creature. Taking the stand in her own defense, she was caught in a tangle of contradictory statements as the prosecution shredded her testimony. Juries were all male at the time, and fearing prejudice from such a group, Daisy chose to be tried by judge alone.

The trial itself was a big media event, and spectators jammed the courthouse. On the day the verdict was to be delivered, unemployed people lined up all night and then offered their places in line to latecomers for £1.

During the trial Daisy took copious notes. As she was taken back and forth to the courtroom, she would happily wave to the crowd. Once she pointed to a group of 300 or so and said to a reporter, "Come and look at this. They're all out just to see me." Obligingly she posed for the press and eagerly read the daily accounts of her trial in the newspapers. Daisy even sent people out to buy any overseas papers that mentioned her case [1].

Even when the crowd showed hostility, Daisy remained defiant. Once the crowd booed her. Another time a woman slipped through the police cordon and tried to hit her. Waving goodbye to a reporter at the end of one trial day, the man replied "Cheerio." Thinking he had said "Cheer up," Daisy laughed, "Cheer up, I'm quite cheerful enough" [1].

Daisy was found guilty of murdering Rhodes and sentenced to hang. In December a judge declared Robert Sproat's will null and void due to irregular witnessing. The will favoring his mother was held to have existed and the sum of £4,147 was ordered paid to the estate of Mrs. Sproat. From jail Daisy declared she had neither cash nor chattels with which to satisfy the order. It was found she owned property worth £3,640, but mortgages against them totaled about that amount.

On December 30, 1932, Daisy de Melker was executed by hanging. She went to her death calmly. What happened to her money is unknown. Daisy never confessed.

Sources

1. Bennett, Benjamin. *Up for Murder*. London: Hutchinson, 1934, pp. 17–75.
2. Gaute, J. H. H. *The Murderers' Who's Who*. London: Harrap, 1979, p. 83.
3. Nash, Jay Robert. *Look for the Woman*. New York: M. Evans, 1981, p. 118.

Elsie Nollen

(1907–1937). *Place:* Denison, Iowa. *Time:* August 29, 1937. *Age:* 30. *Victims:* 7. *Method:* Asphyxiation from automobile exhaust.

When Elsie Jones married Albert Nollen in 1923 she was only 16 years old. Albert was six years older than his wife. The couple settled on a farm 15 miles outside of Denison, Iowa, where Nollen worked as a tenant farmer. The marriage had its problems, since Albert drank a lot. When he was drunk, he was mean and would beat his wife. By the summer of 1937 the Nollens had six children, and Elsie, it seems, was at the end of her rope. Raising so many children and living in such an isolated area — Denison itself was a tiny farming community — must have left Elsie feeling hopelessly trapped.

On Saturday afternoon, August 28, 1937, the Nollens drove into Denison. There they bought school supplies and books for their children, who would be returning to school the following Monday after summer vacation. They arrived home at 6 P.M. Albert decided he wanted to go out again right away, but Elsie refused to accompany him and wanted him to stay home. Albert started to go anyway, and Elsie followed him outside. As they both entered the car, the couple argued. When Elsie asked him where he was going, Nollen refused to tell her. He got mad, told her it was none of her business, and threw her out of the car.

Before he drove off, Elsie scrambled into the back seat of the car and they drove back to Denison. Parking in front of the town's post office, Albert got out and started walking. Elsie trailed behind. More words were exchanged. Elsie returned to sit in the car and wait. Nollen had gone drinking. Elsie hoped that her being in the car might hasten her husband's return. It didn't seem to work, however, and hours passed with no sign of his return. Finally Elsie gave up her vigil and drove home around 11 P.M.

When Nollen found his car gone, he arranged a ride home with Jack Schile who lived on an adjacent farm and was apparently in Denison at the time. The two men arrived at Nollen's place at 2:30 A.M. Sunday morning. It was too late. As the car's lights illuminated the house, the men saw Albert's car backed up to a bedroom window.

When she arrived home, Elsie attached a washing machine hose to the

224

car's exhaust pipe and ran it into the bedroom. Next she carefully "caulked" the house up tightly, sealing all cracks, and then started the car. By the time Nollen arrived his wife and six children — Orvin, 11; Wilbert, 10; Pauline, seven; Carl, six; Leona, four; and Earl, two — had all been asphyxiated. Some of the children had kicked themselves out of their bedclothes as they expired. Others had wandered out of their bedrooms before they suffocated. Mr. Schile said he had a hard time keeping Albert from killing himself when he discovered the bodies. Before the group was buried two days later, a special order for caskets was necessary. There weren't enough in Denison to take care of all the family.

Elsie left behind a six-page note detailing her marital troubles. It read, in part:

> I have tried and tried to live a decent life and raise my kids up right so they would be decent. . . . But they have a father that does not care for them or me either. He don't know any better. . . . Albert was awfully good to me when he wasn't drinking. I couldn't ask for a better husband. But oh, he sure was awful when he got drunk! . . . He has beat me up lots of times and I always forgot about that just because I loved him and wanted to live with him. . . . Now today he got drunk. I never said much to him because I knew it would just be a fight again. . . . I am doing this business because I can see that this family is not going to be raised up right and I think it is a shame to let them grow up and live such a life. . . . I have lots I could tell but I'm getting tired. I hope Albert will be happier when he is rid of us. . . . Oh, my, such a life [2].

Sources

1. "Kills Family of Six and Self by Gas." *New York Times,* August 30, 1937, p. 3.

2. "Mass Rites for Seven Gas Victims." *Council Bluffs Nonpareil,* August 31, 1937, pp. 1, 2.

3. "Nollen Family of 7 Buried." *Council Bluffs Nonpareil,* September 1, 1937, p. 5.

Maureen O'Donohue

(1930–). *Place:* Toronto, Canada. *Time:* November 11, 1957. *Age:* 27.
Victims: 3. *Method:* Hanging.

Maureen Upper was born and educated in Belleville, Ontario, Canada.
In 1951 she graduated as a nurse from Toronto's St. Michael's Hospital. Not
long after that she married Melville O'Donohue, a Toronto lawyer. The
couple had four daughters in less than five years. Neighbors considered the
O'Donohues to be a happy family. One of them, Mrs. Loveland, said, "It
was a house filled with love and tenderness." She recalled that each morning
all the children would line up in the doorway and wave goodbye until Mr.
O'Donohue disappeared from sight on his way to work [3].

In August 1957, shortly after the birth of her fourth child, Maureen
entered the hospital for psychiatric treatment for what was called a nervous
breakdown. Released at the end of September, Maureen continued to go
for regular checkups as an outpatient. Some neighbors regarded Maureen
as a perfectionist. She regularly hired household help only to become
dissatisfied, complain to neighbors that these workers didn't do things
properly, fire them, hire new ones, and then repeat the whole process.

A little after 10 A.M. on November 11, 1957, Maureen got some strong
parcel twine, fashioned four nooses of identical size, and methodically
hung her four children: Maureen, four; Eileen, three, Katherine, two; and
Mary-Jo, six months, from ceiling beams in the basement laundry room of
the family home. The children were strung up in order, from oldest to
youngest.

Then Maureen phoned her husband. Although she didn't tell him what
she had done, he sensed something was wrong. Melville phoned a neighbor
to go next door and see if there was any trouble. The neighbor, Mrs.
Turner, was met at the front door by a sobbing Maureen. A worried Turner
searched the house and found the children, whom she took down out of
their nooses. The police and medical help were alerted. The baby, Mary-Jo,
was revived and recovered. The other three girls were dead. During all this,
Maureen wandered out of the house in a daze, making her way to a nearby
Roman Catholic church. Police took her into custody in the church where
she was clutching rosary beads and praying.

226

Mrs. Robert Hall, a former neighbor, said, "Her youngsters seemed to get on her nerves. She didn't believe in corporal punishment. They were never spanked or their hands slapped if they got into things. To keep them out of drawers she tied up the handles or had a yardstick through the handles of kitchen drawers so they couldn't open them." Another former neighbor, Mrs. Frank Hughes, commented, "Maureen was a perfect mother. Maybe too perfect. The house, the children, herself, they were all beautifully kept. She was meticulous about everything. Early in the morning even, she would look wonderful. I never heard her say a cross word to her children. Most people get mad at their kids sometimes but she didn't" [2].

A few days after the murders the state, on the advice of two psychiatrists, committed Maureen to a psychiatric hospital for an indefinite period.

Sources

1. "Children 4, 3, and 2 Hanged in Leaside, Cut Down, Save Baby." *Toronto Star,* November 11, 1957, p. 1.
2. "Former Neighbors Horrified by Slayings." *The Telegram,* November 12, 1957, p. 3.
3. "4 Girls Hanged, 3 Are Dead, Mother Charged." *Globe and Mail,* November 12, 1957, pp. 1, 8.
4. "Gentle Mother of 4 Veils Face in Court." *The Telegram,* November 12, 1957, pp. 1, 3.
5. "Mrs. O'Donohue Sent to Whitby." *The Telegram,* November 14, 1957, p. 1.
6. "3 Hanged, Baby Survives." *Toronto Star,* November 12, 1957, p. 3.

Bonnie Parker

(1911–1934). *Place:* Southwestern United States. *Time:* 1932–1934. *Age:* 21–23. *Victims:* c. 13. *Method:* Firearms.

In the film *Bonnie and Clyde,* the title characters were romanticized as social protesters and treated like folk heroes. However, the real Bonnie and Clyde were a far cry from their screen image. As robbers they were inept, usually knocking over stores and banks for nickel-and-dime sums. Their propensity to kill — usually pursuing lawmen — for no particular reason gave them their notoriety.

Bonnie Parker was born in 1911 in Rowena, Texas, the daughter of a bricklayer who died when she was four. The Parkers then moved to Cement City, a Dallas suburb. When she was 16 Bonnie married Roy Thornton, a childhood sweetheart. Roy was always in trouble with the law, and mother-in-law problems caused the pair to separate. By then Bonnie had a voracious sexual appetite and would have sex with anybody she could whether she was living with Thornton or not. She would remain so inclined until she died.

Late in January 1930, Bonnie met Clyde Barrow. She had just turned 19; Clyde was almost 21. Working then as a waitress, Bonnie described herself as "bored crapless" and ready for some excitement. Roy was safely out of the way, doing 99 years in prison for murder.

Stories vary on how the pair met, but a likely version is that their lives crossed when they visited an ailing mutual friend at the same time. There was an instant attraction on both sides; Clyde fell for the under-five-foot-tall, 90-pound teenager. Bonnie took him home to her mother's house with her that night, and he stayed so late that Mrs. Parker let him sleep downstairs on the couch. Clyde was still asleep the next morning when the police came for him and arrested him on seven counts of burglary and car theft. Bonnie was more than a little upset that the new man in her life was so suddenly taken away. She was not upset to learn of his criminal tendencies.

Clyde Barrow was born into extreme poverty in Telice, Texas, in 1909. He was one of eight children and was in trouble with the law from his earliest years. As a truant, petty thief, and runaway, Clyde was committed to a boys' school in 1918. Sadistic as a child, he enjoyed torturing animals. His older brother Buck Barrow was admired by Clyde, and the pair often pulled robberies together. When Clyde met Bonnie, Buck was doing time in prison.

After being arrested at Bonnie's place, Clyde was sentenced to two years in jail. Within a month or two Bonnie visited him in jail, slipped him a gun which she had taped to her thigh, and helped him to escape. Freedom only lasted a few days, however, because Clyde was recaptured and returned to prison. This time, the sentence was 14 years. A break came his way in February 1932, when he, along with other prisoners, was released under a general parole granted by the governor of Texas.

Barrow headed straight to Bonnie. When he showed up Mrs. Parker said to him, "Please try to go straight from now on for Bonnie's sake." Clyde promised to try. He did arrange a construction job in Massachusetts, but returned to Texas after two weeks due to homesickness. In March 1932, Bonnie left home for good. "I've got a job demonstrating cosmetics at a store in Houston," she lied to her mother [1]. She was teaming up with Clyde to start a campaign of robbery and murder which would make the Barrow gang Public Enemies No. 1 in the southwestern United States for the next couple of years.

In the very first month the couple stole a car, for which Bonnie was arrested and jailed. When she was released three months later, she rejoined a gang that then included Ray Hamilton and a couple of others. The gang had committed their first murder, killing a jeweler during a $40 robbery, while Bonnie was still in jail. After Bonnie's return the gang held up a gas station in Grand Prairie, Texas, making off with $3,500. It was the biggest haul the gang would ever achieve.

Hamilton was soon arrested, and the gang was reduced to just Bonnie and Clyde. The couple toured around in the fall of 1932 spending what remained of their loot. They patronized good restaurants and hotels. Bonnie was a fussy and immaculate dresser. She also spent a lot of time in beauty parlors.

Soon they were low on funds and went back to robbing. A 67-year-old butcher from Sherman, Texas, was robbed and killed after Bonnie pumped three bullets into his stomach. More robberies followed, including a take of $80 from a bank in Carthage, Missouri.

In November 1932, the pair held up a gas station, kidnapping the attendant, William David Jones. Harboring a romantic image of the then-famous pair, Jones readily joined the gang when he learned who his captors were. It was a decision he would come to regret; when he finally got away he described his time with Bonnie and Clyde as "18 months of hell" [6].

Jones replaced Hamilton's role of fulfilling the couple's sexual demands. Clyde needed help in satisfying Bonnie's incessant sexual appetites.

He also needed a male partner to satisfy his own homosexual needs. Jones grew exhausted with the excessive sexual demands made on him by both Bonnie and Clyde.

The trio continued robbing banks and stores, usually coming away with between $50 and $1,000 for their trouble. Once while stealing a car, they shot and killed the owner's son. Early in 1933 they killed a policeman in a bank who was setting up a trap for another bank robber. In March 1933 the trio was joined by Buck Barrow, newly paroled from prison, and his wife Blanche.

Their killing was often totally capricious. In the summer of 1933 the group was driving through Oklahoma City, Oklahoma. Bonnie was at the wheel when she stopped the car at an intersection to ask directions from a traffic cop. After he responded Bonnie pulled out a shotgun and killed him on the spot.

No exact count exists of the number of robberies and murders the gang committed before they met their own violent end, but they are credited with about 13 murders. During the last year of their lives, the Bonnie and Clyde gang killed at least six policemen in separate incidents as the gang evaded capture. Soon the gang and their exploits made front-page news from coast to coast. Their ability to evade police capture time and time again — largely a result of ineptitude on the part of the law — added to their mystique.

Both Bonnie and Clyde were gun freaks and were overjoyed to own and fire guns. They also loved to take snapshots of each other as they posed menacingly with parts of their arsenal. One Kansas City gangster who sold the pair a couple of submachine guns and a Browning automatic rifle recalled they were "like a couple of kids playing with those guns, running their hands over them, inserting clips and laughing. I thought they were crazy. Bonnie held the Browning and rubbed her legs against it like she was having sex" [4].

Bonnie loved the publicity and was soon nicknamed "Suicide Sal" in the newspapers. Clyde was called "the Texas Rattlesnake." Bonnie went so far as to deluge newspaper editors around the country with samples of her poetry, and many eagerly printed "The Story of Suicide Sal."

In the summer of 1933 the five-member gang was surrounded near Dexter, Iowa, and jumped by a posse of 200 police. Buck was mortally shot and Blanche captured, but incredibly the other three escaped. Later Jones deserted Bonnie and Clyde. Continuing to rob and kill, Bonnie convinced Clyde to get a blonde wig and dress up like a woman. "The police are looking for a man and a blonde, not two blondes," she told him. It was a ploy that seemed to work.

In January 1934, they helped their old partner Ray Hamilton break out of prison, killing one guard in the process. On April 1, Bonnie and Clyde killed two pursuing policemen, gunning them down with machine guns. A week later they killed another cop. On May 23, 1934, Bonnie and Clyde drove into a police trap in Gibsland, Louisiana, where six policemen lay in wait. They were probably given no chance to surrender before the authorities fired 167 rounds into the car. Clyde had his shoes off and was driving in his socks. Bonnie died with a part of a sandwich she had been eating in her mouth. Clyde was hit by 25 shots; Bonnie by 23. One of the cops in the party said, "We just shot the hell out of them, that's all. . . . They were just a smear of wet rags" [1].

Instead of being relieved at the demise of the two killers, the public mourned Bonnie and Clyde when they were taken home to Dallas for burial. Spectators took flowers off the coffins to take home as souvenirs. So many people turned up at the cemetery that Clyde's sister couldn't get within 40 feet of the grave site.

While the general public may have idolized Bonnie and Clyde, top gangsters held them in contempt. John Dillinger summarized that view when he heard of their deaths: "They were kill-crazy punks and clodhoppers, bad news to decent bank robbers. They gave us a bad name" [1].

The end had come much as Bonnie had predicted in the last verse of her poem:

> Some day they will go down together,
> And they will bury them side by side.
> To a few it means grief,
> To the law it's relief
> But it's death to Bonnie and Clyde [5].

Sources

1. *Crimes and Punishment,* vol. 1. New York: Marshall Cavendish, 1985, pp. 150–56.

2. Green, Jonathon. *The Greatest Criminals of All Time.* New York: Stein & Day, 1980, pp. 119–20.

3. Nash, Jay Robert. *Bloodletters and Badmen.* New York: M. Evans, 1973, pp. 39–44.

4. Nash, Jay Robert. *Look for the Woman.* New York: M. Evans, 1981, pp. 316–18.

5. Scott, Harold. *The Concise Encyclopedia of Crime and Criminals.* London: Deutsch, 1961, pp. 45–46.

6. Sifakis, Carl. *The Encyclopedia of American Crime.* New York: Facts on File, 1982, pp. 85–87.

Marie Pasos

(1894–1929). *Place:* New York City. *Time:* February 15, 1929. *Age:* 35. *Victims:* 7. *Method:* Asphyxiation by gas.

Life was a long, hard struggle for 42-year-old Jose Pasos as he struggled to provide for his wife and six children. Even though he worked two jobs, there never seemed to be enough money. From 8 P.M. until 7 the next morning, Jose worked as a deckhand on a ferry. Beginning at seven, he worked in a combination pool room and lunch room that he operated with his brother. Relieved by the brother at 11 A.M., Jose went home to sleep for a few hours before it was time to leave his apartment for the ferry.

Neighbors noted that the family was impoverished and that the children, who ranged in age from one to 13 years, were short of clothing. In other areas, though, the family seemed to be tranquil and lived in harmony. Neighbors could report no other difficulties in the family.

On Thursday, February 14, 1929, Jose left for the ferry as usual. The following day was the youngest child's first birthday. His wife Marie, 35, had struggled long enough with poverty, for some time after Jose departed and after the children were put to bed, she turned on every gas jet in the apartment. To try and facilitate a freer flow of gas, Mrs. Pasos had partially dismantled the stove.

The next morning at the pool hall, a frantic neighbor rushed in to tell Jose that gas was escaping from the Pasos apartment and that no one could open the door. Jose rushed the block or two home and broke down the door, only to find his entire family dead. His efforts to revive them failed. The dead children were Celia, 13; Beatrice, 11; Joseph, 10; Felicia, four; George, three; and Alfred, one.

The Pasos apartment was described as being almost bare of furniture. In the kitchen was found half a loaf of bread and a few vegetables.

Sources

1. "Kills Self and 6 Children on Her Baby's Birthday." *New York Herald-Tribune,* February 16, 1929, p. 3.
2. "Kills 6 Children and Herself by Gas." *New York Times,* February 16, 1929, p. 19.

Popova

(late nineteenth century–early twentieth century). *Place:* Samara, Russia. *Time:* 1879–1909. *Age:* unknown. *Victims:* c. 300. *Method:* Poison.

A brief account of Popova's exploits was published in various newspapers in the United States, including the *New York Times* and the *Chicago Tribune,* but no follow-up appears to have ever been printed. Nor does any account of this mass murderer turn up in print anywhere else.

Identified only as Popova, this woman was arrested in Samara, Russia, in March of 1909. For 30 years she had been dispensing poison to wives who wished to rid themselves of their husbands. Charging only a small fee, Popova executed her work with enjoyment and "much dispatch." Her victims were said to number around 300. She never murdered a woman. The police arrested her after a client, tormented by remorse, denounced her to the authorities.

An angry mob tried to seize her and burn her at the stake but were restrained by the police and by soldiers. Popova reportedly confessed to the murders. She boasted that she did excellent work in freeing unhappy wives from their "tyrants."

Sources

1. "Woman Kills 300 at Wives' Behest." *New York Times,* March 26, 1909, p. 1.

Dorothea Montalvo Puente

(1929–). *Place:* Sacramento, California. *Time:* 1982–1988. *Age:* 53–59. *Victims:* 9. *Method:* Drug overdose.

Overworked social workers in Sacramento, California, often had difficulty in finding accommodation for some of their clients, particularly those who were over 50, those who were ill, and those with mental handicaps. They were happy to find Dorothea Montalvo Puente, who had no objection to renting rooms to such people in her downtown boarding house. Her criminal past, which involved preying on just such people, was either not checked out or was ignored. The people who were referred to Puente's house as roomers often disappeared, never to be seen again. Social workers didn't find this unsettling. Given the transient, down-and-out nature of their clients, it was not unexpected for them to just pick up and go.

Even after the police began digging up Puente's yard, after they had unearthed the first body, after they knew of her criminal past, after a tenant told them Dorothea forced him to lie to them, and after the police told the boarding house operator they expected to find more bodies on the property, Puente was allowed to walk away free. Her freedom was short-lived, but this gaffe brought an enormous amount of criticism onto the Sacramento police, for Puente would ultimately be charged with nine counts of murder.

When arrested, Dorothea Puente was a white-haired, kindly looking, grandmotherly 59-year-old woman. Beneath that surface lay something very dark and sinister. She did what she did in order to get the victim's Social Security checks, which amounted to around $600 a month. If a Social Security recipient was unable to manage his or her own money, the check could be made out to a third party—a landlady, for example—who would manage the money for the person. When Puente's roomers disappeared, their checks, made out to her, kept coming.

Puente claimed to be of Mexican descent, one of 18 children. Her parents were both dead by the time she was five, she said. However, the record showed she was born Dorothea Helen Gray in Redlands, California, on January 9, 1929, to Jessie and Trudy Gray. Her other claims about her background, unverified by any other sources, should remain highly suspect

234

because Puente was a devoted liar. Her marital history is unclear. It seems she was married at least four times, but the details are sketchy. Her first marriage took place when she was 17. Widowed at 19, the next reported union was a four-year marriage to Roberto Jose Puente, which ended in divorce in 1972. Later she married Pedro A. Montalvo. They divorced in 1976.

In 1948 Dorothea had her first run-in with the law when she was convicted of forging checks in Riverside, California. In 1960 Puente was sentenced to 90 days in jail for "residing in a house of ill fame" and also received a 90-day suspended sentence for vagrancy. In denying the allegations, Dorothea explained she was merely staying with a friend, not realizing the house was a brothel. Over the years she worked off and on as a nurse's aide or a boarding house manager, usually with responsibility for elderly, mentally disturbed, and physically disabled persons.

At least one more scrape with the law occurred before 1978. That year Puente was convicted in a federal court of forging 34 U.S. Treasury checks intended for residents of a board-and-care facility in Sacramento she then operated. Her sentence was seven years' probation. More serious alarm bells about the woman started going off in 1980. Esther Busby, 79, had hired Dorothea as a live-in companion. On numerous occasions in 1979 and 1980 Busby had to be rushed to the hospital with mysterious illnesses. Each time she was accompanied by an apparently anguished Dorothea, who struck all as very solicitous and concerned. After a number of such trips to the hospital, a suspicious doctor ordered some extra tests for his patient. Results indicated barbiturates in Busby's system. The drugs had not been given to her by her own physician. Further checks indicated that Puente had been forging Busby's Social Security check. When Busby was informed what had happened, she immediately fired Puente.

One year later, Dorothea was employed as a night nurse for 83-year-old Dorothy Gosting. This woman also made sudden, unexpected trips to the hospital. During one hospitalization Gosting complained to the staff that Puente stole some of her jewelry, rare coins, and blank checks. Somebody at the hospital recalled the Busby case. The authorities were notified, and Dorothea was arrested. On August 23, 1982, she was sentenced to state prison for five years for forgery, grand theft, and administering a drug to commit a felony. Apparently other victims were involved. One account says she would also pick up elderly men in bars, slip drugs into their drinks, and rob them.

William P. Wood, who prosecuted Puente in 1982, described her as "quite cold-blooded," adding, "She looks kind of like a Mrs. Butterworth," the homey figure on the bottle of pancake syrup. Before the trial, Wood said she tried to flee the country. She was arrested with a plane ticket to Mexico in her purse [12].

A presentence report on the woman stated she "was known for her generosity and hospitality to those in need." However, it recommended prison time, asserting that Puente "has demonstrated that she is a danger to elderly persons. . . . She has concentrated her criminal efforts on a segment of the community that is the most vulnerable, the ill and the elderly. Her criminal acts . . . are callous and unconscionable" [16, 1].

While in jail awaiting sentencing, Dorothea showed her manipulative side by writing a pleading letter to the judge claiming that all her brothers and sisters in Mexico depended on her for financial support. "I feel so terrible for the poor people I did wrong to, and my brothers and sisters, they are the ones who are suffering" [1].

At the time of this 1982 conviction, Dorothea was a patient of Sacramento psychiatrist Dr. Thomas E. Doody. A condition of her 1978 federal probation was that she seek psychiatric help. Doody diagnosed her, in 1982, as having "chronic undifferentiated" schizophrenia, a condition commonly associated with delusions and hallucinations. She was, he thought, a very disturbed woman.

Dorothea was released from state prison on February 19, 1985. Because of this state conviction her federal probation was revoked, which resulted in her being sent to a federal prison to serve that sentence. From the federal prison she was sent to a halfway house in July 1985. Two months later she was released from that facility. Her state parole expired March 21, 1986, and she was to remain on federal parole until 1990.

Sometime in the mid–1970s Dorothea met Ricardo Ordorica at a bar where they had both gone to hear a group of Mexican singers. He recalled, "She bought me a beer and sent it over. She was a like a movie star. She was with her husband, a bodyguard and her chauffeur" [6]. Although later divorced, Dorothea remained friends with Ricardo, his wife, and their four children. The children became attached enough to call her their aunt. Late in 1985 Puente moved to an apartment in Ricardo's large house. By early the next year, she rented the entire house from Ordorica, who moved his family to a newer home. Puente paid $600 a month in rent. She had four or five bedrooms she rented out to as many as eight tenants at a time. For their room, two meals a day, and care, they paid Dorothea from $300 to $350 a month.

As a regular visitor to neighborhood bars, Puente was well known. At one such establishment she was remembered for tipping bartenders $10 each month and for buying makeup and perfume for her favorite waitresses. One bartender said, "She was a classy lady—Elizabeth Taylor with white hair." Other recollections were less favorable. At another bar she tried to pass herself off as a wealthy doctor with homes in Mexico and Lake Tahoe. She related that she'd been a prisoner of war during World War II and that a book of her war experiences would soon be published. Another claim she made was that she suffered from cancer and was undergoing chemotherapy. Another bartender observed, "She was like a person living in a fantasy world — always impressing people with money. . . . She's crazy. She's nuts" [12].

Ordorica remembered Puente boasting to him about the famous people she knew. She showed him letters purported to be from the King of Jordan, the Shah of Iran, and the Pope. She turned down a proposal of marriage from the Shah, she told Ricardo, because she thought he should marry someone who could give him an heir. By chance Dorothea met Linda Bloom, 41, in 1987. Linda was her natural daughter whom she had given up for adoption at birth. A distant family member discovered the connection while researching a family tree. The pair exchanged a few letters. Their only meeting lasted a couple of hours, during which Dorothea told Linda she was a doctor with a clinic in Mexico, had been in the movies, and was friends with actress Rita Hayworth.

John Sharp, a tenant in the boarding house, was told by Puente that she was a survivor of the war's Bataan Death March and was in Hiroshima when the atomic bomb was dropped on that city. To Sharp she was a Jekyll-and-Hyde type, helpful and sedate at times, but frequently going out of her head and ranting, raving, screaming, and cursing. He witnessed more than one drunken brawl between his landlady and tenant John McCauley. "They used to get drunk and fight and throw things," he said. "I remember when the rug shampooer and a small refrigerator went down the stairs one night. Dorothea was a woman you just didn't question" [18].

One of those who placed clients at the home was Leo McFarland, the president of Volunteers of America, a group that ran the Inebriate Shelter. "She runs hot and cold," said Leo. "She's the sweetest lady in the world, and then she can be foul-mouthed and crude" [2].

Early in 1986 Puente contacted Peggy Nickerson, a social worker with the St. Paul Senior Center, an agency funded by the Sacramento County Health Division. Dorothea explained she was a widow with a big house who wanted to take in the elderly homeless. She was not put off in the least by the fact that Peggy's clients were drug addicts, alcoholics, the mentally ill, and those whose behavior made them unsuitable for government-run facilities. These people were often belligerent; they would start fights and use vulgarities; they would get drunk, vomit, and pass out; or they would take drugs, hallucinate, and would phone the police to complain about rays coming through the walls. One such client was Dorothy Miller. She was a wanderer, schizophrenic, and alcoholic who would become abusive to women and children in public shelters only to be thrown out on the streets. She became a tenant of Dorothea's. She was also a murder victim.

Given the difficulty of placing such people in accommodations, Nickerson was delighted to refer clients to Puente. Peggy took the woman at her word, not investigating her background. "She seemed genuine," said the social worker. "I didn't have any reason to doubt her. She was rough around the edges. She had a tendency to curse. I felt that with that personality trait it would be complementary with the people she would serve. . . . She was the best the system had to offer" [15]. She provided good meals, kept a vegetable garden that was the envy of the neighbors, and could relate to her tenants. Peggy referred about 13 people to Dorothea until the late summer of 1988. When Peggy would occasionally stop in at the house to see how a client was doing, that person was never there. Puente seemed to always provide a plausible excuse. Nickerson stopped referring clients because of what she called verbal abuse. During a visit she made to the home, she overheard the landlady call one tenant "a lousy S.O.B. who'd never amount to anything."

Peggy was initially so happy to have found Puente's facility that in June 1988 she boasted of this exceptional boarding house for the hard to place to Polly Spring of the county's Adult Protective Services Agency. Once Spring found out who the operator was she exclaimed, "I know her. That woman is crazy as a hoot. . . . That woman has been in trouble." It was a warning Peggy chose to ignore, explaining that she and Spring didn't see eye-to-eye on various aspects of their work. Spring reported her concerns to a supervisor who notified the Department of Social Services licensing agency.

A facility that provided "care and supervision" over and above room and board had to have a state license. Puente's operation had no such license. On the day officials of the licensing agency made an inspection of the home, Puente had four or five tenants. The inspector found only Puente and one other person, a "cousin" just visiting. Dorothea said that on occasion she took someone in from St. Paul but only for an overnight stay, there was never a fee involved. When licensing officials later contacted Peggy, she confirmed the lies. Officials decided no license was required since no care and supervision was taking place. When the bodies were discovered — some of them Peggy's clients — Nickerson was tormented by what she had done. She was trying to do the best for her clients. If she had told the truth, the facility would have been shut down and her clients would have been thrown into the street. There was no place else she could put them [11].

As a condition of her federal parole, Dorothea had been specifically instructed not to work with the elderly or emotionally disturbed and not to handle government checks of any kind issued to others. During 1987 and 1988, federal parole officers visited her home about 15 times. Some of these visits were unannounced. When supervisor Charlie Vernon was asked how his people could have missed the fact that Puente was operating a boarding house and violating parole conditions he said, "That's a question we're asking ourselves" [11].

One tenant at the home was 52-year-old Alvaro Montoya, placed at the house in the summer of 1988 by Veterans of America homeless-shelter street counselor Judy Moise. This man was severely mentally disturbed. Dorothea had authority to cash his Social Security checks. When Judy tried to visit her client, he was never there. Judy thought she was getting the run around from the landlady about his whereabouts. When she persisted in trying to see him, Puente said he had gone to Mexico to visit his relatives. On a later visit the landlady claimed her brother-in-law took Montoya with him on a trip to Utah. Judy later spoke to tenant John Sharp, who told her about holes being dug in the backyard. He also told her of another tenant named Ben who had disappeared recently. After a noisy drunken episode by Ben, Dorothea had told Sharp she would make him behave; Ben was never seen again. Moise went to the police.

On November 11, 1988, the police began to dig in the grounds of the house. Over four days they discovered seven bodies buried. All were unearthed in the fetal position. Most were wrapped in sheets, mummylike. One body was wrapped in 14 separate layers. Before the police questioned her, Puente went to Sharp. She told him to lie to the police and say he had witnessed Montoya moving away. In fear of the consequences, Sharp told this story to the police but also managed to slip them a note saying, "She's making me lie for her." At a later private meeting with the police, Sharp told what he knew. This was before the first body was unearthed.

After the discovery of that first body, Puente was allowed to go to a nearby hotel, where she said she wanted to visit a relative. Despite what the police already knew, Dorothea was neither detained nor was she followed. She did not return to the boarding house. She was also not to be found at the hotel when the police went looking for her after they found the second body. During the previous questioning by the police, the landlady had emphatically declared, "Sir, I have never killed anybody." Asked why the woman had been allowed to walk away a police spokesman said, "At the time we found the first body, the lady was very cooperative. She stood over the grave as we dug. There was no need at that point to follow her" [9]. They were also concerned, they explained, that they not violate her civil rights.

In the meantime, Puente hopped a bus to Los Angeles, where she stayed in a motel for four days in a seedy section of the city near the downtown area. At a bar she struck up a conversation with Charles Willgues, 59. She told him she was 50 years old, had been widowed one month earlier, and has moved to Los Angeles for a change of scenery. Finding out that Charles received Social Security, Dorothea advised him he was entitled to more money than he was receiving. During their 90-minute conversation Dorothea suggested since they were both alone she should come over to his place on Thanksgiving Day to cook them dinner. Then she suggested that perhaps they could live together. Willgues said he would have to think about it. The couple made a date for the following day to go shopping for clothes for her, because she said hers had all disappeared in a taxi.

Later that evening it dawned on Charles that he had seen the woman before, on a morning newscast about the Sacramento murders. The police were informed and Puente arrested. Willgues's request that the arrest be delayed one day until after their date was denied. Sacramento police, who had by then acknowledged an "error" in letting her get away, were more than a little relieved to have her back in custody. On the return flight to Sacramento from Los Angeles, Dorothea told the police, "I have not killed anyone. The checks I cashed, yes. ... I used to be a very good person at one time" [19].

Initially Puente was charged with one count or murder — that of Montoya, whose body was one of the seven unearthed. In April 1989 she was charged with nine counts of murder. In addition to Montoya, the other six buried on her property were Leona Carpenter, 80; Betty Palmer, 80; Dorothy Miller, 65; Vera Faye Martin, 65; James Gallop, 64; and Benjamin Fink, 55. Presumably they all died between 1986 and 1988. The other two were 77-year-old Everson Gillmouth, a former tenant who died in 1985 and whose body was discovered along a river bank in the area, and Ruth Monroe, 61, who died in 1982 from a drug overdose.

All seven bodies on her property were found to contain significant amounts of the drug Dalmane. This drug is said to be especially dangerous in combination with alcohol. It also poses extra hazards for the elderly. Dalmane was obtained by Puente from two physicians, one of whom was Thomas Doody, in an amount far greater than she could possibly have needed or used for herself. The state was highly critical of Doody because he knew her background. Prosecution documents stated, "It may be fairly inferred that Dr. Doody knew the risk Puente posed to elderly and infirm persons over whom she had influence. Under these circumstances, Dr. Doody had a duty to disclose to the appropriate authority Puente's request for drugs with which she could stupefy and kill her victims" [5].

It has not been reported how the bodies made it into the yard. One former tenant related that he had dug a large hole, four feet by four feet by five feet deep, for an "apricot tree." In July 1989, the coroner announced that the cause of death for the seven bodies from the yard could only be declared "undetermined." It was a finding that promised to make the prosecution's case more difficult. The state did have the testimony of a man who claimed he helped Puente dispose of Gillmouth's body in 1985.

While the police were digging in the yard, hundreds of onlookers gathered at the site to watch, some spending virtually all day there, day after day. Among them was at least one street preacher screaming, "Jesus saves." One company sold T-shirts bearing a picture of the house and the text, "She digs Sacramento." Later the house was vandalized by souvenir hunters. In searching through the inside, the police trashed the place and didn't restore it properly, according to Ordorica. His request to the city for $9,000 as reimbursement was denied. Nine months after the discovery of the bodies, cars still streamed by daily for a look. Passers-by asked Ordorica to pose for photos or offered him money to let them take a walk inside [6].

Puente remained held in custody. As of this writing there has been no disposition in the case.

Sources

1. Cox, John D. "Court Papers Reveal Several Years of Lies, Poison." *The Sacramento Bee,* November 16, 1988, pp. A1, A26.

2. Cox, John D. "Landlady's Mixed Past." *The Sacramento Bee,* November 15, 1988, p. A12.

3. Delsohn, Gary. "Early Clues Pointed to Landlady." *The Sacramento Bee,* November 15, 1988, pp. A1, A12.

4. Delsohn, Gary. "He Made Date with Suspect, Then Realized Who She Was." *The Sacramento Bee,* November 18, 1988, pp. A1, A20.

5. Ellis, Virginia. "Death House Landlady Got Drugs from Doctor, Prosecutors Contend." *Los Angeles Times,* March 25, 1989, p. 21.

6. Ellis, Virginia. "The House on F Street." *Los Angeles Times,* July 16, 1989, p. 3.

7. Freed, David. "Friendly Woman in Bar Sure Looked Familiar, Then He Remembered Why." *Los Angeles Times,* November 18, 1988, pp. 3, 40.

8. Grieve, Tim. "Death-house Landlady Seized in LA." *The Sacramento Bee,* November 17, 1988, pp. A1, A30.

9. Grieve, Tim. "7 Bodies Now; Search Widens." *The Sacramento Bee,* November 15, 1988, pp. A1, A12.

10. Hecht, Peter. "5 Days of Freedom End with Telltale Barroom Chat." *The Sacramento Bee,* November 18, 1988, p. A30.

11. Hurst, John. "Social Worker's Agony: She Ignored a Warning." *Los Angeles Times,* November 19, 1988, pp. 1, 36–37.

12. Ingram, Carl. "Landlady's Mystery Grows as 6th, 7th Bodies Found." *Los Angeles Times,* November 15, 1988, pp. 3, 27.

13. Jacobs, Paul. "Landlady Charged with 8 More Deaths." *Los Angeles Times,* April 1, 1989, p. 32.

14. Jacobs, Paul. "Police Knew of Criminal Record of Woman They Let Go in Mass Deaths." *Los Angeles Times,* November 16, 1988, pp. 3, 25.

15. Lindelof, Bill. "Agencies: No Funds to Check." *The Sacramento Bee,* November 15, 1988, pp. B1, B2.

16. Malnic, Eric. "Led Police to Death House Suspect." *Los Angeles Times,* November 17, 1988, pp. 1, 3, 30.

17. Mathews, Jay. "Sacramento Social Worker Anguishes as Body Count Rises." *Washington Post,* November 15, 1988, pp. A1, A8.

18. Miller, Max. "Rooming-house Tenant: She Asked Me to Lie to Police." *The Sacramento Bee,* November 15, 1988, pp. B1, B2.

19. Newman, Maria. "Jailed Landlady: I Didn't Kill Anyone." *The Sacramento Bee,* November 18, 1988, pp. A1, A30.

20. Wilson, Wayne. "Prosecutor Still Seeks Death Penalty for Puente." *The Sacramento Bee,* July 19, 1989, p. B1, B2.

Florence Ransom

(1905–?). *Place:* Matfield, England. *Time:* July 9, 1940. *Age:* 34. *Victims:* 3. *Method:* Firearm.

When 48-year-old Dorothy Fisher failed to keep a regular weekly appointment on July 9, 1940, police were dispatched to her cottage at Matfield, near Tonbridge in Kent, England, about 30 miles from London. They found all three occupants of the residence shot dead on the grounds of the property. In addition to Dorothy, the victims were her 20-year-old daughter, Freda Fisher, and 46-year-old Charlotte Saunders, a servant who lived with them. Dorothy had been shot twice, Freda three times, and Charlotte once, all from very close range. The table had been set for tea for four people. While the house had been ransacked, valuables were not removed. The police surmised that the murderer was known to the victims and that the ransacking was a ruse to make it look like a robbery.

Walter Fisher, six years Dorothy's senior, was an editor of a technical magazine in London and had held important positions with several different firms. The Fishers married in 1913, but it was not a happy union. After the birth of Freda, the second and last child, in 1920, the couple stopped having sexual relations although they continued to live together in the same house for years to come. Mrs. Fisher took a lover. Walter made no objection to this arrangement and was on good terms with the pair. Around 1934 Walter took a lover of his own, Florence Ransom, then about 29. Florence had married in 1925 but was widowed when her husband died in 1930.

The three murder victims had moved permanently to Matfield from London in September 1939, after the outbreak of World War II. Sometime before that Walter and Florence settled on a farm at Piddington, Oxfordshire, where they lived as man and wife. Florence was known in the area as Mrs. Fisher. She ran the farm, while Walter spent 12 hours a day commuting to and working in London. To help out, she hired Mary Guilford as a domestic servant and her son Frederick and his wife Jessie as cowman and dairymaid.

On the surface good relations were maintained between Mrs. Fisher and her lover and Walter and Florence, and they would visit back and

243

forth. Walter had last visited his wife about a week before the murder, and Walter had been summoned by the police to identify the three bodies.

On July 8 Florence went to Fred Guilford and asked to borrow his single-barreled shotgun along with some shells. She wanted to kill some rabbits, she explained. She also got Fred to show her how to operate the weapon. Florence then caught the train to Matfield, got the three women outside the house, and shot them.

Worried that she wouldn't be back home before Walter, she left a note for Mary Guilford which read, "Will you come down and see to Mr. Fisher and the farm and don't let anybody on the farm know I am out. I will try to be back before Mr. Fisher arrives. If not, I shall be back soon after. Burn this" [6]. Walter did arrive home first and found his mistress's absence to be highly unlike her.

One week after the murders, Florence was arrested and charged with the killings. Her only comment at the time was, "I didn't do it." One of the more bizarre revelations uncovered by the police was the fact that the Guilfords were not ordinary servants. Mary was Florence's mother and Fred and Jessie were her brother and sister-in-law. This relationship was unknown to Walter, who said there was nothing in Ransom's conduct to lead him to think she was related to the Guilfords. No reason for Florence to keep all this a secret ever came to light.

At her trial on the one charge of murdering Dorothy Fisher, Ransom maintained her innocence, claiming that she had not left the farm all that day. The Guilfords failed to back up this alibi. In addition, numerous people had seen Florence on July 9 as she made her way to Matfield and back on various trains. One of her gloves was found at the murder scene. Fred turned in the murder weapon, which he had retrieved from his sister.

Relationships between the Fishers and Ransom had not been as cordial as they at first seemed. The police found letters in Florence's possession that indicated "clearly that the prisoner was jealous of Mrs. Fisher" and Freda as well [6]. No other motive for the killings was ever advanced.

Originally Ransom declared that when she was searching for a lost cat on her property she fell down and stunned herself, which accounted for her absence from the house all day. Later she changed her story to claim that she couldn't remember her movements that day because she suffered from a loss of memory.

On November 12, 1940, after 47 minutes of deliberations, the jury found her guilty of murder. She was sentenced to death. This sentence was commuted the following month when Florence was declared insane. She was then confined to Broadmoor Asylum.

Sources

1. "Matfield Murder Case: Woman Charged at Tonbridge." *Tonbridge Free Press,* July 19, 1940, pp. 1, 5.
2. "Matfield Murder Case: Woman Committed." *Tonbridge Free Press,* August 16, 1940, pp. 1, 4.
3. "Matfield Murder Case: Woman Remanded." *Tonbridge Free Press,* August 2, 1940, p. 1.
4. "Mrs. Ransom Certified Insane." *The Times* [London], December 23, 1940, p. 2.
5. "Three Women Found Murdered in Grounds at Matfield." *Tonbridge Free Press,* July 12, 1940, p. 1.
6. "Triple Murder Charge." *The Times* [London], August 14, 1940, p. 9.
7. "Woman Sentenced to Death." *The Times* [London], November 13, 1940, p. 2.

Vera Renczi

(?-?). *Place:* Berkerekul, Romania. *Time:* Early twentieth century. *Age:* 20–35. *Victims:* 35. *Method:* Arsenic poisoning.

With an enormous sexual appetite, a jealous temperament, and a lust for killing, Vera Renczi became one of the more prolific mass murderers. Dates for her killing spree, birth, and death are not reported, but she operated in Romania during the first half of the twentieth century. Vera was born in well-to-do circumstances in Bucharest. She received a good education and grew to be a remarkable beauty. Her mother died when Vera was 10 years old, and she and her father moved to the city of Berkerekul. A series of governesses were hired to care for the child, who was noted for rebelliousness and a selfish nature.

By the time she was 15, she had discovered boys. Once she was caught at midnight in the dormitory of a boys' school. Never without a boyfriend, she would occasionally run away with the current one only to return home a few days later, tired of her companion. Soon she fell in love with a wealthy businessman much older than herself. The couple married and settled down to a life of luxury in his mansion. A little over a year after the wedding Vera gave birth to a son.

A few months after that, a somber Vera announced to friends that her husband had abandoned her. He left, she said, without any warning or explanation. She was adamant that he would never return to her. He wouldn't and, in fact, couldn't. Vera had poisoned him to death with arsenic and had placed his body in a coffin in the basement of the mansion.

Vera's grief over her husband's "desertion" was brief. Quickly she was running around the bars of Berkerekul in the company of a variety of men. When a dissolute young man named Josef Renczi took her fancy more than most, Vera announced she had just learned that her husband had died in a car accident. This paved the way for her to marry Josef. Four months after the ceremony Vera told friends Josef had gone on a long journey and that she didn't particularly care if she ever saw him again. The journey was not very long; Josef had only gone as far as the basement, to occupy a coffin next to Vera's first husband.

Resuming her carousing, Vera had no trouble finding lovers. When she tired of them she dispatched them with arsenic and placed them in coffins in her basement in an ever-growing circle. Inscribed on each zinc-lined coffin was the man's name, age, and date of his murder. Apparently enjoying her victims' suffering, Renczi often gave the poison in small doses, prolonging death from a few days to a number of weeks. In all, Vera murdered 35 men: two husbands, 32 lovers, and her own son. She was then 35 years old.

The thirty-fifth and last victim had only recently married. Feeling some guilt over cheating on his wife, he tried to break off the affair. Seemingly in agreement, Renczi convinced him to come to her place for a farewell meal. Accepting the invitation, he died in agony from drinking arsenic-laced wine. His wife launched her own investigation into her husband's disappearance when he failed to return from a "short business trip." When she had accumulated enough information she went to the police, who picked up Vera. Admitting that the missing man had indeed been her lover, Renczi claimed she had thrown him out of her bed the minute she learned he was married and hadn't seen him since.

The police were willing to take her word for it and drop the matter. However, the wife continued to dig, finding out about other missing men. She returned to the police and demanded that they search Renczi's house. It was, and the authorities found the 35 occupied coffins.

Renczi broke down and confessed to the police. Asked why she had killed them, Vera shrugged and replied, "I could not bear to think that they might love another woman. . . . I dare not let them go to the embrace of anyone else" [1]. In the midst of the coffins was an easy chair because, Vera said, "I liked to go down there in the evening and sit among my victims gloating over their fate" [1]. Her son had been murdered because he threatened to expose his mother's activities.

Vera was tried, convicted and sentenced to death. This sentence was later commuted to life in prison. A few years later, she died in prison.

Sources

1. O'Donnell, Bernard. *The World's Worst Women.* London: Allen, 1953, pp. 181–89.

2. Wilson, Colin. *Encyclopedia of Murder.* New York, 1962, pp. 458–59.

Martha Rendall

(?–1909). *Place:* East Perth, Australia. *Time:* 1907–1909. *Age:* unknown.
Victims: 3. *Method:* Hydrochloric acid poisoning.

Thomas Morris was a railway worker who lived in an unnamed
Australian state in the first few years of this century. For unreported
reasons, Thomas threw his wife out of his house but kept all four of the
couple's children. He soon formed an association with Martha Rendall; the
couple lived together as man and wife. In or around 1906 the family moved
to a different state, settling in East Perth, Western Australia.

While the children were reportedly in good health when they lived with
their natural parents, the new arrangement proved disastrous for them.
Martha was, according to witnesses, cruel to the children in various ways.
Worse still, whenever one came down with a cold or minor ailment of some
sort, Martha insisted on swabbing the child's throat. This led to shrieking
agony on the part of the child; one by one Annie, Olive, and Arthur died
between 1907 and 1909. Each was under 13 at the time of death.

In April 1909, the last child, George, accidentally scalded himself
slightly by drinking hot coffee. Martha was ready immediately to administer a swabbing. A terrified George, fearing the same fate as his siblings, fled the house and ran to the police, telling them that Martha was going to kill him.

When the police finished their investigation, Martha was charged with
murder. As a swabbing agent, Rendall had been using deadly hydrochloric
acid. The acid was found in the house. Martha had sent George out of the
house to purchase more acid while Arthur lay ill. The boy recalled that Rendall put the solution into a cup, took a brush, and went into Arthur's room.
Subsequently Arthur was heard to scream. He died shortly thereafter.

Martha Rendall and Thomas Morris were both tried on one count of
murder—Arthur's. Morris was acquitted, but Rendall was convicted and
sentenced to death. During the trial Rendall, who denied the charge,
showed no signs of emotion, but remained calm and cool. It was a demeanor which the judge found to be astonishing. The judge commented
that no one had suggested Rendall was insane, but if she was in her senses,
she must be "a moral deformity" [1].

The only motive ever advanced for the sadistic crimes was that Martha, who never had children, was jealous in some way of the attention the children got from Morris and thus had murdered her "rivals" for his attention. In 1909 Martha Rendall was executed at Fremantle, Western Australia—the first and only execution of a woman in that state.

Sources

1. "The Murder Trial." *West Australian*. September 15, 1909, p. 2.
2. Nash, Jay Robert. *Look for the Woman*. New York: M. Evans, 1981, p. 328.

Sarah Jane Robinson

(1837–1906). *Place:* Cambridge and Somerville, Massachusetts. *Time:* 1881–1886. *Age:* 44–49. *Victims:* 8. *Method:* Arsenic poisoning.

Considered to be a trustworthy wife and mother and a respected member of the community, Sarah Jane Robinson had a hidden and diabolical side to her nature. Using arsenic, she poisoned eight people to death, all but one members of her own family. Insurance money motivated her to relentlessly manipulate and kill off one insured family member after another.

Sarah Jane Tennant was born in Northern Ireland around 1837. By the time she was 14 her Scotch-Irish parents were both dead. Sarah was then sent, together with her nine-year-old sister Annie, to the United States by ship to live with an older brother in Cambridge, Massachusetts. Once she was settled Sarah turned to dressmaking, a skill she had learned in Ireland. When she was 19 she married a machinist named Moses Robinson. The couple lived in near-poverty, and Sarah was forced to keep on working.

Over the following quarter of a century, the family just barely made ends meet. Frequently they were forced to move from one tenement to another as they tried to keep ahead of their creditors. Sarah bore eight children during this time, three of whom died in infancy or childhood.

As a seamstress Sarah was considered more than competent; she worked for companies as well as doing work for individual families who used her over and over again. People considered her trustworthy, and she was a member of a Congregational church. Unremarkable is the best way to describe her life for that 25-year period — with the exception of money problems. Often in debt, Sarah had a scam in which she rented furniture for her home and then mortgaged it three or more times to different companies. It may have helped for a short time, but produced nothing but trouble in the long run.

Perhaps the money situation had become uncontrollable by 1881, for it was in that year that Robinson claimed her first victim. The family's landlord was an elderly man named Oliver Sleeper who became sick and, after Robinson nursed him, died of what was called heart disease. Sarah sent a nursing bill of $50 to the estate. Instead she got a remission on rent, which she sold for cash. Sleeper was known to have $3,000 in cash on hand when he died. The money was never found; it is not known if Robinson got her hands on it or if she did, what she might have done with it.

The summer of the following year, Moses Robinson suddenly died at the age of 45. He was insured for $2,000, but when Sarah went to collect she found that the man to whom Moses had made most of his regular premium payments had absconded with the money. The company, Pilgrim Fathers, refused to pay any benefits and Sarah sued for the money. The case remained pending years later when she was arrested.

Several years passed before Sarah tried again. Early in 1885 her sister Annie became sick with pneumonia. A nurse and Annie's mother-in-law tended her, and she got steadily stronger. She was well on the road to recovery when Sarah dismissed the nurse. Sarah had a premonition that her sister would soon die, and soon after she had taken over nursing duties, Annie did die.

This left Sarah's brother-in-law, Prince Arthur Freeman, with two small children to care for. Robinson urged him to come and live with her and enlisted some of her friends to help her persuade him. She was worried that Freeman would go and live with his own sister whom, Sarah warned, was only after his insurance. Sarah's daughter took the two Freeman kids home immediately after their mother's death. Freeman followed within a week. It would be a good idea, said Sarah, if he would make her the beneficiary of his life insurance — to care for his children. Freeman agreed.

Within a few weeks, one-year-old Elizabeth Freeman was dead. Sarah was tired of tending her relatives already and complained to friends that Freeman was a "lazy, good-for-nothing fellow who would be better off dead." She added that somebody should "give him a dose and put him out of the way" [4]. At supper not long afterward, Sarah had a little spell. Her husband had just appeared to her, she explained, and had informed her that Freeman would soon be dead. When she sent him off to spend a few days with his mother she told him she might never see him alive again.

One morning in June 1885, Prince ate Sarah's breakfast and set off for work. On the way he was violently sick and went to bed immediately when he came home. In between nursing her brother-in-law, Sarah sent her kids to the insurance company to make sure his policy was in order. Taking no chances, she summoned another company official to her home the next day. Sarah explained she went without food sometimes to pay premiums to Pilgrim Fathers and would need the insurance money, if anything happened, to raise the remaining Freeman child. The company officer obligingly paid the small amount then owing on Freeman's policy out of her own pocket. With the insurance in order, Freeman rapidly worsened and died.

The $2,000 from the policy was paid to Sarah, who went through it in a hurry. Creditors were paid and Sarah bought herself some new clothes, visited her brother in Wisconsin, and moved from Cambridge to a bigger apartment in nearby Somerville. The last of the money was used to buy an insurance policy on the life of her daughter, Lizzie. Within half a year, in February 1886, Lizzie died. Six months later the remaining Freeman child, Tommy—by that time a simple liability—died in July 1886.

Just one month later, a doctor connected with Pilgrim Fathers was called in to treat Sarah's 23-year-old son William, insured with the company. He had become ill after drinking some of Sarah's tea, which had tasted "bad," and was in bed with stomach pains, nausea, and vomiting. The doctor was aware of the many deaths in the Robinson family and kept a watchful eye on the situation. He sent a sample of William's vomit off for analysis. Word came back a couple of days later that the young man's stomach was full of arsenic. All of this was too late for William. Before he died he groaned, "The old woman dosed me." Sarah Robinson, then 49, was arrested and charged with William's murder.

After her arrest authorities exhumed all of the bodies, going back to Oliver Sleeper. Every one contained arsenic. One way the wily Sarah had avoided raising suspicion was to call in different doctors to prepare the death certificates for each victim. The multiple claims with the one insurance company finally aroused doubts and spoiled her plans.

For her first trial, in 1887, Sarah was charged only with William's murder. At her arraignment she reportedly sobbed hysterically, asked if Willie was dead, and said, "I am not guilty of poisoning my own child." A contemporary account described her as a "woman who bears her age well and who presents quite an attractive appearance in court" [8].

The state couldn't introduce any evidence regarding the other deaths and was adjudged to have prosecuted with great ineptitude. This trial ended with a hung jury. The case received a great deal of publicity. One account described the prosecution's efforts as the "work of a windbag." The media tended to upgrade her body count; the *New York Times* reported her as a murderess of 11. In another account Sarah was thought to have been responsible for the poisoning of 109 people with arsenic-laced ice cream at a picnic. No one died, but 50 people were seriously ill. Sarah was, however, not at the picnic. The caterer, whose business understandably had dropped off, thought it would be a good idea to cast the blame on her.

For her second trial, Sarah was charged again with one count of murder—Prince Freeman. The state argued successfully to introduce evidence about Annie's death due to the close connection between the two crimes. Sarah's main defense was that Freeman had been killed by somebody else, perhaps the elderly Dr. Beers, a quack, or Thomas Smith, chaplain for Pilgrim Fathers. Both men were ardent suitors for Sarah's favors. Both were in fact indicted as coconspirators or accessories, with Robinson. Neither of them was involved, and both went free.

During her trials Sarah remained calm and composed. She maintained throughout that she was innocent. At the second trial she was found guilty and sentenced to death, which was later commuted to life in prison. Upon being pronounced guilty, Sarah broke down completely in court and almost had to be carried out of the courthouse.

Sarah spent two decades in prison. She kept pictures of her victims in her cell with her and was an excellent prisoner. Her condition, physical and mental, remained sound. An attempt at obtaining a pardon in 1904 failed. Sarah Robinson died in prison in 1906, when she was almost 70 years old. She continued to proclaim her innocence throughout her incarceration.

At the time of her trial her remaining living son, Charley, had commented, "Mother always seemed to like us and we all cared the world for her" [4].

Sources

1. Folsom, Charles. *Studies of Criminal Responsibility and Limited Responsibility*. Privately printed, 1909, pp. 99–101.
2. "For Wholesale Murder." *New York Times,* December 13, 1887, p. 3.
3. Green, Jonathon. *The Greatest Criminals of All Time.* New York: Stein & Day, 1980, p. 233.
4. Jones, Ann. *Women Who Kill.* New York: Holt, 1980, pp. 121–28.
5. "The Jury Could Not Agree." *New York Times,* December 18, 1887, p. 3.
6. "Mrs. Robinson's Denials." *New York Times,* December 16, 1887, p. 2.
7. Nash, Jay Robert. *Look for the Woman.* New York: M. Evans, 1981, pp. 333–34.
8. "Poisoning by Wholesale." *New York Times,* August 13, 1886, p. 1.
9. "The Somerville Borgia." *New York Times,* August 14, 1886, p. 1.
10. "Spoke Often of Poison." *New York Times,* August 15, 1886, p. 2.
11. "They Find Her Guilty." *New York Times,* February 12, 1888, p. 3.

Amelia Sach and Annie Walters

(1873–1903, Sach; 1848–1903, Walters). *Place:* London, England. *Time:* c. 1900–1902. *Age:* 27–29, Sach; 52–54, Walters. *Victims:* 3 or more. *Method:* Chlorodyne drug overdose.

Amelia Sach was an English baby farmer with a slight twist. Acting as a midwife, Amelia helped to deliver the babies and then offered to have them adopted in good homes if the mother was so inclined. Sach employed a not-too-bright assistant named Annie Walters, who did the actual dirty work of murdering the newborn infants and disposing of their bodies. The pair split whatever money they were able to wheedle out of the mothers.

In 1902, the year they were caught, Sach was 29 years old. Described as a kindly, intelligent woman, Amelia contrasted sharply with the 54-year-old Walters, who was termed "bedraggled," or "squat and ugly." Both women were married, although no husband was present in either case. One account credits Amelia with having children whom she doted on and wanted the best for. Nothing else of their backgrounds was reported.

Amelia had run a "nursing home" in the East Finchley section of London for at least two years. More specifically, she offered a haven for unwed mothers in which to deliver their babies. The newspaper ad she ran to offer her services read as follows: "Accouchement: Before and during; skilled nursing. Home comforts. Baby can remain" [1].

A woman named Harris used Sach's services in July 1902, after which she paid £30 to Amelia to have the child adopted into what Amelia unfailingly promised would be a good home. On the evening of the birth Amelia left the house with the infant; shortly thereafter she returned alone. Theresa Edwards was a servant in the Sach home at the time who was warned by Amelia to keep her excursion a secret from Harris.

In November of that year, a woman named Pardoe gave birth to a baby at Amelia's home. Another £30 was paid over to Sach for "adoption." As before, Sarah disappeared with the child on the day of its birth, only to return alone. In the meantime, Amelia met Annie at a prearranged spot, where the baby was handed over. Annie took the infant to the rooming house where she lived and murdered the infant by administering enough of the sedative drug chlorodyne to kill it. Two days later Walters, taking the corpse away for disposal, stopped in a restaurant for coffee. The waitress caught a glimpse of a very white face and asked if it was a doll. Walters replied that she had just got the baby out of the hospital and it would soon be all right. The body of the Pardoe child was never found.

Another woman who delivered a baby at Amelia's house in November 1902 was named Galley. Sach gave her standard pitch about placing the baby boy with a wealthy woman for £30. This time Amelia had to settle for £25, since that was all Galley could raise. Sach passed the infant off to Walters the day of its birth.

Annie had the misfortune to lodge in the home of a policeman named Seal. The officer had grown a little suspicious the week before when the Pardoe baby arrived and then disappeared permanently within a few days. When Annie came home with the Galley baby she told Seal and his wife it was a little girl soon to be adopted by a member of the coast guard stationed at Kensington. This struck Seal as odd, since Kensington was a long way from any coast. Later when Mrs. Seal had occasion to change the baby, she discovered it was actually a boy. Seal reported these strange events to his superiors, who immediately staked out the house. Two days later, Annie was seen leaving the house carrying a brown paper parcel. When the police stopped her at a train station, the parcel was found to contain the dead Galley baby.

On her arrest Annie said, "I didn't poison the baby. I intended to drown myself tonight." In her possession was a telegram dated the day of the birth. It read, "Come tonight. Same place. Sach" [3]. That led to Amelia's arrest.

Gradually the facts of their crimes came out. Initially Amelia denied even knowing Annie but then admitted having employed her for a time. The infant had been born at 8 A.M.; Amelia sent her telegram to Annie at 11 A.M. The £25 that had been paid in notes by the father of the infant was traced to the two women. A quantity of chlorodyne was found in Walters's room.

Sach and Walters were tried in January 1903. Annie was charged with murdering the Galley baby, while Amelia was charged with being an accessory before the fact. In statements to police Annie admitted giving two drops of chlorodyne to the infant because it was "cross" and wouldn't sleep. Claiming that such an amount would not harm the child, Annie said she was surprised to wake up the next morning to find the baby dead in bed beside her. All the other babies, Annie insisted, had been adopted by wealthy women. Neither woman testified in court, always maintaining silence about their activities.

Medical men testified that two drops of the drug were more than sufficient to kill a two-day-old child. Dr. Wylie testified that he had attended 14 births at Sach's current address over a period of 18 months, as well as four other confinements at a previous address. When the police searched the Sach home, they found a cache of more than 300 infant garments. How many children were murdered by these women is unknown, but the total is certainly higher than the three for which any evidence was uncovered.

Found guilty, both women were sentenced to death. However, the jury added a recommendation for mercy. When the judge asked them why they made this recommendation the foreman said, "Because they are women" [3]. This recommendation was ignored. On February 3, 1903, Amelia Sach and Annie Walters were both executed.

Sources

1. Jesse, F. Tennyson. *Murder and Its Motives*. London: Harrap, 1952, pp. 30–31.
2. Shaw, E. Spencer. *A Companion to Murder*. London: Cassell, 1960, p. 237.
3. Wilson, Patrick. *Murderess*. London: Joseph, 1971, pp. 255–59.

Antoinette Scieri

(1890s–?). *Place:* St. Gilles, France. *Time:* 1924–1925. *Age:* c. 27–28. *Victims:* 6. *Method:* Arsenic poisoning.

After a period of activity as a petty criminal, Antoinette Scieri took an apparent hiatus for almost a decade before she returned to crime as a cold-blooded mass murderer. Very little has been reported on her early life. Born in Italy, probably shortly before the turn of the century, she came to France as a child and later took up nursing in the town of Doullens. During the early stages of World War I, she worked with the war-wounded.

As wounded soldiers were brought to her from the battlefield, Scieri rummaged through their pockets and stole whatever money and valuables she could find. In one case she got hold of an officer's pay book and tried to obtain an advance of several thousand francs from army bankers. Sometimes she found letters from friends and relatives written to the wounded men. Antoinette would write these people asking for money on behalf of the patient—to be sent to her at her address. She succeeded several times in this scam. The authorities caught up with her, and Scieri spent time in jail from 1915 to 1916.

Upon her release, she met an Italian soldier named Salmon. They married, but Salmon returned to the front almost immediately. Over the next two years, Salmon was home only infrequently. Antoinette bore two chlidren and had affairs with many men. When he returned after the Armistice, Salmon learned of his wife's infidelities and returned to Italy permanently. The two children disappeared from Scieri's life as well, perhaps having been adopted out.

One of her lovers from that period was Joseph Rossignol. After Salmon left, Rossignol and Antoinette started living together. Both drank heavily and fought regularly. More than once Rossignol came home drunk and physically beat Scieri. Her screams were loud enough on one occasion to draw the attention of a passing gendarme. Rossignol was brought before a judge and sent to prison for one month for assaulting his "wife." Antoinette took him back that time, as she always did.

Around 1920 the couple settled in St. Gilles in southern France, a town of about 6,000 people. Rossignol worked in the vineyards or as a cartman.

Scieri let it be known that she was available for hire as a nurse. The birth of a daughter in 1922 put a temporary halt to her nursing activities, but she was back in business in 1924.

In December that year Mlle. Drouard, a 58-year-old laundry worker, died suddenly after a period of terrible suffering while she was nursed by Scieri. Heart seizure, said the doctor. On Christmas Day, the couple who ran the grocery store, who were friends of Scieri and were being nursed by her, died under similar circumstances. This time, death was attributed to the couple being poisoned from having eaten birds in a state of a decomposition. One day in March 1925, Joseph took a bowl of mussels prepared by Antoinette to work with him for his dinner. He barely made it home that night before he died.

After a few weeks of grief, Scieri was off to nurse a pair of elderly sisters, Mlle. Marie Martin, 67, and Mme. Doyer, who lived together. Worried about the cost of the nursing, they explained they didn't have much money. "You must not worry about money," said Antoinette. "My mission is to heal and help the sick. Fees mean nothing to me" [4].

The nurse fed the sisters two mugs of coffee one afternoon. Martin drank all of hers, but Doyer drank only a little. Later she explained, "It had a bitter taste and I don't like anything bitter, so in order not to offend Mme. Rossignol, I poured most of it down the sink" [4]. As it turned out, this saved her life. Both women became ill, but Martin was much worse than her sister. Martin died in agony, while Doyer recovered. Martin's death was attributed to eating shellfish.

Despite her "bad luck" with patients, Scieri always managed to find work. Her next patient was 75-year-old Mme. Gouan-Criquet, who died just two days after Antoinette arrived on the case. The doctor attending the woman grew suspicious when her husband mentioned having had symptoms similar to those his wife had before her death. When the police were informed by the doctor, they investigated and found a bottle of green liquid beneath the bed of the latest victim. Analysis showed the fluid to be pyralion and ether, a mixture composed mainly of arsenic that was used for killing vineyard weeds. The bottle contained enough poison to kill 300 people.

The other five victims were exhumed; each was found to contain large amounts of pyralion. Scieri was arrested. Just before the police picked her up Antoinette had been fired by her newest patient, who had become suspicious of a mysterious bottle in the household.

Probably about 25 to 30 years old when she was carrying out the murders, she was described as "no beauty." Her appearance was described as that of a typical Gypsy—swarthy complexion, thick black hair in ringlets. "Her face was heavy and pouched, and her eyes were almost mesmeric in the steadfastness of their gaze," said a contemporary account [3].

Scieri quickly confessed to five of the murders after her arrest, denying only the murder of Gouan-Criquet. She tried to put most of the blame on a neighbor who was not involved at all. So convincing were Scieri's lies that this woman was brought to trial, but exonerated. No motive was ever ascertained for any of the killings. Little or no money was involved, since Antoinette often charged little or nothing for her nursing services. She claimed to have received 800 francs on one death she admitted to, but the authorities discounted that. Police believe Antoinette "had a morbid passion for inflicting suffering" [2]. Antoinette never changed her story, sullenly maintaining her neighbor was the instigator and robbery was the motive.

When Scieri nursed patients she did so with kindness and professed great concern that they recover. Yet she killed without compunction and without remorse. Scieri had aroused the hate of the village she had lived in for a few years to such an extent that she was on the verge of being lynched several times as the police moved her back and forth from jail to courtroom. "Hang her to the nearest trees," yelled the mob.

On April 27, 1926, Scieri was convicted and sentenced to death for her crimes. The judge said to her, "You have been called a monster. But that expression is not strong enough. You are debauched, you are possessed of all vices. You are also a drunkard, vicious, and a hypocrite and you have no shame. I do not believe judicial history contains the records of many criminals of your type" [3]. Scieri screamed with rage at these comments and unleashed some vile oaths at the judge. Pausing, she shrugged and laughed before being led away. Her sentence was later commuted to life imprisonment.

Sources

1. "Daily Telegraphs." *The Times* [London], April 28, 1926, p. 15.
2. "French Nurse Admits Wholesale Poisoning." *New York Times,* April 14, 1925, p. 25.
3. Nash, Jay Robert. *Look for the Woman.* New York: M. Evans, 1981, pp. 341–42.
4. O'Donnell, Bernard. *The World's Worst Women.* London: Allen, 1953, pp. 105–16.

Lydia Sherman

(1825–1878). *Place:* New York City and Connecticut. *Time:* 1864–1871. *Age:* 39–46. *Victims:* 10–11. *Method:* Arsenic poisoning.

Only one of Lydia Sherman's murders could be recorded as a crime committed for financial gain. In the other cases murder was committed because Lydia found herself in an unsatisfactory state. Faced with a depressed husband, an ill child, a husband with whom she had differences, or simply the responsibilities of looking after children, Lydia was quick to turn to arsenic as a solution. Unpleasant or uncomfortable situations called for murder as a way out.

She was born Lydia Danbury in 1825 in New Brunswick, New Jersey. Her mother died when Lydia was about a year old, and her butcher father passed on eight years later. The young orphan was raised by a relative; by the age of 16, she was employed as a "tailoress." Soon thereafter she attended a Methodist church meeting and met Edward Struck, a blacksmith and widower with six children. The couple married around 1845.

Life proceeded quietly for the couple, and they soon had six children of their own. Edward changed professions and became a policeman in New York City. The family lived obscurely until 1863 when a barroom brawl took place on Edward's beat. An off-duty detective, who seems to have been just passing by stepped in and killed a gunman. Some employees of the establishment claimed that Edward had been hiding behind a door outside during the incident, afraid to go in. Edward said he arrived at the bar in response to the call after the incident was over. However, his superiors didn't believe him, and he was tossed off the force for cowardice.

Becoming more and more bitter over his lost job, Edward fell into a depression. At times he was constantly drunk; at times he refused to see anybody, to dress himself, or to get out of bed. At still other times he would beat his wife. Captain Hart, his former superior, had no success in trying to reach Edward and he suggested that Lydia put him in an insane asylum.

One night when Struck was violent, Lydia had to call a policeman from another apartment in her building to restore order. This officer suggested she "put Struck out of the way," since he was "no good to himself or anybody else" [1]. This man may have also been referring to committing him to an asylum. However, Lydia took the suggestion literally and went out the next day to buy 10 cents' worth of arsenic. After eating this in a bowl of oatmeal, Edward Struck was dead one day later, on May 26, 1864. A doctor certified the cause of death as consumption.

Lydia still had major problems. She was a widow with no money and many children to care for. She worked as a nurse and a seamstress, but was hard-pressed financially. "I thought that I could not get along and support them," she later wrote of her kids, "and I came to the conclusion that it would be better for them if they were out of the way. I thought the matter over for several days. I was much discouraged and downhearted" [6]. She found a solution in arsenic, and soon four-year-old Edward, six-year-old Martha and the baby William were dead. Now they didn't have to "grow up to life's cares," as she put it [4]. Doctors attributed death to remittent fever and bronchitis.

Fourteen-year-old George developed "painter's colic" on the job and couldn't return to work. This discouraged Lydia; after she dosed the boy's tea with arsenic, George had no more worries. Daughter Anna Eliza suffered recurrent fever and chills in the winter, which left her mother once again downhearted and discouraged. Lydia took care of "the happiest child I ever saw" [1] — the doctors declared that typhoid fever killed Anna. This left the widow with just one child, an 18-year-old daughter also named Lydia. She died in May 1866. It is not clear if she died from natural causes or was poisoned by her mother.

Widowed and childless, Lydia drifted from job to job, finally moving to Stratford, Connecticut, where she cared for an invalid woman for a wage of $8 a month. During this job she was introduced to a widower named Dennis Hurlbut by a storekeeper who told the old farmer she was "a good woman" to keep house for him.

The 74-year-old man hired her and perhaps expected more than just housekeeping services. In the negotiations that must have ensued Lydia held out for more, since the pair married in November 1868. Hurlbut made a will in her favor, leaving her his entire estate of approximately $10,000.

In the spring of 1870 Hurlbut died of natural causes, according to the physicians. Lydia would later deny she poisoned him; however, when his body was exhumed it was found to contain arsenic. This murder was probably done for money, since the easily depressed woman had no depressing situations in her life during this short union. All she ever admitted was that she "did not get along particularly satisfactorily with him" [4].

The next stop was Derby, Connecticut, where Lydia made the acquaintance of Nelson Horatio Sherman who, she thought, was well-off financially. He was a widower with four children. The couple married in

September 1870. The new Mrs. Sherman immediately found herself in a distressing situation.

In the household lived Sherman's former mother-in-law, Mrs. Jones, who looked after Sherman's infant. Jones always quarreled with Sherman's teenager and both Mr. and Mrs. Sherman wanted Jones out of the house. However, Jones would not leave until Nelson paid her $78 he owed her. It was then that Lydia discovered her new husband had no money. He was also a drunk and took to beating Lydia.

Lydia once gave her husband the money to pay Jones but, instead, he blew it all on booze. A second payment did find its way to Jones; just to make sure that Jones had no reason to stay, Lydia poisoned the seven-month-old baby, which she considered a nuisance anyway. This got rid of Jones, but the marriage showed no signs of improving. In December 1870 Lydia poisoned the teenager, Nelson's favorite child, feeling that she was taking too much of her father's time and attention.

Nelson continued to drink, abuse his wife, and spend her money. By the end of 1870 the couple were sleeping separately, she downstairs and he upstairs. Lydia contemplated getting a divorce. Early in May 1871, Nelson came home after having been away for one full week on one of his binges. His wife confronted him about, among other things, the sleeping arrangements and said, "Don't you think we don't do right in not sleeping together?" [2]. Nelson's answer was noncommittal but his wife had had enough. She laced his brandy with arsenic. Nelson was dead by the middle of May. Later Lydia said of this marriage when it didn't work out, "I felt so bad that I was tempted to do as I had done before" [6].

This time so many deaths in one family in so short a time aroused suspicions, and the three Shermans were exhumed. All the bodies contained arsenic. Hurlbut's body was then exhumed, with the same result.

Lydia was arrested and stood trial in April 1872, charged only with the murder of Nelson. A contemporary account described her as having "a face which, though not exactly prepossessing, is not repulsive. She was neatly dressed in half mourning, and talked with the jailer and her counsel before the opening of Court, laughing sometimes, though not often" [10].

The tabloids called her a "Modern Borgia" and "the Unnatural Wife and Mother." Throughout the trial Lydia insisted she was innocent and had poisoned no one. The jury disagreed, and after deliberating for only 50 minutes they returned with a verdict of guilty of second-degree murder. Lydia was sentenced to life in prison.

Suffering apparently from remorse and guilt, Lydia made a confession in prison in January 1873. In her confession she admitted to all the murders except for her baby William, daughter Lydia, and Nelson. William wasn't mentioned at all, apparently completely forgotten, and Nelson, Lydia insisted, must have accidentally taken poison.

Even in her confession she maintained her "altruism" by claiming her victims "would be better off" dead. Confined to a state prison in Connecticut, Lydia escaped in early 1878 but was soon recaptured. She was then placed in "close confinement." Her health deteriorated, and Lydia Sherman died in prison on May 16, 1878.

Sources

1. Dunbar, Dorothy. *Blood in the Parlor.* New York: Barnes, 1964, pp. 156–82.

2. "The Connecticut Murderess." *New York Times,* July 4, 1871, p. 8.

3. "Death of a Murderess." *New York Times,* May 17, 1878, p. 1.

4. "The Derby Poisoner." *New York Times,* January 11, 1873, p. 5.

5. "Horrible Story." *New York Times,* July 1, 1871, p. 8.

6. Jones, Ann. *Women Who Kill.* New York: Holt, 1980, pp. 116–21.

7. Green, Jonathon. *The Greatest Criminals of All Time.* New York: Stein & Day, 1980, p. 155.

8. Nash, Jay Robert. *Look for the Woman.* New York: M. Evans, 1981, pp. 342–44.

9. Sifakis, Carl. *The Encyclopedia of American Crime.* New York: Facts on File, 1982, pp. 478–79.

10. "Trial of Mrs. Sherman." *New York Times,* April 17, 1872, p. 1.

Mamie Shey Shoaf

(?–1929). *Place:* Lebanon, Kentucky. *Time:* May 24, 1929. *Age:* Unknown.
Victims: 4. *Method:* Knife.

In the end, financial problems overwhelmed Mamie Shoaf. She was the
wife of lumber company employee Carey Shoaf. Originally from Lexington, the couple moved to Lebanon, Kentucky, in 1918. By 1929 Mamie
was the mother of seven children between the ages of two and 17 years.
Family members said that Mamie had been worried and depressed about
financial troubles for some time. On May 23, 1929, she told a family
member, in apparent reference to her money woes, that she would not "go
through another day like this." And in fact, she didn't.

The next day she took the three youngest children, Tom, 2; Ina, 7; and
Catherine, 11, to a nearby cemetery, where she slashed their throats with
a knife. Then she slashed her own throat. A little later two youths walking
past heard groans. They followed them to the dying Mamie, who weakly
pointed to a nearby spot where the bodies of her three children lay.

Sources

1. "Mother Kills Tots, Suicides." *Lexington Herald,* May 25, 1929, p. 1.

Della Sorenson

(1897–?). *Place:* St. Libory and Dannebrog, Nebraska. *Time:* 1918–1923. *Age:* 21–26. *Victims:* 7. *Method:* Poison.

For Della Sorenson, the most minor disagreement with family or friend or the most inconsequential slight would be held as a grudge. The grudge would be nursed and then unleashed in a murderous attack. Five of the dead were children, some her own. When she was arrested, she had her eye on more potential victims.

Della was born around 1897 in rural Nebraska, an area she would call home for the rest of her life. In 1915 she married Joe Weldam, moving to his farm near the community of St. Libory. They would have at least two children over the following few years. Mrs. Cooper was Della's sister-in-law, and the two women did not seem to get along. According to Della, the Cooper woman was always running her down behind Della's back. Years later Mrs. Cooper could recall only that Della was annoyed when she wouldn't attend the church which Della recommended.

Whatever the tiff may have been, it was enough for Della to take drastic and murderous action. As Della would state in a future confession, "Mrs. Cooper always was running down my reputation, and to get even with her, I decided to kill three of her children" [1]. Mrs. Cooper and her 13-month-old daughter Viola were visiting Della on July 23, 1918. Della put some poison she had bought on a piece of candy, which she then gave to Viola. The infant was dead before the day was out.

Living with Della was her mother-in-law, Wilhelmina Weldam. She died in July 1920, a couple of hours after taking some of her medicine into which Della had slipped some poison. The elderly woman was dispatched because, said Della, she "was feeble and childish and a burden on my hands and I wanted her out of the way" [1].

Three months later, on September 7, Della poisoned her three-year-old daughter Minnie to death to relieve the child's suffering. "She ate and tore the clothes off the bed; put her hands on the hot stove, could not talk and suffered terribly, so to relieve her suffering I put some of this poison into a glass of water, which I gave her. She died in a very short time. Soon as the child died I had a feeling of elation and happiness; then after thinking of what I had done I had a feeling of fear and tried to hide what I had done" [1]. Minnie's cause of death was listed as St. Vitus' dance. All of Della's victims suffered the same way, going into violent convulsions and dying soon thereafter.

Later that same month, on September 20, Della poisoned her husband Joe to death. She committed this murder because: "I and my first husband, Joseph Weldam, had a fall out. We had a quarrel, a bad quarrel one day. I had it in for him. ... After he died and I came to, I was sorry for what I had done and wished I had never done it" [1]. Mrs. Weldam purchased the poison at a hardware store, signing the register with her correct name.

Joe's brother Frank was a visitor in the Weldam home at the time of his brother's death. "When I went to their home," he recalled, "my brother was ailing and died within a few days. There was nothing in the actions of his wife to indicate anything was wrong. Her sorrow seemed heartfelt. That he was a victim of poisoning never entered my mind" [5].

Feeling sorry for his widowed sister-in-law, Frank stayed on at the farm for several months to help Della get the place in shape so she could sell it. Frank described Della as "agreeable, a good cook and housekeeper, and pleasant when callers came," although he personally never "took much of a shine to her" [5].

Five months after her husband's death, Della married Emmanuel Sorenson following a courtship that lasted only two weeks. She moved to her new husband's home in the community of Dannebrog. They had two children.

Old grudges were not forgotten, however. On August 20, 1923, Mrs. Cooper came to visit Della in Dannebrog, bringing along her four-month-old son Clifford. Della fed the child poison on some candy, bringing about his death that day. Doctors certified this death as due to "acute indigestion with overheating contributory." Two months later the unsuspecting Mrs. Cooper and her daughter Bessie paid a return visit. Sorenson put poison on some bread and butter, which she gave to the child. Bessie got very ill but recovered. "Every time I gave poison to one of Mrs. Cooper's children," Della confessed, "I said to myself, 'Now I am going to get even with you'" [1].

Early in the next year, Della struck again. "On February 13, 1923, I put some poison in my baby Deloris' mouth and then let her nurse. She only lived a couple of hours after that. I gave this baby the poison because it made me nervous and irritable and because it was not feeling very good and was continually fussing and crying. This baby died on its first birthday" [1].

One week after that a friend of Della's, Christina Brook, came to call, bringing her baby Ruth along. Sorenson claimed she felt sorry for the infant since its mother did not properly care for it. Slipping a grain of poison into Ruth's mouth, Della murdered the 18-day-old child on February 20,

1923. "Acute indigestion with exposure to cold contributing," was the cause of death, said doctors.

Della also wanted to kill her daughter Margaret Weldam, born in 1920. After Della had put poison in her medicine Margaret refused to drink it so, said Della, "I told my husband to drink it and maybe she would if she saw him. He drank some of the medicine, but there wasn't enough poison in it to kill him" [7]. Mr. Sorenson got sick but recovered. On another occasion Della tried to kill her husband by putting poison in his food after the couple had an argument. Once again Emmanuel became ill, but recovered.

By 1923, people in Dannebrog had begun to gossip about Della. The sudden illnesses followed by convulsions and death connected to the Sorenson woman didn't go unnoticed. Other visitors to the Sorenson home had been taken acutely ill but survived. The finger of suspicion was pointed at Della. After the deaths in February 1923, town leaders resolved that at the next case of suspicious circumstances connected with the woman they would take action.

The town got its chance in February 1925, when neighbor Mrs. Knott dropped in to visit Della with her year-old infant Lillian. Mrs. Knott stepped outside for a minute. When she went back inside Della was holding the baby, feeding it a piece of candy. Lillian later became sick but survived. Three days later Sorenson visited Mrs. Knott. While Knott was occupied, Della gave Lillian and three-year-old Lyle Knott cookies spiked with poison. Both children became violently ill but pulled through. Mrs. Sorenson later admitted to this attempt at murder, saying, "Their father stole my wine and I felt like I wanted to get even with him" [7].

Dr. Pedersen had tended the Cooper family and was suspicious of the children's deaths. He had thought of launching an investigation at the time but backed off, limiting himself to advising Mrs. Cooper to keep her children and herself away from Della. After the Knott poisonings, Dr. Pedersen, with the support of town leaders, called in state officials who took samples of the Knott children's vomit away for analysis. Poison was found and an investigation was started. On April 17, 1925, Della was arrested. She then had two living children, Margaret and a 15-month-old by Sorenson. Emmanuel expressed faith in his spouse, saying, "My wife is not guilty. Why I've been sick lots of times. People said she tried to poison me. Anybody can get sick for a couple of hours. Why last year, I had quite a spell of intestinal trouble. I had to have a doctor" [3].

Della quickly confessed to the long string of murders and attempts remarking, "I had feelings which would steal over me at times, forcing me to destroy and kill. I felt funny and happy. . . . I like to attend funerals. I'm happy when someone is dying" [2]. She attended the funerals of all her victims. A shaky and nervous feeling crept over her when she felt a desire to kill, she said.

Future victims spared by the woman's arrest included Mrs. Cooper. "I wanted to kill Mrs. Cooper but I never got a chance," complained Della. That was because Cooper never returned after Bessie's illness. Della had also been estranged from her father and stepmother, Mrs. and Mrs. Sidel, since marrying Weldam against their wishes. After Joe's death, Della would sometimes visit the Sidels. "I often wanted to kill Mrs. Sidel and hunted all over the house for some poison but couldn't find any," asserted Sorenson. "I had a good chance to for I could have put it in her medicine" [7].

An insanity hearing was held on April 18. Dr. Flippen said he treated Della for about 18 months in 1919–1920, finding that at times she acted "queerly" with her mind going "blank." Evidence was introduced that Della quarrelled at least several times with Emmanuel. One fight was over some jewelry of Mr. Sorenson's that was missing. He was taken ill after that fight. Della's brother Joe Sidel told of a fire at his parents' home right after a visit by his sister.

Della was examined by a panel of physicians that included Dr. Fast, the superintendent of Ingleside Hospital for the Insane at Hastings. Dr. Fast called the woman illiterate and incapable of learning. "She is abnormal mentally suffering with dementia precox [sic]," added the doctor [2]. The hearing adjudged Della to be insane, a "paranoiac victim." The physicians agreed that Della was dangerous, an "imbecile," and had the mind of a seven- or eight-year-old child. She was committed to Ingleside on April 20. No criminal charges were brought against the woman.

Immediately after signing her confession Della became hysterical, screaming "I'll never do it again. I want to die, too. ... I don't want to be electrocuted. Please send me to the hospital right now so that I can get out in a couple of weeks and return to my children. I was out of my head each time. It was horrible—like a dream—but I had that feeling that I wanted to kill. I killed when I had that feeling. They can't do anything to me for that, can they?" When Mr. Sorenson arrived at the jail she cried out to him, "Don't let this break up our home. I will be out of the hospital soon, and then we will be happy again" [8].

When Dr. Fast was asked by newsmen how long Della might be confined to the Ingleside hospital he replied, "Such cases do not recover in a short time. She should remain here for many years. She is a moron and has been defective since childhood. Her condition should have been recognized years ago and would have been disclosed by a mental test. Cause of Mrs. Sorenson's condition might be traced back several generations" [5].

Sources

1. "Confession of Mrs. Sorenson, Nebraskan, Slayer of Seven." *Omaha World-Herald,* April 20, 1925, p. 1.

2. "Desire to Kill, Mrs. Sorenson Gives as a Motive." *Omaha World-Herald,* April 19, 1925, pp. 1, 3.

3. "Mate Defends Woman Suspected Poisoner." *Omaha World-Herald,* April 19, 1925, p. 1.

4. "Mrs. Sorenson Under Watch by Town for Nearly 3 Years." *Omaha World-Herald,* April 19, 1925, pp. 1, 3.

5. "Omaha Brother Tells Poison Victim's Death." *Omaha World-Herald,* April 22, 1925, p. 7.

6. "Poisoned Children Listed as Dead of Acute Indigestion." *Omaha World-Herald,* April 22, 1925, p. 7.

7. "Poisoner of Twelve Taken to Asylum." *Omaha World-Herald,* April 21, 1925, pp. 1, 3.

8. "Sorenson Admits Poisoning Eight." *Omaha World-Herald,* April 20, 1925, pp. 1, 2.

9. "Victims' Kin Says Poisoner Should Die." *Omaha World-Herald,* April 23, 1925, p. 10.

Mariam Soulakiotis

(c. 1900–?). *Place:* Keratea, Greece. *Time:* 1940–1950. *Age:* 40s. *Victims:* 177. *Method:* Beatings, torture, starvation.

Father Matthew, a Greek Orthodox priest, grew upset in 1923 with some of the changes taking place within his church. Resigning from the Church, Father Matthew vowed he would continue to serve Christ by founding a new sect more in keeping with his own views. This he did that same year by establishing his new sect on a slope of hilly land, known as the Mount of Pines, just outside the Greek village of Keratea. He was then about 65 years old.

Men and women slowly trickled in to join the unnamed group. Among the first was a young former factory worker by the name of Mariam Soulakiotis. One account describes her as a woman who "spoke glibly and managed to give her words an air of authority. She was certainly prepared to work, and she had a shrewd head on her young shoulders. She was comely for a peasant, not tall, but had a pair of eyes that could be passionate about something or someone" [1].

Soon Mariam took charge of the day-to-day running of the place. She also took over direction fo the building construction. Some of the men complained, but Father Matthew gave her his full backing. It left him time to withdraw from everything to a greater degree. A monastery for monks was constructed, along with a convent for nuns. A third building was a joint-use chapel. Father Matthew renamed himself Archbishop Matthew. This new order lived an austere and devoted life. Long hours of manual work in the fields were followed by long hours of prayer and secluded devotion. Mariam had been Sister Mariam after joining the sect, but soon she redesignated herself Mother Mariam.

In 1939, Matthew died. Mariam was named heir in his will, which gave her title to various properties given to Matthew over the years. It seemed to bring out the greed in the woman. On Matthew's death Mariam ascended to leadership of the sect, then known in Greece as the Calendarists. It was an unopposed transition, for the woman had been leader in all but name for some years.

Beginning in 1940, Mariam set the order on a new course of intensive recruiting. Nuns and monks, the youngest and most personable, were dispatched to all points of Greece to bring in new members. Before setting off Mariam gave her missionaries a crash course in selling her way of life. Mariam was primarily interested in recruiting women to the sect — preferably women who had plenty of material goods. The message was that being well endowed with goods was a terrible burden. If this burden was cast aside — given to the sect, of course — then a spiritual life infinitely more rewarding than the temporal one could be assumed.

It might have been a very old con, but it worked. Over the years a steady stream of newcomers arrived at the Mount of Pines. The convent was enlarged. Residents in Keratea noticed the increase in new recruits and they wondered, for while many women entered the convent, few were ever glimpsed on the grounds when townspeople walked by the walls. Travelers passing the place after dark claimed they heard muffled cries and groans from inside. People from Keratea then would sometimes climb the walls at night to listen. They soon agreed that something sinister was going on.

One night a couple of villagers, fortified by alcohol, sneaked in to find an old woman, emaciated and filthy, chained to a wall. This woman refused their offered aid. The two men carried the story back to the village. An unspoken pact was reached whereby the incident would not be mentioned. From then on the villagers would not talk about the Calendarists to themselves or to strangers. They treated the place as though it did not exist.

Everything that was going on at the place started to break open in March 1950, when a woman by the name of Helen Papas wrote a letter to the Public Prosecutor in Athens. She claimed her mother had been accepted into the order only to be forced to sign over her possessions to Mother Mariam, who by then styled herself Popess and insisted on being addressed as such. The prosecutor turned the letter over to the police, who started an investigation.

The authorities established that about 500 people had been recruited to the sect during the 10-year recruitment drive. All were forced to sign over their possessions to Mariam. They were then beaten and subjected to penances. Recruits were denied sleep and food. They were flogged and forced to live in their own filth. No doctors were permitted on the grounds.

When the police raided the place, half the inmates were found to be suffering from tuberculosis. Mother Mariam was arrested. Soon inmates who had escaped from the place came forward to relate their personal horror stories to the authorities. A woman of 70 was stripped of her possessions the day she arrived. She was then kept like an animal and refused permission to write to relatives. A mother from Thebes entered the convent with her four daughters between the ages of 22 and 26. Within six months of signing over their worldly goods as "dedications" to the sect, all five women were dead. Ileana Spirides was a 22-year-old of Greek ancestry born in Toledo, Ohio. On a trip to Greece she entered the convent, never to be seen again.

When the nuns who assisted Mariam in her work were asked why there had been so many death in the convent their stock answer was, "Because so many of those who came to us were old." Another answer was that the monks, resenting the rise of Mariam to sect leadership, were chiefly responsible for the "trouble" that had befallen the Calendarists [1]. In January 1951, this sect was proscribed and prohibited from any further activities.

Typically a new inmate would first be given a form on which to list a complete inventory of possessions and property. Signing it all over to the sect was the next order of business. Mariam explained that the new recruit could never attain grace in the hereafter if she refused to sign everything over. The women who did make this sacrifice would be rewarded for such self-denial, said Mariam, by becoming "the brides of Christ in the next" world [1]. If this gentle persuasion didn't do the trick the inmate was chained in a cell, starved, burned on her body's extremities, forced to drink a narcotic-laced fluid, and beaten with a knotted rope.

Once the donations were collected, a week followed in which no sleep was allowed. The recruits were subjected to hard manual labor, endless prayer, and rigorous fasting. A rule of complete silence was imposed. An inmate who broke the silence rule was forced to kiss Mariam's boot. The inmate was then beaten on the face by Mariam, using this boot, which she took from her foot. One woman who objected was held by two nuns. Mariam then beat her unconscious, leaving her lying on the floor choking on her own blood, with no medical attention.

Mariam was tried for the first time in 1951 on the sole charge of illegally detaining a child. She was convicted and sentenced to two years in jail. The state did this solely to keep her in custody while they prepared the major charges, which took the state longer than it expected. In two separate trials held in 1953, Mariam was found guilty both times. A sentence of 10 years was imposed at the first trial, followed by four more years at the second trial. It was a remarkably light sentence considering that the state established that during the period from 1940 to 1950, 177 inmates of the convent, ranging in age from 20 to 80, died as a result of the treatment Mariam meted out.

Sources

1. Gribble, Leonard. *The Hallmark of Horror*. London: John Long, 1973, pp. 135–46.

Hieronyima Spara

(?–1659). *Place:* Rome, Italy. *Time:* To 1659. *Age:* Unknown. *Victims:* 100 or more. *Method:* Arsenic poisoning.

Preceding the murderous footsteps of Toffania was Hieronyima Spara, who shared her fellow Italian's hatred of men. Nominally Spara made her living as a fortune-teller, but in reality she dispensed poison potions to her numerous clients to help them get rid of unwanted husbands. This self-styled witch operated in Rome, Italy, until the year 1659. At that time she was said to be getting on in years. No accurate body count exists for Spara, but one source puts it in the hundreds.

Most of her clients were married women who consulted her about the quickest way to eliminate their spouses. Hieronyima boasted that she never sent a client away disappointed. Each one went off with a phial of poison. Spara apparently used a concoction that was mainly arsenic. With the poison, each client received lessons in acting from Spara so that she could carry out the murder without arousing any suspicions.

Mysterious deaths of men in Rome occurred so frequently that the papal police of Pope Alexander VII finally launched an investigation. So serious was the matter that they violated the confessional, where a few women had confessed to murdering their husbands, to get onto Spara's trail. A female papal spy was dispatched to enter Spara's world. She found a sect of women who met at Spara's home. After they performed satanic rituals, poison would be sold, at a high price, to any woman who needed it.

The spy pretended to be a wealthy society woman with a tiresome husband. After performing various mystical antics, Hieronyima produced a phial of poison, gave it to the spy with instructions to covertly slip it into her husband's food or drink, and was told that if she followed instructions she would soon be free. This led to Spara being arrested, along with many of her clients.

Subjected to torture on the rack, Spara soon confessed to being a wholesale poisoner. Spara and a few other women were publicly humiliated and then hung as witches and murderers. A number of others received only the public humiliation, which consisted of being driven half-naked through the streets of Rome and beaten by a whip. The year was around 1659.

Sources

1. Nash, Jay Robert. *Look for the Woman.* New York: M. Evans, 1981, p. 348.

2. O'Donnell, Elliott. *Women Bluebeards.* London: Stanley Paul, 1928, pp. 20–21.

Marybeth Tinning

(1942–). *Place:* Schenectady, New York. *Time:* 1972–1985. *Age:* 30–43. *Victims:* 8. *Method:* Suffocation.

Marybeth Tinning and her husband Joseph were described by neighbors as a nice couple who kept mostly to themselves. A run of incredible bad luck seemed to dog the couple. From 1967 to 1985, Marybeth gave birth to eight babies. A ninth was adopted by the Tinnings. By the end of 1985, all were dead. Not one of these children lived to see its fifth birthday. Some of the neighbors grew suspicious and a certain amount of gossip made the rounds, but the deaths continued. The police investigated on a couple of occasions, but only in a cursory way. The investigators in each case were unaware of other deaths in the family or even of other investigations.

In high school, the somewhat outgoing blonde Marybeth Roe had been president of the Future Homemakers of America. She noted in the school yearbook that she "hated bookkeeping." William Barnes was a few years older than Marybeth but recalled riding the school bus with her to Duanesburg High School. Two and a half decades after Marybeth's 1961 high school graduation, Barnes would be one of the police officers who questioned Tinning. Of those teen years, Barnes described her as a girl who was explosive, quick to lose her temper.

Marybeth's plans to attend college never materialized. Instead, she was employed as a nurse's aide at Schenectady's Ellis Hospital. Around 1964 she met and married Joseph Tinning. Their first meeting was a blind date. Joseph was then employed as an apprentice at the General Electric plant in Schenectady. By the mid–1980s he was a foreman. Originally hoping to get an engineering degree, Joseph spent two years at Southern Methodist University in Texas but left without earning a degree. When Marybeth was arrested in connection with the deaths of her children, Joseph would be questioned but quickly dismissed as not being a suspect. Police Chief Richard Nelson called him "a hard-working Joe, laid back," compared to Marybeth, whom Nelson categorized as "a very dominant individual" [14].

Over the years Marybeth worked sporadically. For a time she was a school bus driver. In the 1970s she worked at an establishment called the

Flavorland Restaurant as a waitress. Later she worked in the coffee shop at a J.C. Penney department store. During the early 1980s Mrs. Tinning spent one-and-a-half years as a volunteer for the Duanesburg Rescue Squad working as a driver and first-aid person. Coworker Linda McDougall recalled Marybeth as a regular member of the squad who worked one six- or 12-hour shift per week. "I think she just wanted to help people," said McDougall [10]. When traveling between her home and this volunteer job proved too difficult Tinning quit, around 1984. She rarely discussed her personal life with her coworkers. At the time of her arrest, Marybeth was unemployed.

Alton Roe, Marybeth's father, died unexpectedly of a heart attack in October 1971. In pretrial testimony, Tinning claimed that when she was a child Alton sometimes beat her with a flyswatter and locked her in her room. A couple of months after his death Marybeth gave birth to her third child, Jennifer. This infant died on January 3, 1972, seven days old. She never got out of the hospital. The cause of death was listed as respiratory failure due to meningitis. After investigation, this would be the only death of a Tinning child the police did not view as "suspicious."

Dates of the other deaths and causes listed at the time are as follows: Joseph died January 20, 1972, at the age of two years of cardiorespiratory arrest; Barbara died March 2, 1972, at the age of four-and-a-half years of brain edema; Timothy died December 10, 1973, at the age of 14 days of sudden infant death syndrome (SIDS); Nathan died September 2, 1975, at the age of five months of acute pulmonary edema; Mary died February 22, 1979, at the age of three-and-a-half months of SIDS; Jonathan died March 24, 1980, at the age of three months of cardiopulmonary arrest; Michael (the adopted child) died March 2, 1981, at the age of two-and-a-half years of pneumonia; and Tami died December 20, 1985, at the age of four months.

Sometime between December 10, 1974, and May 1, 1975, police became aware of a report that Tinning tried to murder her husband. The couple had fought over money. When Joseph took away his wife's checkbook Marybeth responded by putting barbiturates into his iced tea. Joseph got sick and required hospital treatment but recovered. No charges were laid, and the case was not pursued. Over a decade later, when arrested in connection with the children's deaths, Marybeth admitted this poisoning attempt to the police.

When Timothy died, Marybeth took him to the emergency ward of a local hospital where she told the staff she found him dead. Since he died unattended, policy dictated that the hospital inform the county medical examiner, then Dr. John L. Shields. This doctor knew of no previous deaths in the Tinning family. During his exam he declined to perform an autopsy saying, "You've got a distraught mother standing there with a dead baby and you sign it out as a crib death. Now you wouldn't do that today, but that's the way it was 12 years ago. When this boy was admitted, there was no reason to suspect anything, so we signed it out as a crib death." A successor to Shields, the medical examiner at the time of Tinning's arrest, Dr. Robert L. Sullivan, commented on the lack of an autopsy in Timothy's case by saying, "That was really a complete — not a mix-up, I won't say that. It just should have been done" [12]. The file on Timothy was lost sometime over the years, making it impossible to determine if other agencies investigated the infant's death.

Two years later, Marybeth rushed the dying Nathan to the hospital. While this death was ruled natural, Medical Examiner Dr. Henry Damm noted "a history of other children and sudden death" at the time. For the first time the police became involved. Detective Daniel O'Connor investigated Nathan's death but found no cause to file any charges. A decade later O'Conner was described as unavailable for comment.

When Marybeth took her dying daughter Mary to the hospital in 1979, the police were again called in. This time Detective Robert Imfeld investigated. One of the ambulance squad members who carried the baby into the hospital thought the death was suspicious and notified the police. Imfeld was unaware of the five previous deaths of Tinning children. He was also unaware of the previous investigation by O'Connor. Imfeld conducted, by his own admission, a cursory investigation. He simply checked the coroner's report, saw it listed SIDS as the cause of death, briefly questioned the Tinnings, then closed the case. "Let's face it, once the coroner's office rules SIDS, you don't have a case," said Imfeld. "Who's going to go out and interrogate a couple who've lost their kid to SIDS?" When asked if he would have handled the case differently had he known of the prior deaths, Imfeld replied, "No comment" [4]. Sullivan said that no one reported this death to his office, neither the police, the hospital, nor the doctor who signed the death certificate. All unexplained deaths — which is what SIDS, or crib death is — are supposed to be reported to the county medical examiner.

When baby Jonathan died in 1980 he was pronounced dead in a hospital in the city of Albany, New York. The doctor who performed an autopsy listed death as due to natural causes but advised his superiors that he was suspicious and to keep the case open for further investigation. However, the medical examiner in Albany failed to notify Sullivan, who had jurisdiction only in Schenectady County. It was, as one writer noted, a problem in communication. No action was taken in the death of Jonathan.

In February 1981, social workers from the Schenectady County Child Protective Unit visited the Tinning home to investigate after being notified that Michael needed medical care in a hospital after falling down a flight of stairs. The workers found no evidence of wrongdoing. A couple of weeks later Marybeth rushed the dying Michael to the doctor. Sullivan was called in to investigate this time. By then he was partially aware of the number of Tinning deaths, for he noted down "Sixth child in Tinning family to die since 1972." Michael was actually the eighth. Sullivan was still then unaware of the demise of both Mary and Jonathan.

Based on the "past record" of the Tinnings Sullivan ordered an autopsy, but no evidence of foul play was uncovered. While the cause of death was ruled as natural, one of the members of the investigating team of physicians warned authorities to keep an eye on Marybeth in case she had more children.

On December 20, 1985, Tami was transported by ambulance to a hospital, where she was pronounced dead. This time alarm bells went off everywhere. Hospital staff notified the medical examiner and a recently established state hot-line for potential child abuse reports. The state informed the county child protection unit, which notified the district attorney's office. All of this culminated in a full investigation of Tami's death, followed by the arrest of Marybeth on February 5, 1986. Thomas Oram, a hospital chief pathologist, said, "Up to the sixth or seventh death people were still thinking it was some medical curiosity. I think we were blinded to the fact there may have been something else because of the reaction of the family . . . on a rational level it just couldn't be put together. There was a grasp to find a natural cause" [12]. Tests revealed Tami died of suffocation.

Initially Chief Nelson stated that the police had conducted full probes the times they had been called in. In light of Imfeld's statement, he had to retract that and agree that the investigations were not "in depth." Said Nelson, "Just about everyone who came into contact with the family — the hospitals, doctors, social services workers — was suspicious and communicated that suspicion to each other, many from the very beginning. Everyone did their jobs, but when you have a legitimate cause of death, where do you go from there?" [14]

After Tinning's arrest, Medical Examiner Sullivan commented on the failure to act earlier: "There were so many of us in on it, I guess. If anyone is negligent, I suppose I am. I probably should have said, 'There must be more to it than this.' But we all think, and don't do. . . . Everyone says, 'How could it happen?' But if you look at the cases one by one you could see how it could happen. There were too many people involved in too many deaths. Only when they started happening with greater frequency did we suspect anything. The doctors thought: Natural deaths do occur. You think this is either terrible luck or maybe it's something in the genes. . . . Now it looks bad. Nobody paid that much attention. At the time it looked OK" [14, 6].

One person whose suspicions weren't aroused was Larry Daly of the Daly Funeral Home. His company handled all nine of the Tinning funerals. Daly considered the deaths strange but until hearing of Tinning's arrest on the radio ascribed the deaths to fate, just bad luck. "We've never seen anything like this before, he said. "They seemed like a model — a very, very nice couple. If you met them, you wouldn't believe this. . . . There was plenty of emotion on their part in the services as there would be for anyone who lost a child. It would be the same as anyone else, the same grief, the same emotions" [1].

The Reverend Roger Day consoled the family the morning Tami died. Having heard from the funeral home about the previous deaths, Day initially suspected something other than bad luck. However, when he went to the Tinning home he found himself believing that what Marybeth told him about finding Tami blue was correct. Finding a well-kept home and a woman who seemed interested in her child, Day left the home convinced there had been no foul play.

In her neighborhood Marybeth was often seen pushing a baby carriage on her way to the market. On warm summer nights she might sit outside on the porch for hours with a baby in her lap. Although the Tinnings didn't try to make friends with their neighbors, they would say "hi" on the street, and Marybeth welcomed any attention paid to her neatly dressed children. The few times neighbors asked Marybeth about her tragedies, Tinning would say the children died of congenital heart ailments or SIDS. One neighbor, Dorothy Posluszny, said, "I knew she had lost five children and I had my suspicions. But who was I to point the finger?" A second neighbor commented, "When I read about it I said 'We could have saved this one. How could we all have been so dumb?'" A third neighbor remarked, "When the last child was born I asked myself, 'How long is this one going to last?'" [14].

Joseph Tinning expressed faith in his wife's innocence, although Nelson felt he probably suspected something but never confronted his wife about it. "There were things to make me suspect, but you have to trust your wife," Joseph said. "She has her things to do and as long as she gets them done you don't ask questions" [14].

Another who believed in the woman's innocence was her brother Alton Roe, Jr. He described his sister as just a "home person." According to Alton, adopting Michael brought a little sunshine into the Tinning lives. Alton said the couple really loved Michael. After his sister's arrest Roe said, "We didn't suspect anything. We still don't suspect anything. . . . She's always very interested in helping other people. She goes out of her way to help somebody if they need help. . . . She's real protective over the kids. . . . I don't know if you'd call her a religious person or not. She believes in God, but I know they talked to ministers" as the children died [3].

During police interrogation after her arrest, Marybeth gave the police a statement which read, in part, "I did not do anything to Jennifer, Joseph, Barbara, Michael, Mary, Jonathan. Just these three, Timothy, Nathan and Tami. I smothered them each with a pillow because I'm not a good mother. I'm not a good mother because of what happened to the other children" [2]. Marybeth suffocated Tami because "she was always crying and I couldn't do anything right." Timothy was smothered because he was making "gurgling noises" from a cold he had. She wanted him to be quiet so she put a pillow over his face until he stopped making the noise. She told police it was out of frustration, saying, "I mean, whatever I did just didn't turn out right." While driving her car with Nathan, the infant began to cry. She put a pillow over his face until he stopped. Officer Barnes recalled the interrogation and that Tinning stated, "She was not a good mother. She never felt that she was worth anything. Her self-esteem was low. She couldn't even stop her children from crying" [13].

Marybeth stood trial on one count of murder—that of Tami. She didn't testify and was largely emotionless until the end, when she broke down sobbing. During the trial Tinning followed the proceedings closely, taking copious notes. When her defense attorney, Paul Callahan, finished his summation and sat down Marybeth leaned over to tell him something. Callahan then objected to a point made by the state. While he had the judge's attention he asked if he might continue his summation as Marybeth had pointed out an omission to him.

On July 17, 1987, after four weeks of testimony and 15 hours of deliberation, Marybeth Tinning was convicted of second-degree murder. She was sentenced to a term in prison of from 20 years to life. Of the verdict Joseph said, "I still think she's innocent, that's all I can say"—despite the fact he had previously stated Marybeth had admitted in front of him that she killed Tami.

Sources

1. "Area Mother Charged with Killing Her Baby." *The Knickerbocker News,* February 5, 1986, pp. 1A, 5A.

2. Boorstin, Robert O. "Schenectady Child-Suffocation Case Goes to Jury." *New York Times,* July 16, 1987, p. B2.

3. "Brother: Accused Babykiller 'Loved Children.'" *The Knickerbocker News,* February 8, 1986, pp. 1A, 4A.

4. "Earlier Child-Death Probes 'Not in Depth.'" *The Knickerbocker News,* February 7, 1986, pp. 1A, 6A.

5. "Hot-line Call Prompted Baby Death Probe." *The Knickerbocker News,* February 6, 1986, pp. 1A, 6A.

6. "Medical Examiner: 'At the Time' Tinning Deaths 'Looked OK.'" *The Knickerbocker News,* February 7, 1986, p. 6A.

7. "Mother Guilty of Murdering Her Daughter." *New York Times,* July 18, 1987, pp. 29–30.

8. "Mother Is a Suspect in the Nine Deaths of Young Children." *New York Times,* February 6, 1986, p. B5.

9. "Mother's Trial Starts in Baby's Death." *New York Times,* June 28, 1987, p. 42.

10. "Neighborhood Refrain: 'If You Met Them, You Wouldn't Believe This.'" *The Knickerbocker News,* February 6, 1986, p. 6A.

11. Smith, Greg. "Baby-Slay Verdict Spurs Review of Other Deaths." *The Knickerbocker News,* July 18, 1987, pp. 1A, 4A.

12. Smith, Greg. "Communications Snarl Blocked Baby Death Probes." *The Knickerbocker News,* February 13, 1986, pp. 1A, 4A.

13. Smith, Greg. "History of Marybeth Tinning, Family Studied in 6-week Trial." *The Knickerbocker News,* July 18, 1987, pp. 1A, 4A.

14. Wallace, Amy. "After 9 Babies Die in 14 Years, Mother Is Held." *New York Times,* February 8, 1986, pp. 1, 30.

La Toffania

(1653–1723). *Place:* Naples, Italy. *Time:* 1670–1719. *Age:* 16–66. *Victims:* c. 600. *Method:* Arsenic poisoning.

Today she is known only as La Toffania (or Tofania), her full name lost to history. Her name may be unknown, but her deeds are not, for she was one of history's biggest mass murderers, male or female, with her victims numbering in the hundreds.

Born in Italy in 1653 she operated out of Naples, where she specialized in concocting and dispensing poisons. She started about 1670 and continued her murderous ways for almost 50 years until she was apprehended in 1719. In her teens she murdered a man in Palermo, perhaps a husband or relative. In turning to poisoning as a profession, La Toffania seemed to be motivated by a hatred of men more than by greed. Her deadly poison potion was an arsenic compound named, in honor of its maker, "aqua toffania." It was said to produce symptoms unlike those usually found with arsenic.

Some people she killed herself, but she was usually just the supplier. Clients came to her and bought her potions to do away with others. The typical client was a society woman who wanted to rid herself of a husband or lover to ease her way into other affairs. Almost all of La Toffania's victims were men.

So popular was aqua toffania that it found buyers as far afield as France, Spain, and even England. To safeguard buyer and seller, the concoction was sold as a preparation for the complexion. On the phial containing the liquid was the inscription "Manna of St. Nicholas of Bari" [1]. The poison could kill quickly if a lot was administered or slowly, prolonging the suffering, if a smaller dose was given. La Toffania displayed her hatred for men by urging her clients to give small doses and enjoy the resulting agony for as long as possible. Not all of her clients took this advice.

Sometimes naïve people were steered her way and believed they were buying a potion that could cure all diseases, and that the liquid actually periodically flowed from the tomb of St. Nicholas. When these honest purchasers were men, Toffania exhorted them to drink it themselves. If they were women she advised them to give it to those of their male acquaintances who were ailing.

Authorities caught on to her in 1719, and the Viceroy of Naples issued an order for her arrest. Married men had been dying off at such a rate that it was finally noticed and acted upon. Some people had long noted the fact that when a bottle of aqua toffania appeared in a house, a death invariably followed. Some of this potion was examined and found to be mostly arsenic. The authorities then set out to identify the maker and vendor. La Toffania already had a bad reputation among the men of Naples. She was known as the head of a group of militant feminists who met in secret and who, thought these men, plotted darkly against the male sex. Before she could be picked up, her female spies warned her of danger. La Toffania tried to avoid arrest by taking refuge in a convent, believing that the authorities wouldn't try to violate the sanctity of a church.

An appeal to the convent by the viceroy to have the murderess turned over to him was rejected. Her popularity was still quite large in the city, at least in some quarters. The authorities were stonewalled—at least until someone spread a rumor that La Toffania had poisoned the cisterns that supplied drinking water to Naples. This aroused public indignation and emboldened the viceroy to send troops into the convent. They dragged the poisoner out and threw her into a dungeon, a move that was still controversial. The local archbishop became incensed and demanded she be returned to the convent.

Under torture, La Toffania confessed to being responsible for the deaths of some 600 victims. This figure may be an exaggeration, but it is far from impossible.

She readily named names, and it was reported that later many noblewomen were tried and executed based on her evidence. At the conclusion of her trial, in 1723, Toffania was ordered strangled to death. After this was done her corpse was thrown over the wall into the convent where she had sought sanctuary.

Sources

1. Green, Jonathon. *The Greatest Criminals of All Time.* New York: Stein & Day, 1980, p. 156.

2. O'Donnell, Elliott. *Women Bluebeards.* London: Stanley Paul, 1928, pp. 16–19.

Jane Toppan

(1854–1938). *Place:* United States, New England area. *Time:* c. 1880–1901. *Age:* 26–47. *Victims:* 31 or more. *Method:* Morphine and atropine poisoning.

She was respected wherever she went as the embodiment of a selfless, nurturing woman. Nurse Jane Toppan worked long and hard over her various patients. Esteemed physicians had no hesitation in recommending Jane to patients in need of private nursing. However, there was a dark side to this dedicated nurse. She lied and she stole; but worst of all, she murdered her patients. Jane killed because she enjoyed it. The act of murder excited her.

Toppan was born Honora A. Kelley around 1854 to impoverished Irish immigrants. Her birthplace seems to have been in Massachusetts. Mrs. Kelley died when her child was a year old. This left Peter Kelley, a tailor, to try and raise his four daughters alone. Unequal to the task, he suffered some sort of breakdown and was confined to an insane asylum. Forty years later he would still be there when his daughter became notorious. A grandmother next tried to look after the children, but she became destitute. The four girls were turned over to the Boston Female Asylum for Destitute Girls.

The Abner Toppans of Lowell, Massachusetts, adopted Honora from this home when she was five. The first thing they did was to rename her Jane Toppan. The adoption arrangement was such that the Toppans could send her back to the institution at any time up to the age of 18 if the child proved to be unsatisfactory. Jane was brought up strictly but fairly, although she never seemed to have obtained the status of an "equal" family member. When Mrs. Toppan died she left Jane nothing in her will. It all went to her two daughters, who were grown when Jane was taken in.

At that time the Irish were regarded as an inferior race and were much discriminated against in the United States. The Toppans told Jane that while she couldn't help being Irish she didn't have to be a "Paddy." To avoid the stigma, Jane was passed off as an Italian child whose parents had both died of ship fever on their way to the United States. One of Jane's sisters, Ellen, was committed to an insane asylum when in her twenties.

Jane seemed to have had a pleasant childhood. She was cheerful, clever, had a sense of humor, and enjoyed telling stories. Her propensity to lie was noted even then. At school she did well, and she faithfully attended church. Among her peers she was the proverbial "life of the party" at picnics and at skating and boating parties.

When in her early twenties, Jane fell in love and became engaged to a Lowell office worker. This man gave her a ring with a bird engraved on it. A better job came along, and he moved to Holyoke. Just a few weeks after that a shocked Jane received a letter from him in which he explained he had married the daughter of his landlady. So upset was Jane that never again could she look at even a picture of a bird without screaming, "Take it away!" Depressed, Jane retreated into herself and didn't socialize much. Buying a dream book, she made copious notes in an attempt to read the future. Reportedly she attempted suicide once or twice.

By around 1880 Jane had pulled herself together and had determined that nursing was the occupation for her. Jane enrolled as a student nurse at a hospital in Cambridge, Massachusetts. Described as a quick learner, Toppan was considered competent and popular with the other students. What set her apart was a morbid interest in autopsies and operations, which other nurses found unsettling. Toppan was believed to have stolen sums of money from time to time while at the hospital.

After one or more patients under her care died mysteriously, Toppan was dismissed without graduating. No investigation of the matter was pursued. Much later Toppan would admit to murdering during this period, calling them "practice" killings. Lying about her background, Jane managed to obtain a post as head nurse at another Cambridge hospital. She was fired when it was discovered she had forged her graduation diploma. As a head nurse Jane had continued to pilfer sums of money on occasion and at least twice had falsified the temperature record of patients.

After being dismissed as head nurse, Toppan would work from then until her arrest in 1901 as a private-duty nurse. One writer noted that "she had the reputation of being the best nurse in Cambridge. She was eagerly sought after and was almost without exception very much in demand in families where she had once worked. ... Toppan's name was put at the head of the list by one of the most prominent Cambridge physicians after he had known her for years" [2].

Over the years she murdered many of her patients, never drawing any suspicion onto herself. Although she often stole money and other items from their homes, again she was never suspected. When Jane was arrested, she claimed to be broke and without funds for her defense. She habitually traveled around without even enough money on her person for bus fare. Generous on occasion to friends, she owed well over $2,000 to various people at the time of her arrest. What she did with her money is unrecorded.

Around employers, prospective employers, physicians, or others to whom it was important, Jane was the model of decorum and propriety. She abstained from alcohol and coffee and was moral, modest, and respectful. The real Jane drank beer, large amounts of strong coffee, told "broad" stories, and could be very vulgar in her speech. The real Jane was also a morphine addict and had been for some years prior to her arrest.

For the most part Toppan worked in Massachusetts, but she may have been employed — and committed murder — in other areas of New England. In 1899 she poisoned one of her adoptive parents' daughters, Mrs. Brigham. Apparently she entertained the hope that Mr. Brigham might marry her. A year later she killed his housekeeper, Florence Calkins. In February 1900, she murdered a woman in order to get that person's job. She succeeded. Other victims of her poison concoction included Myra Connors of Woods Hole and Mrs. McNear of Watertown.

Toppan killed by injecting her victims with morphine and atropine, the latter a derivative of belladonna. The technical knowledge she possessed as a nurse helped Jane escape detection. Death from morphine poisoning causes the pupils of the eyes to dilate. By judiciously mixing the two poisons, Toppan could leave the victim dead but the eyes normal.

Death from these poisons was considered painless, but Jane often stretched the procedure out for some time. Often she would build a patient up, encouraging the attending physician and decreasing the frequency of his visits. Then Jane would begin to feed the victim a little poison each day. The patient would slowly sink and die after several days. At times she seemed to repent and work feverishly to bring the patient back from death only to send him back to the brink, and over it, after recovery seemed possible. This was perhaps Toppan's way of extending the murder process, which she enjoyed.

As the climax of death approached Jane became more and more excited; later she said, "It wasn't my fault. I had to do it. They hadn't done anything to me and I gained nothing from their deaths except the excitement of watching them die. I couldn't resist doing it. . . . Everybody trusted me. It was so easy. I felt strange when I watched them die. I was all excited and my blood seemed to sweep madly through my veins. It was the only pleasure I had" [5].

In the summer of 1901 Jane ran into Mattie Davis, an old friend of the family who wanted the nurse to pay her some money she was owed. This elderly woman injured herself slightly in a fall from a train, and Toppan ended up nursing her. For weeks Davis got better and worse by turns until she finally died of poisoning on July 4. Jane attended the funeral and then went to the home of Mr. Alden Davis at Cataumet on Cape Cod, where she stayed as a guest. Also staying with Davis were his two married daughters, Mrs. Harry Gordon and Mrs. Irving Gibbs.

Just a couple of weeks after Mrs. Davis's funeral people were saying it was a good thing that nurse Jane had stayed on, for Mrs. Gordon had taken ill. Toppan nursed her night and day, but the woman worsened and expired on July 31. Soon Mr. Davis was likewise feeling poorly and died. The last person remaining at the house was Mrs. Gibbs. Four days after her father's death, she too died.

Before Mrs. Gibbs's death Jane had asked her if she might be forgiven the $500 she owed the Davises, since both were dead. Mrs. Gibbs declined to forgive the loan. The Gordons had a couple of children whom Jane was fond of, and after their mother's death Jane asked Mr. Gordon if she might move into his house to look after them. Mr. Gordon felt it would look too scandalous and refused her offer. Jane told friends that Mr. Gordon made the suggestion and she refused it.

After Mrs. Gibbs died, Toppan left Cataumet and stopped briefly in Lowell to visit Mr. Brigham. Another visitor there was Edna Bannister, Jane's other foster sister. When they met Jane told Edna she looked poorly and needed a tonic. Edna refused, but Jane insisted and prepared the tonic. Edna had been on her way to Buffalo but never made it there, dying four days after Mrs. Gibbs.

Meanwhile Irving Gibbs, a sea captain, returned from a voyage only to receive the shocking news about his wife and her family. He was suspicious and went to the sheriff. His wife's body was exhumed and it was determined that she had been poisoned. A detective was dispatched to arrest Toppan.

Jane was then working on a case in Amherst, New Hampshire, where she was caring for George Nichols and his sister. Toward the end of October 1901, the police caught up with her and arrested her at the Nichols home. The nurse waived extradition and returned to Massachusetts, telling the police, "I have a clear conscience. I wouldn't kill a chicken, and if there is any justice in Massachusetts, they will let me go." After she was exposed, Jane grinned devilishly and said, "I might have killed George Nichols and his sister that night if the detective hadn't taken me away" [3].

Toppan was held in such esteem in the community that there was great indignation on the part of many well-to-do families in Massachusetts who couldn't believe that the efficient nurse they remembered was a killer. A defense fund was established by such people on her behalf.

An alienist by the name of Dr. Henry Stedman visited Jane many times in jail. He took his time and finally got the truth out of her. She blurted out that she had killed them, she had killed them all; that she had fooled the stupid doctors and the dumb relatives. Nor was she sorry. They were better off dead, she told Stedman. "Most of the people I killed were old enough to die, anyway, or else had some disease that might cause death. I never killed children. I love them" [3].

Altogether she enumerated the names, dates, and addresses of 31 murder victims. All checked out. Permission to exhume was denied by relatives in many cases, but of those bodies that were exhumed and examined, all had been poisoned. Once this revelation was made, the defense fund was stopped and the money that had been collected was quietly returned to the contributors.

The accusation that she may have used arsenic angered the woman, who claimed, "If I had used arsenic, my patients would have died hard deaths. I could not bear to see them suffer. When I kill anyone, they go to sleep and never wake up. I use morphia and atropia, the latter to hide the effects of the former" [3].

Jane was only tried for the murder of Mrs. Gibbs. Her defense attorney admitted to 11 murders by Jane, but no more. A plea bargain was struck in which Jane was found not guilty by reason of insanity. In return she would be confined for life to the Taunton mental hospital on the condition she would never attempt to secure her release. On June 24, 1902, Jane was committed to that facility. More than a little angry at being judged insane, she lashed out at the judge, saying she knew she was doing wrong when she was committing her murders and that fact proved she was indeed sane.

In a later confession the nurse told newsmen, "I have given the alienists the names of 31 persons I killed, but, as a matter of fact, I killed many more whose names I cannot recall. I think it would be safe to say that I killed at least 100 from the time I became a nurse at a Boston hospital, where I killed the first one, until I ended the lives of the Davis family" [4]. Most, but not all, observers regarded the figure of 100 as fanciful.

Awaiting her trial, Jane gained 50 pounds. During her first couple of years in the asylum, she seemed normal but then signs of disturbances set in. Jane began to worry because she suffered no remorse for her crimes. She accused the nurses of trying to poison her. Becoming increasingly violent, she was confined to a straitjacket for years. Jane almost died in 1905 but recovered and mellowed over time. Writing love stories was her favorite way to pass the time.

On August 17, 1938, when she was 84 years old, Jane Toppan died in that asylum. Officials then described her as a quiet old lady who never gave them any trouble. However, from time to time she would beckon to a nurse and say, "Get some morphine, dearie, and we'll go out in the ward. You and I will have a lot of fun seeing them die" [3].

When she first confessed, she said to Dr. Stedman, "Do you know what I want to be? I want to go on, and on, and on. I want to be known as the greatest criminal that ever lived. That is my ambition" [3].

Sources

1. "Admits to Killing Thirty-one Persons." *New York Times,* June 25, 1902, p. 3.

2. Folsom, Charles. *Studies of Criminal Responsibility and Limited Responsibility.* Privately printed, 1909.

3. Manchester, Harland. "Jane Toppan, Champion Poisoner." *American Mercury,* 49:340–46, March, 1940.

4. "Miss Jane Toppan, 84, Mass Poisoner, Dies." *New York Times,* August 18, 1938, p. 15.

5. Sifakis, Carl. *The Encyclopedia of American Crime.* New York: Facts on File, 1982, p. 716.

6. Nash, Jay Robert. *Look for the Woman.* New York: M. Evans, 1981, pp. 362–68.

Ruth Urdanivia

(1918–). *Place:* Allentown, Pennsylvania. *Time:* October 14, 1959. *Age:* 41. *Victims:* 5. *Method:* Barbiturates overdose.

Ruth Strawbridge was born in 1918 in Allentown, Pennsylvania. When she graduated from Allentown High School in 1935 the school yearbook listed her as being the "strong, silent type . . . silent but wise." Moving on to San Francisco, Ruth was working as a clerk in the local FBI office toward the end of World War II when she met and married Peruvian diplomat Jose Urdanivia. Jose, the son of a Peruvian army colonel, had been educated in Germany and Switzerland. Before taking up his diplomatic post as consul in San Francisco, he had served in the Ministry of Foreign Relations in Lima.

The couple had two children in San Francisco and two more during a period when they lived in Lima. Their fifth and last child was born in Washington, D.C., where Jose served as second secretary at the Peruvian Embassy from 1954 to 1957. For Ruth it was a world of status and prestige. The couple were both well known in Washington diplomatic circles. Presidents Eisenhower and Truman were two of the people Ruth met at diplomatic functions.

The future looked bright for the couple as Jose was promoted to first secretary in 1957. Not long after he was named consul-general at Yokohama. As Jose boarded the plane for Japan in November 1957, he collapsed and died of a heart attack. He was 42 years old. Ruth's world came crashing down, and she never really recovered from it.

By January 1958, Ruth had returned to Allentown and settled into a rented five-room apartment with her children. She paid the first six months' rent in advance. Because Jose was a diplomat, he paid no U.S. taxes on his salary, or Social Security, making Ruth ineligible for benefits. She was entitled to a pension from Peru amounting to about $50 a month. However, Ruth declined to apply for it, telling friends there would be too much language difficulty even though Ruth spoke Spanish fluently, as did all her children. Upon Jose's death the embassy staff took up a collection for the widow, giving Ruth around $2,000. Later Ruth would say the amount was only $250.

After resettling in Allentown, the Urdanivias were considered to be a model family in every way. The children were all well dressed, well behaved, did well in school, and had lots of playmates. Mrs. Urdanivia presented the face of an in-control mother to the world. The apartment was attractively furnished and was always spotless. Ruth paid the rent, and all her bills, on time. Among the furnishings was a new television set. Closets were full of clothes. Several cartons of canned goods stocked the kitchen.

Yet through it all, Ruth was worried. In April 1958, she was working as a clerk in Hess Brothers where she earned a little more than $200 per month. Apartment rent was $80 a month. That month she applied for welfare from the Department of Public Assistance. Ruth was told she wasn't eligible since the welfare limit for a mother with five children was $196.20, an amount Ruth exceeded with her salary. The Department told Ruth she could collect that sum if she quit her job and stayed home. They also suggested that there were other agencies Ruth could try for assistance.

Speaking to an employee at another government agency, Ruth told the man she needed financial assistance. She asked this man if it were true that if her father legally adopted her youngest children they would then qualify for Social Security benefits. The employee checked and found out that Ruth's information was erroneous.

Ruth's job required her to work on Thursday evenings and all day Saturday, which made child care difficult. Therefore she jumped at a chance for an 8-to-4 Monday-to-Friday job. On October 12, 1959, Ruth started work as a clerk in the admitting office of Sacred Heart Hospital. On October 16, Ruth had an appointment to make the final settlement on a house she was buying in suburban Allentown. Houses in the suburb sold for $11,000 to $12,250. Ruth never kept that appointment, for on October 14, she murdered all five of her children and tried to take her own life.

On that tragic day, after she finished work, Ruth picked up two of the youngest children at her brother's house, where they had been living temporarily to ease their mother's financial burdens. She told her brother she would bring the children back in a day or two. They all seemed to have colds, she explained, and she wanted to take all five to the doctor for a check-up on the following day. That evening, at a little after 9 P.M. Ruth gave her children an overdose of barbiturates. Ever since the death of her husband, Ruth had been saving a 100-tablet bottle of the drug Nidar with the thought that if things didn't get better, she would kill the children and herself. Jose had used Nidar occasionally to control tension. Ruth knew it was potent, for she once took one when she had a toothache and slept almost 24 hours.

Ruth ground up the pills and put them into fruit juice glasses with sugar and orange juice. She tricked the children by telling them it was medicine for their colds. When they complained of the bitter taste, Ruth added more sugar and then gave each child a peppermint patty candy. The children—Carol Miriam, four and a half; Marie, seven; Louis, nine; Ruth Lucille, 10; and Christina, 12—then went to bed, where they all died that night. Urdanivia wrote out a will and a letter to her father before taking her share of the pills. All 100 pills were consumed. The four youngest received about 50 pills, while Ruth and the eldest child took the rest.

It was daylight when Ruth woke up. She thought it was Thursday. As she went to get a drink of water she passed one of her children and realized what she had done. It was actually Monday, October 20. Ruth had been in a stupor for close to five days. The children's bodies were bloated, decomposing, and had turned black. Dismayed that she was still alive, Ruth broke a glass and tried to slash her wrists, but only succeeded in inflicting very minor cuts. Then she unlocked the front door "in case somebody wanted to come in." Giving up on slashing her wrists, Ruth turned on the gas stove and lay down on the kitchen floor. Later that evening the building caretaker came upon the scene when, at the urging of people who couldn't reach Ruth, he entered the apartment to investigate.

Urdanivia was revived from a semiconscious state. Taken to a hospital for treatment, she readily confessed to killing the children. In her statement to the police, Ruth said she was "tired of seeing my children living in a pigsty and eating inferior food" [4]. Investigating officers agreed the home was not a pigsty nor was the food on hand in either short supply or inferior. Ruth added in her statement that "I went everywhere to get help, but couldn't get any. . . . No one wanted to help a widow. . . . I did it. I know it's a sin. If only I could have gone with them," [11] and "Who wants a widow with five children? . . . The children are now with their father. I'm sorry I didn't finish the job so I could be with them too" [6].

Neighbors were all shocked by Ruth's actions. At the school, where she sometimes brought the children herself, teachers remembered her as a devoted and loving parent. Mrs. Mae Peters, who operated a corner store Ruth patronized, said, "She was a wonderful mother. She loved the children and seemed worried about raising them and sending them through school. . . . I think she was mourning her husband. She couldn't seem to forget his death, and talked about him a lot." Another neighbor remarked, "She was always smiling, and I never heard her complain about a thing. She was one of the nicest women I have ever known, and those children were beautiful. They were well trained. I wish there were more children like that" [6].

Yet there were some cracks in Urdanivia's facade just before the end. She had worked just three days at her new job; however, some of the staff noticed she was upset. Some felt the change of jobs might have upset her—

made her worried about how she was doing. Coworker Mary Schellenberg recalled Ruth's last day of work, Wednesday: "That woman was emotionally upset. . . . Her hands shook when she sat down to type. . . . The change came over her from about noon Wednesday until 4 P.M., when she quit. You could see it in her eyes. She was shaking and trembling. During the afternoon I heard her say—'This has got to work out. Oh! It has to work out.' I said, 'What did you say, Ruth?' She didn't answer me" [8]. Ruth was well liked at the hospital. So proud of her children was she that one day she brought some of them in to meet some of her coworkers.

After her arrest, Ruth kept threatening to kill herself. A couple of days later she was transferred to the Allentown State Hospital for a period of psychiatric observation. Psychiatrists ruled her competent to stand trial and her trial began in April 1960, with a charge of one count of murder— that of her oldest daughter Christina. Her attorney had her "stand mute," a plea of not guilty, planning to argue she was not mentally competent at the time of the killings. Jury selection had begun when Ruth insisted on a conference with her attorneys. Upon her insistence, and over her lawyer's objections, Ruth changed her plea and entered one of guilty of murder generally—technically a plea to second-degree murder—in all five cases.

Three judges then heard evidence for a day to determine the degree of guilt. Police Captain Aldo Candia said Ruth told him she was looking for aid, not charity, for her family. "She said she was rejected everywhere because she was married to a foreigner, a Peruvian" [7]. A psychiatrist, Dr. Fiedler, who examined Ruth at the state hospital testified for the defense. He described the woman as having great love and affection for her children. He declared her psychotic since the death of her husband. "The loss of her husband represented the end of everything for Mrs. Urdanivia, loss of security, prestige, and status," he testified. "She developed an increase in her natural hostility. She became a person of grandiosity as a defense to her loss of prestige. She became the victim of mental and emotional factors beyond her control. She was in the acute exacerbation of her illness when she killed the children and was incapable of exercising judgment at the time" [10].

The judges found her guilty on April 7, 1960, of second-degree murder and sentenced her to five concurrent indefinite terms in the Industrial Home for Women at Muncy, Pennsylvania. They agreed she was suffering from some form of mental illness but were also convinced it was not sufficient to relieve her of responsibility for her actions.

While incarcerated, Ruth upgraded her office skills and received psychological advice and therapy. On January 18, 1967, Ruth was released on parole. She started work in an office job at a hospital in central Pennsylvania. Reportedly she "was doing very well on the outside" [5].

Sources

1. "Child Slayer to Start Term Early Next Week Facing Up to 20 Years." *Evening Chronicle* [Allentown], April 8, 1960.

2. "Death of 5 Children Shock to Their Friends." *Evening Chronicle* [Allentown], October 20, 1959.

3. "Distraught Mother Threatens Continued Suicide Attempts." *The Morning Call* [Allentown], October 21, 1959, pp. 1, 9.

4. "5 Murders Charged to Mother." *The Morning Call* [Allentown], October 20, 1959.

5. "Mrs. Urdanivia Paroled—Working in Hospital." *The Morning Call* [Allentown], July 25, 1967.

6. "Mrs. Urdanivia's World Changed on Husband's Death." *Evening Chronicle* [Allentown], October 20, 1959.

7. "Ruth Urdanivia Gets Indefinite Term for Slaying 5 Children." *Evening Chronicle* [Allentown], April 7, 1960.

8. "'She Was Shaking and Trembling,' Hospital Worker Says." *The Morning Call* [Allentown], October 21, 1959.

9. "3-Man Court Will Decide Guilt Degree." *The Morning Call* [Allentown], April 7, 1960.

10. "Urdanivia Guilt 2nd Degree, Court Rules Indefinite Term." *The Morning Call* [Allentown], April 8, 1960.

11. "Victims Given Drug Overdose 6 Days Ago." *The Morning Call* [Allentown], October 20, 1959.

Sophie Ursinus

(1760–1836). *Place:* Berlin, Germany. *Time:* 1790s–1801. *Age:* 30s–41. *Victims:* 3. *Method:* Arsenic poisoning.

As a member of the German upper class, Sophie Ursinus didn't quite get away with murder, but her life-style in prison was consistent with what she enjoyed prior to her arrest. Sophie Charlotte Elizabeth Weingarten was born the daughter of an Austrian diplomat in 1760. Marriage to an elderly privy counsellor named Ursinus followed in Berlin in 1779.

The young Sophie started to stray from her husband and had one affair with a Dutch officer named Rogay. He died suddenly at a fairly young age, probably in the 1790s. Consumption was the cause of death, according to the medical men. Ursinus himself died in 1800. Then Sophie's aunt, Christina Witte, expired only four months later, in 1801.

Sophie had one confidante, a servant named Benjamin Klein. The servant told the police that Sophie had fed arsenic to Rogay because he had planned to leave her. She had poisoned her husband to get rid of a "useless old man" [1]. And she did in her aunt to inherit Witte's estate.

Klein came forward when he too was poisoned by his mistress — although he recovered. Sophie didn't take kindly to Klein's intention to leave her employ. He also knew too much. Sophie was tried and convicted on one count of murder — Witte — and sentenced to life in prison.

Her sentence was served in a massive fortress at Glatz, where Sophie was given a suite of rooms near the top — an apartment usually reserved for the warden. Sophie was allowed to furnish her rooms, to have servants, and to keep her fortune. While prisoners housed underneath her starved and worked to death in chains, Sophie paraded around in fine clothes, giving elaborate dinner parties for aristocrats living nearby and for traveling dignitaries in the area. Things continued that way for more than three decades until Sophie died of natural causes at the prison on April 4, 1836.

Sources

1. Nash, Jay Robert. *Look for the Woman.* New York: M. Evans, 1981, pp. 370–71.

Waltraud Wagner

(1959–). *Place:* Vienna, Austria. *Time:* 1983–1989. *Age:* 24–30. *Victims:* 49 or more. *Method:* Injection, drowning, strangulation.

Starting in 1982, Waltraud Wagner worked as a nurse's aide in Pavilion 5 of Vienna's Lainz General Hospital. Earning a base salary of $635 to $715 a month, Wagner and the other nurse's aides were paid about half of what a nurse earned. Their duties were supposedly limited to feeding, cleaning, and assisting patients. However, with the shortage of nurses at the hospital, the aides regularly took on responsibilities such as administering injections.

The country of Austria was shocked and horrified early in April 1989, when Wagner and three other aides, Maria Gruber, 25, Irene Leidolf, 27, and Stefanie Mayer, 50, were arrested and implicated in a large series of murders that had taken place in the hospital. Chancellor Franz Vranitzky called it "the most brutal and gruesome crime in Austria's history" [3].

Apparently Wagner was the instigator and ringleader. She began to murder elderly patients around 1983. The average age of the victims was 80, with the youngest one being 75. While they were old and feeble, none were terminally ill. Patients were murdered for no apparent reason other than because the aides found them burdensome. Said one of those arrested to the police, "The ones who got on my nerves were dispatched directly to a free bed with the good Lord" [3].

Waltraud started by killing one patient a month. Later she was reportedly murdering three a month. One method of killing consisted of giving the victim a lethal injection of insulin or of a tranquilizer such as Rohypnol. Strangulation was employed in a few cases. A third method involved holding a patient's nose closed while forcing water down their throats until they drowned. Wagner showed the others how to make up lethal injections. She also let them watch while she demonstrated the other methods.

One year before the arrest, hospital administrators were alerted to the possibility of mass murder in their facility. Wagner was the subject of a police investigation into one suspicious death at that time, but the case was dropped due to a lack of pathological evidence. The murders were finally uncovered in April 1989 when two ill patients were discovered to have received insulin overdoses. A second account of the discovery has it that the aides were discussing their killing in a local bar. A doctor from the hospital overheard the remarks and reported them. This led to a tight monitoring of their activities, which resulted in their arrest.

Initial news reports were that the aides confessed to killing at least 49 patients. Authorities estimated that the final toll could be as many as 300. One of those arrested, Leidolf, believed Wager murdered at least 100 patients a year herself for the previous two years. Waltraud admitted to the police she murdered so many she could remember only the names of a small number. She killed them because "they had irritated her during the night shift or had been unpleasant" [4]. Waltraud later withdrew parts of her confession, admitting to only nine murders.

Police and hospital officials criticized each other after the arrests over who to blame for not discovering the murders much earlier. Dr. Franz Xavier Pesendorfer, the head of Pavilion 5, was suspended from his post a few days after the arrests. Pavilion 5 was closed. By the middle of April a news blackout was imposed on the case, which prevented any details of the case from being published. The tabloid press was left to rely on its imagination. Rising to this challenge, they printed stories about a victim found in a pile of rubble in the hospital two years after he disappeared, about Wagner having organized sex and booze parties during the night shift to buy doctors' silence. This story also claimed Wagner worked as a prostitute on her off-duty nights under the nickname "The Swine," charging £350 for her services. No disposition of this case seems to have been made or reported in the North American press.

Sources

1. "Angel of Death in Sex Parties." *Daily Express* [London], April 24, 1989.
2. "Doctors Knew of Hospital Killings." *Sunday Express* [London], April 16, 1989.
3. Protzman, Ferdinand. "Killing of 49 Patients by 4 Nurse's Aides Stuns the Austrians." *New York Times,* April 18, 1989, p. A1.
4. Traynor, Ian. "Silence Shrouds Murder Horrors Inside Ward D." *Sun* [London], April 16, 1989.
5. "Vienna Nurses Held for 44 Killings." *Sun* [London], April 10, 1989.

Marie Walkup

(1905–1937). *Place:* Flagstaff, Arizona. *Time:* July 23, 1937. *Age:* 32. *Victims:* 5. *Method:* Knife, strangulation, firearm.

The Walkups of Arizona were a prosperous family who seemed, on the surface, to have few problems. James Walkup was a World War I veteran who after the war moved to Flagstaff, where he met and married Marie Green. The couple had four children. James served several terms as a member of the board of supervisors in his area and in July 1937, he was chairman of the Coconino County Board of Supervisors. In addition, Walkup was secretary of the Flagstaff Chamber of Commerce.

The only problem the family had was 32-year-old Marie's health. She had suffered for some time from a chronic, but unnamed, intestinal ailment. On July 22, 1937, Marie consulted her physician, Dr. Fronske, about her illness. Apparently she was quite despondent over it and expressed a concern to the doctor that her children might have contracted the illness. This was not the first time she had expressed such fears. She was very depressed over the idea that her children might contract it. That evening at 10 P.M. she phoned Dr. Fronske, who was out. Marie left a message requesting that he stop by her house the next morning. She was very specific that Fronske was not needed that evening. James Walkup was out of town on business.

Sometime in the early morning hours of July 23 Marie went into the bedrooms of her children, where she stabbed and then strangled Daniel, 10; Rose Marie, eight; John, four; and Elizabeth, 20 months, in turn. Only Rose Marie showed any evidence of having awakened and resisting her mother. When this grisly work was complete, Marie drove to a nearby golf course, taking with her a rifle from the house. Attired in nightgown and robe, Marie placed the rifle pointing toward her body and discharged it with her toe. Her body was found around dawn.

When the police entered the Walkup house, they found a neat and orderly scene. Coroner Max Miller said that Marie had accomplished "the slayings with such dispatch that not an object was out of place in the home. The children, their night clothes and bedding neatly arranged, were tucked into their beds as though asleep" [1]. The previous evening's call to Fronske was thought to be part of Marie's orderliness to ensure that the children were found.

At the home a note had been left telling the milkman not to leave any milk. Another note contained instructions as to how the five bodies should be disposed of. The note to Fronske directed the physician to enter the house and go to the children's bedrooms. The fourth and last note was to James. It read, "Because of my lack of discipline, the children are happier this way. Only grief would come to them. You are strong in faith, never doubting — mercy, mercy to my people. I loved you, and I have failed" [2].

Sources

1. "Mass Funeral Is Scheduled." *Arizona Republic,* July 25, 1937, p. 2.
2. "Mother Kills Four Children, Ends Own Life." *Arizona Republic,* July 24, 1937, pp. 1, 4.

Margaret Waters

(1835–1870). *Place:* Brixton, England. *Time:* 1866–1870. *Age:* 31–35. *Victims:* 16–35. *Method:* Starvation.

Baby farming was Margaret Waters's specialty. Adopting babies into her home for a fee, Margaret murdered them. The motive was money, although the amounts were small. Apparently she was unable to dispatch the infants quickly, but instead allowed them to die from starvation. To cover the cries and screams of the hungry children, she kept them in a drugged state. Their deaths were slow and painful.

Waters was born in England in 1835. She married and then emigrated to Newfoundland, where she reportedly lived in respectable circumstances. The death of her husband prompted Margaret to return to England; she opened a lodging house around 1866 in Brixton. Margaret was then 31 years old. Helping her out in her business was Sarah Ellis, her 23-year-old sister, who was separated from her husband.

To drum up business, Margaret placed ads in local newspapers. She was partial to advertising in *Lloyd's Newspaper*. A typical ad would read: "Adoption — A good home with a mother's love and care is offered to a respectable person wishing her child to be entirely adopted. Premium £5, which sum includes everything. Apply by letter only to Mrs. Oliver, Post Office, Goar Place, Brixton" [1].

Margaret's response to replies to her ads was standard. She would meet the person in a public place, always refusing to give out her own address. This was necessary, she explained, as she feared the person might try to reclaim the child. She never used her real name, continually charging her alias. All correspondence would be picked up at the post office.

To the persons wishing to give up their infant, Margaret would relate that she was childless and had a husband in a good position. If a reference was requested, Waters would give the name of Sarah Ellis. Sarah, of course, never failed to praise the character of Mrs. Oliver. Women giving up their babies in this fashion often sought secrecy as much as Waters. While Margaret asked for £5, the deal struck usually ranged from £2 to £4. A little extra would be made by pawning whatever clothes the children came with. A few children were not "adopted," but boarded for a weekly fee.

By June 1870, the police were investigating Waters. What got them involved is unstated. Police Sergeant Relph responded to one of Margaret's ads. Her letter in response said, in part, "The child would be well brought up and carefully educated, he would learn a good trade and be to us in all respects as our own. We have been married for several years but have no family. We are in a comfortable position, have a good business, and a home in every way to make a child happy. We are both very fond of children, and should you entrust your little one to our care, you may rely upon his receiving the love and care of a mother" [1].

Relph met Waters at a train station. As usual, she would not reveal her address. However, she was followed home, and on the next day, June 11, the police raided her place. Before they entered, Margaret told the police she didn't board children and wasn't Mrs. Willis—the name she had given to Relph. Once inside, the police were confronted by a poorly furnished, four-room house that smelled vile. In one room, where the stench was described as overpowering, five babies, unwashed and wrapped in shawls, lay on a urine-soaked sofa, apparently asleep. Asked if any other babies were in the house, Margaret said, "A few." Five more were found in the back yard. They ranged in age from a few weeks to 30 months. Ellis claimed one of the children as her own, while Margaret denied knowing the names and origins of the other nine.

Police found quantities of laudanum in the house, used to drug the children. Under more questioning Margaret admitted to being "in the business" about four years. She estimated 40 children had been in her care over that time. One baby was removed from the house that day—its grandfather came with the police to identify it. However, it was two days later before the police returned to take the other children away, despite their condition, and arrest the two women. Police found 92 pawn tickets in the home, all of which had been issued to Waters for baby clothes. As the sisters were taken away Waters said, "Believe me, what my sister has done has been entirely under my direction. I am the sinner and I must suffer" [1].

The badly emaciated babies were removed to a workhouse. All were filthy, with bones protruding through their skin and raw buttocks; some could not cry, and all had been drugged. Four- and five-month old infants weighed between five and seven pounds. Five of the 10 infants died within two or three weeks of their discovery. The others would survive. Doctors attributed death to insufficient food and the administration of narcotics.

As the case was publicized, women came forward who had given their children over to Waters. Two teen-aged girls who had separately worked in the house as servants for Waters testified about the treatment handed out to the babies. One of those servants, Ellen O'Connor, reported buying laudanum for her employer. Ellen was told to carry the babies to the back room if anybody called. Seven babies slept in Margaret's bedroom, four at the foot of the bed, two on pillows on chairs, and one in a bassinet. In the morning they were brought downstairs and placed on the sofa, where they stayed all day.

One of Ellen's jobs was to go to various post offices to collect mail addressed to different names. During her three months of employment at the house, Ellen said that no babies died; however, four "disappeared." The second servant reported that two babies disappeared. Waters would go out in the late evening with a baby in a shawl. She returned only with a shawl. When an infant died, Margaret would take the corpse and toss it in any convenient place, an archway or under a railroad bridge. One such corpse was found wrapped in an item owned by Waters.

In September 1870, both sisters stood trial on one count of murder. Despite public appeals, four of the dead infants were never identified. Police only knew the name of the child identified by its grandfather, Mr. Cowen. A clerk for *Lloyd's Newspaper* produced copies of 27 different ads placed by the women. Sarah Ellis was acquitted. Later she pleaded guilty to obtaining money by false pretenses. For this she was sentenced to 18 months in jail. Waters was found guilty and sentenced to death. Margaret protested that the condition the children were found in was greatly exaggerated. She added, "The Cowen baby was a very fine child and I was much pleased with it, but it did not get on, whatever I did" [1].

Waters did admit that five babies had died in her care over the years. Of the 40 which she said passed through her hands, only the five who survived when removed by the police were definitely alive. Five of those removed died; Waters admitted five others who died, plus the six "disappearances" reported by the servants. The remaining 19 were unaccounted for. While awaiting execution Waters made a statement: "If I did not give the children suitable food, it was from an error of judgement, and I think it hard I should be blamed for the deaths of those who died in the workhouse so long after they were removed from my care. ... As to the Cowen child, I employed a wet-nurse for it, and it did not die until a fortnight after it was removed from my house. I think it hard I should be blamed for its death. I think too that parents of illegitimate children are more culpable than persons like myself, for if there were not such parents, there would be no baby-farmers" [1].

On October 11, 1870, Margaret Waters was executed.

Sources

1. Wilson, Patrick. *Murderess*. London: Joseph, 1971, pp. 158–66.

Jeanne Weber

(1875–1910). *Place:* France. *Time:* 1905–1908. *Age:* 30–33. *Victims:* 8–20.
Method: Strangulation.

One of the most gruesome of all female mass murderers was Jeanne Weber. This Frenchwoman specialized in killing young children by strangulation. The ineptitude of so-called expert medical witnesses allowed her to escape punishment on two occasions and thus to add to the total of the children she murdered. No motive was ever ascertained; it appears that Weber got sexual release from her crimes.

Jeanne was born in 1875. A Breton, she was the daughter of poor parents in the Côtes du Nord. Her father was a fisherman. One of eight siblings, Jeanne grew up in poverty and often went to bed hungry. Her wardrobe was limited and her education rudimentary. Physically strong, she was described as a shy youngster. Often morose, she spent hours lost in a world of her own. When she was just 14 years old her parents sent her off to work as a maid in the house of a local family.

The break with her family was complete, for she never returned to her family home — not even for a visit. Bored with the tedious drudgery of being a servant, Jeanne quickly quit her first job and began to wander around France, taking jobs when needed. By 1893 she had worked her way to Paris, where she eked out an existence in the slums. In those slums she met Marcel Weber, who was employed as a timekeeper and whose financial condition was only marginally better than her own.

The couple married and had three children, two girls and a boy. The two daughters died mysteriously and close together, perhaps early in 1905. In light of her following activities they were most likely Weber's first victims. Always fond of booze, Jeanne drank more and more after those deaths. Her in-laws attributed it to her grief.

Early in March 1905, Jeanne's sister-in-law asked her to watch her two young children while she did the family laundry at the washhouse. Jeanne readily agreed and accompanied her relative home. Soon the other woman was off, and Jeanne was alone with the kids. A short time later the mother was interrupted by a neighbor at the washhouse who said, "You must go home at once. I think something is wrong with Georgette. I heard her cry

303

out as I was about to pass your place, and looked in. Your sister-in-law had Georgette on her lap and the poor little mite sounded as though she was choking" [2].

Mother ran home to find Jeanne holding 18-month-old Georgette with one hand inside the child's clothes. "I'm rubbing her. Something seems to be wrong with her breathing," said Jeanne. The child had gone blue in the face. The sister-in-law grabbed the baby and ministered to her. She recovered quickly, and the mother returned to the laundry, leaving Jeanne to baby-sit again. Once more her chore was interrupted when husband Pierre arrived at the washhouse and said, "Look, come on home. Something's very wrong with Georgette. I think she's had a fit." The couple were too late, for when they arrived the baby was dead. Its face was dark, the eyes bulged out, and there were black-and-blue marks around the neck [2].

A doctor was summoned; while the group waited, the neighbor pointed at the curious marks and told the couple to report them to the doctor. It's not known if they did or did not. In the event, the doctor's exam was cursory and a death certificate listing the cause as convulsions was issued. Certainly the parents had not the least bit of suspicion toward Jeanne, for less than two weeks later she was called to baby-sit the remaining child, Suzanne, who was not quite three years old.

When the parents arrived home, they were shocked to find their daughter dead in circumstances similar to those of Georgette's death. Suzanne's face was dark, foam was on her mouth, her legs were contracted, and her teeth clenched. Her neck bore ugly black-and-blue marks. Still no suspicions were raised, and another death was attributed to convulsions.

Just two weeks after that, near the end of March, a different sister-in-law, the wife of Leon Weber, asked Jeanne to mind her seven-month-old daughter Germaine while she went to the store. When the mother left, the baby was sleeping peacefully. She had only gone a block when the infant began to shriek. Upstairs in another apartment, the baby's grandmother heard the cries and came down to find the baby being held by Jeanne. Germaine was gasping for breath and losing color.

The grandmother took the infant, who then settled down. When the mother returned, Jeanne asked her to go to the store for her. Jeanne explained she would go herself, but her legs were bad and bothering her greatly at that time. The mother obliged and left. When she returned, she found Jeanne holding the baby who was having a fit. The grandmother and other neighbors had responded to more shrieks. A doctor was summoned, but Germaine seemed fine by then.

When the two women were alone again, Jeanne sent her sister-in-law to the store on another pretext. When she returned she found Germaine having another fit and Jeanne bent over the crib, bearing down on the baby's chest. Very small children can be suffocated by compression on the chest. The mother had to pull hard at Weber to make her stop. Once again the baby settled down. Amazingly, the mother still had no suspicions and went out again. This time she returned to find her relative in a tearful state, cradling a corpse. "She had another of her strange turns," said Jeanne. The cause of death was diphtheria, said the doctor.

Three days later, on the day Germaine was buried, Jeanne's only remaining child, seven-year-old Marcel, died of similar "convulsions." He had slept with his mother that night. Diphtheria was also listed as the cause of his death, but it didn't explain the marks on his neck. Weber was the object not of suspicion, but of pity. She had lost all her children. In fact, the Weber clan wondered if they might not be tainted in some way; they had lost so many children so quickly. No one seemed to take note of the fact that Weber was the only person present at all the deaths.

Early in April, two sisters-in-law called on Jeanne. They were the wives of Leon and Charles Weber. Charles's wife brought her 10-month-old son Maurice. After Jeanne had prepared lunch and the group had eaten she complained of her legs bothering her and said, "I ought to go and get some needles. Of course, if Marcel had been here he would have gone for me." The mention of her dead son was enough to send the one sister-in-law to the store. A moment later Jeanne suddenly remembered she needed something else. The second sister-in-law volunteered, and Jeanne was alone with Maurice [2].

The infant's mother came back first to find Maurice in Jeanne's arms, having convulsions. The mother grabbed the infant — who was dying — and screamed, "You miserable woman. He's choking to death while you look on — like the others did." A doctor was called who was suspicious of the marks on the child's neck. He had two other doctors carry out an exam at a hospital, and all concluded that Maurice had died of strangulation. A police surgeon confirmed the findings, and Jeanne was arrested. With that memories were jogged; other children, not relatives, had also reportedly died in the arms of Jeanne Weber.

Hate filled the streets of Paris as news of the child murderer was reported. The judge in charge of examining the case called in a medical expert by the name of Professor Thoinot of the Paris Faculty of Medicine. The professor examined Maurice and declared death was due to natural causes. The judge ordered other bodies exhumed; Thoinot said none of them had died of strangulation. Two other doctors were called in. Before they delivered their findings, they consulted with the eminent Thoinot and then issued findings that confirmed his.

In January 1906, Jeanne Weber went on trial amid much public agitation. Outside the court a mob chanted, "Death to the ogress." Mothers denounced her, while the mob demanded her head. The Weber family would have been content to have her placed in an asylum. Psychiatrists who examined Jeanne found her calm and lucid but noted that she suffered from "nervous upsets and hysteria as a result of mental disorders caused by the loss of her children and certain gynaecological troubles" [2].

The trial became a forum notable for the level of disagreement among the medical experts. Eighteen experts contradicted each other, and Weber's lawyers took advantage of the confusion. Thoinot prevailed, and the unexpected verdict of not guilty was returned. Weber was free to kill again. The mob did an emotional flip-flop and largely came around to her side.

Rumors still persisted in some quarters, however, and Jeanne left Paris to disappear for 15 months. Her husband had left her, convinced of her guilt. During those months she worked sporadically as a maid, and perhaps as a prostitute. She surfaced again in April 1907, in Chambon, France, as Madame Blaise. She was living with a man named A. M. Bavouzet who had taken her on as mistress/housekeeper. He had three children; one of them, Auguste, aged seven, died of convulsions that month. The boy was dressed in a fresh nightgown, and when the doctor asked Madame Blaise why she had done this after his death she said it was because he had vomited.

The doctor found bruises on the boy's neck and refused to issue a death certificate immediately, saying he was out of them and would come back. Instead, he reported the death to the police, who examined Auguste and found many bruises — on the stomach, thighs, and forehead, in addition to those on the neck.

That same day, Auguste's sister searched through Blaise's room. She found news clippings of the trial of Jeanne Weber. Some had photos, and it was obvious to the girl that Weber and Blaise were the same person. This was enough for the police to arrest Weber.

The second inquiry went as poorly as the first. Medical experts contradicted each other again. Thoinot was there to again say that no strangulation had taken place. A group called the League for the Rights of Man staged protest rallies, claiming Weber was being persecuted. The judges looked askance at the jumbled evidence and accepted Jeanne's lawyer's plea of judicial error. Weber was free to kill again, almost without even being tried a second time. Journalists were coming to portray her as a martyr.

Jeanne moved on, again changing her name to Marie Lemoine. A sympathizer named M. Bougeau ran a private sanitarium for infirm children. Mistakenly believing Weber to be a victim who needed companionship and a purpose in life, he gave her a job at his institution. Just two weeks after she started work she was found with her hands around a young boy, strangling him. Her attempt was interrupted and he survived. Bougeau fired her immediately but he never reported the incident, not wishing to appear a fool.

Weber went back to Paris and paid a surprise visit to the Chief of Police, saying, "I feel I must confess to the murders of my nieces and nephews. I strangled them." The chief knew she had been acquitted on those charges and that she couldn't be tried again. He asked her if she murdered Auguste. Weber categorically denied it, and the chief threw her out [2].

Her next stop was Saint-Remy, where she was reportedly a prostitute for a time before moving in with a man named Emile Banchery. They lived at an inn run by the Poirots, who had two children. One day Jeanne asked the Poirots if one of their children could share her bed that night, since Emile beat her frequently and he would be less inclined to do so if a child were present. The Poirots agreed, and sent six-year-old Marcel upstairs to her room.

Late that night, screaming was heard; when her door was forced open, Jeanne was found bending over the dead body of Marcel. Blood poured from his mouth and his face was turning black. Three handkerchiefs covered in blood were hung over the bed. Weber was in a state of frenzy when discovered and had continued to tear at the body even after the boy's death. Mr. Poirot had great difficulty in dragging her off the body of his son and had to strike her several times. Before strangling the child, she had bitten out his tongue.

Once again, Weber went on trial. This time the only conflict was over her sanity. Thoinot was heavily scored in the media for his previous stance, but he never admitted any error on his part. In 1908 she was found guilty but insane and sent to an asylum for the criminally insane at Mareville. Jeanne deteriorated rapidly, both mentally and physically. She was often found in the midst of a fit of some kind, trying to choke imagined throats while fighting for air. She also foamed at the mouth and wailed loudly. One morning in 1910 officials found her dead, her fingers tightly locked around her own throat.

Sources

1. Green, Jonathan. *The Greatest Criminals of All Time.* New York: Stein & Day, 1980, p. 211.

2. Gribble, Leonard. *Such Women Are Deadly.* London: John Long, 1965, pp. 94–106.

3. Nash, Jay Robert. *Look for the Woman.* New York: M. Evans, 1981, pp. 377–81.

4. Wilson, Colin. *Encyclopedia of Murder.* New York: Putnam, 1962, pp. 548–50.

5. "Woman Thrice Held as Child Slayer." *New York Times,* May 17, 1908, part 3, p. 3.

Catherine Wilson

(1822–1862). *Place:* Boston and London, England. *Time:* 1854–1862. *Age:* 32–40. *Victims:* 5–7. *Method:* Colchicum poisoning.

Systematically and ruthlessly, Catherine Wilson spent the better part of a decade poisoning at least five and possibly as many as seven people to death. The motive was money, although she reaped only small financial benefits from her murdering spree.

Wilson's early life remains almost completely unreported. She was born in Boston, England, around 1822, but did not surface publicly until 1853 when she answered an ad for a housekeeper in the town of Boston. Catherine then passed herself off as a widow. There is nothing to indicate one way or another if she had had a husband or if there had been one, whether he may have been her first victim. At any rate, in 1853 she was alone, and she liked to spend more money than she had.

Mr. Mawer was the widower who advertised; he claimed to be quite prosperous. His health was good except for attacks of gout, which he treated with colchicum. In small doses, colchicum was often prescribed by doctors, but in large doses it was a deadly poison.

Catherine landed the job, and over the following year Mawer found her to be a hard-working and trustworthy woman. Soon they were good friends, and Mawer's gout improved, a fact he attributed to Wilson's tender care. To show his gratitude, he told his employee he had redrafted his will and was leaving everything to her. That was it for Mawer.

Wilson's greed, together with the availability of the poison already in the house, was too much of a temptation. Mawer died in October 1954, after 10 days of vomiting and violent diarrhea. Wilson pretended to be heartbroken, and no suspicion was raised against her even though a nurse noticed Mawer always got worse after drinking tea prepared for him by his housekeeper.

The fortune inherited from Mawer turned out to be less than Catherine had anticipated, but it kept her for a time. She next turned up in London, where she rented rooms in the house of Mrs. Soames late in 1855. Wilson was then traveling and living with a man named James Dixon, whom she passed off as her brother. Also traveling with her was a large amount of colchicum which she had left over from Mawer's disposal.

Catherine was already tiring of Dixon, who didn't produce enough money to satisfy her. The Mawer legacy was also almost gone. In addition, Dixon had returned home drunk one night and had hit her. Wilson had become close with Mrs. Soames and learned that her landlady had a fair amount of money.

First, however, Dixon had to go. One day he became sick with terrible pains and soon died. Consumption was the cause, cried his "sister," even though Dixon had appeared in excellent health. The doctor wanted to do a postmortem to ascertain the cause of death, but Wilson pleaded with him not to. Dixon, in life, had always told her he wished to be spared such indignity, explained Catherine. However, the doctor prevailed. He found the lungs to be in perfect shape. Somehow Wilson managed to escape detection, because the doctor apparently didn't look too closely and attributed death to natural causes.

Mrs. Soames and Wilson became even closer friends after Dixon's demise, and the boarder learned all the facts about her landlady's life and affairs. Maria Soames had an income from property she owned, but Wilson managed to wheedle most of it away from the woman. By October 1856, Maria was forced to borrow money from her brother.

One morning Maria went out to pick up some money that was due to her. On her return Wilson invited her up to her room; after that, Mrs. Soames's days were numbered. The next morning she was too sick to get up. She lingered for a few more days until she died on October 18. Catherine appointed herself nurse and rarely left the bedside of her friend, even going so far as to catch a few hours' sleep in a chair in Soames's bedroom so her friend would not be alone. Maria had died after suffering from severe vomiting, diarrhea, and burning of the chest and throat. The doctor was suspicious as to why a formerly healthy woman of 50 had died so suddenly and ordered an inquest. Catherine quickly spread a story around that Maria had become the mistress of a man who had gone on to deceive her. This, said Wilson, caused Maria to commit suicide by drinking poisoned brandy. When a listener asked Wilson how she could let Maria drink the deadly liquid Catherine replied, "It wasn't my business" [3]. No one bothered to report this story to the authorities, even when letters arrived for Maria supposedly from this mysterious lover—letters forged by Wilson. Once again a cursory autopsy was performed which found nothing suspicious. Death was attributed to heart disease and peritonitis.

Wilson could not inherit from her landlady since Soames had a number of relatives, but she profited by having borrowed sums of money from her before her death. These loans were kept secret from the estate. Catherine also presented the estate with the demand for payment of £10, which she claimed Soames owed her. That sum was paid when Wilson produced a signed promissory note. This later proved to be a forgery.

During part of 1859, Wilson frequently visited Mrs. Jackson of Boston. After this woman withdrew £120 from the bank, she was dead four days later. The money was never found.

That same year Catherine maintained a friendship with Mrs. Ann Atkinson from Cumberland, in the north of England. She was the aunt of the late James Dixon. The two women went shopping one day when Atkinson came down to London, and Atkinson was shocked to lose her purse containing £51 in notes. Catherine feigned sympathy, but after her friend caught a train back home, she was £51 richer.

Generally Mrs. Atkinson made one major shopping trip each year to London, and when she came in October 1860, she was carrying £120 in notes. Wilson was then passing herself off as the wife of a man named Taylor. Ann's visit was good timing from Catherine's point of view, since she was once again out of funds. She even faced the threat of eviction because she was behind in her rent. Wilson put her landlady off for a bit by explaining her wealthy friend, Mrs. Atkinson, would lend her enough money to pay all her debts. The landlady was therefore pleased to see the woman arrive from the north and share Wilson's rooms during the shopping expedition.

When his wife had been away for four days Mr. Atkinson received a telegram stating that she was dangerously ill. He hurried down to London, but by then Ann was dead. A grief-stricken Catherine Wilson had taken to her bed and was so distraught as to be unable to provide a coherent account of his wife's death. The doctor who was called in was puzzled over the cause of death and suggested a postmortem. Wilson found the strength to suppress her grief long enough to inform Mr. Atkinson that his wife's dying wish was that her body not be "cut up." Mr. Atkinson, not wanting to dishonor his wife's wish, denied permission, and no examination took place.

When Atkinson went through his wife's belongings, he was surprised to find no money at all. He knew how much money she had brought with her and that she couldn't possibly have spent it all at the time of her death. He asked Wilson, who innocently told him that his wife arrived in London with only a few shillings and her return ticket. When the shocked husband expressed surprise, the grieving friend inquired whether he had not received the explanation in a letter. He said he had received no letters, although he had expected some. Mrs. Atkinson had written but left the letters with Wilson to be posted; she promptly destroyed them.

Catherine told the confused husband that his wife "wouldn't tell him the bad news. I'm sorry to say that she was robbed of all her money at Rugby." That stop was news to the husband, and he asked Wilson why Ann had gotten off the train there. Wilson replied, "She was taken ill in the train and when it stopped at Rugby she got out. Soon afterwards she became faint again, and when she recovered she found she had been robbed. Then she came on here and told me, and I've been lending her money to get about" [1]. After this speech, Wilson collapsed sobbing.

Mr. Atkinson traveled back home, apparently entertaining no suspicions about his wife's friend. During the next week Catherine paid off all her debts, bought some new clothes, and flashed a diamond ring that was ostensibly a token of gratitude from Mr. Atkinson for looking after his wife. It was actually removed from the dead woman's finger.

Mr. Taylor left Wilson a few months later, apparently after an illness. At the end of 1861 Mr. Atkinson received a letter signed with the name of the girl who had been Ann's servant during her final illness in London. This letter told of Wilson's mistreatment at Taylor's hands, including being locked out of the house one rainy night and suffering a miscarriage. Other such letters followed, begging for money for Wilson. Atkinson sent £10 to his wife's faithful friend. These letters had all been forged by Wilson herself.

April 1862 found Wilson once again low on funds. She was close to a Mrs. Carnell then, who was estranged from her husband. For some reason Carnell had chosen Catherine to try and act as an intermediary to arrange a reconciliation. During tea one afternoon Mrs. Carnell became ill, and Wilson put her to bed. Quick as a flash she rushed off to a drugstore and returned with some medicine. Carnell tried to drink some when Wilson offered it, but immediately spit it back up, with some landing on the bedclothes. So strong was the medicine that it burned holes in the linen. Carnell came close to death, but did survive.

The authorities were summoned in, and Wilson put the blame on the druggist who, she insisted, must have sold her the wrong medicine. The angry druggist proved that what he had sold was harmless and any noxious additions must have been made by Wilson. The police went to place Wilson under arrest for attempted murder. By then she had disappeared, and it was six weeks before she was captured. In addition to the victims mentioned there were possibly one or two others, bringing Catherine's body count to between five and seven.

Both awaiting trial and during the trial, Wilson maintained a cool demeanor and said very little, occasionally protesting her innocence. The case against her regarding Carnell was largely circumstantial and the jury returned a verdict of not guilty. A smiling Wilson walked out of the courthouse a free woman.

The police were then aware of her background and exhumed the bodies of her victims, finding poison in all of them. Wilson was rearrested only a few days after the end of her first trial. She faced a second trial on one count of murder—that of Mrs. Soames. The state intended to proceed victim by victim in case they bungled along the way.

This second case was tight, and the jury quickly found her guilty. She was sentenced to death. When Justice Byles passed sentence he remarked, "the result upon my mind is that I have no more doubt that you committed the crime than if I had seen it committed with my own eyes" [1]. Wilson was said to have left the dock with a look of contempt on her face; she retained a sneering posture until the end. She showed no remorse or repentance and never admitted guilt. Catherine Wilson was hung on October 20, 1862. The public execution took place outside London's Horsemonger Gaol before a crowd, said one source, of 20,000 people [2]. It marked the last public hanging of a woman in London.

Sources

1. Kingston, Charles. *Remarkable Rogues*. London: John Lane, 1921, pp. 197–211.
2. Nash, Jay Robert. *Look for the Woman* New York: M. Evans, 1981, pp. 389–90.
3. Wilson, Patrick. *Murderess*. London: Michael Joseph, 1971, pp. 131–36.

Martha Hasel Wise

(1883–?). *Place:* Medina, Ohio. *Time:* 1924–1925. *Age:* 41. *Victims:* 3. *Method:* Arsenic poisoning.

A grim tragedy overtook the Gienke family, who lived in the area of Medina, Ohio, in January and February of 1925. On New Year's Day the father, Fred, the mother, Lillie, and six children ranging in age from nine to 24 were all taken violently ill with symptoms of searing stomach pains and violent diarrhea. On January 4, 53-year-old Lillie died. Whenever the family seemed to be on the way to recovery, they would get violently ill again, and then again. On February 8, 59-year-old Fred died.

Authorities were suspicious. They quietly began an investigation on February 12. They thought the first attack may have been due to botulism or food poisoning from the family's holiday dinner, but that didn't explain the other attacks of illness. Eventually they discovered arsenic poisoning was the culprit. One of the Gienke children mentioned that the coffee they drank had recently burned the mouths of some of the drinkers. Despite this, when the coffee package was analyzed it contained no arsenic. The Gienke home contained no poison at all, not even rat poison. No domestic trouble existed within the family, nor did the Gienkes have any known enemies.

In charge of the investigation was State Prosecuting Attorney Joseph Seymour, who released what information he had to the press on March 12, admitting he was completely "at sea" since there seemed to be no motive at all for poisoning the family. By releasing the facts he had, Seymour hoped something might break when the public was made aware of what had happened. Seymour thought, "Administration of the poison appears to have been accidental or the work of a moron" [1].

A couple of days later, a third name was added to the list of dead victims: 69-year-old Sophia Hasel, who had died on December 13, 1924. Stricken at her own home, her symptoms were identical to those of Fred and Lillie. Sophia and Lillie were sisters. Seymour no longer thought the poisonings were accidental: "I fully believe the deaths and illness of the other members of the family can be laid to the hands of a crazed person" [3]. The Gienke children were parcelled out to various people in the vicinity. One son was being housed and cared for by 41-year-old Martha Wise, Sophia's daughter and Fred and Lillie's niece.

Seymour's idea of going public with the information paid off, for less than a week after the news account appeared he received an unsigned letter that read: "I just want to make a suggestion — see if you can find out if there was ill feeling between Martha Wise and Lillie Gienke. I know something of the treachery of this Martha Hasel Wise and also her craftiness to evade suspicion. She is what you might call a moron. Could it be to get rid of her mother and get the property and of Lillie for suspecting her. She claimed to have been made sick too, but that may be a lie too" [4].

Born around 1883, Martha Hasel spent her life in the Medina area in hamlets such as Valley City and Hardscrabble. From the outset a strange child, Martha was set apart from the others. One who knew her as a child said, "She was never able to learn anything." Another remembered her as "always crying and every time anyone spoke to her she would burst into tears." A former teacher of the child remarked, "Martha was the dullest child in school. She was even too dull to make trouble." Retreating into a world of her own, Martha conjured up imaginary friends as she trudged her solitary way. She heard these "friends," it was said, and carried on conversations with them [10].

Martha was the only daughter of four children born to the Hasels. Everyone in the family did work on the small farm they owned in order to eke out a modest living. In due course, perhaps in 1906, Martha married farmer Albert Wise. Financially nothing changed for Martha, who simply moved from one threadbare existence to another. For several months each winter, the mud that was everywhere on the farm made getting out of the house difficult. The couple had five children, one of whom died in infancy. Albert died around 1923 of natural causes, leaving his widow a very long way from easy street but financially better off than she had ever been. For the first time in her life Martha did not have to slave from dawn to dusk each day. She could relax a little. However, she seemed ill equipped for it. Restlessness overcame her. Many times she spent an entire sleepless night walking through the woods near her home. And just as when she was a child, her imaginary friends went with her.

As soon as Seymour received the anonymous letter, he had Martha taken into custody for interrogation. Questioned by Ethel Roshon, wife of the sheriff and jail matron, Wise soon confessed to the crimes. On November 24, 1924, Wise had bought some arsenic at a drug store. Then she put some of it into the water bucket at the Hasel home. This water was used for cooking food, making coffee, and other uses. Three times during the first month of the next year she did the same thing to the Gienkes' water bucket. Martha regularly went to the Gienkes' to get milk and thus had easy access to the bucket.

After hours of interrogation Ethel said to Wise, "Didn't you poison them?" Martha replied, "Well, maybe I did." Roshon countered, "Hadn't you better leave out the maybe?" Finally Martha said, "Yes, I did it." When Ethel asked her why, all Martha could reply was, "The devil did it." Not satisfied, Ethel asked the poisoner who she was aiming at when she poisoned the water. "I don't know," was the reply [4]. Altogether 16 people became ill after being poisoned, including two of Martha's brothers, who ingested arsenic while visiting their mother. The others took sick after visiting either the Hasel or Gienke home. All survived the poisoning except three.

Martha's statement of confession read, in part, "On the day before New years, in the evening, when I went down to Gienkes after milk I put some arsenic in the water pail. About two weeks after that I put some more arsenic in the water pail. The water pail was always sitting on the cupboard in Gienke's kitchen. I don't know why I did it. I just couldn't help it. The devil was in me. Mrs. Gienke used the water in the pail to make coffee and cook the meals in. The day before my mother, Mrs. Sophia Hasel, took sick I was at her home. I put a small quantity of arsenic in the water bucket. . . . Along the latter part of January or the first of February, I can't just remember which, I put more arsenic in the water bucket at Gienkes'. That is the last time I used any arsenic. . . . I bought the arsenic at the drug store on the corner in Medina. He asked me what my name was and where I lived and wanted to know what I wanted the arsenic for. I told him I wanted to kill rats. I bought about two ounces. . . . I don't know why I did it I just couldn't help it. Something seemed to make me do it. I lost my mind. My mind wasn't right since last summer. It has been working on me since last summer. After I did it, it bothered me and worried me. I worried about it all the time. I feel better now" [17].

In addition to the poisoning, Martha admitted to setting fire to three barns in the area, the first being in 1922. She also confessed to stealing jewelry from relatives and friends. No reason was offered for committing these acts. A day after her confession, authorities interrogated her again but could get no reason from her for the poisoning except for Martha repeating that the devil made her do it. This time she told questioners that she had a mania for attending funerals. When there wasn't one, she decided to have one.

The first few days in custody Martha spent much of her time praying. She was allowed visits by the pastor of the Lutheran church she had attended all her life, but denied visits by her children. Martha repeatedly asked Ethel why she, Martha, had committed such a crime. Psychiatrists who observed her defined her as mentally deficient. Even Prosecutor Seymour felt she was suffering from "mental dementia."

On May 4, 1925, Martha stood trial for the murder of Lillie Gienke.

Only Lillie's body was exhumed. It contained arsenic. Several of the witnesses still suffered effects from the poisoning and had to be wheeled into court on hospital carts in order to testify. The defense was content to try and show Martha was insane. Several relatives testified that they had seen Martha foam at the mouth and roll her eyes in a "queer manner." A man by the name of Harry Obermyer, described as Wise's lover, testified that on one visit when he entered Martha's home he found her on the floor "barking like a dog." When he asked her what was wrong she told him, "I couldn't say. I don't get those spells as often as I used to" [16].

One defense witness told the court he had seen Martha in the summer of 1924, during which time she had one of the "fits" others had testified about. The prosecutor's assistant suddenly challenged the man and got him to admit it was all a lie that the defense attorney had him tell. He admitted he hadn't seen Martha for more than two years. Strangest of all, the defense attorney sat mutely at his table while this drama unfolded, not once objecting.

A second dramatic event during the trial came when Edith Hasel committed suicide by slashing her throat. She was Martha's sister-in-law. Edith, her husband, and son had all suffered severe physical damage from the poisoning. Apparently Edith couldn't bear it any longer. Throughout her trial and upon hearing of Edith's death, Martha remained calm and indifferent. On May 13, Wise was found guilty of first-degree murder with a recommendation of mercy. The jury returned the verdict after one hour of deliberations. Martha was sentenced to prison for the rest of her life. Said Martha, "I don't feel very well but I am satisfied. They did their duty" [15]. Following sentence, Wise posed for news photographers in the yard of the jail, excited and flattered by the attention.

Two days after the trial ended, Martha suddenly announced everything was the fault of 59-year-old Walter Johns, another man in her life. Martha's mother had disliked the man because he was of a different religion. Johns used to visit Wise a couple of times a week. Martha claimed he put her up to the poisoning. She failed to say anything earlier because she feared Johns. Taken into custody, Johns was grilled through the night for several days before being exonerated. Part of the grilling included being confronted by Wise in person, who repeated her accusations against him in a voice, said a newspaper account, "that would have wilted many an innocent man" [13].

While Johns had testified on Wise's behalf at the trial, he never visited her after the arrest, did not answer her one letter from the Medina jail, or look her way in the courtroom. Perhaps revealing her real motive in accusing him Martha said, "If he had spoken or even looked at me once I would have carried this whole thing to the grave" [13].

A week after the trial, Martha was transferred from the local jail to the state prison to begin her sentence. At that time she said, "I need the punishment and I expect to take it." Her siblings and her attorney all said they never wanted to see her at large again. They all agreed if by some chance she should be pardoned, they would take immediate action to have her recommitted to jail. The six Gienke children all survived, but didn't fare too well. Four months after the poisoning, three of them were described as "crippled for life." One was confined to bed flat on her back, unable to even move her arms enough to feed herself [11].

Sources

1. "Chemist Says Arsenic Took Victims' Lives." *Akron Beacon Journal,* March 13, 1925, p. 1.
2. "Finds Arsenic Killed Medina County Couple." *Akron Beacon Journal,* March 12, 1925, p. 15.
3. Hardy, J. R. "Family Enemy Described by Stricken Son." *Akron Beacon Journal,* March 16, 1925, pp. 1, 10.
4. Hardy, J. R. "Medina Woman Enjoys Good Night's Rest After Relating Details of Killings." *Akron Beacon Journal,* March 19, 1925, pp. 1, 17.
5. Hardy, J. R. "Prosecutor to Charge First Degree Murder." *Akron Beacon Journal,* March 20, 1925, pp. 1, 33.
6. Hardy, J. R. "Test Finished by Chemist in Medina Murder." *Akron Beacon Journal,* March 21, 1925, pp. 1, 13.
7. Wolf, Howard. "Drops to Floor on His Way to See Prosecutor." *Akron Beacon Journal,* May 8, 1925, p. 1.
8. Wolf, Howard. "Jury May Get Arsenic Case Early in Week." *Akron Beacon Journal,* May 9, 1925, pp. 1, 17.
9. Wolf, Howard. "Man Named by Medina Widow Given Freedom." *Akron Beacon Journal,* May 20, 1925, p. 1.
10. Wolf, Howard. "Martha Wise Will Welcome Prison as Haven of Rest After Life of Oppression, Hardship." *Akron Beacon Journal,* May 14, 1925, p. 17.
11. Wolf, Howard. "Poisoner Goes by Automobile to Marysville." *Akron Beacon Journal,* May 23, 1925, p. 13.
12. Wolf, Howard. "Question Cleveland Man on Charges Made by Convicted Woman." *Akron Beacon Journal,* May 16, 1925, pp. 1, 17.
13. Wolf, Howard. "Stoutly Denies Charges Made in Poisonings." *Akron Beacon Journal,* May 19, 1925, pp. 1, 17.
14. Wolf, Howard. "Widow Is Sent to Marysville for Life Term." *Akron Beacon Journal,* May 13, 1925, pp. 1, 8.
15. Wolf, Howard. "Widow on Trial Who Confessed Poisoning Act." *Akron Beacon Journal,* May 4, 1925, p. 1.
16. Wolf, Howard. "Women in Tears as Cripples in Medina Case Tell Stories." *Akron Beacon Journal,* May 7, 1925, pp. 1, 19.
17. "Woman Tells How She Placed Poison in Water in Her Complete Confession of Murder Case." *Akron Beacon Journal,* March 19, 1925, p. 1.

Anna Zwanziger

(1760–1811). *Place:* Pegnitz, Germany. *Time:* 1806–1809. *Age:* 46–49. *Victims:* 3. *Method:* Arsenic poisoning.

Life seemed to be a series of disappointments, frustrations, and failures for Anna Zwanziger. At middle age she found herself without prospects or means. Described as unattractive, she nevertheless set out to snare a wealthy husband. More failure followed, the bitterness and rage finally spilled out as Anna sought revenge through the use of poison. In the end the practice of poison seemed to be the end itself for her.

She was born Anna Maria Schonleben in Nuremberg, Germany, about 1760. Her beginnings were better than most, for her father was a successful innkeeper and the family didn't lack for money. Mr. Schonleben doted on his daughter. Her home life might have been somewhat monotonous, for Anna married the first man who came along, a waster named Zwanziger who described himself as a lawyer. He turned out to be a bully and a drunkard who was only interested in the money Anna received when her father died.

The most charitable physical description of Anna is that she was "no beauty." Another account calls her "ugly, stunted, without attractions of face, figure, speech . . . this misshapen woman whom some people likened to a toad" [1]. Anna endured much misery at the hands of her husband, who mistreated her for years before dying from the effects of alcohol abuse. Any rejoicing was tempered by the fact that no money was left, only debts.

Anna tried to make a new start and somehow managed to scrape up enough money to open a small confectionery shop. It failed. She tried again, this time selling toys. This also failed. She became despondent and, according to her, attempted suicide. Anna was said to be partial to "gloomy fiction of the romantic type."

Moving on to Frankfurt, she tried her luck as a cook in a couple of different households but didn't last long. Vienna was next; she did odd jobs there before she returned to Nuremberg. She then went to Mainbernheim to stay with a married daughter. Anna was then on the run from the police, having stolen a diamond ring from the house of a woman where she had worked as a servant. When her son-in-law chanced onto a police description of the thief, he told his mother-in-law to move on. Then in her forties, Anna's life was not going well and she had taken her initial foray into crime.

She eluded the authorities and took to the road again, working as a restaurant cook, a nursemaid, and doing needlework. Finally she settled in the small German town of Pegnitz, near Bayreuth. By day she earned money through her needlework, and by night she stole things from houses.

Around the year 1806, Anna became preoccupied with the thought of marriage. With minimal natural attractions at her disposal, she developed a strategy. She would get a job as a housekeeper to a wealthy single man and through hard work and graciousness become indispensable to him. He would marry her. To this end she applied for a job and was hired as housekeeper to Judge Glaser.

Believing the jurist to be a widower, Anna was horrified to find he was in fact only separated. In her own mind Anna felt he had shown interest in her as a woman as well as a servant when he hired her. When Anna delved further and found that the quarrel which caused the separation was not necessarily decisive, the first flicker of murder must have crossed her mind.

Recovering from her initial shock, Anna set to work on Glaser. She urged him to take back his wife, using various arguments. At the same time she wrote letters to Frau Glaser saying her husband regretted the separation and wanted her back. A visit was arranged between the couple, and they were soon reunited. Both expressed deep gratitude to Anna.

Frau Glaser had been home only a few days when she became ill. Three doses of arsenic, in tea, coffee, and wine, did the trick; she died vomiting and in agony. Anna retreated to her room to grieve alone. Of this poisoning she later recalled, "In one cup I handed her the powder was so thick that I feared she would see it. She did not, however, and as I watched her drinking it all unsuspectingly I said to myself, 'That will do the trick.' And it did" [3].

According to Anna's plan, Glaser should have been easy to console and cajole into marrying her. However, a stinging rebuke came her way. Glaser was not friendlier, but instead became morose and unresponsive. Perhaps blaming himself for the time lost in the separation from his wife, Glaser determined his future life would be entirely solitary. Glaser fired Anna.

He did, however, give her an excellent reference, good enough to land her a post as housekeeper with another jurist, Judge Grohmann. Zwanziger made sure this man was single. He was 38 years old and suffered from gout. Tending to his infirmity, Anna was again horrified when she discovered her employer was considering marriage to a young and pretty woman. The housekeeper tried to break up the romance by intercepting letters and by a few other tricks, but nothing worked. Grohmann remained indifferent to his servant.

Enraged, Anna burned like a spurned lover. Grohmann had to go. First she gave a small dose of arsenic to two other servants in the household. They had, for some reason, displeased her. They got arsenic in their beer, and Anna later recalled, "I intended to give them the beer by degrees, not in order to kill them, but only to make them sick" [3]. They did recover after being ill.

Grohmann died after receiving a much larger dose of the poison in his soup. Doctors certified the death as being from natural causes, as they had with Glaser. During the days of the illness before Grohmann expired, Anna nursed him assiduously and became a sort of heroine in the village on the basis of her self-sacrificing qualities.

This devotion was what caused a magistrate named Gebhard to come forward and hire Anna as nurse to his children and maid for his wife, who was expecting a child. Again Anna fancied her employer saw her as more woman than maid. She imagined herself as a wife again, and after a short period of her nursing Frau Gebhard lay dead.

During the poisoning Frau Gebhard became suspicious and shared her fears with her husband. No attention was paid, though, as it was put down to the ravings of a delirious person. Anna insisted that she be left in complete charge of the sick room and that absolutely no one else should enter.

After the funeral, Zwanziger was elevated to the position of housekeeper and curried favor by being overly solicitous to her master. The other servants, who had wondered about her link with death, came to openly dislike her. Anna dosed two of them with arsenic. One was a pretty maid Anna feared could be a rival, and the other was her boyfriend. Both recovered.

Some time after his wife's death Gebhard decided to have a dinner party; he felt he had a duty to his living friends, and did not want to become a hermit. For some reason this infuriated Anna, whose vigorous protests were overruled. She seemed to accept this graciously, but it aroused a hatred in her for everyone attending the party. As the cook, she dosed the food of everyone present, except the host, with arsenic. The party turned into a nightmare, since all became violently ill. None of them died.

Gebhard dismissed his housekeeper two days later—not that he suspected anything; he didn't. Anna had pleaded a mistake with ingredients. He told her he couldn't keep a cook who made so many mistakes. By then Anna seemed to be into poisoning for its own sake. She dosed the noon meal on her last day of work, and all the servants got sick. One of them suggested Gebhard have the food analyzed. The magistrate did so and the chemist reported the presence of arsenic. The shocked magistrate, fearful of any scandal, did nothing. He hoped Zwanziger would be gone from his life when she left that night.

That night Gebhard's infant became violently ill. Anna had given the child a biscuit soaked in milk just as she left. The magistrate changed his mind and called in the police. When the authorities investigated, they found that Zwanziger had been busy before she left. All of the salt, sugar, and coffee containers in the house had been liberally dosed with poison.

The slow-acting police made no move for about nine weeks to arrest Anna, who had settled temporarily at Bayreuth, from whence she wrote Gebhard several letters upbraiding him for his ingratitude and urging him to take her back. He didn't reply. Meanwhile, the bodies of all three victims were exhumed and found to contain arsenic.

Anna moved on briefly to Nuremberg, where she couldn't find work, and then to Mainbernheim. Her daughter couldn't support her and Anna returned to Nuremberg, where the police finally arrested her on October 18, 1809. On her person the police found a number of packets of arsenic.

When she was brought to trial, it dragged on for over a year. Initially Anna denied everything and implicated Glaser, who was briefly arrested before being cleared. Bavarian law at the time required that a person could not be convicted of murder unless some type of confession was made, which caused the trial to take so long. One day, the previously composed Zwanziger suddenly broke down in court and screamed out that she was the murderer, saying, "Yes, I killed them all, and would have killed more if I had had the chance" [1]. With that she collapsed on the floor. She was sentenced to death.

In July 1811, Anna Zwanziger was beheaded by axe. Her passion for poisoning and death had usurped her quest for a husband, for just before her execution she wrote, "It is perhaps better for the community that I should die, as it would be impossible for me to give up the practice of poisoning people" [3].

Sources

1. Barry, Philip Beaufoy. *Twenty Human Monsters*. Philadelphia: Macrae Smith, 1929, pp. 157–74.

2. Green, Jonathon. *The Greatest Criminals of All Time*. New York: Stein & Day, 1980, p. 159.

3. Gribble, Leonard. *Sisters of Cain*. London: John Long, 1972, pp. 127–39.

Index

Albany, New York 28
alcohol use: Bolin 40; Collins 57;
    Deshayes 90–91; Falling 107, 109;
    Ford 121; Foster/Powell 126–30;
    Graham 148; Jackson 169–70;
    Juenemann 186; Puente 236–37;
    Scieri 257; Toppan 286; Weber 303
Allentown, Pennsylvania 290–93
arsenic poisoning: Archer-Gilligan
    10–12; Barfield 16–19; de Brinvilliers
    44–49; Cotton 66–71; Cunningham
    74–77; Doss 92–96; Fazekas 112–17;
    Gibbs 136–37; Gottfried 142–45;
    Hahn 162–65; Jegado 177–80;
    Klimek 192–95; Lyles 199–201;
    Martin 213–16; de Melker 219–22;
    Renczi 246–47; Robinson 250–52;
    Scieri 257–59; Sherman 260–62;
    Spara 273; Toffania 282–83; Ur-
    sinus 295; Wise 313–16; Zwanziger
    318–21
arson: Cooper 64; Dcyzheski 87–88
asphyxiation: Fiederer 118; Fuller 134;
    Hultberg 167; MacDonald 206–07;
    Nollen 224–25; Pasos 232
atropine poisoning: Jeanneret 173–76;
    Toppan 284–88
automobile, as weapon: Ford 120–21;
    Foster/Powell 126
axe murder: Cooper 64; Gunness
    157–60

baby farming: Dyer 98–100; Sach/
    Walters 254–56; Waters 300–02
beating, to death: Beck 28; Cannon
    54; Gonzales 140–41; Soulakiotis
    271–72

Berkerekul, Romania 246–47
Berlin, Germany 186–87, 295
Blountstown, Florida 107
bludgeoning, to death: Campbell 51;
    Cannon 53; Columbo 62; Dcy-
    zheski 87–88; Jackson 169–70; King
    189
Boston, England 308–10
Bremen, Germany 145
Bristol, England 98–99
Brittany, France 177–80
Brixton, England 300–02

Calgary, Alberta 42–43
Cambridge, Massachusetts 250–52,
    285–88
Cataument, Massachusetts 286–87
Center, Texas 78–79
Chambon, France 306
Cherryvale, Kansas 35–37
Chicago, Illinois 28, 192–95
childhood: Barfield 15; Beck 26; de
    Brinvilliers 44; Columbo 59; Cot-
    ton 66; Doss 92; Falling 105–06;
    Ford 121; Foster/ Powell 128–29;
    Gibbs 136; Gottfried 142; Graham
    147; Gunness 155; Jeanneret
    172–73; Lehmann 197; Malcolm
    208; Martin 213–14; de Melker 218;
    Puente 234–35; Robinson 250;
    Sherman 260; Tinning 275; Toppan
    284–85; Urdanivia 290; Weber 303;
    Wise 314; Zwanziger 318
Cincinnati, Ohio 162–65
colchicum poisoning: Wilson 308–11
confession: Barfield 18–19; Bearce
    24–25; Beck 29; de Brinvilliers 49;

Cannon 54–55; Collins 57–58;
  Cooper 65; Cunningham 76–77;
  Curtis 78–79; Dcyzheski 88; Dyer
  100; Falling 109–10; Fiederer 118;
  Ford 121; Foster/Powell 130–31;
  Godfrida 138; Gottfried 145; Hultberg 168; Jeanneret 176; Jones,
  Roxanne 185; King 190; Lehmann
  198; McAninch 204; MacDonald
  206–07; Martin 216–17; Nollen 225;
  Renczi 247; Scieri 259; Sherman
  262–63; Sorenson 267–68; Toppan
  288; Urdanivia 292–93; Walkup
  299; Wise 315; Zwanziger 321
Cordele, Georgia 136–37

Dannebrog, Nebraska 265–68
dating clubs and agencies 26–27, 94,
  157–58, 192
Denison, Iowa 224–25
Derby, Connecticut 262
digitalin poisoning: Becker 32–34
drowning: Beck 29; Brar 42–43;
  Campbell 51; Wagner 296–97
drug overdose, to kill: Beck 28–29;
  Godfrida 138–39; Puente 234–41;
  Sach/Walters 254–56; Urdanivia
  290–93; Wagner 296–97
drug usage: Archer-Gilligan 12; Barfield 16; Ford 121–22; Foster/
  Powell 128–30; Godfrida 138;
  Graham 149; Jeanneret 176; Toppan 286
Durham, England 66–70

East Perth, Australia 248–49
elderly victims: Archer-Gilligan 10–12;
  Becker 33–34; Godfrida 138–39;
  Graham 151–53; Puente 234–41;
  Wagner 296–97
Elk Grove Village, Illinois 59–62
Emporia, Kansas 94
execution: Barfield 19; Beck 30; de
  Brinvilliers 49; Cotton 72; De-
  shayes 91; Dyer 100; Gottfried 145–
  46; Hahn 165–66; Jegado 181;
  Juenemann 187; Malcolm 209;

Marek 211; Martin 217; de Melker
  223; Rendall 249; Sach/Walters
  256; Spara 273; Toffania 283;
  Waters 302; Wilson 312; Zwanziger
  321

financial motives for murder: Archer-
  Gilligan 10–12; Beck 28; Becker 33;
  Bender 35–37; de Brinvilliers
  44–48; Cannon 53–54; Collins
  56–57; Columbo 60; Cotton 67–72;
  Dyer 98–100; Godfrida 138–39;
  Gonzales 140–41; Gottfried 142–45;
  Gunness 156–60; Hahn 162–65;
  Klimek 192–95; Marek 210–11; de
  Melker 218–22; Puente 234–41;
  Robinson 250–52; Sach/Walters
  254–56; Soulakiotis 270–72; Ur-
  sinus 295; Waters 300–02; Wilson
  308–11
firearms: Beck 27–28; Bolin 39–40;
  Collins 57–58; Columbo 62; Curtis
  78–79; Foster/Powell 126; Jones,
  Annie 183; Jones, Roxanne 184;
  McAninch 204; Parker 228–31;
  Ransom 243–44; Walkup 298
Flagstaff, Arizona 298–99
Fresno, California 102–03

Gary, Indiana 74–76
Geneva, Switzerland 174
Germany 142–45
Glasgow, Montana 51
Grand Rapids, Michigan 29, 148–53
Greenwich, Connecticut 14
groups in support: Cotton 72; Falling
  109; Toppan 287; Weber 306
Guern, France 177–78

Hammond, Indiana 56–58
hanging, to kill: O'Donohue 226
Hungary 20–23
hydrochloric acid poisoning: Rendall
  248

infanticide and child murder: Bearce 24–25; Beck 28; Becker 14; Bolin 39–40; Brar 43; Campbell 51; Cannon 53–54; Cooper 64; Cotton 67–71; Cunningham 74–76; Curtis 78–79; David 85; Dcyzheski 87–88; Deshayes 90–91; Doss 92–96; Edwards 102–03; Falling 106–09; Fiederer 118; Fuller 134; Gibbs 136–37; Gottfried 143; Gunness 156, 160; Hultberg 167; Jones, Annie 182; Jones, Roxanne 184; Juenemann 186; King 189–90; Lyles 199–201; McAninch 204; MacDonald 206–07; Martin 214–16; Nollen 224–25; O'Donohue 226; Pasos 232; Rendall 248; Robinson 251–52; Sach/Walters 254–56; Sherman 260–62; Shoaf 264; Sorenson 265–68; Tinning 275–80; Urdanivia 290–93; Waters 300–02; Weber 303–07

Jacksonville, Alabama 92–93
Johannesburg, South Africa 219–22

Keretea, Greece 270–72

Lake George, New York 24–25
Lakeland, Florida 107–08
La Porte, Indiana 156–60
Lausanne, Switzerland 173–75
Lebanon, Kentucky 264
Lexington, Kentucky 126–31
Lexington, North Carolina 93
Liege, Belgium 32–34
Locmine, France 178
London, England 208–09, 254–56, 310–12
Lorient, France 178
Lumberton, North Carolina 15

Macon, Georgia 199–201
Madison, Maine 182

Mahwah, New Jersey 206–07
marital discord: Bacher 14; Barfield 16–19; Bearce 24; de Brinvilliers 46–47; Collins 56–58; Cooper 64; Cotton 67–70; Curtis 78; Doss 92–96; Gottfried 142; Lehmann 197; MacDonald 206–07; Nollen 224
Matfield, England 243–44
Medina, Ohio 313–16
mental condition: Archer-Gilligan 12; Bathory 22; Bearce 24–25; Brar 42–43; Cooper 64–65; Cunningham 74–76; Curtis 78–80; Dcyzheski 88; Doss 97; Dyer 98, 100; Edwards 102–03; Falling 106–09; Fiederer 118; Ford 124–25; Fuller 134–35; Gibbs 137; Jeanneret 172–75; Jones, Annie 182; King 188–90; McAninch 203–04; O'Donohue 226–27; Puente 236; Ransom 244; Sorenson 267–68; Toppan 288; Urdanivia 290–93; Walkup 298–99; Weber 307
Minneapolis, Minnesota 167–68
Mobile, Alabama 213–16
Montgomery, Alabama 213–16
morphine poisoning: Jeanneret 173–76; Toppan 284–88

Nagyrev, Hungary 112–15
Naples, Italy 282–83
New Orleans, Louisiana 169–71
New York, New York 232, 260–61
Norwalk, Iowa 203–05

occult practices: Bathory 20; Bender 35; Deshayes 89–90; Fazekas 112–16; Lyles 200
Oklahoma City, Oklahoma 230

Paris, France 44–48, 89–91, 303–07
Passaic, New Jersey 118
Pegnitz, Germany 318–20
Perry, Florida 108
phosphorus poisoning: Lehmann 197–98

poisoning: Cannon 53; Deshayes 89–91; Popova 233; Sorenson 265–68
poverty: Curtis 78–79; Dcyzheski 87; Deshayes 89; Falling 105–08; Foster/Powell 128–29; Fuller 134; Jones, Roxanne 183–84; Juenemann 186; King 188–90; McAninch 203–04; Pasos 232; Robinson 250–52

Reading, England 99–100
Reliance, Delaware 52–54
religion: Barfield 16–19; Brar 43; Cotton 66; David 82–85; Falling 105; Ford 121–22, 124; Gibbs 136–37; Gunness 161; Jegado 179; Jones, Roxanne 184; Soulakiotis 270–72
Rennes, France 179
Reno, Nevada 120–23
Reseda, California 183–84
Rome, Italy 273

Sacramento, California 234–41
St. Gilles, France 257–59
St. Libory, Nebraska 265–68
St. Pauls, North Carolina 15
Saint-Remy, France 307
Salt Lake City, Utah 83–85
Samara, Russia 233
San Francisco, California 134
San Francisco del Rincon, Mexico 140–41
San Juan de Los Lagos, Mexico 140–41
Saxonville, Massachusetts 87–88
Schenectady, New York 275–80
sexual abuse: Barfield 15; Beck 26; de Brinvilliers 44; Foster/Powell 128; Graham 147
sexual aspects of murder: Bathory 22; Beck 28, 30; Becker 32–33; de Brinvilliers 46–47; Columbo 60–61; Gonzales 140–41; Graham 152; Renczi 247; Toppan 286; Weber 307; Zwanziger 319–21
sexual behavior: Bathory 21–22; Beck 27–28, 30; Becker 32–33; Bender

37; de Brinvilliers 44–48; Columbo 60, 62; Cotton 67–70; Deshayes 90; Falling 106, 109; Foster/Powell 128–29, 131; Godfrida 138; Gottfried 142; Graham 148–51; Gunness 157–58; Jackson 169–70; Klimek 193; Parker 228–30; Renczi 246–47
Sherman, Texas 229
Somerville, Massachusetts 250–52
stabbing, to death: Bacher 14; Bearce 24–25; Bender 36; Cannon 53; Columbo 62; Foster/Powell 126; Jackson 169–71; Malcolm 208–09; Shoaf 264; Walkup 298
starvation, to death: Juenemann 186; Soulakiotis 271–72; Waters 300–02
strangulation: Beck 28; Dyer 98–100; Edwards 103; Falling 106–09; Malcolm 208–09; Wagner 296–97; Walkup 298; Weber 303–07
Stratford, Connecticut 261
strychnine poisoning: Gunness 156–60; Hahn 162–65; de Melker 219–22
suffocation: Graham 151–53; Tinning 275–80
Switzerland 172–76

thallium poisoning: Marek 210–11
throwing to death from tall building: David 85
Tiszakurt, Hungary 112–15
Toronto, Canada 226
torture: Bathory 20–23; de Brinvilliers 49; Deshayes 90; Gonzales 140–41; Soulakiotis 271–72; Spara 273; Toffania 283
Tulsa, Oklahoma 95

Upper Arlington, Ohio 39–40

Valparaiso, Indiana 74
Vienna, Austria 210–11, 296–97

Watertown, Massachusetts 286
Watsonville, New York 64–65
Wetteren, Belgium 138–39
Windsor, Connecticut 10–12
Woods Hole, Massachusetts 286
Worms, Germany 197–98

Xenia, Ohio 188–90